The Psychology of
Musical Ability

The Psychology of Musical Ability

SECOND EDITION

ROSAMUND SHUTER-DYSON
AND CLIVE GABRIEL

METHUEN

LONDON AND NEW YORK

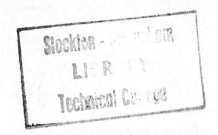
To Jim and to Doreen

First published in 1968
Second revised edition 1981
Methuen & Co. Ltd
11 New Fetter Lane, London EC4P 4EE
Published in the USA by
Methuen & Co.
in association with Methuen, Inc.
733 Third Avenue, New York, NY 10017
First edition © Rosamund Shuter-Dyson 1968
Second edition © Rosamund Shuter-Dyson and Clive Gabriel 1981
Printed in Great Britain
at the Cambridge University Press

British Library Cataloguing in Publication Data

Shuter-Dyson, Rosamund
The Psychology of musical ability. — 2nd ed.
1. Musical ability — Psychological aspects
I. Title   II. Gabriel, Clive
155.4'13   ML3838
ISBN 0-416-71300-9

Contents

Acknowledgements

Thanks are due to Schott Music Publishers, London for permission to use Figure 8 from p.99 of *The Musical Experience of the Preschool Child* and to the University of Iowa Press for permission to reproduce Table 32 from *Studies in the Psychology of Music*, Volume V, by E. Gordon. Rosamund Shuter-Dyson is grateful to the Hatfield Polytechnic for sabbatical leave to gather material for the revised edition and to the British Academy for some financial support to visit the United States for that purpose.

Introduction to first edition

The common man of today is far richer in music than the prince of two centuries ago. Through radio and television he can command the services of not just one orchestra, but of many. Though he may not be able to commission an ode in celebration of his birthday, he can, for the price of a record, have the finest artists performing in his own home any music that happens to suit his mood at the moment. Yet relatively few people take full advantage of this wealth. Many who do try to listen attentively are often only too well aware how much they are missing of the real meaning of the music. Almost everyone understands his native language, but many people cannot sing in tune, much less play an instrument. Most people learn to read; far fewer are musically literate. We may wonder whether this is due to a lack of interest or of opportunity to learn. Or is it necessary, in order to understand and appreciate music, to have some special gift?

What in fact makes a musician? What distinguishes the musician from the rest of mankind? Why should one infant in the cradle seem so much more responsive to music than another? Why should one, but only one, of the small-town German musicians at the beginning of the seventeenth century have been the progenitor of the amazing Bach family who produced in six generations no fewer than 47 musicians of talent or genius? Was this due to heredity or to family background? Is there a sense in which we are all musical? How can we educate children to enjoy and truly appreciate a wide variety of music?

It is with questions such as these that this book is primarily concerned. It evolved from a doctoral thesis and from the writer's ponderings on the barrier to advanced achievement in music which she had earlier encountered and which, in spite of her own and her teachers' efforts, had proved insurmountable. The writer's aim has been to collate and evaluate psychological studies of musical ability and attainment in order to make the results more widely accessible to all who are interested in music, whether as performers, teachers, or listeners. Much less research has been carried out into musical ability than into other abilities, e.g. 'intelligence'. However, though fragmentary, studies of some aspects of musical ability have produced interesting and important results. The present book is not concerned, except incidentally, with the psychology of sound, nor with the aesthetic aspects except in relation to ability to compose or appreciate music, nor with music therapy which is fast becoming a specialist area.

Historical background

Interest in the psychology of music is as old as experimental psychology itself, the birth of which may be dated at 1879 when Wilhelm Wundt opened his 'Psychological Institute' at the University of Leipzig. Wundt and many of his associates were physiologists by training. They concentrated at first on measurements of sensitivity to auditory, and other sensory stimuli, and of simple reaction time. Gradually, however, their attention turned to the measurement of perceptual span and the rate of learning. The need for rigorous control of experimental conditions soon became apparent; for it was found that even such factors as the wording of instructions could significantly influence the results obtained. The acoustical studies of the pioneers of experimental psychology such as Hermann von Helmholtz and Carl Stumpf (both professors in the University of Berlin) are discussed in Geza Revesz's *Introduction to the Psychology of Music*.

Stumpf was himself a cellist and as early as 1883 had already devoted considerable thought to possible tests of musical aptitude. He had become interested in individual differences in ability after observing the varying responses obtained with musical and unmusical persons during his study of tones. He carried out experimental tests with David Popper, a celebrated cellist, and with Pepito Areola, an infant prodigy. Revesz was in many ways Stumpf's direct successor. He too studied – for five years – an infant prodigy and experimented with tests which closely resembled those given traditionally by music teachers. He left his native Hungary after the First World War and settled in the Netherlands. Though greatly influenced by the Gestalt school of psychology then prominent in Europe, his own theories were too wide to be easily classified. Among the many investigations he carried out was a study of the popular notion that there is a connection between mathematical ability and a talent for music.

On the theoretical side, the first important book on the psychology of musical ability, *Wer ist musikalisch?* appeared in 1895. The author was Theodor Billroth, a Vienna physiologist and music lover. The characteristics of the musical person which he listed are of a relatively objective nature. He recognised the importance of a spontaneous interest in music and memory for musical material, as well as the sensory capacities he had studied as a physiologist. Another physiologist with musical training, Johannes von Kries, wrote in 1926 a book with a similar title to Billroth's in which he attempted to collate all the characteristics of the musical person.

The value of the research into problems in the psychology of musical ability in that period was limited by the lack of controlled tests. The inheritance of musical talent was studied by Francis Galton's methods of drawing up family trees on the basis of reputation or – a later refinement – of answers to questionnaires. Galton himself realised the importance of trying to make the most accurate possible assessment of individual abilities and of finding statistical methods of comparing different groups of people and the results of different tests. Among his many inventions was the Galton whistle for determining the highest audible pitch. He believed that powers of sensory discrimination were directly related to intellectual powers. It was not long before he was proved wrong as far as general intellectual ability was concerned.

Meanwhile in the United States the full resources of the psychological laboratory were being brought to bear on the problems of providing objective tests of musical ability. Around 1890 W. E. Scripture set up at Yale University a psychological laboratory on the lines of Wundt's at Leipzig. Numerous experiments were carried out on vision, hearing and the other senses. It was here that the first measurements of pitch discrimination were made by a group test. Here too Hughes was the first to compare the scores obtained under laboratory conditions with an outside criterion of musical ability.

But the most important of the pioneers at Yale, from the point of view of music, was Carl Emil Seashore. In 1897 he went to the State

University of Iowa where he stayed for forty years and later became director of the Psychology Laboratory. His pioneer work included the invention of the voice tonoscope, which gives a visual picture of a tone, thus enabling the singer to see the sound he is producing, and the audiometer, an instrument for measuring the threshold of hearing for the intensity of sounds at various frequencies. In his books *The Psychology of Musical Talent* (1919) and *The Psychology of Music* (1938), Seashore emphasised that his aim was to apply the technological apparatus and methods of his laboratory for *the service of music*. His Measures of Musical Talent, published in 1919 after twenty years of experimentation, were intended to select for training gifted children whose talents might otherwise be neglected, and to save the unmusical and their teachers from the discouragement of failing to progress. The publication of his measures was followed by many efforts to check their validity in actual prognostic situations. Criticisms were directed at Seashore on several accounts: James Mursell of Columbia University Teachers College doubted whether measurements of isolated, specific capacities could have much relevance to functional musical activities. Paul Farnsworth of Stanford and Robert Lundin then of Hamilton College, New York, besides producing evidence of the deficiencies of the measures, also attacked Seashore for his assumption that the capacities he was seeking to assess were innate and unaffected by training. Seashore himself was well aware of the more complex aspects of musical perception and performance but believed that the capacities he was testing were as basic to musical aptitude as they were to sound itself. Paradoxically, this author of the most objective, laboratory-bound tests was prone to make *ex cathedra* pronouncements which seem, in these less confident days, not wholly in the spirit of scientific enquiry. He was not himself a musician, though he is said to have played the organ when he was young. But the sincerity of his interest in music cannot be doubted. Many who have criticised his approach to testing musical ability have themselves adopted his aims.

   The criticisms of Seashore suggested that tests based on musical material might prove more satisfactory provided that they could be properly standardised. During the 1930s three successful batteries were in fact developed. Kate Hevner, the only woman author of a test that has gained an international reputation, produced the Oregon Music Discrimination test. Raleigh Drake, a musician as well as a psychologist, devised during a course of postgraduate study in London a musical memory test of lasting worth. Herbert Wing, who had practical experience of schoolteaching as well as being a musician and psychologist, developed a comprehensive battery of aural acuity and musical appreciation tests. His research at University College, London was guided by Cyril Burt whose immensely wide interests included music. Burt had concluded from his early experiments with the Seashore tests that they were unsatisfactory.

Since 1940 other tests based on musical material have been produced. Validation studies of these and the earlier tests have been continued and tests have gradually come to enjoy increasing use both in educational situations and as research tools. More sophisticated forms of statistical analysis have been applied to the results obtained with the tests to throw light both on exactly what the tests are measuring and on the complex nature of musical ability.

Tests have not been the only source of data for the psychologist of musical ability. Intensive case studies have also been made. Concerned for example with the early development of individual children, or with the exceptional displays of talent of the musical prodigy or of the idiot savant. Psychological experiments have also been carried out where one 'variable' is selected for study, all the other factors in the situation being as far as possible controlled. For example, many experiments have been devised to try to determine the effect of a particular type of training on the singing or performing ability of an experimental group of 'subjects'. The results on some standard task before and after the training are compared with a 'control' group who have not received the training.

Observations, both of spontaneous behaviour and of responses induced by the experimental conditions, can be a valuable source of data. Best results are obtained when the behaviour to be studied has been specified beforehand and where more than one observer works independently.

Definitions and plan of the book

'Musical ability' is the term generally adopted throughout this book, as being in Farnsworth's words 'the broadest and safest', since it suggests power to perceive and act without any *a priori* implication to the extent of heredity. (Farnsworth, however, believes that we should speak of musical abili*ties*.) 'Talent has been used similarly, but usually with the implication of some positive degree of ability. 'Musical' is taken to mean simply 'having musical ability'. The reservation 'musical ability as assessed by the such and such test' frequently needs to be read into the text. Other writers on the psychology of musical ability have preferred other terms. Thus Holmstrom uses 'musicality' and Teplov, 'sens musical', while both musicians and laymen speak of 'an ear for music'. The term 'musical ear' should, of course, include not only the sensory and perceptual system, but also the integrating and interpreting power of the human mind.

But the possession of a fine ear, important prerequisite though it is, does not make a musician. To perform or sing, the motor mechanisms of the mind and body must be brought into play. Therefore in practice a useful distinction can be drawn between the perceptual and the muscular aspects.

To speak only of ability to perceive and understand music or to play it with nimble fingers would be to leave out of account the heart of the matter. For music is an art, music is beautiful. Its power to move, to excite and to charm has always been recognised. As Curt Sachs tells us in his fascinating essay 'The Lore of Non-Western Music', all over the ancient world from Egypt to China, beautiful women with musical training were a typical gift to royal friends or suzerains.

The contrast between the ability, if such it can be called, to respond emotionally to music and what we mean by musical ability is epitomised in two characters described by Stendhal in his *Life of Rossini*. One, an elderly clerk from the War Office, possessed the gift of absolute pitch to such a degree that if he happened to hear a couple of workmen on a building site chipping a block of stone with their hammers, he could tell instantly the exact notes which the two sets of hammer blows were emitting. He could also copy down any tune he heard. However, music apparently gave him no pleasure whatsoever; as an art it was meaningless to him. The other, a young Venetian nobleman, was incapable of singing four notes on end without committing the most excruciating cacophony. Yet he adored music with a passionate intensity, rare even in Italy.

Such an extreme contrast is in reality quite unusual. More commonly, emotional and intellectual elements combine in the highest type of aesthetic experience.

June 1967

Introduction to second edition

In the last chapter of the first edition, the book was called a 'progress report'. Even as those words were being written, many new research projects were in progress. Since then, new tests, especially of aural achievement in music and of the musical ability of children as young as four or five years of age, have been devised. Very considerable development in studies of the child from birth onwards has occurred. So important have become the areas of perception, memory and cognition of music and its physiological correlates that it seemed wise in the second edition to include a section on this research. While little attempt has been made in the past to link these areas within the traditional ways of studying and assessing musical ability, ultimately all of the research studies the same processes from different aspects and at different levels.

The general purpose of the book remains the same: the evaluation of psychological studies of musical ability and attainment to make the results of such research more widely accessible to all who are interested in music, music education or psychology.

Primary responsibility for Parts 1, 2 and 3 rests with Rosamund Shuter-Dyson and for Part 4 with Clive Gabriel but we have worked together on the whole with the aim of providing a reasonably unified style and approach.

In Part 1, we shall discuss the concept of musical ability, then how musicians and psychologists have tried to find ways of assessing musical ability and achievement that would prove useful in education and in research, followed by a discussion on what light the results of such research throws on the nature of musical ability and its relationship to other abilities. Part 2 deals with the development of musical ability from birth to adulthood, Part 3 with the determinants of musical ability. Part 4 is concerned with cognitive and neurological studies relevant to musical ability. In the last section conclusions will be summarised and some implications for education in music discussed.

R. S-D.
C.G.

January 1981

Part 1

The concept and assessment of musical ability

1

The concept of musical ability

Many questions arise when the psychologist seeks to investigate musical ability. For example, how right are we to speak of musical ability rather than musical abilities? While the nature of musical ability is generally admitted to be complex, opinions differ on the extent to which its various aspects are consistently related.

At one extreme, Seashore believed that musical capacity may be divided into a number of sharply defined talents which are unrelated and can be present or absent in individuals in varying degrees. He claimed that the capacities measured by his tests were as basic to musical aptitude as they are to sound itself. Moreover, 'each one of these capacities runs as an independent branch, not only in sensation, but through memory, imagination, thought, feeling and action' (Seashore, 1938). Thus, a 'sense of rhythm' depends on the basic capacities of time and intensity discrimination, and tonal memory upon pitch discrimination.

On the other hand, Wing (1968) believed that there is a general ability to perceive and appreciate music. When he was developing his battery of tests, one criterion he used in deciding whether or not to include a test was that it should correlate to a reasonable (but not too high) degree with the total for the whole battery. Wing did not deny that rhythm might be a separate factor, but included only one test of rhythm, being concerned with producing a set of tests that could be administered within an hour.

More recently, Gordon (1965) has produced tests where the rhythm element is given as much prominence as the melodic and harmonic. While agreeing that as they exist in music 'rhythm and melody interact in an inseparable way', he believed that providing separate scores is helpful in diagnosing the strengths and weaknesses of the learner in music.

In a temporal art, memory must play an important role. Drake

(1933) suggested that specific talents as measured by the Seashore tests might all depend on, or be knit together by, musical memory. A fuller discussion of experiments based on models proposed by cognitive psychologists that are relevant to music appears in Chapter 17. For the moment, we should note that the memory process includes (*a*) the immediate auditory image which may fade rather rapidly unless it can be 'rehearsed', (*b*) memory for a phrase to be sung back immediately (in the case of group tests of musical ability some judgement is used such as asking the listener to note which note has been changed when the phrase is played again), and (*c*) long-term storage which enables the mind to make meaning out of new material. Seashore himself recognised the importance of 'auditory imagery', i.e. 'the capacity to hear music in recall, in creative work, and to supplement the actual physical sounds' (1938, p. 168). Indeed he believed that it is perhaps the most outstanding mark of the musical mind.

Even in the last quarter of the twentieth century, the need to be able to feel the presence of a tonal centre is a vital aid to enabling the listener to 'make sense' of music, leading to a sound basis for its appreciation.

Much cognitive activity is involved in keeping track, for example, of a musical theme through modulations and rhythmic or melodic transformations. A different kind of 'appreciation' seems to be involved in grasping the 'meaning' of music. This latter will be discussed in Chapter 17. An important contribution to perception of music, as well as to its performance, comes from our muscular system, as we shall note on p. 64.

A further question which arises in the psychological discussion of musical ability is: how far is it possible to distinguish musical potential (inborn, or at least present at birth) from musical ability as it functions at a given point in life? What do we mean by 'inherent'? Does it refer to 'species-specific' activity or does it refer to differences in the ability of individuals to deal with the music of their own culture which may be attributable, at least in part, to hereditary factors?

As we shall see in Chapter 7, there is evidence that infants respond to tonal patterns in a special way that is similar to response to language elements. To be human is to be capable of music, just as to be human is to be capable of speech. Blacking (1971) pursues this concept of universal musical competence in discussing his anthropological studies among the Venda in Africa. The Venda takes universal capacity for music-making for granted – even the deaf should be able to dance. Some might argue that western music is more complex, hence fewer people can master it. This view may fail to do justice to the creative ability behind an apparently simple folksong. Again, though Venda instruments may not be technically difficult, the criterion of worth is the creative and expressive use of the instrument. The Venda seem to be able to imitate chromatic intervals or European chord sequences if required to do so, but often prefer to make creative adaptations of the music of the west. They do, however, recognise that some persons perform better than others. Children born into certain families may be expected to show exceptional talent for music. Only a few of these may emerge as exceptional, due to their devoting more time and energy to music. As in the case of the traditional Gagaku musical families in Japan, the child is in a favoured position to acquire his father's skills through imitation and example.

A member of a gamelan in Bali may during a performance take his small son on his lap and guide his tiny fingers to the proper metallophone keys at the proper time (Small, 1977, p. 42). A musician in the west would also guide his child's fingers at the piano, but hardly during a public performance and herein may lie a fundamental cultural difference . . . .

We have to recognise with Zuckerkandl (1973) that music in the western world has come to be equated with compositions that are characterised by their tonal polyphony. Composition and interpretation have become the business of experts; some special sensitivity seems to be required of the listener who is to 'appreciate' them. A distinction between 'musical' and 'unmusical' thus comes to be drawn, even though it may be conceived of as a continuum rather than a dichotomy. Though we shall not lose awareness of the 'species-specific' concept of inherited capacity for music, we shall be primarily concerned with ability to deal with the music of the west, with individual differences of the extent to which this is manifest and the effects of interaction with the environment. Part 3 is devoted to a consideration of such questions.

For the present we may usefully consider the question of distinguishing between 'aptitude' and 'attainment' in their relationship to 'ability'. Both Edwin Gordon and Richard Colwell seek to draw such a distinction. 'Aptitude is a measure of one's potential to

learn, and achievement is a measure of what one has learned. . . .
Although one who displays high achievement must possess at least
equally high aptitude, one who possesses high aptitude will not
necessarily display high achievement' (Gordon, 1979*a*). Colwell
(1970*a*) suggests that aptitudes develop over a long period of time
and may cease to improve despite further training, whilst achievements are measurable within short periods.

It may be helpful at this point to consider definitions that have
been found useful within the field of intelligence. Hebb (1949, pp.
294-6) put forward the view that the word 'intelligence' has *two*
valuable meanings. One, Intelligence A, is *innate potential*, the
capacity of the central nervous system for forming, retaining and
recombining concepts and schemata, while Intelligence B is *present
mental efficiency*, i.e. it refers to the effectiveness of the individual's
present behaviour or thinking, acquired through the interaction of
his genetic endowment and the stimulation offered by his environment. Intelligence B is culturally conditioned by the environment
provided by the social and ethnic group into which the child is
born, especially by incidental learning acquired at home and in the
child's leisure pursuits. Such a concept is echoed by Gordon when
he says (1979*a*): 'Immediate impressions and intuitive responses
are developed in correspondence with the level of a child's innate
capacities and the quality of his early informal environmental
experiences in music.' Vernon (e.g. 1968) designates the results of
intelligence testing Intelligence C. The value of intelligence tests
lies not in their measuring innate capacities but in their predictive
value in sampling useful mental skills.

Cattell (1965) draws a distinction between fluid general intelligence (Gf) and crystallised general intelligence (Gc). Gf is a kind
of mental energy that can be applied to deal now with this problem
and now with that; it is acquired under incidental learning conditions. As ability to perceive relationships in any material, new or
old, it reaches its maximum level at about the age of 14 or 15 when
the brain finishes its growth. Gc is the outcome of cultural
influences (acculturation) and is determined by the extent to which
the individual has the opportunity and desire to apply himself to
areas such as linguistic or scientific pursuits. Development may
continue well into adulthood, at least in those fields where the
individual exercises his skills. Gc is, however, distinguishable from
general school achievement in being what is acquired by applying

fluid intelligence to school opportunities. In a rough sense Gc is dependent on Gf since the acquisition of intellectual skills depends not only on the cultural and educational environment but also on the level of fluid ability which enables the individual to benefit from his experiences. However, Horn and Donaldson (1980) cite evidence that individual differences in Gf are not necessarily more determined by hereditary influences than those in Gc. This suggests that it is unsound to point to any close relationship of skills developed through interaction with a cultural environment as necessarily proving that heredity is of little importance in their development.

In Chapters 3 and 4 'aptitude' tests will be discussed separately from 'achievement' tests. But all aptitude tests are to some extent achievement tests, just as all achievement tests necessarily reflect the initial aptitude of the individual. Attainment depends not only on aptitude but also on the teaching received and the child's interest in music and willingness to learn.

We may also enquire into the place of musical ability in relation to other abilities. How far does it depend on general intelligence? How is it related to abilities in the other arts and to mathematical ability? This topic will be dealt with in Chapter 6, which ends with a discussion on musical ability and personality factors.

2

Problems of testing

The professor struck a chord on the piano. 'What chord is this?' he asked. 'It's a major chord, sir,' replied the candidate. 'What else can you tell me about it?' After a pause in which the candidate could not elaborate on his answer, the professor sounded a discord. 'That's a major – no, minor seventh . . . .' 'Try again,' said the professor. But, though he played three more chords, he had already decided to reject the candidate. The second candidate was more fortunate; he possessed absolute pitch and had no difficulty in identifying the chords.

By such an arbitrary method were the candidates for places in the music department of an august British university selected not so very long ago. It does not take a psychologist to point out the deficiencies of such a procedure. The test was very brief and confined to only one type of item. With so much depending on their success, the candidates were likely to be nervous and had no time to settle. It is probable that a chord test had considerable discriminatory value with candidates who must have already passed through other screening examinations at earlier stages in their musical training. The successful candidates were no doubt found to be quite satisfactory by the professor, who after all had selected them himself. But he had no means of knowing how well some of the rejected candidates might have succeeded in the course.

Music teachers and examiners usually employ much more rational procedures. In fact, Wing (1968, p. 5) remarked that the organisation of a well-conducted musical competition is as close an approximation to a psychological test as it could be hoped to obtain in an aesthetic activity. The conditions are made as standard as possible, with the assessment being done on a scale of marks. However, the music festival adjudicator falls short of the demands of the psychologist in that his marks tend to vary with the standard of the competition. In addition to standard tasks and an objective scoring procedure, the psychological test includes tables of the scores made by representative groups, so that it is possible to compare the testee with others of similar age.

It is no easy matter, as Lowery (1929) pointed out, to devise tests of musical ability,

> since a passage of music involves numerous factors which, in general, are not readily isolated from one to another; so that the experimenter who would have his subjects attend to the variation of some one factor in a series of presented phrases is often at a loss how to obtain phrases in which the special factors to which attention is to be given may be pointed out quite unambiguously.

Lowery (1952) elsewhere relates that, when he first tried to formulate a cadence test on 'giving the test to both children and adults, chaotic results were obtained in spite of careful efforts to ensure the subjects understood what was required.'

Most of the tests so far developed have for practical reasons been intended for group application. Group tests enable results from the large numbers necessary for standardisation to be collected within a reasonably short time. They also enable the user to classify one or more classes of pupils at one session.

Readers who are interested in the task of developing a test battery will find a detailed account of the evolution of Wing's harmony test in his Monograph (1968). Briefly, the procedure is as follows: After deciding which aspects of musical ability he wishes to assess, the test author selects a number of possible items which seem suitable for his purpose. He then has to try them out on a variety of children or adults or both to see which are the most satisfactory. In the early stages it may not be possible to judge whether any unsatisfactory results are due to the music used, or to the method of application, or whether they are inherent in the style of test.

Each item of each subtest has to be carefully examined to see whether it is contributing its share to the total marks. This is done by item analysis which shows how many subjects obtain the correct answer to each item and also whether those who get the right answers are the subjects who are believed to be musical. After item analysis, unsatisfactory questions are revised or discarded.

Work can now begin on compiling the norms, i.e. the normal score that would be obtained by the 'average' child of a specified age. The groups whose scores are going to be used for the norms against which, when published, the results of testing will be compared must be as representative as possible of the whole population on which the test is likely to be used. The norms can be presented in various ways, e.g. by percentiles or by grades. With percentile ranks the score of the individual is interpreted in terms of what percentage of other individuals makes scores above (or below) his score. For example, if only 20 per cent of the group on which the test was standardised exceeds his score, he is said to have a percentile rank (PR) of 80. PR 50 is the median or middle point of a range of scores. In other tests, the scores are divided into grades, e.g. the top 10 per cent may be called 'A', etc.

In America, grade levels are often used instead of age levels. Since the age of entrance to school is 6, grade 1 would consist of 6-year-olds, but later grades might have more heterogeneous ages.

As well as providing tables of norms, a test author can be expected to publish evidence of the *reliability* and *validity* of his tests. Reliability refers to the consistency of a test in yielding the same, or closely comparable, results if given to the same subjects on subsequent occasions. It is shown statistically as a coefficient of correlation, i.e. a measure of the degree of resemblance of two sets of scores or of two orders of merit. When calculated directly from scores, the coefficient is indicated by the symbol r, when rank orders are used, by p (rho). If the two sets of scores corresponded exactly, the coefficient would be $1 \cdot 00$. Given a reasonably large sample, a coefficient of $\cdot 80$ or $\cdot 90$ is a very high correlation, such as is obtained by duplicate sets of a good intelligence test. A coefficient of $\cdot 40$ or less indicates only a slight resemblance between the two sets of scores and is quite consistent with many considerable differences in the position of individuals. A resemblance between the two sets of scores no greater than would happen (on the average) by mere chance would be represented by $\cdot 00$. If the two sets of figures are exactly the opposite to one another the figure would be minus $1 \cdot 00$.

A point that should be borne in mind is that the proportion of variance of a dependent variable determined by the independent variable is r^2, known as the coefficient of determination. Thus, a correlation of $\cdot 5$ may seem sizeable till we remember that r^2 would equal $\cdot 25$. That is, only one quarter of the variance between, say, a test of pitch discrimination and one of sight-singing, can be attributed to what they have in common, and threequarters is left unaccounted for.

In interpreting correlation coefficients, the range of abilities of the group studied must be kept in mind. A correlation will be lower for a very selected group than for one with a wide range of abilities. The reliability of a test depends on a number of factors. One is length. The longer the test, the more likely it is to be reliable, at least till the point is reached where scores may be affected by fatigue or boredom. Another important factor is the suitability of the test for the people on which it is being used. If there are, for example, too many difficult items, a large proportion of the answers may be based on guesswork. The reliability of a test can be assessed by giving it to the same group of people on two different occasions and correlating the results. This is the *test retest* method. Alternatively, two equivalent forms of the test might be given to the same group. A practical modification of this method is to compare odd and even items of one testing. This is known as the *split-half* method. A correction formula is applied to the result to compensate for the reduction by half of the number of items.

Another technique for estimating reliability was devised by Kuder and Richardson. Based on an analysis of the subject's performance on each item it in fact provides a measure of consistency between the items.

A test is said to be valid in so far as it measures what it purports to measure. Thus a test that claims to measure musical aptitude is valid only so far as it measures that and not, for example, intelligence or some other trait. One means of validating a test is by item analysis, as mentioned above. This ensures that it is internally consistent and that each item is measuring what all the other items are measuring. Other methods involve comparing test scores with some outside criterion of musical ability. This may be teachers' ratings, examination marks for music or success in music as a profession.

It is not usually easy to obtain reliable ratings from class teachers, especially in the case of a subject like music. A teacher probably knows the very able pupils and the very weak ones, but may find it very difficult to rate all the members of a class. Teachers of specialist music classes or of instrumental pupils are familiar with the work of the individual pupils, but these are usually selected and unrepresentative of the general population. However careful and unbiased the rater tries to be, his judgements may be subjective and inaccurate. When a low correlation between test and rating is obtained, it is often difficult to decide whether this is due to deficiencies in the test, or to the unreliability of the rating, or both.

The researcher who has identified a criterion which he wishes to assess may find multiple regression analysis a useful means of judging how much various factors (test scores, home environment, etc) contribute to the criterion. This statistical technique is intended to determine the amount of variance in a criterion variable, such as teachers' ratings of student talent, and the degree to which each predictor bears a significant relationship to the criterion. Thus, weightings can be calculated to find the best predictors to suit the given situation, allowing redundant tests to be discarded.

Another means of validating a test is suggested in Mursell's remark: 'We must try our developed tests on individuals known to be conspicuously musical and those known to be conspicuously non-musical to try to discover where the most crucial and significant performances are located.' If a music test has any validity at all, recognised musicians can be expected to make higher scores than persons of average or low ability. A test that can discriminate not only between those with a marked degree of ability and the definitely unmusical, but also between the more and the less able members of a highly talented group can be considered to have superior validity.

The results of comparing groups should be tested to see whether the difference obtained is actually 'statistically significant'. Significance in connection with differences of scores does not mean 'worth noting'. It means that the likelihood of such a difference, however large or small, arising by mere chance is so slight that it is not worth considering. If a difference is reported to be highly significant, the likelihood of its being due merely to chance is less than 1 in 100.

The statistical procedure of factor analysis is sometimes adopted to isolate the significant variables of musical ability and to validate the appropriate tests. Factor analysis is a means of resolving a set of intercorrelating tests into a few factors which are regarded as being the fundamental underlying variables (see further Chapter 5).

A further method of validating a new test is by comparing it with an existing established test. This has become possible only comparatively recently in the case of musical ability tests, owing to the lack of previous tests of proven validity.

Tests can be broadly divided into two types: those of attainment where the aim is to assess what has been learned, and those of aptitude or potentiality which seek to predict future success. In music, attainment tests may take the form of questionnaires on musical knowledge, or of scales against which vocal or instrumental performance can be compared. Most prognostic tests so far developed deal only with the aural side; the motor skills required for musical performance have been but little investigated. It has usually been the aim to try to devise tests that are as little affected by previous experience of music as possible. However, some tests, though mainly aural, require a knowledge of notation. In addition, efforts have been made to find means of assessing interest in music.

3

Tests of musical aptitude

This chapter is divided into three parts. The first deals with earlier attempts to test musical ability that were not commercially published. This may have been because the author was primarily interested in research or because he was unable to spare the time to produce a standardised version. In the second section we shall discuss the more important of the tests which are commercially available. Finally, mention will be made of more recent attempts to develop tests which have not been fully standardised.

Detailed description of tests which are commercially available, or which have at least enjoyed some use for research purposes, can be found in Appendix I, in the order in which they are discussed in this chapter.

Earlier unstandardised tests

In the 1880s Stumpf devised a few simple tests that are similar to those traditionally given by music teachers: singing a note that had been struck on the piano; judging which was the higher of two notes played successively; and judging degrees of consonance for pleasantness. These were successful in discriminating between experienced musicians and fourteen self-confessed 'unmusical' students.

In 1920 Revesz produced a more extensive battery of tests which, like Stumpf, required individual application. For example, the subject was asked to imitate by clapping rhythmic patterns played on the piano or to sing the notes of chords. He also attempted to test 'regional pitch', a sort of approximate absolute pitch. Eight notes between G_2 and A^3 were played on the piano in irregular order, the subject being asked to find each note on the piano. A test which Revesz believed to be particularly important was singing back melodies. He played nine bars of a tune; then repeated the first two bars, the subject being required to continue the melody. Revesz used the scores on this test as a criterion with which he correlated all the other tests. Playing from ear correlated ·77 and the pitch tests about ·60 with this criterion in his experiments with children aged 7-12.

Revesz (1946) recommended the use of his tests of rhythm, regional pitch, two-note chords and ability to grasp and sing a tune as measures of the 'lower grades of musicality'. For the 'higher grades of musicality' he proposed tests of relative pitch, harmonic apprehension and response, playing familiar tunes by ear and creative fantasy (singing the ending of a familiar, unfinished melody). Franklin considered the two rhythmic tests to be among the best in Revesz's battery and used them in a modified form for his own investigation (see p. 58). His results largely verified Revesz's. Revesz did not standardise his tests and did not intend them as group tests.

Schoen (1923; 1925) devised three tests intended to supplement the Seashore battery. In the test of relative pitch, the subject has to compare 100 paired intervals and say whether the second is larger or smaller than the first. For rhythm he has to state whether or not two rhythmic patterns played on one note are the same, and, if different, whether the first or second phrase has been changed. In the tonal sequence test, the listener has to judge the relative merits of four possible endings to a melody. The evidence of validity provided by Schoen is based on a comparison of scores with teachers' estimates for only 10 pupils.

Lowery (1926; 1929) produced three tests. In one, two cadences are played and the listener has to judge whether the second is 'more or less complete than the first'. Cadence tests are difficult to apply to subjects without musical training owing to the difficulty of describing them and because, in any case, two chord cadences present a certain ambiguity of key. Lowery also worked out a tone memory test which required the subject to recognise a theme after certain changes, e.g. after transposition to another key, and a phrasing test in fact involved memory to rather a high degree. The retest abilities obtained with 130 girls, aged 12-14, were quite promising (·75 and ·71).

Mainwaring (1931) constructed tests of perception of pitch differences and rhythmic patterns, and of recall. His primary purpose was to study the cognitive processes involved in musical ability. He began with a consideration of the four physical attributes of sound. He assumed that everyone who could hear at all could perceive differences in loudness and distinguish for example between a saxophone and a harp. He therefore confined his attention to pitch and rhythm. For details of the tests see Appendix I. Mainwaring, like Lowery, never fully standardised his tests.

Madison (1942) stressed the importance of the interval as the basic perceptual unit in music and carried out an extensive study of ability to discriminate intervals. As can be seen from Appendix I, this 'Test of Tonal Imagery' correlated significantly with success in musical activities. Christy (1956) reported promising results from its inclusion in the college records of the School of Music, Indiana University.

Lundin (1944; 1949) worked on a battery of tests that would measure objectively the aspects of music commonly taught in music theory courses, which include in the USA aural exercises as well as written work. The five tests (intervals, transposition, melodic and rhythmic sequences, and a type of chord analysis) cover quite a comprehensive range of musical abilities. The results Lundin obtained from his own experiments were on the whole promising, but the tests have not been published.

Standardised tests

The Seashore Measures of Musical Talents

The Seashore measures were the first standardised tests of musical ability to be published. Twenty years of intensive experimental work preceded the publication of the first edition in 1919.

Seashore's intention was to measure what he considered basic capacities for music, one at a time, before training has begun and, therefore, before they have been affected by musical training. He insisted that the scores for each subtest be used to provide a profile and not totalled to give a composite score. In most cases where they have been successfully applied, for example at the Eastman School of Music and in the Rochester (NY) public schools, a general classification based on composite scores has been employed. The total score has much greater reliability than the single tests.

Under ideal laboratory conditions Seashore claimed that a reliability coefficient of over ·90 could be obtained. In practice, much lower coefficients have been reported by users of the test, at least for the 1919 version. In the 1939 version the number of items in the subtests was reduced. Theoretically this should have reduced the reliability but results from the longer version were liable to be affected by inattention or fatigue, as Franklin (1956) showed in a detailed analysis of test and retest answers. Where the coefficients were relatively low, Seashore emphasised the importance of interpreting in broad categories only, and of retesting, if important decisions were to be based on doubtful performances. Retesting may, however, create other problems; the later results may be influenced by practice. In the case of musical subjects lower scores may be obtained since they are liable to become bored.

Sergeant (1973) reported evidence that the conditions of testing in a classroom are unsuited to the discrimination of fine differences of pitch. Music students made significantly more errors in a testroom situation than in a sound-attenuating booth or when listening through headphones.

While Seashore would have accepted Sergeant's point, he would most probably have strongly disagreed with Sergeant when he goes on to advocate the use of complex tones, not only because they are less liable to variations in intensity in a large room, but also because they enable experienced music students to demonstrate their superiority to a greater extent than do pure tones. Seashore would say that this is precisely why he chose pure tones. The validity Seashore claimed for his tests was 'an internal validation in terms of success in the isolation of the factor measured and the degree of control of all other factors in the measurement'. His critics did not deny that the pitch discrimination test, for example, is an objective and valid measure of sensory capacity but did question whether the results of such testing have much relevance to functional ability.

When the Eastman School of Music was opened, Stanton was appointed psychologist to the School, with full facilities for introducing a programme designed to validate the tests. After some promising experimentation during which the Seashore scores were compared with teachers' estimates of talent (see Schoen, 1940, pp. 181-3), a method of classifying entrants into five classes: 'discouraged, doubtful, possible, probable and safe' was worked out. Of the discouraged group, only 17 per cent completed the four years' course in the standard time, compared with the 60 per cent of the safe group who successfully graduated. Unfortunately, the predictive value of the Seashore tests alone cannot be determined from these data, since an intelligence test *was used as well as the measures in the classification of entrants. No correlations are given, or indications of the weightings attributed to each. The music tests seem to have been considered the more important.

Larson (1955) claimed that a selection programme based on the Seashore tests which she had carried out for twenty-five years among the school children of Rochester, NY had proved of great worth. Less favourable conclusions were reached, however, in an extensive study carried out by Taylor who investigated how effectively the subtests of the Seashore and Kwalwasser-Dykema batteries (see p. 19) could forecast (1) success in a college of music and (2) success in music as a profession. Marks for dictation, sight-singing, harmony and performance were used as criteria of college success. Professional success five years after leaving college was assessed by very careful enquiries from at least one person competent to judge. Compared with marks for dictation, all the Seashore test correlations were below ·30 and with sight-singing only intensity reached the ·33 level with around 150 students. From the 93 cases graded into five groups from the highly successful to the complete failures as professional musicians, correlations of between ·34 and ·47 were obtained. Two more recent studies of the use of the measures with professional musicians are discussed on p. 59.

The validation studies of both the 1919 and the revised version of the measures suggest that the tonal memory and pitch tests are the most satisfactory. A comparison with sight-singing scores gave co-efficients of ·60 with pitch and ·65 with tonal memory (Salisbury and Smith, 1929) and ·61 with pitch and ·63 with tonal memory (Dean, 1937). However, most of the correlations quoted in Appendix I fall well below ·50. Seashore himself protested against attempts to validate his measures against such criteria. It did indeed seem illogical to McLeish (1950) to try to demonstrate the worth of a test that was supposed to provide a more reliable assessment of ability than teachers' opinions by comparing the scores with music grades and teachers' ratings. He therefore undertook a factorial study in which he tested a hundred students with the 1919 version and with the Wing and the Oregon tests (see below). He came to the conclusion that the measures were 'adequate for their original purpose, to measure the most elementary abilities required for the understanding and appreciation of music'. Comparing the Seashore and Wing batteries he concluded 'that Wing's tests measure much the same kind of ability as Seashore's but measure it at a higher or at least a different level, namely, that of musical meaning'. The measures, McLeish added, will be 'most effective if the scores are weighted in accordance with the calculated regression coefficients and if used in conjunction with other tests of musical appreciation'. Sheldon (1964) found both the pitch and tonal memory tests predictive of ability to sing on pitch among college non-music majors, but found prediction could be improved by a multiple regression equation.

Kwalwasser-Dykema Music Tests

Kwalwasser and Dykema published in 1930 a set of tests in which musical notes are used on the same lines as Seashore uses sensory material. Like Seashore's, the K-D battery contains measures of pitch, intensity, time, rhythm, timbre and tonal memory. Except for tonal memory, however, the corresponding tests in the two batteries do not appear to measure the same variables. To these, four tests have been added: tonal movement, melodic taste, pitch imagery and rhythmic imagery. The test manual does not mention reliability or validity. Studies on the reliability of the tests suggest that being shorter they are much less reliable than the Seashore tests. The most satisfactory seems to be the tonal movement test, the next best being tonal memory. But the reliability of the other subtests and even of the test as a whole is very low.

Because the battery is more musical and less tedious to take than the Seashore, it enjoyed considerable popularity in the United States. Holmes (1954) therefore thought it worthwhile to develop new directions together with a new set of weighted scoring keys and new norms. As a result of his revisions, Holmes obtained considerably improved coefficients with high school pupils.

However, the validity of the tests is still open to doubt. Lundin's (1967) table of validity studies reported by five different investigations shows 17 instances where a negative correlation was found between a subtest and the criterion and only four examples of validities of ·40 or over and one of ·59. For example, the results of a study by Bienstock with over 100 students enrolled in the High School of Music and Art in New York showed that intelligence tests predicted individual success in the music courses better than did the K-D tests. This may have been because the tests do not contain enough discriminating items at certain important levels. Taylor found the pitch imagery and the K–D tonal memory tests the two outstanding subtests from the K–D and Seashore batteries in her investigation described above.

In his book Kwalwasser (1955) refers to several researches carried out by his students which show that his tests separate the most from the least musical children in a class, and that music students make appreciably higher scores than liberal arts students.

Farnsworth (1969) sums up the differing results of validity studies of the K–D tests in the words: 'Perhaps the modal forecast value for the battery as a whole would lie in the neighborhood of ·40, with that for the individual tests being considerably lower.'

The Drake Music Tests

Drake, a musician as well as a psychologist, produced the first test based on musical material that had really satisfactory reliability and validity. He experimented with four tests: interval discrimination, retentivity, intuition and musical memory. In the retentivity test the subject is required to remember a musical interval, a beat given by a metronome, and a three-note sequence. He then has to judge whether each of several intervals is greater or smaller than the original and whether a single note was the first, second or third note of the three-note sequence. (This ingenious test, intended 'as a test of absolute pitch or memory for isolated tones' seems to offer scope for the development of some really difficult musical puzzles!) The intuition test was supposed to measure 'intuitions' for phrase balance, time balance or key centre. Only the musical memory and interval discrimination tests gave satisfactory results with more than one group (Drake, 1933).

Drake, therefore, concentrated on standardising the musical memory test and in 1942 a recording was published. In 1954 Drake produced a rhythm test, which is in fact a test of whether or not the subject can keep a steady beat in his mind during a period of silence. This is of course an important ability for all types of musical performance.

The reliability of the two tests is high, especially for musical groups. (However Gordon (1961) reported some disturbingly large discrepancies between two testings of 20 subjects.) The advantage of measuring only two kinds of performance is that the subtests can be longer, thus improving reliability. The memory test alone takes 20-25 minutes, as compared with the 12 minutes required for the first three Wing tests.

The validity data given in the test manual is on the whole good, though the range of the coefficients is wide. Drake offers no explanation of the variations, apart from referring to the inaccuracies of the raters. Correcting for unreliability of the ratings would raise, for example, coefficients of ·70 to ·90. The validity figures obtained by Lundin (1949) and by Christy (1959) were much lower. Ferrell (1961) concluded from a study of the memory test with 180 pupils from three high schools that it successfully identified students that had superior musical aptitude. From comparisons of professional musicians, music majors and non-musicians, Griffin and Eisenman (1972) concluded that the test was useful as a gross indicator of success in music courses.

In the case of the rhythm test, Manturzewska (1978) reported that it was the only one of many music tests she used with international piano competitors, and music students and students of other disciplines which did not discriminate between the music groups and students whose special subjects were theoretical. Indeed musicologists gained higher scores than instrumentalists. (Cf. Tomita and Kurosu's results, p. 228.) The mean scores of music school students on the Drake memory test fell in the range above the 95th percentile for the population of general (musically unselected) Polish schools. Within the music students, the highest 10 per cent compared with the lowest 10 per cent, scored higher, especially on Form A.

The Drake memory test has survived for more than 40 years, and won considerable approval. The rhythm test is the only published test available that specifically measures ability to keep in time.

The Oregon and Indiana-Oregon Discrimination Tests

In 1930, Kate Hevner experimented with a test based on material from the compositions of accepted composers. The subjects had to listen to four versions of each item and judge which was the original, and which had been distorted by a mutilation of the rhythm, harmony or melody.

Keeping in mind four versions of a melody proved, however, too difficult a task for general use. In 1935, therefore, Hevner devised and published an easier and more useful form of the test, where only one distorted version had to be compared with the original. Besides stating which version he prefers, the subject also has to decide which element – rhythm, harmony or melody – has been altered. Hevner found that the earlier test had considerable discriminatory value in distinguishing between psychology students and advanced music students and that results with the later form were similar. A second version of the test also requires the hearer to state the degree of confidence he feels in his judgements.

The Oregon tests have usually been regarded as tests of taste and appreciation, as distinguished from ear acuity tests. However, ability to perceive the differences between the accepted and distorted version is obviously required. Moreover, building up a listening repertoire of good music with which to compare the versions must partly depend on general auditory efficiency. McLeish found quite moderately high correlations between the test and both the Seashore and Wing tests. Of these three batteries, the Oregon seemed to demand the highest degree of musical ability, particularly the score based on judgement of the nature of the change.

The Oregon tests enjoyed wide use and considerable esteem (Lundin, 1967, and Farnsworth, 1969) for a number of years, though reports on experimental studies involving these tests have been few in number. Long (1971; 1978) has worked on a revision of the tests under the guidance of Hevner. Thirty-one items were selected for reconstruction. To these were added 75 excerpts from piano, organ, string quartet and woodwind literature, mutilations being composed for each. A tape recording of these items was submitted to a panel of musicians who rated the items for probable difficulty and screened out those of doubtful validity. A 43-item test was eventually produced. Later shorter versions were devised for use with schoolchildren. Attempts to adapt the test for use with elementary school children showed that, while they were able to make an overall judgement of distorted versus original, they were unable to judge with any consistency which element had been altered (Long, 1972).

To provide a third choice, some items were repeated. The reliability figures for all three versions of the test rise to above ·8, at least with testees of 15 or over. The elementary school children version produced a reliability coefficient of ·59 with 383 children between six and ten. Besides depending on 'expert' opinion and a rather limited analysis of the most discriminating items, Long claims a correlation of ·7 with a music experience inventory used with 'a diversified population'. The scores of graduate music majors correlated ·48 with Madison's test of tonal imagery and ·49 with a test of dictation.

Now that the test has been published, future research will be able to investigate how the new version compares with the original and with other tests.

The Wing Standardised Tests of Musical Intelligence

Wing first started to work in the field of music tests in 1933. After a thorough survey of such tests as were then available, he decided 'to compile a comprehensive series of new tests, to assess their relative merits, and . . . to select a short series of proved diagnostic value'. There were 21 tests in the pilot survey. These were revised and later increased to 25. In addition to tests of a cognitive type, Wing sought to include tests of appreciation – 'the fundamental quality that all musicians would desire to find in any person who claims to have an interest in the art' (Wing, 1941*b*, p. 70).

After various modifications the seven most suitable tests were standardised. Further revisions have since been carried out, any item that appeared at all doubtful being removed or modified. The first three tests deal with aural acuity and the last four with taste or preference. The reliability of the whole test and of the first three subtests certainly seem to be good. The reliability of the four appreciation tests is less well established.

To establish the validity of his test Wing investigated the relationship between his test results and ability to persevere with the playing of a musical instrument. 333 boys, aged 14 to 16, were divided into Above Average, Average and Below Average groups according to their test scores. Wing (1968) then found that 40 per cent of those with below average, and 27 per cent of those with average ability, who had started to learn an instrument, had let their playing lapse, while only 2 per cent of those of the above average group had ceased to play. A similar study of 718 adults showed that 83 per cent of the below average group, 30 per cent of the average group and only 9 per cent of the highest ability group had given up playing (Wing, 1954).

Independent studies have confirmed the validity of the test (see Appendix I). Newton's (1959) study was carried out at the Admiralty with a view to reducing failure during training among the junior musicians at the Royal Marines School of Music. In his report Newton recommended that the test should be incorporated in the selection procedure and that a score of 70 (out of 136) should be adopted as a discretionary minimum. While candidates with lower scores would not necessarily be excluded, more stringent regard would be paid to their educational standard and personal qualities.

Bentley (1955) included the Wing tests, along with Gaston's test, and the Farnum Music Notation test (see below) in a critical study of music tests then recently published. He matched 110 instrument-playing music students of a California high school with 110 non-instrument-playing students on the basis of sex, IQ, grade placement and socio-economic status. Of all the tests included in his study the Wing tests were the most discriminating between the instrument-playing group and the non-instrument-playing group (many of whom had had music lessons). Correlation with an index of interest in music was higher than that of any of the other music aptitude tests. Bentley concluded that where a critical analysis of individual capacities is required for guidance purposes, the Wing battery was the best test to use. When only a short time is available for testing, the first three Wing tests were the most satisfactory.

In Manturzewska's research, Wing's tests produced comparable results to those of Drake's memory test. Wing tests 1-3 were, however, rather more discriminatory between the highest and lowest 10 per cent of music students.

Though the battery was intended to be used as a whole to provide a general assessment of musical ability, some evidence is available on the relative value of the subtests:

Test I: chord analysis. This has proved to be a most effective test over a wide range of aptitude. The opinion of Stumpf and Revesz as to the value of chord analysis as a diagnostic test of talent would seem to be justified. Even among the 41 professional students tested by Wing at the Eastman School of Music, it successfully separated the good student from the very good one (see Shuter, 1964, p. 386).

Tests 2 and 3: pitch change and memory. McLeish (1950) regarded these as being the best validated of the whole battery, in the sense of showing the highest loading on a general music factor. This also proved to be the case with a group of students of average musical ability, studied by the writer. However, among highly select Eastman students these two tests were too easy to be really discriminating. Both Whittington (1957) and Newton found tests 2 and 3 to be among the three most effective. The pitch test was particularly good at picking out the junior musicians who were below average. The most efficient of all with the RMSM group was the memory test. 24 (out of 27) of the Above Average boys made above average scores, while 17 out of 28 Below Average boys scored lower than the mean of the total group of 223. In Bentley's results, the pitch test was the most effective single measure of pitch discrimination used in his study, and the memory test the most effective measure of memory.

Tests 4 to 7: appreciation of rhythm, of harmony, of intensity and of phrasing. Wing found that the majority of the items of these four tests were too difficult for most children of nine years and under. Their usefulness increases with age and with level of musical ability. With the RMSM junior musicians the harmony test was second only to the memory test in efficiency in discriminating the good from the average and the weak from the average of the total group. The Eastman students, however, found it rather too easy to be highly discriminating.

The last two tests are especially liable to be affected by fatigue and loss of concentration, particularly with less talented students. However, in Wing's own factorial study (1941a), the phrasing test gave the highest loading on a general music factor and Whittington found it one of the three most satisfactory for discriminating between his musical and unmusical groups. Whellams (1973a) found it was by far the best discriminator between professional and non-professional students.

Martin (1979) sought to derive a formula that would help identify children who should be encouraged to join a school orchestra. He experimented with various multiple regression analyses of data obtained by testing 180 secondary school pupils (see also p. 203) with the Wing, Indiana-Oregon and Hoffren tests and from a questionnaire on their experience of music. The most effective formula consisted of three variables: (*i*) total scores of Wing tests 4-7; (*ii*) self-assessment of instrumental ability and (*iii*) whether or not the pupil had studied an orchestral instrument for at least two years. It would be interesting to see whether this formula would be predictive in other schools.

The Gaston Test of Musicality

Gaston aimed at providing a general assessment of the subject's musical ability and interest in music. The latest version of this test, issued in 1958, presented all the tonal items on one continuous record.

The test consists of 40 items, the first 18 of which are in the form of a questionnaire seeking to assess interest in music. This leaves only 22 actual tonal test items. Reliability of the test is good. However, as Bentley points out, the validity evidence put forward by Gaston shows that the association between teachers' ratings and the scores reached a significant level only in the case of older children and of the total group studied by Gaston. The seven melodic memory items were, of all the tests Bentley investigated, most discriminating in distinguishing the instrument- from the non-instrument-playing group. The other items proved too easy for his subjects. In some situations, the testees may feel the interest questions reassuring at the beginning of the testing session.

The Gordon Musical Aptitude Profile (MAP)

McLeish (Buros, 1972) hailed the MAP as 'without a doubt, the best test of its kind on the market. It conforms to all the criteria of excellence not only in test construction and validation, but in musicality.'

Published in 1965, the battery is intended to be administered on three days, and consists of three parts: tonal imagery (melody and harmony), rhythm imagery (tempo and metre) and musical sensitivity (phrasing, balance and style). The musical examples are all original tunes composed by Gordon himself for violin and cello and are performed by professional players. The phrasing and style tests are designed to assess interpretative ability. The balance test is supposed to be related to melodic and rhythmic creative ability, at least indirectly. Gordon's approach to establishing the 'better' version for his sensitivity tests was to begin by asking professional musicians which of two interpretations of specially composed items they preferred. Both versions contained intended musical faults, but one was designed to be a 'better' rendition than the other. Only when nine out of ten of the musicians agreed on the correct version and their judgements had been confirmed by field trials were the items incorporated into the final version of the test.

A notable feature of the MAP is the provision of a possible 'in-doubt' answer. This arises from Gordon's mixing easier with more difficult items, instead of proceeding from easy to difficult (as e.g. do Wing's memory test and the Bentley pitch discrimination test). Presenting the easier items first may cause the talented child to become bored; if the child does not know the right answer, Gordon believes that it is better to ask him to mark an 'in-doubt' column than to tell him to guess.

As we should expect with these longer tests, reliability is excellent. The validity evidence published in the manual was very promising. A three-year longitudinal study was published in 1967. Some 250 pupils, aged ten to eleven from eight class-rooms in five different schools were tested before the beginning of instrumental music lessons. The teachers were not told their pupils' scores. At the end of each year the children's achievements in music were compared with their test scores. The criteria used to evaluate progress were (*i*) ratings of melodic, rhythmic and expressive aspects of tape-recorded performances of short études (these were composed by Gordon in consultation with the teachers as to their suitability for the stage reached); (*ii*) the teachers' ratings of each pupil's progress as compared with others in the group; and (*iii*) scores on an early version of the ITML (see p. 39). The profile was shown to be a valuable predictor of achievement.

Since an important objective of the MAP was to provide teachers with a profile of strengths and weaknesses, a logical extension was a study of the progress of children who would volunteer to learn an instrument and who would be pretested with the MAP and then divided into two matched groups; both groups would be taught by the same teachers, in the case of one group the teachers would be told the MAP scores of the pupils, in the other, they would not.

Besides the curriculum that the teachers would normally have used, supplementary exercises were given appropriate to the musical talents measured by the MAP. The 190 children who took part in the experiment received one 30-minute lesson a week in classes learning similar instruments and comprising pupils of all aptitude levels. Both the results achieved at the end of the first year (Froseth, 1971) and at the end of the second year (Gordon, 1970) showed that the pupils whose teachers had knowledge of their MAP scores achieved more than the other group. This was particularly true for the highest scores (PR 90+) and the lowest scores (PR 24−). It has sometimes been held that when teachers know that certain pupils have low IQs they tend to expect less of them and that this lack of expectation communicates itself to the children, who hence achieve less than they might have done. This was not true of the present study. This may have been because the teachers were not only 'forewarned' but 'forearmed' in that they had materials to hand that would help them to provide suitable exercises for the lowest as well as the highest scorers.

Hatfield (1967) studied the association of the MAP to activities such as improvising a variation, rhythmic and interpretation tasks; his subjects were 105 members of a university band. Scores on the melody and harmony tests correlated highly with ability to perform with good intonation in unison and in parts, respectively. Scores on the sensitivity tests were substantially correlated with musical expressive abilities, talents for improvisation, and perception of appropriate tempo in the performance of music. The relationships between the MAP rhythm tests and Hatfield's rhythmic tasks were less strong. Young (1976) also found the test with the greatest predictive power for development in pitch ability and performance on a band instrument was the MAP tonal subtest (see further p. 4).

The length of the MAP may seem to create a problem, at least for researchers whose access to pupils may be limited. Brown (1969) investigated whether it would be possible to reduce the length of the subtests without reducing reliability; this did not prove possible. Gordon (1968a) discussed the contribution of each test to overall validity. He concluded from a multiple regression analysis of data from the three year study that the tests of metre and balance did not contribute significantly to the prediction of musical success. That the balance subtest did not prove more useful was, Gordon believed, due to the study not providing scope for the pupils' creative abilities. That the metre subtest did not provide a significant contribution may have been due to the teachers being more concerned with ability to maintain a consistent tempo than with ability to perceive metre. Schleuter (1977) is experimenting with an abbreviated form of the MAP containing 40 tonal, 24 rhythm and 54 sensitivity items for use as a college entrance test for potential music majors. Reliability for the tonal items ranged between ·75 and ·83, for sensitivity between ·63 and ·88. The rhythm items were less satisfactory (generally in the 50s), due partly to the small number of items and a lack of variation in the scores. Previous attempts to extend the use of the MAP to college students (Lee, 1967; Young, 1972; and Schleuter and Chambers, 1976) had found sufficient variability in the full version of the MAP to make it useful as a diagnostic tool and as a guide to the optimum courses to suit students whose college studies of music might be limited to a single course.

The Bentley Measures of Musical Abilities

Arnold Bentley's tests (1966) arose from his interest in the musical development of children aged 7 or 8 to 14. The pitch discrimination test returns to the use of smaller than semitone differences as Seashore had done. A pilot test of pitch discrimination, based on a comparison of melodic intervals from a semitone up to a tenth proved too easy. A possible means of increasing the difficulty would have been to mask the pitch change by adding concurrent notes, as in Wing's test. Since, however, the harmonic aspect of music seemed to have little appeal to young children (cf. Chapter 9), and because artistic performance on pitch-variable instruments seemed to require subtle deviations from exact intonation comparable to *rubato*, Bentley decided to introduce smaller than semitone differences. In the current version, the twenty items range from one semitone (26 Hz difference at A = 440 Hz) to 3 Hz. His experiments with differences as low as 1 Hz suggested that 3 Hz was the smallest useful pitch difference that could be included in a group test.

Bentley's chord analysis test is similar to Wing's, although it contains a higher proportion of two-note chords. Tonal memory and rhythm memory are tested separately. This makes the requirements of both tests less confusing for younger children.

Misgivings have been expressed by reviewers (Buros, 1972) about the inclusion of a 20-item test of chord analysis, when the memory tests have only 10 items each. Bentley (1966) makes it clear that, although the test is difficult for younger children, 14 per cent of 10-year-olds make scores of 11 or more (well above the theoretical guessing average), the justification for including it being its effectiveness in identifying 'early starters'.

The reliability figures, at least for the tests taken as a whole, are good. Since their publication, Bentley (1970; 1977) has collected further evidence of the stability and the validity of the scores. Candidates for entry to the choir of New College, Oxford are selected by the organist on criteria of vocal quality and range, ability to sing back tunes and the singing of a prepared song. All the candidates for some years took the Bentley test. The scores were referred to only after the selection had been made. The lowest musical quotient analogous to IQ among successful candidates over six years was 155 and the mean MQ 180. Eighty per cent of some 500 children in the UK from widely differing social and ethnic backgrounds who have been retested at intervals ranging from 7 to 12 months achieved remarkably consistent scores. Movement between adjoining grades might occur, but children with initially high grades were not likely to drop and those with very low scores were not likely to rise to the highest grades on a later occasion.

From a comparative study of the Bentley test and the MAP, Young (1973) concluded that, despite their short length, the Bentley measures could be considered to possess a moderately high validity for the purpose of assessing the musical potential of children around 14. A coefficient of ·58 was obtained between the composite MAP score and the total of the Bentley tests.

Mawbey (1973) found a connection between ability as measured by the Bentley tests and perseverance in the learning of a musical instrument. Of 118 secondary school pupils, 50 per cent with grade A or B ability gave up music lessons, 72 per cent of C grade and 75 per cent of D and E grade dropped out. In the case of 330 children aged 7 to 11 33 per cent of A or B grade, 49 per cent of C grade, and 84 per cent of D or E gave up learning an instrument.

The Gordon Primary Measures of Musical Audiation (PMMA)

Though Gordon believes that musical aptitudes do not stabilise till a child is about 9, he has devised these measures to serve as a diagnostic aid to the strengths and weaknesses of children between 5 and 8 (Gordon, 1979*a*). The test is in two parts: tonal and rhythm. The child has to listen to a pair of short phrases and decide if they are the same or different. If they sound the same, the child draws a circle around the pair of faces which are the same on the answer sheet; if they sound different, he draws a circle around the pair of different faces. The patterns used were selected on the basis of children's perception of tonal and rhythm patterns (Gordon, 1977; 1978). The tonal phrases are all performed at the same tempo and in the same key. At least one phrase of the pair includes the tonic, and the tonic is included in both patterns in the pair in strategically placed items in the test. The differences are due to one or more pitches, the melodic contour, or both being changed. The rhythm phrases include tempo beats which may or may not be systematic in length, the melodic rhythm being performed on a synthesizer in a different timbre and louder than the rhythm beats.

Gordon reports good reliability even with kindergarten children. The rhythm test is rather less reliable, due, Gordon suggests, to some of the children having had little experience of rhythmic movement. If the children have had any experience at all of a written test, the results are likely to be more reliable. A longitudinal study of the test's validity is under way. Children who were receiving tuition in music made higher scores than unselected children (see further p. 233). To obtain evidence of congruent validity, 227 children aged 9 were tested with the MAP and the PMMA. Though the PMMA was too easy for 10-year-olds, the correlations were promising. In short, this latest of the Gordon tests seems set to prove both useful in music education and a valuable tool for research with younger children. It is already being translated into Hebrew for use in Israel.

Zenatti Tests Musicaux pour les Jeunes Enfants

This battery of tests has been developed from Arlette Zenatti's extensive researches with 7000 younger children (see further Chapters 8 and 9). The tests are intended to be administered to children between 4:0 and 7:11, individually. As with individual intelligence tests, such as the Stanford-Binet and the Wechsler tests, a great deal more can be learned from the manner in which the person tackles the test than is expressed in the quantitative score. Zenatti presents the tests in a 'play' situation. For example, in the test of identifying two melodies, practice is given in learning 'Which is the song the dog likes?' and 'Which is the song the horse likes?' During the test the child has to point to a picture of the dog or horse, or else to name the animal. The aesthetic tests make use of judgements of e.g. consonance/dissonance, or tonal/atonal melodies. These are scored only for consistency of response, each item being presented for a second time in a different order. In spite of there being rather few items, reliability of test and retest are satisfactory. Like Gordon, Zenatti intends to undertake a longitudinal study to establish the validity of her test. Zenatti presents suggestions for the use of the tests with adults and children in pathological cases; she is researching further the application of the tests in pathology.

Tests not commercially available

Though some attention has been given to the testing of a comprehensive range of musical abilities, test authors have also tended to explore more specialised areas, such as aesthetic and rhythmic aspects of musical ability.

The basis of Franklin's research (1956) at the University of Gothenburg was that a melody ends on the tonic. If the subject can find this tone, he has thereby demonstrated his musical ability. Franklin, therefore, sought to construct a series of short two-part melodies which would be interrupted immediately before the final tone, the subject then being required to complete the melody by singing the final note. Later, Franklin constructed a group version. Though the music for the individual form of the tests has been published in Franklin's thesis no recorded version is available.

The reliability, in the 80s, seems very promising for a 15-minute test. The validity compared with a teachers' ranking was ·51. These coefficients refer to the individual form of the test.

Mueller (1956) commented on a need for assessing the intellectual processes involved in the appreciation of music and described a testing procedure. A complete composition is presented to the listeners and repeated three or four times. After the first presentation of the piece, the listener checks his answers to a list of questions. During two or three more hearings he continues to study the same or more difficult lists. Such questions may be as simple or as difficult as the experimenter desires. Mueller describes an experiment in which over 100 students at Indiana University listened to the third movement of Mozart's Symphony No 40 in G minor. After listening to the piece the student was given five minutes to write a brief description of it. He was then asked to read through a list of 43 brief questions and to check with the number one his degree of assent on a scale as follows: strongly disagree, probably disagree, no opinion, probably agree, strongly agree. During the second and third playing of the movement the student had the list in front of him and recorded his observations on each question with '2' and '3' to indicate second or third hearing, either during or after the hearing of the piece. The questions included 'piece includes three-four time' and 'harp and piano are heard'.

The reliability of the scale was ·80, the correlation with music training was ·56 and with an interest in music scale ·70. Mueller's experiment produced interesting results and her procedure could usefully be adapted to obtaining information on the appreciation of many different types of composition with various sorts of listener.

Hoffren (1964) of Jacksonville University has tried to produce a test of expressive performance of music that would resemble as closely as possible the judgement required in an actual musical situation. The ingredients of expression which he included were: rubato, smoothness, articulation, phrasing, unity, continuity, dynamic and agogic accentuation. Each test item consists of two versions of the same musical excerpt. One version of each pair is deficient in one or more of these elements of expression. The testee is asked to select the more appropriate version. He is not told which element of expression is lacking. Reliability coefficients range from ·53 to ·66. Hoffren's primary means of validation depended on agreement among judges drawn from the staff and graduate students of the University of Illinois School of Music as to which was the better version. A correlation of ·35 with the corresponding subtests of the Wing battery was found. Musicians as compared with subjects with less training and experience of music gained significantly superior average scores.

Leon Crickmore (1968; 1973) has attempted to obtain a quantitative measure of the aesthetic response to music. Starting with the suggestion (Bell, 1914; Langer, 1942) that an aesthetic response or emotion may exist, Crickmore developed a test to recognise it. The test comprises only seven items which need a cross each and is to be completed at the end of the piece of music heard. Crickmore's test decides that an 'aesthetic response' has occurred if a particular profile of scores is achieved. Crickmore has correlated results on his test with Wing scores using engineering students and the results were low, not surprisingly given that the testing situation might evoke an analytical rather than a synthetic attitude on the part of the listener. Although an initial attempt has been made to standardise the test (Gabriel and Crickmore, 1977), it proved not to show test-retest reliability, perhaps due to the intrinsic elusiveness of aesthetic experience.

After experimenting with several different sorts of rhythmic tests for adults (see p. 63), Thackray (1972) turned his attention to tests of rhythmic ability for children. More musical material was introduced into the six tests adapted from the adult version. The age span to which the tests can be applied ranges from 8 to 18. The reliability of the whole test seems to be satisfactory, though that of test 2 and of test 5 was low on retest. Thackray believed that, in the case of 2 ('steady counting'), this might be reflecting the frequent observation of teachers that ability to keep a steady tempo sometimes varies from day to day. Test 5, comparing rhythms, proved to be more reliable with children of 13 and over. As it seemed to be a highly discriminating test, Thackray did not drop it from his battery. Evidence of the validity of the test which Thackray cites was based on the superior performance of students specialising in music and dance. Thackray has also devised three tests of rhythmic performance for children, but gives no details of their reliability. (See further Chapter 4.)

Creative ability is hard to test, even by individual methods (Wing, 1968). Vater (1934) and Vidor (1931) gave their subjects tasks like a tapped time pattern on which to build a tune. Recently, Vaughan (1977; Vaughan and Myers, 1971), has experimented with the possibility of producing a music creativity test modelled on the Torrance Tests of Creative Thinking. Two types of items are used. A rhythmic or melodic pattern is presented and the child asked to improvise an answer; or else a basic outline or ostinato is set up and the child makes up a pattern to go with it. The making of an *interesting* response is emphasised. The test has been used with good effect with children as young as seven as well as with adults. A problem is the evaluation of results produced. Vaughan scores the responses on four criteria: fluency (ease of responding regardless of quality); rhythmic security; ideation (how often patterns occur which are more than note-for-note response) and synthesis (how well the ideas come together). Reliability among judges have ranged from ·67 to ·90. Correlations with the Bentley measures are positive but low, as are those with the Torrance test.

Gorder (1980), too, has tried to produce measures of musical divergent production. The beginning notes of a phrase (in two cases also the final note) are presented and the subjects are asked to improvise as many phrases as possible within three minutes. The tape-recorded improvisations are scored for fluency (number of phrases produced), flexibility (shifts of musical content), elaboration (varied use of musical content), originality (rarely used content) and 'music appeal'. Except for fluency, the scores of all the parts showed sizeable loadings on a factor which was associated with rating of musical creativity by the school band director and a test of improvisation ability. The test was designed to be undertaken by students with the minimally acceptable music abilities at junior high school level. The test requires individual administration, taking only about 20 minutes including instructions. The scoring, however, calls for time, effort and expertise. Consistency of response was promising. However, reliability among judges was variable. Associations with the Seashore tests and the Drake rhythm test, with IQ and with the Torrance figural tests were low.

Davies (1971) devised tests that he hoped would measure 'bedrock' basic capacities from which all types of musical abilities develop and which would be as little affected by experience of music as possible. Having found that the accuracy of pitch judgements of a musically trained group was not significantly affected by change of timbre, but that a musically untrained group performed worse with certain wave-forms, Davies decided to use sine-waves. At the same time, he insisted that a valid measure of melodic memory must be based on intact tunes (as opposed to changes of single notes of the Seashore, Wing and Bentley tests). For his melody test he used tonal sequence based on statistical approximations to music in the equal-tempered scale (see Davies, 1978, pp. 75-8), while envisaging the production of sequences based on a scale not common to any culture in an attempt to reduce effects of experience still further. After considerable experimentation to produce items easy enough, he succeeded in producing a test battery in which at least the melody test and the composite score had reasonable reliability. The tests seem to differentiate musical from randomly selected groups.

Davies's approach would seem worth further investigation in these days of electronic music. So far the tests seem to have been used mainly in his own experiments (see further Chapter 17).

Kai Karma (1975; 1979) in Helsinki is experimenting with a test based on the ability to structure acoustic material, which he considers to be the central factor in musical aptitude. In one version of his test the subjects have to divide the first section of each item into three similar parts in their minds and then decide whether the second section is similar. Pitch, loudness or length of note may be changed in the 'answer'. Reliability figures range between ·60 and ·80. Research is continuing with the test. It seems already to be proving useful in aiding the selection of candidates for music school.

Stankov and Horn (1980) have developed for their own research purposes auditory tests intended to be analogous to established tests in the visual modality. (See further Chapter 5.)

Sergeant (1979) has paid particular attention to producing a test that would eliminate the problem of children having to understand 'higher' and 'lower' in a pitch discrimination test, without sacrificing the number of choices and the greater reliability gained thereby. In his test, therefore, five tones are presented, one differing in pitch; the child has to determine which of the five is different. With younger children the introductory instructions include a simple auditory task : identifying the mewing of a cat from four examples of a dog barking.

The test consists of 30 sequences of square wave tones, approximating to an organ 'string-tone' stop, at the basic frequency of 290 Hz, with one of the five tones varying from the other four by from $\pm$ 20 to ± 1 Hz. In his experiments with children between 6 and 9 years old, Sergeant obtained a reliability coefficient of ·76. In an investigation comparing five types of test, Sergeant and Boyle (1980) report K-R reliability coefficients of ·77 and split-half ones of ·86 with 65 children aged 11 and 12.

This would seem an excellent measure of pitch discrimination to use whenever the children concerned cannot be assumed to know the meaning of 'higher' or 'lower' with regard to pitch. It certainly seems easier than the two-step judgement (same vs different, if different, higher or lower?) as required, e.g., in Bentley's test. However, the ability to hold the possibility of two steps in mind may have its own virtues (cf. p. 70).

Summary

From the pedagogic view, we can say that useful tests of musical aptitude have been developed. The Seashore measures, once their limitations as predictors of functional musical achievement have been accepted, can now be more dispassionately judged as valid for the measurement of specific abilities. As Lundin (1958) suggested, we should try to find 'the specific performances where these abilities are needed' before discarding the measures. Is it, for example, true, as Seashore asserts, that the violinist requires the fine ear for differences in pitch as measured by his test in view of the place of vibrato in performance which Seashore's measurements of performance reveal? (See further p. 59.)

Gordon's Musical Aptitude Profile, with its attention to melodic, harmonic, rhythmic and appreciation aspects, would now seem to reign supreme for aptitude testing for children of 9 and over. For a quick assessment of the musical ability of children from 8 to 14, the Bentley measures have won an established place. For the provisional assessment of the aptitude of children still younger (5 to 8), Gordon's new Primary Measures of Music Audiation seem most promising. Is there still a place for the older tests, Drake, Wing and Gaston? Drake's two tests have justified continued use, as has the Gaston for those who wish to explore interest along with response to tonal items. The recording of the Wing tests may sound rather less than perfect and the instructions perhaps didactic to some modern ears. Notoriously, the hi-fi enthusiast is not necessarily the person most sensitive to music. While an improved recording would be most welcome, the intrinsic worth of the present test remains without real challenge.

All these tests have research uses. Many researchers aspire to produce *ad hoc* tests. This may of course often be necessary, but if a standardised test already exists, it would seem sensible to use it. At the least an established test can serve as a reference point in relation to which new tests can be judged. There is of course always a need for the collection of additional data on existing tests.

4

Tests of attainment, of performance, and of interest in music

The last few years have seen the publication of several notable tests of musical achievement. These include: Colwell's Musical Achievement Tests (MAT), and Gordon's Iowa Tests of Musical Literacy (ITML) at the school level and Bridges's Australian Test for Advanced Music Studies at the college entrance level. These all have aural items requiring musical aptitude as well as a knowledge of notation. They thus differ from pencil-and-paper tests than can be answered by those who have acquired a factual knowledge about music.

The Colwell Music Achievement Tests (MAT)

The general purpose of the MAT are to enable the teacher to determine how well each pupil has mastered the basic auditory objectives of the school music programme, to offer information as to the pupils who will most profit from instrumental instruction and to provide data for evaluation and improvement of the curriculum.

The tests were developed by Colwell between 1962 and 1969 and published between 1969 and 1970 (the first edition was called Elementary Music Achievement Tests). There are now four tests which range in difficulty from short pitch tests to recognition of cadences and tests of musical style, and span grades 3 to 12. Each test can be used independently, according to which skills the teacher regards as important.

Reliability of the total scores is excellent. The reliabilities of certain subtests, especially with younger children, are much lower. One explanation may be the large number of low scores and hence of guessing (Colwell, 1970*b*). The validity of the test content was based on having examined a leading series of music textbooks and consulted with experienced music educators. Correlations between teachers' selections of their best five and poorest five pupils and test scores were high. Colwell also quotes studies of predictive validity. In one, less than 5 per cent of the pupils scoring above 49 in test 1 dropped instrumental music at the end of one year, while 50 per cent of those scoring 35 and below failed to complete the course. The MAT certainly seems to provide an effective means of evaluating achievement in a number of important music skills and to be enjoying widespread use in the USA.

The Iowa Tests of Music Literacy (ITML)

Gordon (1970) has concentrated upon providing assessment of 'fundamental musical achievement' of tonal and rhythm concepts. Each of the six levels is divided into tonal concepts and rhythmic concepts. Each of these divisions includes three subtests: aural perception, reading recognition, and notational understanding. From level 1 which is concerned with major or minor tonal concepts and duple or triple metre, the levels progress to including 'unusual tonality' such as Dorian mode or to the non-tonal, and to 'mixed' metres (e.g. including triplets) or unusual metres (such as $\frac{5}{8}$). The reliability coefficients of the tests are very high, but, as with the MAT, drop where for example the children are not familiar with unusual modes. Gordon emphasises the importance of content validity and of the teacher convincing himself that the skills measured are those he wishes to teach. Mohatt (1971) undertook an investigation of the validity of the ITML in a school situation. He gave all six levels to 164 13-year-old pupils. During the subsequent school year the pupils were evaluated on their understanding of musical concepts that directly corresponded to those of the ITML. They were given tasks such as circling a word on an answer sheet to indicate the mode and metre of 30 musical excerpts, completing the notation of short pieces composed by Mohatt and sight-reading short pieces. The tonal concepts were more successfully predicted than the rhythmic ones, but Mohatt concluded that the information gained from the ITML groups results approximated to that from the time-consuming process of individual evaluation. Schleuter (1971) showed that the ITML was much more strongly related to the MAP than to intelligence tests or to personality factors (see further p. 91), though both the Gordon batteries seemed to serve, as intended, distinct purposes.

Young (1976) reported a valuable comparative study of the MAT and the ITML. Over 400 pupils were tested with test 2 of the MAT and level 1 of the ITML. The intercorrelations of the subtests and composite scores were, as might be expected, mostly moderate to strong. The composite scores in both cases correlated well with teachers' ratings: the MAT ·59 and the ITML ·69. Young concluded that if time permitted the most comprehensive measurement of achievement would be attained by using all the subtests from both batteries. Otherwise, the most efficacious combination would be the three Gordon tonal concepts tests, his tests of rhythmic aural perception and reading recognition, and the Colwell audio-visual rhythm discrimination test. Young, however, emphasises that each teacher must decide for himself what aspects of musical achievement best reflect his philosophy. Most of Young's teachers of band instruments seemed to rate high the pupils who also scored highly on the tests involving rhythm.

The Farnum Music Test

This is an enlarged version of the Farnum Music Notation Test originally published in 1953 – one of the more satisfactory of the earlier tests of musical achievement for children. It is claimed to be an indicator of readiness to learn an instrument.

The first part of the test incorporates the original 40 items. Each of these consists of a melodic example which is played once, the testee being required to compare it with notation and mark the number of the bar in which a change from the notation has been made. The difference may be in pitch, in rhythm or in both. In fact more than 75 per cent of the changes are in pitch. Three new tests have been added. One is a cadence test which resembles the K-D tonal movement test in that a last tone is missing and the testee has to say whether it should move up or down. A tonal pattern test is similar in principle to Seashore's memory test. An unusual test is the symbol test intended to measure speed of eye focus and reaction time. Obviously eye and hand coordination is important for playing; but the value of the symbol test needs to be verified by further research. While the first three tests can be found in other batteries, it may be useful to have in one package tests that have proved to be among the more successful type of test. Total cut-off scores are provided by way of norms. As Farnum suggested in the case of the original test, users might profitably compile norms based on their own scholastic standards.

The Simons Measurements of Music Listening Skills

Published in 1976, these are the first tests specially intended for children aged 6 to 8 to be made available. Simons aimed to provide objective measurement of the achievement of groups of young children in nine separate music listening skills, as an aid to teachers and researchers. The tests aim at evaluation of groups rather than individuals, but may help to identify musically talented children.

Ability to read or write is not needed, since the child has only for example to circle the pictures of two dogs if a tonal pattern is the same on a second playing or a dog and cat if it is different. Like Colwell's Silver Burdett Competency Tests (see below), the Simons Measurements are 'criterion-referenced', i.e. not intended to differentiate between the poorest and the best students, but to measure minimum competencies for everyone. If the skills correspond to those that have been taught, each question should be correctly answered by most of the pupils.

The tests certainly cover basic skills that might reasonably be expected from young children. The coverage is comprehensive; unfortunately this means that each subtest has only five items. Norton (1979) used seven of the tests in a study of six-year-old children (see p. 135 below) and obtained a reliability coefficiency of ·77. The tests seem to be enjoying use in the USA. Simons intends to revise them.

The Silver Burdett Music Competency Tests

These tests are the result of the collaboration of a leading American publisher of material for use in school music and Colwell whose special concern for the problems of evaluation in music we have already noted.

Published in 1979, they provide three tests for each book of Silver Burdett Music, 1 to 6. Most of the questions involve aural perception of the basic qualities of music: rhythm, tonality, form, etc. Colwell believes that with a criterion-referenced test, appropriate for a single level, it is adequate to test a narrow range of abilities on several concepts. However, successive evaluations, carried out soon after the material of each third of the book has been taught, are envisaged, so that a cumulative record of progress can be built up. The tests can be used to evaluate individualised instruction, since they do not have to be given to a whole class. It is suggested that inspection of data from one or more classes will help the teacher to identify weaknesses in instruction, taking into account time available for music, background of the pupils, etc.

Colwell's manual presents comparison data from a wide sample of American schools which the teachers may use in interpreting the scores obtained by their own classes – again having regard to differences in circumstances.

The type of reliability that seemed most appropriate was test-retest. Colwell cites the results from 567 pupils retested after three days; as might be expected, means scores rose somewhat on the second testing, but coefficients ranged from ·69 to ·94, most being in the ·80s. Computing the correlation between items using the same concept with 457 pupils resulted in correlations from ·78 to ·97.

The tests are based primarily on content validity and on the extent to which they measure the objectives of the Silver Burdett Music programme, the critical appraisal of which Colwell had been involved in for some time. (For a favourable critique from the UK of the Silver Burdett Music Scheme, see Peggie (1980).) This seems to accord with the oft-heard plea that scientists should be brought in at the design stage of equipment. There is an obvious danger that the mediocre teacher will latch on to such a programme and its evaluation as a panacea, and apply it in robot fashion. Such a teacher might do even worse without a good programme. A 'ready-made' programme is clearly likely to be useful to teachers who are not music specialists but whose duties require them to teach music. The bright teacher may feel constrained by a programme, though its scope does not extend to performance, improvisation and any other activities that the individual teacher may wish to foster. It is often salutary for such teachers to check that they are not neglecting basic skills. Indeed some may come to consider more seriously the importance of evaluation of achievement and aptitude in music. If any feel challenged to produce a better music programme and means of evaluating it, they should be encouraged to try.

College entrance level

The Aliferis Music Achievement Tests

The first really well standardised music achievement test to be published was the James Aliferis Music Achievement Test College Entrance Level which appeared in 1954. Aliferis's aim is to assess the student's power of auditory visual discrimination, i.e. his ability to visualise the musical notation of what he hears, and to hear inwardly what he sees. The tests are divided into three sections: melody, rhythm and harmony. In each section there are both 'elements' and 'idioms'. By a melodic element, Aliferis means an interval. By a rhythmic element, he means a figure of one-beat duration. By an idiom, he means a four-note figure pattern. The rhythmic idioms consist of a combination of two rhythmic elements. When taking the test, the subject has to select, for example, which of four intervals is the one that is being played on the piano.

The standardisation of the test was very thorough, norms being collected from different types of colleges in four regions of the United States. As we can see from the figures in Appendix I, the test appears to be of good reliability, except perhaps for the rhythmic section considered separately. The correlations with success at college music are satisfactory, although Aliferis exaggerates when he calls them 'high'. Wing considered that it might well prove to be a sound diagnostic test of general musical aptitude at college entrance level (see Buros, 1959).

Encouraged by the success of his college entrance tests Aliferis published in 1962 a test on similar lines for use at the end of the second college year. It includes comparison with the notation of harmonic elements (chords) and of melodic and rhythmic idioms.

Norms are again provided for various types of colleges and regions in America. The reliability is quite good except again for the rhythm test considered on its own. The validity figures which Aliferis quotes in his manual are rather lower than those for the college entrance level. Wing (Buros, 1966) in fact found its discriminatory power disappointing and considered that more easy and more difficult items were needed.

Educational Testing Service Music Tests

Among other tests concerned with achievement in music at college level are those offered by the Educational Testing Service of Princeton. The Graduate Record Examinations Advanced Music Test is designed to help the assessment of the qualifications of applicants for advanced study in music. The scores are intended to indicate the students' mastery of the subject matter emphasised in many undergraduate programmes. Since it is a standardised test, it allows comparison of students from different institutions with different programmes. About 40 per cent of the questions deal with music theory, including concepts related to jazz and contemporary composition, the rest dealing with music history and literature. The reliability of total scores on recent editions is about ·96. Two advanced placement examinations are offered in music : one on music listening and literature and another on music theory. They are intended for students who have completed in secondary school music studies comparable to first-year college courses for the music major or for the non-major with a serious interest in the field. Each includes a strong aural component. An examination in music education is included in the National Teacher Examinations, the purpose of which is to measure the candidates' academic competence in the subject matter they hope to teach. Reliability is claimed to be in the ·90s.

All these examinations can only be taken at specified centres on specified dates, since the material is confidential and revised every year. They would seem to fulfil for the USA the function performed in the UK by the music examinations of the General Certificate of Education and of the Associated Board of the Royal Schools of Music. However, the American tests have received much greater psychometric attention.

The Australian Test for Advanced Music Studies

This is a very interesting test – both for the student who takes it and for the test user. It arose from the need to provide objective assessment at college entrance level in the context of the Australia-wide system of music examinations; but the problem of varying standards is not confined to Australia and the test is likely to prove valuable in many countries.

The test uses aural stimuli from recorded passages of vocal and instrumental music covering a wide range of timbre and textures. The musical examples are not restricted to the tonal idioms of the eighteenth and nineteenth centuries, but are drawn from art music of the fourteenth to twentieth centuries as well as from folk, ethnic, jazz and pop music. A desire of the author was to discover whether students can conceptualise their musical learning and apply it in diverse musical contexts. Very reasonably for a test for students aspiring to study music at college level, it was aimed to measure such developed aural abilities and general musical intelligence as students with special interest in music might reasonably be expected to have acquired during secondary schooling.

The test consists of three parts or 'Books'. Book 1 requires no knowledge of musical notation or terminology. It is concerned with aural perception and memory applied to various components of music, e.g. pitch, rhythm, tonality and style. Book 2 aims to assess ability to read and understand musical notation and to audiate the sounds represented by visual symbols. Book 3 seeks to evaluate how well the student can comprehend and apply the musical material which he can be assumed to know; it includes aural recognition of intervals, tonality, triads, and time signatures presented in a musical context and ability to discriminate between styles of particular composers. Bridges (1979) states that the test has much in common with the Advanced Placement Test of the Educational Testing Service.

The data which Bridges has so far been able to collect on the test's reliability and validity are certainly promising. Essentially, the validity criteria show that those students that embark on music courses and succeed are those who make higher scores on Bridges's test. So far, percentile norms are not available. However, the test user who sees the unique value of the test should be able to arrive at a grading of scores appropriate to his situation. Aliferis based his tests on the materials used in 'traditional' music courses (are melody, harmony and rhythm the equivalent of the three R's at music college level?) so that success in such courses is evidence of the worth of his test. Bridges's approach being wider ranging, the test manual is less psychometrically rigorous than Aliferis's. Bridges herself readily admits that many more follow-up studies are needed to establish the predictive validity of her test. Hopefully, such studies will soon be carried out in Australia and in other countries, in these days when not only are music programmes being liberalised, but courses in jazz and other music are being offered. Important, too, is the diagnostic forecasting for the student whose interest in music leads him to seek enrolment in a music class. If his capabilities turn out to be too limited for him to make satisfying progress, his enthusiasm for music of any kind may wane. On the other hand, tests such as Bridges's, may help channel talented, if inexperienced, students into courses that lead them to a life-time of enjoyment of music.

Performance tests

The Watkins-Farnum Performance Scale (1954) remains the most important attempt to provide an objective grading of instrumental performance that has so far been published. It consists of fourteen sight-reading exercises which are graded in difficulty. The easiest is intended for pupils who have only been studying the instrument for three months, while the most difficult would be an exacting test after several years of study. The system of scoring takes account of pitch and rhythm accuracy, correct tempo, the observation of expression marks, slurs and repeat signs. The reliability claimed is around ·9. The correlation between test scores and the ranking of students by their teachers had a median value of ·83. The instruments for which the scale is available include most of the woodwind and brass instruments, and the snare drum. The exercises, being originally developed for the cornet, vary in difficulty for different instruments. Stivers (1972) concluded that they were not suitable for the French horn and clarinet. However, his study of 100 band performers tested twice one week apart, confirmed the high reliability of the test – ·93 to ·97 for the equivalent forms (A and B) and for test and retest on the same forms. The scores also correlated ·71 to ·90 with sight-reading ability and ·63 or higher with rankings by band instructors, except in the case of French horn and saxophone. The reliability with which judges scored the performances was also very high. How far the scale is being used by teachers in the assessment of learning even in the USA is difficult to find out. It certainly appears to be enjoying much use for research purposes.

In 1969 Farnum produced the Farnum String Scale which provides a grading chart based on fourteen of seventeen exercises given to fifty violinists in different parts of the USA. No data on reliability and validity are presented.

Abeles (1971) devised a scale for the rating of performance on the clarinet based on those traits which seemed most salient to experienced judges. After analysing opinions of experienced teachers and the literature on the aural aspects of memorable performances, he produced a rating scale on which teachers rated the performance of 100 junior high clarinetists. A statistical analysis of the results yielded six factors (e.g. intonation, articulation, tempo) for each of which he selected the five most satisfactory items. Three different sets of ten performances were then rated by three judges, with an inter-judge reliability of ·9 for the whole scale and a validity coefficient of ·8. Cooksey (1977) has used similar methods to construct a rating scale for the evaluation of high school choral performances. He evaluated statements from experienced judges and teachers to produce 147 statements for an initial pool of items. Fifty judges were asked to rate two performances out of 100 recorded choral performances gathered from various parts of the USA. A five-point scale was used with which the judges marked from 'strongly agree' to 'strongly disagree' with statements such as 'Top voice flat at times', 'Excellent feeling of ensemble'. The results were analysed and compared with a National Interscholastic Music Activities Commission scale. Further refinements were produced by additional trials and analyses. Eventually a seven-factor rating scale was produced to rate seven categories (such as diction, precision, tone control) with high inter-judge reliability and whose scores had strong relationships with global performance rating.

Fiske (1977) has concerned himself with factors involved in the evaluation of performances by adjudicators. He cites Eysenck's 1939 study that concluded that consistency of judgement is much greater with from seven to ten judges, as opposed to only one. Fiske (1975) found that it seemed not to matter whether or not the judges are specialists in the instrument they are called upon to rate, at least in selection/rejection situations, though it might be valuable to have critical comments by specialist judges in diagnostic situations. Fiske believed that it is best if judges concentrate on overall performance. Vasil (1973) found that taped performance elicited equivalent judgements to live ones and that performing beyond fifteen seconds may make little difference to judges' decisions.

Motor Performance Tests

Seashore (1926) devised a 'Rhythm Meter', a gramophone with contacts embedded in the turntable at various points. A number of different rhythms can be provided for the subject who had to try to make his taps on a telegraph key coincide with the clicks he is hearing. Nielson (1930) found significant correlations between this type of rhythmic performance and the rankings of superior compared with poor music students. Williams (1933) adapted the device in order to study the motor rhythmic performance of young children.

As mentioned in Chapter 3, Thackray (1969; 1972) developed tests concerned with rhythmic performance; the tests are administered individually. See Appendix I.

Gilbert (1979) has devised a test of motoric music skills, i.e. of the facility in the motor performance aspects of the striking skills used in instrumental music. The tasks entail striking a musical instrument (drums, xylophone, etc) with a mallet through use of vertical arm and hand motion. Believing that the ages of three to six were particularly important in the development of motor skills, she tested 800 children within those ages with a 44-item test. The internal consistency of the test is high ($\cdot$78 to $\cdot$89). Test-retest reliability ranged from $\cdot$84 to $\cdot$96 for small numbers of children retested up to 30 days after the initial test and remained sizeable after a year (Gilbert, in press). Correlations of from $\cdot$50 to $\cdot$78 were obtained when she compared performance on her test with selected items of the Lincoln-Oseretsky Motor Development Scale. As might be expected, correlations with teachers' rankings of children on (1) eye-hand coordination; (2) general motor coordination; (3) motor speed; and (4) range of movement varied considerably from one class of children to another, greater accuracy being obtained with the older groups. This certainly sounds an interesting and promising test.

Assessment of interest in music

As mentioned in the last chapter, part of Gaston's test of musicality is concerned with assessing the child's interest in music. In many cases questionnaires or interest in music and on experience of playing and listening will provide all the information that is needed.

However, scales have been devised specially as objective measures of attitude to music and of interest in music compared with interest in other vocational or leisure-time pursuits.

Hevner and Seashore (see Mueller *et al.*, 1934) adopted the method developed by Thurstone for the construction of attitude scales. Their test is composed of fifty statements about music with which the subject is asked to agree or disagree. Examples of the statements are: 'Living would be a much more dull and drab affair were it not for the beauties of music' and 'I believe the world would be just as well off if there were no music in it.' Each item on a Thurstone scale has been pre-judged by a large group of people and rated as indicating a completely favourable, or a completely unfavourable attitude, or one that falls between these values. The reliability of the Seashore-Hevner scale for college students is ·90. Farnsworth (1964), having found the scale valuable for research purposes, provided a new set of weights, fifteen items receiving significantly different weights from the original.

Time permitting, it would seem preferable to ascertain preferences for various types of music by playing recorded selections for rating by the listeners. Le Blanc's test of generic style music preferences will be discussed in Chapter 10.

Another recent attempt to measure attitudes was made by Chalmers (1976; 1978). He presented in random order 50 items consisting of 10 each of Baroque, classical, romantic, early twentieth century (Stravinsky, Copland, Bartok, etc.) and experimental (Messiaen, Cage, etc.), for rating on a seven-point scale of like-dislike by college students. High test-retest reliability was found between two administrations of the test to 20 students after a month. Chalmers has also sought to validate his measure by comparing the ratings with self-reports of the students on their preferences for musical styles and their possession of records, and by video-taping their reactions while listening to the excerpts. The tapes were analysed by specialists in non-verbal behaviour for indications of 'approval' or 'disapproval'. Percentile norms were drawn up for the general student population on the basis of testing some 100 University of Kansas students. Chalmers believes his measure can help collect data that will be important in planning music courses.

Two of the well-known attitudes scales, the Strong-Campbell Vocational Inventory Blank and the Kuder Preference Records and

Interest Surveys provide means of assessing interest in music as compared with other vocational or leisure-time activities. The most obvious use for these would be in a counselling situation, when some choice had to be made among courses or careers. Manturzewska (1978) found the Kuder Preference Record (Vocational) contributed usefully to the total picture of characteristics that distinguished music students from unselected school children, and the top 10 per cent of music students from the lowest 10 per cent.

Summary

During the last few years tests for aural achievement have become available for ages ranging from six to college entrance level. For school children the ITML is anchored soundly on tonal and rhythm tasks, progressing from the discrimination of simple major/minor patterns and duple/triple differences to modal and non-tonal music and to mixed and uncommon metres. The Colwell MAT has become well established and will appeal to the teacher who wishes to introduce objective evaluation of a wider spectrum of musical skills. Both the new Bridges test and the Aliferis tests at college level have their uses, depending on how far a course is based on 'traditional' aural skills.

Whatever the judgement of the teacher as to what is the most appropriate evaluative tool, its psychometric worth is important. One would hope that teachers will increasingly make use of objective tests to check the progress of their classes and in the planning of curriculum.

5

What is musical ability?

In this chapter, we shall take up some of the questions raised in Chapter 1. Do we get the clearest understanding of the nature of musical ability if we think in terms of musical ability as one broad factor, different aspects of which may be sampled by different tests, or as composed of separate abilities which, however, may overlap and seem to work together? Is there some useful distinction between sensory and 'higher' levels of musical processing? Is there any difference in the way music is processed by men as compared with women? Does research with blind persons help us to understand the 'earmindedness' required for music?

In seeking to answer such questions we shall consider how far the various tests intercorrelate and how far they seem to depend on underlying factors. We shall also discuss experiments relevant to musical abilities.

In trying to evaluate theories on the nature of musical ability, we need to bear in mind that the results of correlation studies and the factorial analyses derived from them depend on the tests chosen and the subjects tested. The reliability and validity of the tests are also of crucial importance in assessing the meaningfulness of the results. (Correlation studies of musical ability are discussed rather more fully in Shuter-Dyson, in press.)

Factor-analytic methods

When different tests of ability are correlated, the correlations found are usually all positive. This suggests that they are to some extent measuring some underlying common factor. Various statistical techniques have been developed to investigate such factors and to aid in their identification. From a matrix of intercorrelations between a group of tests, a factor matrix can be obtained. This is a table which shows the weight or loading of each of the tests on each of the factors. It is expressed on the same type of scale as are correlation coefficients: from $+1\cdot00$ through zero to $-1\cdot00$. A common or general factor has positive loadings from all the tests used in a particular study. Group factors are found when only certain tests have positive loadings, the others being zero or negative. The nature of a particular factor can be deduced from examining the tests which had high loadings on that factor and trying to discover what psychological processes they have in common. This might, in the case of music ability tests, be concerned with the perception of pitch. If several tests of chords or harmony were included in the study, a factor separating melodic from harmonic aspects of pitch might also be found.

It is customary to represent factors geometrically as *reference axes* in terms of which each test can be plotted. The position of the reference axes is not fixed by the data, the original correlation matrix determining only the position of the tests in relation to each other. The axes can therefore be rotated to obtain the most satisfactory and easily interpretable patterns. Criteria for rotation include the rotation of axes to such a position as to eliminate all significant negative loadings and of 'simple structure' which means that each test should have loadings on the factors ideally near to ± 1 or 0. The aim is to obtain factors that can be readily and unambiguously interpreted. In practice, however, results are rarely clear-cut and much room is left for subjective interpretation – or misinterpretation.

The general effect of rotation is to minimise the importance of general factors in favour of a number of 'primary' factors of more nearly equal status. If such primaries are themselves correlated, further analysis can be used to produce 'second-order' factors, e.g. Cattell's Gf and Gc (see p. 6). Examination of the loadings of the primary factors on these 'super factors' or dimensions shows the relative contribution of each to the underlying unity. For detailed information on factor analysis, see Nunnally (1978).

In the earlier studies in the field of musical ability rather small numbers of subjects and a variety of methods of analysis were used. A valuable piece of work has been carried out by Whellams (1971) in re-analysing using the same approach as many previous factorial and correlational studies, to show the extent to which diverse studies might be found, at least tentatively, to produce similar results.

The theory of specific capacities

If Seashore were correct to believe that musical ability is composed of separate elements, we should expect that intercorrelations among music tests would be very low and that the search for underlying factors would yield only highly specific ones.

Correlation studies of the Seashore measures do suggest that they test relatively distinct abilities. Yet near zero correlations are rare. With the exception of pitch and tonal memory, correlations between pairs of tests average around ·3 or less (Teplov, 1966, p. 63; Drake, 1939 and Gordon, 1969). The connection between rhythm and time or intensity appears to be no greater than the intercorrelations of supposedly unrelated capacities. Pitch and tonal memory do, however, correlate more often around ·5 (e.g. Drake, 1939; Franklin, 1956; Fleishman, 1955; Rainbow, 1965; and Gordon, 1969).

Some of the agreement between the correlations is probably attributable to intelligence. But, even with intelligence held constant by statistical methods, Drake found a common factor and two group factors, and McLeish a general factor. However, there seemed to be more that was specific than common in what the tests were measuring. In Whellam's re-analyses of Seashore studies, the three more frequently occurring factors all involved the tonal memory test, though none seemed to be a factor of memory as such (see below). In the first study by Horn and Stankov (see below), all the Seashore measures except loudness were used and all appeared on one factor, 'discrimination among sound patterns'.

The theory of a general musical ability

Wing's thinking about musical ability appeared to be greatly influenced by what is required for successful performance. The various aspects of music are so intimately connected that a reasonable minimum of all-round efficiency is needed for playing and, indeed, for listening.

Wing's tests do tend to intercorrelate more highly than do Seashore's, depending on the group studied. In his factorial study (1941*a*), the intercorrelations of the first three tests all exceeded ·5 and the general (unrotated) factor accounted for 40 percent of the variance. McLeish, too, found quite high correlations among the first three tests and the harmony test (·44 to ·67). Shuter (1964; 1968) was interested in comparing the results of testing selected groups – talented children with talented adults, male with female college students of above average musical ability, and students whose scores were close to average on Wing's norms. Among those groups test intercorrelations were low, zero or even negative. When Whellams combined the groups and added in the results for other college students as well as for students at the Royal Marines School of Music, the intercorrelations of the first three tests and harmony rose to range between ·32 and ·56.

How far any common factor found by factorisation is evidence of the unitariness of musical ability depends, of course, on how successfully the tests cover all aspects of the ability. The comprehensiveness of the Wing battery depends on how wide was his original choice of tests and how valid is his claim that 'no vital test is missing from the short series' (Wing, 1968, p.49). The seven tests did correlate highly with thirteen wider ones, which in turn correlated very highly with the original twenty four with which he experimented.

Mainwaring (1947) expressed doubt as to how well Wing's seven tests covered the rhythmic aspect of music. In Wing's view, the word rhythm should be reserved for 'the realization of the idea of movement towards points of climax and response . . . conveyed by the tune shape (which also implies cadence points), the style of the time used (e.g. 6/8 or 4/4) and the accenting of certain important notes in the melody'. (Wing, 1968, pp. 25-6.)

Support for Wing's view comes from Thackray (1969, p. 34) who concluded from his study of the rhythmic abilities of adults that the 'best single test for measuring general rhythmic ability is one in which the subject is asked to reproduce the rhythm of a melody'. Most of Thackray's subjects, physical education students, claimed that the melodic element of his test both made it more interesting to do and the items easier to memorise. In fact the task was more demanding than the reproduction of time patterns, since the time values, the grouping of notes and loudness had to be observed, implying ability to distinguish between staccato and legato, to show accents, tone gradations and sensitivity to phrasing. The reproduction of melodic rhythm correlated ·58 with the reproduction of time patterns. Wing reported that out of 171 intercorrelations which he had calculated among 18 tests, the correlation between his rhythm appreciation test and a time-pattern dictation test was among the highest twelve. On the other hand, the Wing rhythm test correlates to only a very low degree with the Seashore and with the Drake rhythm tests (Tanner and Loess, 1967) and with the other tests of rhythm studied by Bentley (1955) and with the Revesz-Franklin rhythm tests (Franklin, 1956).

Wing (1941a) reported two minor factors: one which distinguished ability to judge harmony from ability with melody or rhythm, another which sorted persons and tests into two types – analytic (the first three tests) and synthetic (the last three tests), the harmony test having a zero loading. These two different attitudes might be habitual in some listeners, but also the same listener might deliberately choose to listen analytically or holistically on different occasions or for different purposes, depending perhaps on the familiarity of the music. Wing thus foreshadowed a distinction which has been the subject of much recent discussion (Chapter 18).

Primary factor studies

Whellams (1971) extracted from his re-analyses fifteen factors of some significance. Having regard to the poor reliability of many of the tests, and the differences in content in the different batteries, the results seemed to be reasonably plausible and consistent. In Table 5.1 factors which appear to be similar are grouped together.

Before discussing Whellam's factors, let us consider the recent researches of Horn and Stankov in so far as they relate to musical abilities. Four studies have been reported:

1. 241 male convicts, mean age 26, mean IQ 100 (Stankov and Horn, 1980; Horn and Stankov, in preparation);
2. 113 children, aged 11-12, from a working-class suburb of Belgrade (Stankov, 1978);
3. 90 children, aged 10-15, 30 blind, 30 partially sighted and 30 sighted; (Stankov and Spilsbury, 1978; Stankov, 1980);
4. 47 adults from adult education classes at Sydney University; 29 firemen, and 22 adults from evening classes; mean age 34, mean years of education 12 (Stankov, in preparation).

The first study included an extensive battery of visual, speech and 'musical' auditory tests, including Seashore's, Drake's and Wing's first three tests. The tests used with the Yugoslav children were

Table 5.1 Primary aural musical ability factors

Description	No of studies in which factor appeared	Tests	Tests loaded
Pitch imagery (pi)	13	Seashore	Pitch and tonal memory
	2	K–D	Tonal memory and pitch
	9	Wing	Pitch change and memory
Kinaesthetic factor for development of pitch perception (kp)	10	Seashore	Rhythm and tonal memory
	2	K–D	Rhythm and tonal memory
Harmonic ability (h)	7	Seashore	Consonance and tonal memory
	5	Wing	Chord analysis and harmony
Tonal separation (t)	10	Wing	Chord analysis and harmony
Rhythmic ability (r)	4	Gordon (MAP)	Tempo, metre
Experience (xp1)	3	K–D	Tonal movement, memory
Experience (xp2)	2	K–D	Tonal movement, rhythm imagery
Musical judgement (j)	3	Gordon (MAP)	Phrasing, style
Wing test (j1)	7	Wing	Intensity
Wing test (j2)	6	Wing	Phrasing
Wing test (j3)	4	Wing	Rhythm

more limited, while visual tests were omitted in the last two studies. For their research purposes, Horn and Stankov did not feel bound to use more than the number of items of the standardised tests than was necessary for reliability. The easiest items were chosen (Stankov, private communication). Considering the differences between the subjects, reasonably stable factors were produced.

When certain speech tests are not included in the study, DASP tends to become a narrow factor of tonal memory. It still remains, however, a somewhat broader factor than Whellams's pi. Stankov believes that it involves memory for sounds, and suggests that the

Table 5.2 *Primary auditory factors found by Horn and Stankov and by Stankov*

Factor	Tests loaded
Discrimination among sound patterns (DASP)	Seashore; Wing pitch and memory; tonal classification; chord matching
Auditory cognition of relationships (ACoR)	Tonal series; chord series; chord decomposition; chords parts decomposition; tonal analogies; Wing chord analysis; Wing and Seashore pitch; Drake memory
Maintaining and judging rhythm (MaJR)	Drake rhythm A and B; Seashore rhythm
Temporal tracking (Tc)	Tonal and speech re-ordering; detection of repeated tones
Auditory immediate memory (Msa)	Tonal figures; verbal span (especially numbers backwards)
Speech perception under distraction/distortion (SPUD)	Various speech tasks

relationship among tones represents a critical datum of musical memory. DASP, however, differs from 'mere' memory span, since Msa formed a separate factor. Faulds (1959), too, reported no correlation between digit span and the Wing and Seashore pitch and memory tests. ACoR is described as showing how well the listener can comprehend the relationship between sounds. Examination of the content of the tests would seem to confirm that they may well require a more advanced form of processing. Wing's chord analysis test loaded ·42 on this factor. As we noted above this is a test which seems to discriminate well among talented musicians. Many of the ACoR tests involve chords, so that the factor would appear to be similar to Whellam's tonal separation. MaJR received its major loadings from the Drake rhythm tests. While it seems to correspond to Whellams's rhythm factor, only the Seashore test was common to the studies from which he drew his data and those of Stankov. An interesting factor not found before either by psychologists concerned with general intellectual abilities or by those interested in music is Tc. The tasks require the listener to attend carefully to the order in which sounds occur and then be able to re-order them in the mind's ear. Stankov (in press) suggests that while this factor may be only a simple measure of working memory, the 'bottleneck' which gives rise to individual differences on Tc tasks derives from the need to keep track of the order on which stimuli have arrived. Tc could be expected to be important in music, but the point remains to be elucidated.

Pitch/tonal memory factors

Considering the prominence accorded to pitch and tonal memory in music test batteries, it is not surprising that both appear in factor analyses. Sometimes memory has been stressed, sometimes pitch. Karlin (1941) found evidence for a pitch factor and for two different types of memory factor. The tests he used included a simplified version of the Seashore battery, and Drake's memory, retentivity and intervals tests. He claimed to have found evidence for a pitch factor and for two different types of memory factor. As no fewer than three tests of memory were included, it is not surprising that some distinction between 'memory for form' (i.e. the ability involved in Drake's memory test) and 'memory for elements' (as in Drake's retentivity test) emerged. It is interesting to note that echoes of such a distinction have appeared in more recent research, where differences of processing of melodic contour and of intervals have been postulated (see further Chapter 17). Franklin (1956) included the Wing tests, the Seashore pitch and memory tests, as well as his own TMT test and two tests of rhythm in two studies. His main interest seemed to be in drawing a distinction between ability to discriminate fine pitch differences as in the Seashore test and 'judicious-musical' pitch – judging pitch changes in a musical context. However, in Franklin's own results as well as those of other researchers, the correlations between the Seashore and Wing pitch tests and between the Seashore and Wing tests of tonal memory are far from zero. Thus:

Correlations between Seashore and Wing pitch tests: ·49; ·67; ·62 (Franklin, 1956); ·63 (McLeish, 1966); ·53 (Faulds, 1959);

Correlations between Seashore and Wing tonal memory tests: ·64; ·75 (Franklin, 1956); ·74 (McLeish, 1966).

Correlations between the Drake and Seashore memory tests are of a similar order (Lundin, 1967; Farnsworth, 1969; Rainbow, 1965).

Even the Gordon melody test correlates ·40 with Seashore pitch
and ·42 with Seashore memory; the correlations of the Gordon
harmony test with Seashore pitch and memory are slightly higher
still (Gordon, 1969).
Wing and Franklin might of course argue that what is important is
the variance which the Wing and Seashore tests do *not* have in
common. Some at least of such variance would have to be attributed
to 'error' factors due to the less than perfect reliabilities of the tests.

Holmstrom (1963) claimed to find two pitch factors in studies in
which he gave simplified versions of the first three Wing tests and a
rhythm test of his own to children aged around eight and ten. The
first factor, 'Alpha', might have a physiological basis and be but
little influenced by experience of music, while the second, 'Beta',
factor involved the more musical tonal memory tests. However,
Holmstrom's Alpha factor differs from Franklin's 'acoustic-mech-
anical' factor in not being restricted to the perception of minute
pitch differences. Indeed Holmstrom points out that the individual
with fine pitch discrimination is likely to be helped rather than
hindered when he attempts the more musical tests. This is a valid
point which Bruton-Simmonds (1969) seems to confirm.

Bruton-Simmonds and his assistant judged the performance of 15
well-known musicians as giving them 'intense pleasure'. They then
persuaded these musicians and 10 others with comparable training
and technical accomplishment to take the Seashore tests. None of
the criterion group, nine of whom were pianists, scored less than the
75th percentile on the pitch, loudness, rhythm and tonal memory
tests; many scored much higher. The other musicians made inferior
scores. Bruton-Simmond believed his evidence showed that at the
highest level of musicianship, fine discrimination of pitch is required
by the pianist and a high discrimination of loudness by the violinist.
Also at the level of the professional musician, pitch discrimination
below 10 cents (a cent is a hundredth of a semitone) may critically
depend on the timbre of the musician's own instrument, at least in
the case of string and wind players (Meyer, 1978).

On the other hand, Henson and Wyke (private communication)
tested 21 members of a leading orchestra with the Seashore tests.
They achieved a PR of 99 on tonal memory, but their average PR on
pitch was 68 and on rhythm, 74. The musicians' scores fell below the
median of Seashore's norms on loudness time and timbre.

Jane Siegel (1972) discussed the contributions of pitch discrimination and tonal memory to absolute pitch. Was it due to exceptionally fine pitch discrimination or at least acute sensitivity at specific points along the pitch continuum? Or was the critical determinant ability to store pitch information in memory, or at least to acquire a number of internal standards against which to compare the tones? Her own experiments provided direct support for none of these hypotheses. She proposed a modified hypothesis which held that persons with absolute pitch have stored a limited number of points along the pitch continuum in long-term memory and that they can use this information for classifying pitches. Rakowski (1979) found that a musician with absolute pitch used the same strategy as one with good relative pitch when asked to tune a pure tone to the same frequency as a standard after periods up to three to five minutes. After a long delay a different strategy is adopted which suggests that absolute-pitch listeners permanently remember a number of standard pitches corresponding to the chromatic scale. The best subjects can reproduce from memory most of these pitches with an accuracy of 10 to 20 cents. When faced with the task of tuning to a pitch outside the permanently stored pitches under the condition of a long delay, they estimate pitch with reference to their internal standard. Thus 1000 Hz would be estimated as 'somewhat higher than B♭'. For a detailed discussion of absolute pitch, see Ward (in press).

The value of possessing absolute pitch is open to question. A more important characteristic of the musician seems to be the ability to perceive tonal intervals in categories as surely as, for example, 'p' and 'b' can be distinguished in speech. In a series of experiments, Jane and William Siegel (1976; 1977*a*; 1977*b*) have demonstrated that musicians with excellent relative pitch and ability to name intervals are remarkably poor at identifying mistuned intervals. Six subjects were asked to judge 13 intervals ranging from 20 cents flatter than a perfect fourth to 20 cents sharper than a perfect fifth, arranged in 20-cent steps, against a standard perfect fourth, augmented fourth and perfect fifth. The subjects were accurate *between* the interval categories, but discrimination *within* an interval category was unreliable. Only 37 per cent of the intervals were judged as out-of-tune when in fact 77 per cent were. Even a subject who was a highly proficient performer of Indian music categorised (1976). Burns and Ward (1978) found that it was possible to train musicians to discriminate pitches in the troughs between categories. Locke and Kellar (1973) reported that while all musicians categorise, some show sharper category boundaries than others. The Siegels (1977*a*) found that subjects without musical training were inconsistent in their use of categories, except in the case of unison. Some of Locke and Kellar subjects, classified as non-musicians, showed evidence of categorisation or at least of increased discrimination at category boundaries, but in fact many had had considerable musical experience, with which the results appeared to be correlated.

Categorisation can also occur in the perception of tempo. In Wapnick's (1980) experiments speed-change relationships that only very roughly approximated to the doubling or halving of tempo might be perceived as exact.

This attention to the role of pitch in music does not, however, mean that Franklin was wrong to emphasise the importance of a sense of tonality. One of the characteristics of effective listening is the apprehension of music as interrelated parts of a whole. Musical perception is necessarily structured in terms of the musical language of a particular culture. Meyer (1956) drew attention to the importance of expectations created while listening to music, e.g. of a return to the tonic, of a certain chord being followed by a certain other as a fundamental source of its power to create excitement and fulfilment.

Carlsen (1976) reported evidence concerning which note is most likely to follow another in a cross-cultural study among music majors in Hungary, West Germany and the United States, by presenting pitch intervals as the beginnings of a melody which the subject was asked to continue as he would have expected it to proceed. Highly significant differences were found between Hungarian and American students, but not between the Germans and either of the other two groups. From the point of view of musical ability, an important finding was that strong expectations may lead to inaccurate perceptions. Thus in melodic dictation, exercises which did not conform to the patterns expected resulted in many errors.

A musician when he first encounters music in a different cultural idiom is likely to perceive it according to the convention of his own culture and hence to misperceive and misinterpret it. It seems important to distinguish between persons whose ears are not particularly keen and who have not become well acculturised to their own music from those who have (in the western world) an excellent sense of tonality, but who need to make additional efforts to cope with exotic or even atonal music. Much evidence exists on this point. Gordon (1917) found that 'musical' subjects were more affected when asked to sing melodies when they were played backwards than were 'unmusical' subjects. None the less, they were much more efficient at singing the melodies played backwards than were the unmusical group at reproducing the tunes when played forward.

Taylor (1976) asked 63 college students to listen to 7-, 11- or 15-tone melodies and to sing back the note they thought represented the tonal centre of the melody. The higher the score they gained on a test of sight-singing and singing back phrases, the stronger were their estimates of tonality for the melodies that outlined a key. Estimates of tonality for melodies *not* outlining a key were not affected by test scores. The lowest scoring students showed little difference in their perception of tonal strength for either type of melody.

Tan (1979) found that college students with little experience of music were somewhat better at recognising a two-tone 'target' in a tonal sequence when the target did *not* contain the tonic. Those with considerable experience of music did tend to perform better with the tonic target, but only if they applied a 'tonality' strategy to the problem. Those who had been trained in singing tended to do this. The musically experienced were more able to use specific interval size (as opposed to 'large' or 'small' intervals) and to associate the target tones with parts of familiar tunes (cf. Chapter 17, pp. 238–57).

Experiments involving tonal versus atonal sequences usually show that the tonal sequences are easier, but that 'musical' subjects are relatively better with atonal ones than are naive subjects. (See, for example, Dewar, Cuddy and Mewhort, 1977). (In such experiments, 'musical' tends to mean musically trained. With college students this may be partially valid, though 'trained' is not synonomous with 'talented'.)

Rhythmic abilities. Not without justice, Davies (1978) speaks of rhythm as having been too often regarded as 'tonality's poor relation' and urges that the role of rhythm needs more emphasis than we tend to give it. Obviously, it is not only tonal tests that require memory. Thackray (1969) speaks of memory as 'an important ingredient in rhythmic ability'. The Gordon rhythm tests are just as dependent on memory as are the tonal ones. Sizeable correlations are found between the tonal and rhythmic parts of the MAP (Gordon, 1965; 1969; Tarrell, 1965). In the case of the PMMA, the intercorrelations of the tonal and rhythm tests are approximately ·50 (Gordon, 1979*a*).

For his study of the rhythmic abilities of adults, Thackray (1969) devised tests of rhythmic perception, auditory and visual, rhythmic performance and rhythmic movement. His own factor analysis (unrotated) suggested that there was a general factor, though this was complex, both in the case of the auditory and of the visual perception tests. He suggested that this factor might be identified as 'the ability to perceive and memorize a rhythmic structure as a whole, and to analyse it consciously'. A second, less clearly defined factor might be concerned with accent. With groups of physical education students, he found the following intercorrelations: aural perception and performance ·63, perception and movement, ·55 and performance and movement ·59.

With his tests for children, Thackray (1972) found almost identical correlations among 40 children aged 11 as among 40 children aged 8 when he compared the perception and performance tests (·69 and ·68). General factors were again found, with ability to maintain a steady tempo emerging as a highly specific ability.

Hiriartborde and Fraisse (1968) have also tried to study the nature of rhythmic abilities among physical education teachers, using some of the Wing and Seashore tests, as well as eleven tests of their own devising. Validation of their results was attempted by comparison with dance examination scores and rating by instructors. They concluded that several independent factors are needed to account for a 'sense of rhythm'. These include the perception of rhythmical structures, the ability to synchronise with them and a third of elaborating complex movements with one or several limbs when accompanying or reproducing rhythms.

Kinaesthetic factor. Kp has no counterpart in Horn and Stankov's researches. Besides the loadings on the rhythm and memory tests of Seashore and Kwalwasser-Dykema (see p. 56 above), Whellams interpreted a factor which loaded heavily on the MAP melody and harmony tests and which also had sizeable loading on MAP tempo and metre and on Seashore pitch and memory as a kp factor. Kp also appeared more strongly on a factor associated with helping McLeish's students to judge which element in the Oregon test had changed than in their judgement of 'original' versus 'distorted'. Whellams's kinaesthetic factor thus seems to draw together into a broad factor the rhythmic and tonal elements of music; he suggests that it may represent an important central activity influential in the development of various overt musical behaviours and of the higher-level imagery required for advanced tasks such as musical dictation. Certainly it would seem to draw attention to the importance of feedback from the muscles stressed in contemporary models of skilled behaviour, and long noted in connection with the development of musical abilities. Mainwaring (1933) found that both children and students of education tended to translate auditory into kinaesthetic cues in order to recall tunes they had listened to well enough to answer questions about them. Vernon (1931) noted the value of kinaesthesis in making the perception of music definite, but both he and Sergeant (1969*b*), believe it may be of less importance among adult musicians.

Leontiev (1969) provided some interesting evidence on the role of ability to sing a pitch and discrimination of basic pitch thesholds. A high correlation, ·83, seemed to exist between these two abilities. Adults with high pitch thresholds, when asked to sing the pitch of tones presented to them always improved. Some subjects could not 'tune' their voices correctly to a calibrating device. After training sharp drops in the threshold of discrimination occurred, particularly where they had learned to tune their voices correctly. However, Leontiev found that it was not sufficient for a person to be able merely to be able to tune his voice to the tone he hears; he needs to incorporate this in his perception of pitch. Leontiev here seems to have identified the heart of a problem which we shall encounter in Chapter 16 – on the carry-over between singing and discrimination.

Leontiev went on to experiments where the subjects were asked to discriminate pitch without overt singing. First it was suggested that they should not begin to sing till the sound had been cut off, i.e. the subject had to soundlessly tune his vocal apparatus to the pitch of the tone. Later they learned to discriminate pitches beyond the range of their voices.

Leontiev's research sets out nicely the process that seems to be involved in building up pitch discrimination through singing. Ward and Burns (1978) have recently taken up the question from a different point of view. Noting that auditory feedback information for the singer is active only for the last portion of a tone, a successful pitching of the voice at the beginning of a phrase without opportunity for rehearsal implies a sense of 'absolute kinaesthesis'. During the phrase going from one pitch to another may involve an awareness of change in ongoing kinaesthetic cues, a 'relative kinaesthesis'. Ward and Burns asked eight singers, four trained and four amateur, to sing up and then down a diatonic scale, with and without a masking noise being fed into their ears by headphones. Without noise, all were very well able to maintain the starting pitch and to return to it. In noise, the starting note was sung sharper and the descent was begun higher than the note at the end of the ascent. But enormous individual differences were found; the deterioration in performance was consistently less for the trained musicians. Delayed auditory feedback (whereby a time delay is introduced by means of a microphone and receivers over a performer's ears) seems to be as disruptive in music as it is in speech. For example, Gates, Bradshaw and Nettleton (1974) found that keyboard players trying to perform pieces as fast as they could under the condition of simultaneous immediate and delayed auditory feedback increased their total playing time for all delays between 0·1 and 1·05 seconds; maximum increase occurred at about 0·2 seconds. Individual notes tended to be repeated or an extra note added to a scale passage, suggesting that auditory feedback operates at a level of performance organisation which governs motor commands for the playing of individual notes, rather than groups. Gates and Bradshaw (1974) had subjects play on an electronic keyboard instrument whose speakers could be switched off so as to eliminate immediate auditory feedback. This hardly interfered at all with performance. It would therefore seem that the disruption caused by delayed auditory feedback can hardly be due simply to interference with immediate auditory feedback. It may be that when a discrepancy arises between feedback from hearing and some other modality, then hearing dominates. For a more extended discussion of feedback in music performance, see Sloboda (in press).

We may well wonder about the relationship of kinaesthesis and mastery of the rhythmic aspects of music. Bond (1959) found that among 78 negro girls, aged 14 to 17, relationships between the Seashore rhythm test and tests of motor performance (such as jumping or the motor learning of table-tennis) rather low. Huff

(1967) could find no significant differences in scores on the Seashore rhythm test and a visual counterpart using flashing lights as between athletes and dancers compared with students who had no athletic or dancing experience. A long-term effect of limitation of muscle movement was, however, shown by Moog (1979) to affect rhythmic perception. He compared the performance of children, aged 10 to 11 (*i*) with physical handicaps, (*ii*) with mental handicaps, and (*iii*) normal children, on discrimination of rhythmic patterns presented in a melodic, or non-melodic, context. Limitation of movement since earliest childhood reduced rhythmic perception as much as did low intelligence. Thus children with physical handicaps tended to use pitch, rather than rhythmic, perception to discriminate rhythm patterns. Among normal junior high schoolchildren, Boyle (1968) studied the effectiveness of using bodily movement as an aid to teaching band instrumentalists to read rhythm patterns correctly. Those junior high school bands who used movements for an experimental semester made significantly greater increases in both rhythm reading scores and on the Watkins-Farnum performance scale.

The relationships between the detection of errors in a musical passage and melodic dictation (perceptual tasks) and sight-singing might be regarded as indicative of the connections between perceptual and motor aspects of musical ability. Larson (1977) obtained high correlations: error detection with dictation ·59 to ·80, error detection with sight-singing ·50 to ·62 and dictation with sight-singing ·55 to ·77. The lowest correlations occurred for atonal items.

An attempt was made by Burroughs and Morris (1962) to relate eight trials at reproducing a melody with results on the first six Wing tests, and the Mainwaring pitch and immediate recall tests. Whellams (1973*b*) re-analysed the data; he showed that the Wing memory test rose in importance up to the third trial and then declined. At the fourth trial chord analysis (probably the test least affected by memory) came to the fore and retained its importance for the rest of the trials. This suggested to Whellams that ability to perceive rather than remember is what matters in the ultimate success in the task of learning to sing back a tune.

Bain (1978) claimed support for the hypothesis that the six-year-old child receiving a Suzuki-Kodaly music programme for 30 minutes a day would be more aware of postural and kinaesthetic

aspects of his body, while bilingual children would be more cogniz-
ant of the arbitrary relationships between sound and meaning in
language. The 'music' group scored higher on two tests of body
percept and the bilingual children on tests of verbal facility.

Performance skills

We have attempted to discuss the interaction of kinaesthetic and
perceptual aspects of musical ability. Aural abilities may be a prerequisite for, but are no guarantee of, performing ability. As we
noted in Chapter 3, tests of aptitude for the executive side of
performance have received much less attention than those for the
aural side. Wyke and Asso (private communication) have experimented with an extensive battery of tests of rapidity of hand
movements and of manual dexterity. A group of highly talented
performers were compared with subjects who had no musical training. Wyke and Asso's general conclusion was that there was no
difference in performance between the two groups when using their
dominant hand, but the musicians performed better than non-
musicians with the non-dominant hand. On all tests the musicians
had a smaller discrepancy between hands and were almost equally
skilled with both hands. The twelve musicians were as unequivocally right-handed as the non-musicians; their family histories of
handedness were similar. Both Oldfield (1969) and Bryne (1974)
found that left-handedness among instrumentalists was no greater
than among musically unselected students. However, Bryne did
show that among a group of musicians there was a large proportion
of mixed-handedness. While Wyke and Asso's results might suggest
that playing an instrument tends to develop the non-dominant
hand, Bryne's would seem rather to support the view that the
ambidextrous are at an advantage when learning an instrument.
Here we may note that Deutsch (1978a) reported evidence that
moderately left-handed students were more likely to be superior at
pitch memory judgements.

In an exploratory study, Schleuter (1978) found no influence on
the achievements, as rated by himself and their music teachers, of
preference for hand, foot or eye among over 100 beginning instrumental players.

Morton (1979) reported limb asymmetries in rhythm tapping.
The task was to tap a steady beat with one hand then, in time, tap the

'How's your father. All right' rhythm with the other. Few other than musicians succeeded except with the 'easy' combination, i.e. left hand tapping the beat and right hand the melody: the same was true for the feet. Left-handed subjects who showed asymmetry had exactly the same bias as the right-handers.

Second-order factors

Horn and Stankov further analysed their primary factors to produce second-order dimensions. In the first study, besides Gf, Gc, and Gv (visual organisation), a Ga (auditory perception) and an Ac (auditory acuity) emerged. In Stankov's Yugoslav study, most of the auditory/musical tests loaded on a factor which he interpreted as Gf measured through the auditory modality, but probably embracing short-term memory factors. He rejected the possibility of it being a Ga dimension because some of the primaries involved required relatively complex manipulation of stimulus input, not just perception. Also it included two visual primaries. Ga loaded only on the Drake rhythm and Seashore rhythm tests and on masked speech. The Stankov and Spilsbury study produced only one second-order factor interpreted as Gf with loadings of Tc, Msa, ACoR and lesser loadings of SPUD and DASP. In the fourth study the second-order factor was composed mainly of loadings of DASP, Tc and ACoR which Stankov accepts as Ga, agreeing that Tc has a loading on both Gf and Ga.

The relationship between the auditory/musical tests and Gf will be discussed below (p. 81). The Ga dimension derived by Horn and Stankov from their convict study supported the idea of there being organisation among auditory perceptual processes at a general level. The loadings of the primaries were as follows:

DASP ·50
MaJR ·35
Tc ·29
ACoR ·23
Msa ·22

(Speech and Listening Verbal Comprehension ·11;
Auditory Acuity −·01.)

In an earlier discussion of the investigation, Horn (1973) noted that

DASP was a more prominent component of Ga than the more 'cognitive' factors. As the subjects were musically unselected, it is not surprising that they may have been operating at a rather basic 'melodic' level rather than a more advanced 'harmonic' level (cf. pp. 145–9 below). Different results might have been obtained with trained musicians.

The zero loading of auditory acuity (left and right ears tested at 500, 100 and 4000 hz) on Ga confirms evidence that mere acuity of hearing is not related to the performance of music tests. Fieldhouse (1937) found zero correlations in the case of the Seashore battery and Mainwaring's tests of pitch and rhythm. Wing (1968, p. 67) concluded that deafness at least up to a loss of 15 db did not affect ability to perform his tests. Sherbon (1975) tested 30 music and 30 non-music undergraduates with the MAP tonal, the ITML reading recognition, Seashore's pitch, timbre and loudness and the Gaston tests. Auditory acuity did not show a significant association with any of the test scores. In Horn and Stankov's study, SPUD, speech detection under distraction (such as a background of cafeteria noise), did have a strong loading on Ac and a listening verbal comprehension primary factor had a moderate one. In the case of Stankov's Australian study, the subjects were older and auditory acuity did show some relationship to DASP, MaJR and Tc.

Horn and Stankov claim that the distinction between Ga and Ac is evidence of a distinction between sensory and perceptual organisation. We should note that the Seashore tests load on the same dimension as the more musical tests, not on the acuity one.

A hypothesis which Stankov entertained to account for the general factor of auditory perceptual functions is that the emergence of Ga might depend on competition between the ears. Besides the competition involved in SPUD tests and in Drake's 'B' form of the rhythm test, Stankov noted that in the Wing pitch and chord analysis tests which both involved chords, performance suffered when they were presented to both ears, as compared with either ear separately. Among tasks which tap competition of a kind that derives from differences in sensory organs and requires very simple judgements, he investigated binaural diplacusis. This is a phenomenon where the same tone presented to the two ears sounds different. He found some low correlation between diplacusis at frequences 2000 to 3000 Hz and DASP, Tc and MaJR factors, but none for frequencies 3100 to 4100 Hz. Sherbon (1975) also investigated

diplacusis and reported it to be not a significant factor in performance of the music tests he used in his investigation (see above).
Diplacusis was related to a pitch-matching task which was in turn
associated with the Seashore pitch test. Individuals with an uncom-
fortable degree of diplacusis might of course have problems with
pitch perception.

A more interesting aspect of Stankov's investigations of competition in auditory processing was his dual task. One way to increase
the loading on a more general intellectual factor is to present a more
complex task. Another procedure is to increase the effort required
by asking the subjects to cope with two problems at the same time.
The dual task did indeed produce higher correlations between tonal
memory and re-ordering than when they were presented singly – the
correlation rose from ·26 to ·55, thus indicating an increase in the
loading on a general factor.

FIG. 5.1 Example of Stankov's 'dual task'

The subject was not told till after he had listened to the item, to
which voice he would be required to respond.

Such a 'contrapuntal' task would seem of considerable relevance
to music. But, again, this would have to be investigated.

Second-order musical ability factors

It will be obvious to the reader that the primary aim of the research
of Horn and Stankov is to throw light on auditory capacities in the
context of intellectual functioning as a whole. How relevant is their
work to the understanding of musical abilities?

From the point of view of music, it would be desirable to use the
tests they devised with groups of contrasting degrees of musical

aptitude. It would also be important to find out how their ACoR and Tc tasks compare with standardised music tests such as Gordon's. The relationship of Ga to appreciation of music needs to be investigated. If we accept a Ga at a perceptual level, ought we to distinguish between the abilities involved in verbal processing and those required for music? As we shall note in Chapter 17, Deutsch has reported evidence that pitch is processed on a separate channel from words. In Chapter 18, we shall discuss experiments which suggest that at least for some music material in some circumstances the right hemisphere is more important, while for words the left hemisphere usually plays the dominant role.

Horn and Stankov (in preparation) put forward a systemative representation of the place of auditory functions within intelligence. Figure 5.2 is a speculative attempt to represent how such a system might apply in music.

At the 'sensory detector' level we have used a box for the kinaesthetic factor noted by Whellams. This is connected with the auditory factors. At the level of associative organisation, short-term acquisition retrieval (as required by such tests as Wing's and Sea-shore's tonal memory) may be specifically musical; the same would apply to tertiary storage retrieval. A general music ability factor might usefully be divided into 'fluid' and 'crystallised.' The visual system is involved in music in such activities as the reading of notation and the visual cues utilised in performing on an instrument.

The connecting lines should be thought of as operating in both directions, to represent, for example, the role of long-term memory in the processing of incoming musical stimuli. In Horn and Stankov's system, TSR is conceived of as the ability to recall information from the relatively distant past (of one's own development) and to bring it to bear in the solution of a problem, as measured for example by tests requiring the retrieval of stored exemplars of a concept. The musical equivalent of such a test might be to require the subject to recall as many tunes as possible beginning with 'soh doh'' in one minute. While long-term memory is certainly involved in such short-term memory tasks as the Seashore, Wing and Drake memory tests, attempts to assess long-term memory have usually involved the recognition of tunes (often distorted in some way) on their recall (see further Chapter 16). Agnew (1922) asked musicians, and musically unselected adults and children, to assess how clearly they could imagine the tune 'America' as played on a

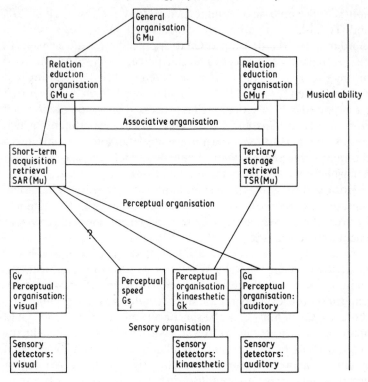

FIG. 5.2 Schematic representation of intellectual functions as applied to musical ability (Mu)

piano. Bergan (1967) compared a score obtained by self-rated musical imagery with a pitch identification test and with Drake's memory test. Musical imagery produced a sizeable association with pitch identification, but little with the Drake.

Both at the perceptual and associative organisation levels Horn and Stankov include speed factors. Speed must presumably be a potent factor in the processing of music. Specific evidence from tests is, however, sparse. McLeish (1950) found that 'speed at the higher levels measured by Cattell's timed intelligence test has an appreciable influence on the Seashore memory and pitch tests'. Woodrow (1939) reported a factor on which the Seashore tests were heavily loaded that also had lighter loads on speed of copying. Whellam's (1971) analysis with young children using the Bentley and Wing tests 1-3 and a variety of other tests produced factors on tapping and formboard (timed), but the loadings of the music tests on these were slight. Such matters require further research.

The processing of music by the blind

Blind persons are sometimes supposed to develop superior powers in their other senses to compensate for their lack of sight. It is probably nearer the truth to say that the sighted do not use their auditory and tactile senses to the full.

Though some differences between the blind and sighted on the Seashore and K–D tests have been reported (Kwalwasser, 1955; Juurmaa, 1967), on the whole the blind are not superior to the sighted (Seashore and Ling, 1918). Sakurabayashi, Sato and Uehara (1956) in Japan administered the Seashore measures to 282 non-music students, to 148 music students and to 150 blind non-music students and to 17 blind students of music. The music students scored better than the non-music students, but no clear difference between the sighted and the blind was found. Drake (private communication) tested 15 students available at a blind academy. The average score for musical memory was very superior to his norms. It would seem understandable that the blind should be superior in musical memory rather than pitch discrimination considering their long experience of dealing with meaningful stimuli perceived in succession. Pitman (1965) found higher average scores for the first three Wing tests, while Heim (1963) obtained results that were quite similar to Wing's norms, except that there were rather more at the higher and lower extremes of talent among his blind subjects. Stankov and Spilsbury (1978) reported that their blind subjects were better than their sighted counterparts especially on DASP abilities, but inferior on rhythm (especially on Drake's B rhythm test). If the development of rhythm partly depends on being able to move around freely in space (p. 66 above), this would be understandable.

Witkin, Oltman, Chase and Friedman (1971) administered a slightly adapted version of White's auditory embedded-figures test (see p. 87) to 25 children aged between 12 and 19 who had been blind from birth, and to a matched group of sighted children. The verbal IQs of both groups were similar, averaging around 115. The performance of the blind on embedded tunes was significantly superior (mean = 84·9 compared with 66·7). A group of children who had had vision early in life were also tested; their scores were around 82·5.

Sex differences in musical ability

Most test authors have found differences in scores between males and females small enough to disregard. Where differences have been found, they have turned out to be attributable to the women having received more instrumental training than the men with whom they were compared (Gilbert, 1942).

However, McGuinness (1976) claimed that sex differences in sensory capacities are present in infants before they have been affected by selective reinforcement, girls showing interest in auditory stimuli and boys in visual. As evidence, McGuinness cites studies such as an investigation carried out by Kagan and Lewis (1965) who found that at six months boys attended to an intermittent tone, while girls paid more attention to a more complex excerpt of unusual jazz. Unfortunately, from the point of view of music, the stimuli used were very limited in their range. From her own research (1972) she found no sex differences among 25 male and 25 female college students on pitch discrimination, when differences in musical training were taken into account, nor in loudness thresholds. What she did find was a very highly significant difference between the decibel level at which a subject reacted when instructed to adjust an attenuator to the point where a 'fairly loud' tone became 'too loud'. The average level for men was 83·3 db and for women 75·5. These figures were close to those reported by Elliott (1971) for children aged 5 and aged 10, using white noise. Shuter-Dyson found some confirmatory evidence that women students began to rate a folksong as 'too loud' at a lower decibel level than men. (See Shuter-Dyson, 1979, for a more detailed review of the sex difference question.)

Wing (1941*b*) reported that after the age of 14 girls seemed rather better than boys at his appreciation tests, though the two sexes were still equal in performing the ear acuity tests. The difference amounted to about 4 out of 80 marks. One explanation that Wing put forward was that the greater number of introverts among women tend to make them 'better listeners to music that requires appreciation'. Whellams (1973*a*) compared the Wing scores for two groups of women college of education students with three groups of males, along with data relating to instrumental music students. By a discriminate function analysis*, he reached two equations of weighted Wing scores. These were:

$$X = 1 \text{ Chords} + 2 \text{ Intensity} + 4 \text{ Phrasing and}$$
$$Y = 2 \text{ Chords} + 3 \text{ Pitch} + 5 \text{ Memory} + 4 \text{ Rhythm} - (4 \text{ Harmony} + 5 \text{ Intensity} + 6 \text{ Phrasing})$$

Women students tend to have higher X-scores than men. In a mixed group males whose X-score is greater than the mean X-score for women may have high musical potential. Y-scores are more characteristic of men than of women, and of instrumentalists than of non-players. Thus a woman who makes a high score may have high potential for success in instrumental music. Whellams suggested that these results indicated the possibility of the operation of a sex factor that could lead to the development of different types of musicality. The negative weightings awarded to the appreciation tests, with the exception of rhythm, in the case of the Y equation would seem to confirm Wing's surmises. In various other rhythmic tasks, boys may equal or even surpass girls. Shuter-Dyson (1979) suggested that this might be connected with the well-documented superiority of males in spatial abilities. McGuinness (private communication) reported that in a study on rhythm perception in speech patterns females *without* musical training scored significantly worse than males with or without training and females with musical training. Shuter (1964) reported that while appreciation of rhythm loaded more strongly on an (unrotated) general factor based on the Wing scores for males, appreciation of intensity was more evident in a broad factor obtained from testing women of comparable age, education and level of musical ability. This also seemed to support Wing's view that girls are more interested in music as a means of expressing feeling – hence appreciation of changes in intensity might be a more important component of their musical ability.

Sex differences in the personality of musicians and in the greater proportion of boys who experience singing difficulties will be discussed in later chapters.

---

*A technique for assessing the relative strengths of variables which discriminate between two criterion groups.

Summary

On the basis of the evidence now available we have presented a model which we believe reflects, if only in a much simplified form, the complex nature of musical ability. The model is intended as a basis of discussion and of further research. While recognising the contribution of the various musical elements to music listening and performance, we have emphasised the importance of the inter-relations and coordination that music requires.

6

Ability in music and other abilities

How far is musical ability related to general intellectual ability and to academic attainment? Many highly intelligent people do not seem to be able to hear the difference between 'God Save the Queen' and 'The Star-Spangled Banner', while some mental defectives can play by ear.

Other questions to be considered in the present chapter are: Is there a broad ability which embraces all the arts? Is there any basis for the persistent notion that musical and mathematical abilities go together?

Musical ability and intelligence

Sergeant and Thatcher (1974) and Phillips (1976) provide evidence that comparisons of children classified into groups according to intelligence or type of school attended will produce highly significant associations with musical ability. Sergeant and Thatcher re-analysed data collected by Taylor (1973). Taylor had obtained the following correlations between a verbal reasoning test and his music responseness tests (see further p. 150) with 70 children aged 10 to 11 years: ·40 (melody), ·37 (rhythm) and ·58 (harmony). The highest correlation was, not unexpectedly, with the hardest test. In the case of his music discrimination test, correlations for 100 children were ·42 and ·47. Sergeant and Thatcher's re-analysis demonstrated a highly significant linear relationship between five divisions of IQs and the music tests. Sergeant and Thatcher also reported three experiments with the Bentley tests. In the first, 54 children aged 10 to 11 whose mean scores on the Schonell Essential Intelligence tests were 115, were divided into six groups according to their IQs. Their Bentley scores were close to the population mean of Bentley's norms. Again, highly significant linear association was found between the groups. A second group, of 78 children aged 10 to 11 much lower both in non-verbal IQ and on the Bentley, also showed linear trends. Ninety children out of over 500 tested were selected to provide six groups whose mean verbal IQs should range from 75, to 85 up to 125. Their mean Bentley scores increased in parallel (though the IQ 85 group was only 1·2 better than the IQ 75 group). Linear and highly significant associations were found between IQ and the total Bentley and all the Bentley tests taken separately.

Sergeant and Thatcher then tested 75 children, aged 10 to 11, with the Cattell Culture Fair Scale 2 (supposedly a test of Gf). The children were selected so as to represent the full range of socio-economic status. They were taught to clap a short rhythmic figure, repeating it after the experimenter till it was accurately reproduced. Four short melodic figures were then heard and the child had to identify which contained the rhythm they had learned. A test-retest reliability coefficient of ·625 was obtained from the fifteen items of this test. A similar test of melody was given (the child had to identify the phrase he had learned to sing), a test with a reliability of ·72. A direct linear relationship was found between the music measures and IQ. (Significant relationships were also found between IQ, music measures, socio-economic status and home music background – see further Chapter 15.)

Phillips (1976) tested 194 children from four Newport (Gwent) schools. The children at School A came from the best residential area in the town; those at B were 'lower-middle' class, those at C 'working-class', while School D was situated in the depressed docks area. Phillips used the Wing tests 1-3 (re-recorded) and the Thackray tests of rhythmic perception (omitting the steadiness test). The Thorndike-Hagen 'Cognitive Abilities Test' was used to provide verbal, quantitative and non-verbal scores and total IQs. Both the Wing and Thackray scores for School A were significantly superior to those for School B. Since School B provided an exceptionally stimulating musical programme, Phillips felt that this was disappointing. (Perhaps a more encouraging result might have been obtained had an achievement in music test been used. Jamieson (1951) found that pupils of a school in a working-class district where the headmaster was particularly keen on music knew comparatively more songs and were able to recognise more tunes than might have been expected on a linear socio-economic class hypothesis.) The musical backgrounds of Phillips's subjects from School A as compared with those from School B were not significantly different. In the case of the Wing tests, Schools B and C but not C and D were significantly different; with the Thackray tests, the only difference that was not significant was between Schools B and C. Phillips concluded that his findings were in agreement with those of Sergeant and Thatcher, i.e. that the home that fosters musicality is also likely to foster intelligence.

When we turn to the studies based on correlations between intelligence test scores and musical ability tests, tabulated in Appendix II, a different picture emerges. Nearly all of the correlations are positive but low, not far from the ·3 which both Kwalwasser and Wing refer to as being indicative of the association to be expected with ordinary unselected subjects. It is true that most of the correlations refer to college students or high school groups, for whom intelligence would not be very likely to be important in success with performance of musical ability tests. Wing (1948) observed that he found good agreement between low intelligence and low scores on his tests, but that disagreement occurred where a high IQ was accompanied by a low musical ability score. This is partly why Sergeant and Thatcher prefer to compare groups of subjects rather than individual scores – since anomalous cases reduce correlations.

Edmunds (1960) also found that low intelligence and low musical ability appear to be closely related, but that when a certain level of general ability is reached, around IQ 90 for children aged 12 to 13, intelligence no longer plays a significant part, i.e. children may be musical or unmusical. Zenatti (1975) reported that the acuity of perceptive discrimination and tonal acculturation of some 400 subnormal children were related to their mental, rather than to their chronological, age.

While the ability of backward children at music may appear high when compared with their achievements on more academic subjects, they may well only rarely be as good as the normal child of the same age. Nevertheless, some intellectually dull children seem to have average or superior musical aptitude. Thus, McLeish and Higgs (1968) tested educationally subnormal children, in pairs, to allow for slower responses, with the Seashore, Wing and Bentley tests. Except for tests where memory was highly involved, their mean scores were reasonably comparable with those made by children in ordinary primary and secondary schools. As Wing (1955) pointed out, it is important that such children should receive opportunities for developing their musical gifts. The correlations reported by Whellams for his own investigation are often above ·5. All his subjects were learning the recorder; their scores were at least as good as average on Bentley's pitch test, but somewhat lower than average, for the ages on the other music tests he used. Their non-verbal ability test scores were about average, but their reading ages were some two years lower than the norms given for the reading tests used in his study. Whellams (1971) noted that higher correlations with intelligence are often reported with younger children.

In the case of younger children and at the lower levels of intelligence, the connection between intelligence and musical ability is probably at least partly due to adaptation to the testing situation, willingness or capacity to concentrate and so forth. Though the correlations with other abilities which Gordon (1979*a*) obtained are quite low, he reports finding that if any type of pencil and paper test had been administered to kindergarten children previously, the reliability of the PMMA increased. On a different type of musical task, auditory conservation of tonal and rhythm patterns, Norton (1979) found an almost zero correlation with a picture vocabulary test among children, whose average age was 6.1.

Considering the abstract nature of music we might expect non-verbal intelligence tests to be more closely related to music tests than are verbal ones. The trends are, however, inconsistent – towards the non-verbal side in the case of Lundin's and Gordon's results, towards the verbal in Whellams's. Again, Roderick (1965) obtained correlations ranging from ·20 to ·35 between the Minnesota Tests of Creative Thinking and the Wing and Aliferis tests. Correlations with the Drake memory test were even lower. There was no significant difference between music students, art students and a randomly selected college group.

We may also ask, 'Are some aspects of musical ability more closely related to general intelligence than others?' Again our table does not show many consistent trends. This may be partly because many of the subtests are much less reliable when considered separately. As might be expected, memory tests give relatively high correlations, but pitch tests are often slightly higher still. Some tests of rhythm, for example, Holmstrom's and Gordon's, show rather higher correlations than tonal tests with intelligence. Thackray's tests seem to show sizeable (·55) correlations with IQ, both in his own research (1971) and in Phillips's (1976). Phillips's correlations are admitted to be 'surprising' and should probably be disregarded since they may be due to the 'humps' in the distribution of scores which roughly correspond to the schools.

With children aged 12 to 16 in Yugoslavia, Rados (1980) reported that the association with intelligence depended on the music test used and the musical experience of the testees. With children without musical experience, the Seashore and Wing ear acuity tests also measured verbal ability. With children in music school the Wing appreciation tests were independent of intelligence.

We may now return to our conceptualisation of musical ability and enquire how Stankov's interpretation of factors loaded on DASP tests in the cases of his Yugoslav study and of his study with the blind as Gf can be reconciled with our view. If Gf is a general ability that can be applied to incidental learning situations which the child encounters, it should facilitate the development of musical ability. Indeed achievements in music, such as the mastery of notation, might be one area in which Gf crystallises. Among older children, Stankov appears to agree with the view that differentiation of abilities takes place, giving rise to separate factors of verbal, numerical and reasoning abilities, etc. Certainly, we shall note in Chapter 8 evidence that the newly born react to auditory tonal patterns in similar ways to verbal (or pre-verbal) ones. In Chapter 15 we shall find that a programme intended by Kucenski to stimulate musical sensory learning among infants between three and nine months also produced gain in language.

However, due account must be taken of other evidence that specifically musical abilities appear very early in life, even in circumstances when high Gf would find relatively little material upon which to operate. Cases of precocity in music are described in Chapter 11. These include Revesz's study of the prodigy, Erwin Nyiregyhazy. Revesz tested Erwin with the early version of the Binet-Simon intelligence scale and came to the conclusion that he was at least two years ahead of his chronological age. Revesz considered that the questions in an intelligence test did not do justice to the brilliance of Erwin's intellect, particularly to the precision with which he grasped and tried to answer questions about music.

That the musically great men of history did possess far better than average intelligence is well established. Cox (1926) included eleven musicians in her careful study of the biographies of great men, whose intelligence was estimated from evidence of the activities of which they were capable at various ages. Bach's IQ was thought to lie between 125 and 140; Beethoven's between 135 and 140; and Mozart's between 150 and 155. Taken as a group, however, the musicians were among the lowest in IQ of all the eminent persons she studied. A later investigation of their versatility placed them among the least versatile (White, 1931), perhaps through lack of time due to the demands of their music.

Also discussed in Chapter 11 are idiot savants. The so called idiot savant is an individual of very low general intelligence who shows some special aptitude, such as for music. The typical musical accomplishments of idiot savants somewhat resemble those of infant prodigies, especially with regard to memory. Thus they are able to play tunes, often after hearing them only once, and can play familiar tunes by ear, sometimes with 'correct' harmonisation – suggesting excellence of long-term memory.

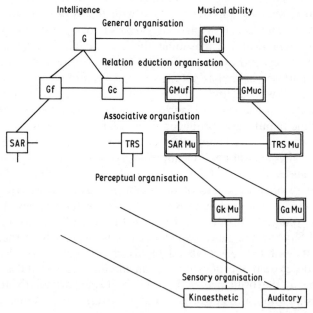

FIG.6.1 Diagrammatic representation of the very highly talented musician. Double lines indicate an exceptional degree of ability.

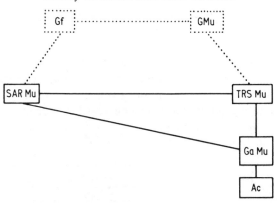

FIG. 6.2 Diagrammatic representation of a musical idiot savant. Ability mainly at perceptual and memory levels, due, apparently, to lack of adequate general intelligence

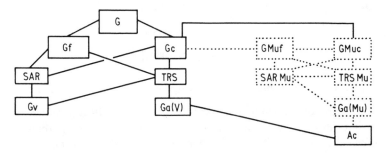

FIG. 6.3 Diagrammatic representation of the highly intelligent person with low aptitude for music. (Dotted lines indicate a weak degree of ability.) A line between Gc and GMuc to indicate that the intelligent person is likely to learn music symbols and terminology without difficulty. The main link of the auditory system is to words (here called Ga Verbal).

Figures 6.1, 6.2 and 6.3 indicate how we might conceptualise the intellectual functions of the highly talented musician, the idiot savant and the individual of high intelligence with low aptitude for music. Only those connections which seem of particular relevance to music have been shown. No implications as to whether the talent is inborn is intended, since the question will be discussed in Part 3. Nor has the vital role of motivation in the development of talent been illustrated. It must be admitted that these diagrams may overemphasise the specificity of musical abilities and give too much attention to anomalous cases. A more acceptable view that would be applicable to the majority of children would envisage a general intelligence which comes in part to be crystallised in the direction of music, perhaps through favourable environmental influences which focus the child's interest on music, given a reasonable measure of Ga and resulting in musical achievements which depend largely on how much time and effort the individual is prepared to invest in them and his opportunities to learn (see Figure 6.4).

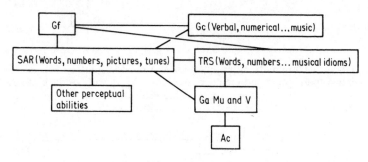

FIG. 6.4 The average child

Musical achievement and intelligence/scholastic achievement

We might expect that achievement in music (GMuc) might be rather more closely related to intellectual functioning than is musical aptitude. The answer depends partly on the criterion of musical achievement.

Mursell (1937) inferred from data such as teachers' estimates of musical ability or marks for school music that musical achievement shows a close association with educational attainment. It is difficult, however, to assess how far personality factors like willingness to work hard influence such results. More teachers' marks are liable to be contaminated by what is known as the 'halo effect' of the pupils' other school work. 'Halo effect' is a term used for the tendency to generalise from achievement in one sphere. Indeed, Gordon (1968*b*) reported that, whereas performance of études and a music achievement test were most highly correlated with scores on the MAP, teachers' ratings of the pupils' progress in music showed a higher association with intelligence and scholastic attainment than with MAP scores. This he attributed to halo effect. Nevertheless, quite substantial correlations (around ·60) were found for the études and the early form of the ITML used in the Three-Year Validity Study (see p. 27 above) for 28 nine-year-olds from whom satisfactory scores on intelligence were available.

However, with the standard form of the ITML, as with the MAT, low correlations are found with tests of intelligence and scholastic achievement (see Appendix II), as we might expect with tests with a high aural content.

Students undergoing professional training are likely to be partly selected for their general intellectual brightness. Cooley (1961), reporting on 180 students majoring in music, stated that their scores on intelligence tests placed them on the sixtieth percentile rank compared with other college students. Students at the Warsaw Academy of Music reached PR 90 on Raven's matrices and PR 60-70 on a Polish version of the Army General Classification Test compared with children in general schools (Manturzewska, 1978). Shuter (1964) found evidence that in the case of the junior musicians at the RMSM some of the musically weaker ones came from grammar as opposed to secondary modern schools, their educational attainments being possibly in some measure held to compensate for lower musical potential. In all the music groups that Kemp studied (see p. 92), higher than normal intelligence was present, as measured by Cattell's 'B' factor, claimed to be a mixture of Gf and Gc (Cattell, 1965). Kemp believed that the lesser academic achievements of the music students were not due to a lack of ability but rather to their decision to devote their efforts to music.

The progress of children beginning to learn an instrument is likely to be influenced by their level of general intelligence. Webber (1974) found that the best predictor of some 1500 ten-year-olds' performance after a year of instruction on the Watkins-Farnum scale, as well as on a notation and terminology test, was a measure of scholastic achievement. The correlation of Watkins-Farnum and intelligence/scholastic achievement is around ·5 (Stivers, 1974). Mitchum (1968) also used the Watkins-Farnum scale after six months of music lessons to assess the progress of 76 students. Performance on the scale was better predicted by tests of intelligence and scholastic achievement than by the Wing tests. However, the Wing pitch and memory tests combined with social status and IQ and scholastic achievement produced a multiple R of ·55.

Colwell (1964) compared in all some 4000 children in grades 5 to

12 on music achievement tests and IQ and grade level. One group of the younger children was receiving extra vocal practice, a second extra instrumental practice, a third the vocal practice plus piano lessons outside school and a fourth instrumental practice in school and piano lessons outside. Their scores on the K–D tests, the Knuth achievement test (which required matching music heard to one of four notation choices), on IQ and on grade levels followed the same order. With older groups where music was completely elective, the piano-instrumental pupils had IQs which averaged 123, compared with the mean IQ 100 of their schoolmates. As we shall see in Chapter 15, the parents who provide opportunities for piano lessons are likely to be of higher socio-economic status, a factor which interacts with superior intellectual ability. It could be that brighter pupils are attracted to music because of the challenge that mastery of an instrument offers; or because they can more easily cope with the demands of music lessons as well as their school work; or it might be true that the practice of music promotes general intellectual development. All these points may be valid, but in different degrees for different individuals.

Musical ability and other abilities

The table in Appendix II shows correlation coefficients obtained by comparing tests of musical ability with tests of various other abilities. Oral French showed a moderate correlation with musical ability, confirming the popular view that musical children have an advantage when it comes to learning to speak a foreign language. Some success has been obtained with using certain of the Seashore tests as predictors of success at learning foreign languages. For a review of research, see Leutenegger and Mueller (1964) and Leutenegger, Mueller and Wershow (1965).

As one might deduce from the low correlation with other ability tests, factor analytic studies of music tests tend to produce separate music factors, which however, show certain links with other tests. With students of speech and of psychology, Hanley (1956) found that verbal facility and the Seashore tests formed two separate factors. Solomon, Webster and Curtis (1960) tested 90 naval recruits with the same and other tests. A factor on which tonal memory and pitch were especially loaded also had sizeable loadings on tests of verbal facility. Pitch, loudness, time and tonal memory also had some loadings on a factor of ability to perceive verbal material that had been distorted by noise masking and perception of nonsense syllables had some loading on the Seashore verbal facility factor. These recruits who undersood the abstractions in the Seashore and nonsense-word tests did well on these tests, the others did not.

Several studies have suggested that certain factors of speed and of memory may span the visual and auditory modalities (Karlin, 1942). White (1954) found that a hidden tunes test (spotting whether or not a 3-, 4-, or 5-note melody is embedded in a more complicated one) correlated with its visual counterpart (embedded figures) ·66 and had correlations in the ·50s with three other visual tests. In Fleishman, Roberts and Freidman's (1958) study hidden tunes had a major loading, ·62, and the Seashore rhythm test one of ·56 on a factor which involved tests of ability to detect the dots and dashes of Morse code. Beard (1965) found that in a factor defined by Wing tests 1 and 2 and a shortened version of Seashore's rhythm test the Gottschaldt test (finding simple figures among more complex ones) had a ·3 loading. She suggested that the factor might not be a purely auditory one but might depend on a more general ability to recall Gestalten after a short interval. In her study the easier part of the Gottschaldt test was connected to the music factor in the case of girls, but the harder part in the case of boys. Wing test 1 had a fair loading on a factor involving flexibility in recognition of a pattern amid a distracting background. Horn (1973), however, concluded that while there is some common variance between comparable visual and auditory tests, there is more common variance *within* the auditory and the visual modalities.

Musical ability and the other arts

Feis (1910) noted that the parents of great musicians have often been distinguished in the other arts or literature. This suggested to Mursell and Glenn (1931) that distinctive talent is a manifestation of a high level of all-round ability and particularly of artistic and literary ability. Bühler (1935) concluded from her extensive studies in Vienna of young children that they will take up any art that happens to be readily available in the environment as a means of expressing themselves.

It does not follow, however, that individuals would be equally good at any art. Correlations are low (See Appendix IIb). Both Carroll (1932) and Rigg (1937) compared the Oregon music tests with literary appreciation tests constructed upon somewhat similar principles. Thus, as far as such appreciation tests permit, little correspondence was evident.

Egger and Ivinskis (1969) found that music students were significantly superior to students of art who were in turn superior to students who had never learned music and professed to be untalented at art on a melodic discrimination task. This required the subject to listen to four notes and to set keys to copy the sequence at the different pitch. In Freeman's (1974) study musical ability appeared to overlap somewhat with artistic in a group of musically talented children as compared with artistically talented children, but ability to draw was confined to the latter (see further Chapter 15). Wing (private communication) could find no correlation between the paintings of students, as judged by an expert artist, and the results of his test.

Conceivably, at some elusive 'aesthetic' level, music, poetry and art may show stronger connections. Beldoch (1964) presented 89 students with representations of ten emotions in three media. They were asked to identify the emotion conveyed (*a*) by the voice in samples of speech of neutral verbal content, (*b*) in graphic art work of abstract representation of the same emotions, and (*c*) in short musical compositions composed to communicate the emotions. Though a vocabulary test was related to all three measures, significant intercorrelations remained with intelligence held constant, as can be seen in table 6.1. Previous training or current interest in the arts did not contribute to the success of the judgements. High scorers did describe themselves as more sensitive to emotional expressions than did the low scorers. A personality factor of tender-minded was shown both by musical children and by professional music students, but it did not clearly distinguish them from non-musical groups. Martin (1976, see also p. 91) interpreted this to mean that it was common to all whose interests lay in the arts.

Musical ability and mathematical/scientific abilities

There would seem to be a similarity between music and mathematics in that both involve thinking in relationships and abstractions. However, one difficulty which arises in trying to investigate

Table 6.1 *Correlations for 89 students, divided into two groups, in their judgements of the same emotion conveyed in three different media*

	Music	Art	Intelligence partialled out Music	Art
Speech	·64; ·43	·56; ·27	·59; ·34	·46; ·08
Music		·53; ·55		·46; ·38

the connection between ability for music and that for mathematics is the very different treatment they receive in school. Considerable attention is given to arithmetic and other branches of mathematics and its utilitarian value is made apparent. Music, except for the very talented, may be presented as less important, except as a hobby. For the very talented, music requires a great investment of time and effort – no doubt often at the expense of other studies. Even if they had aptitude for mathematics, many musicians may have little time or opportunity to develop it. Revesz (1953) found that only 9 per cent of professional musicians had mathematical talent or interest in mathematics. We may wonder what percentage of the population of comparable socio-economic status to musicians *would* express an interest in mathematics.

The results of correlating music and mathematics tests do not reveal any close connection. For example, Shuter (1964) found zero correlations between the Wing tests and the Admiralty mathematics tests. These were largely arithmetical and must have been considerably affected by the candidates' previous experience. However, Whellams (1970) contrasted junior musicians rated as 'A' with those rated as 'C' by their instructors and also buglers, from whom lower standards of musicianship were required. The mathematics, especially the algebra component, were the highest discriminatory tests among the non-music tests. In Manturzewska's comparison of the 10 per cent most successful with the poorest 10 per cent of academy of music students (see also p. 21), the good students were especially distinguished from the poor by their high scores on the scientific and mechanical scales of the Kuder Preference Record. Over 50 percentile ranks separated the leading from the poor students in the case of the spatial subtest of a Polish version of the Army General Classification Test. A spatial ability factor with loadings on artistic and musical interests was reported for over 500 further education students by Smith, Howes and Shepherd (1976).

Considerable evidence exists that at an advanced level mathematics involves a high degree of spatial ability (see MacFarlane Smith, 1964, Chapter 3). This would explain Vernon's (1933) data which showed that 60 per cent of scientists were members of the Oxford University Music Club during the year 1927-8 compared with 15 per cent for the university as a whole. Revesz (1946; 1953) sent a detailed questionnaire to over 500 Dutch mathematicians, physicists, physicians and writers about their composing, performing and concert-going activities. The percentages classified as musical were: mathematicians 56 per cent; physicists 67 per cent; physicians 59 per cent and writers 71 per cent. Only six of Revesz's questions were concerned with aural ability, and two of these related to absolute pitch. It is not clear how much weight was given to these in assessing the results. In any case it is questionable how far trying to assess musical ability by questionnaire is a valid procedure. The writers may have answered the questions less objectively than the scientists, though they may in fact have been sensitive to nuances of sound. But if we adopt a rather broad definition of mathematical ability, Revesz's evidence may be better than he believed.

Webster (1979) found that figural creativity (i.e. with pictures) correlated more significantly with musical improvisation than did verbal creativity. Little difference was found when 'composition' or 'analysis' (making imaginative observations on a section of Bartok's *Mikrokosmos*) was used as the musical counterparts.

If any test of musical aptitude is related to spatial ability, Karma's test of acoustic structure might seem to be that test. In his earlier studies Karma did find higher correlations (·33) with spatial ability than with verbal (·09). In later research this tendency was reversed – the correlation with verbal ability rose to ·45 and ·47, while those with spatial ability fell to ·32 and ·06. Karma (1979) tested the hypothesis that two ways of processing musical material might exist: the verbal and the spatial. Since boys are known to be better on spatial tasks and girls on verbal, a sex difference might be influential. The average difference confirmed this. But classifying his results by sex and by spatial/verbal dominance did not confirm this hypothesis. He finally concluded (Karma, 1980) that the essential difference was in the amount of experience of music his subjects had had. Thus, untrained persons tend to process acoustic materials 'verbally'; spatially talented persons do not use their full potential in acoustic structuring. Musical training seems to increase the individual's possibilities of using spatial abilities in processing acoustic materials. This makes the difference in the *levels* of the performance of spatial and verbal individuals disappear, but may not affect the different *styles* in the processing of musical material. It might also be true in the early stages of learning music, as with learning number, verbal ability plays an important role.

Musical ability and personality factors

Intuitively, one feels that there is likely to be an association between musical talent and personality. Early attempts to establish connections did not lead to clear-cut results, perhaps in part because the personality tests used in some of the research were of dubious validity.

Garder (1953) and Kaplan (1961) both studied high school instrumentalists. Using the Guilford-Zimmerman Personality Survey, Garder reported that the instrumentalists were less objective and unskilled in personal relations; Kaplan (see Kemp, 1979), from results, on the Manifold Interest Schedule, found self-confidence, self-control and intellectualisation to be prominent characteristics. Garder interestingly showed that male musicians were less active and less masculine than their non-musical peers, while girl musicians were lower in restraint, stability and friendliness.

Other studies using the Cattell personality factor questionnaires suggested that factor I (tender-mindedness) and Q_3 (high self-esteem) might be characteristic of musical persons (Cattell, *et al*. 1970; Shuter, 1974).

Schleuter (1972) could find a significant relationship only between intelligence (Cattell factor B) and the MAP and the ITML scores of 12- and 13-year-old pupils. Thayer (1972) showed significant correlations exist between Cattell factor A (warmheartedness), B intelligence, submissiveness (E−) and I and the MAP and ITML composite scores of 12- and 13-year-olds; also, with the exception of intelligence, with their Seashore test scores. With 60 pupils aged 14 only intelligence correlated with the three musical ability batteries and I with the MAP and ITML.

Martin (1976) tested 78 academy of music students, 140 college of education students, as well as the 200 secondary school pupils further described on p. 203, finding intelligence and factors I higher than the average of the norms in all groups. Martin's results suggested some interesting differences among different groups of musicians and between the sexes. However, he concluded that factors associated with home and social environment were more important than personality factors in the making of a musician.

Much more positive results have come from an extensive study of the Cattell personality factors of some 200 professional musicians, 688 music students from conservatoires and nearly 500 children aged 13 to 17 who were receiving special training in music recently completed by Kemp (1979). With these large numbers, Kemp has been able to analyse the profiles characteristic of various types of performers, of musicians whose main study is composition, and to point up sex differences. The personality traits of the musician are highlighted, in the case of the music students and secondary school musicians, in contrast with students possessing little interest in music or creative activity.

Kemp made use of Cattell's formulae for obtaining second-order factors. This enabled him to show that the components of such second-order dimensions as anxiety or introversion may be different for different groups. For example, among musical secondary school children, introversion was composed of J (individualistic) and Q_2 (self-sufficient); among music college students, introversion came from A− (aloof), F− (serious) and Q_2, while the introversion of the professional musicians came from A− and Q_2.

Talented children at residential music schools were characterised by introversion and anxiety, while pupils who were attending ordinary schools but who had won scholarships for instrumental tuition at conservatoires tended to be extraverted, well-adjusted and had the G (conscientious persistence) and Q_3 which make up the dimension of 'good upbringing'. The 'hothouse' competitive atmosphere of some of the residential schools may partly explain the difference (Kemp, 1980).

Compared with the norms for the general population, fewer sex differences were found among musicians, i.e. the women were more 'masculine', the men more 'feminine'. This androgyny appeared to increase with the length of time spent in the music profession.

One of Kemp's general conclusions is that his data suggest that the personalities of musicians should be regarded as polymorphous rather than heterogeneous.

Summary

Aural abilities are primary prerequisites for music learning. Given an adequate endowment of perceptual abilities, 'Ga', intelligence is an important factor in the level of attainment in music that the individual will achieve. There seems to be general agreement that not all highly intelligent persons show talent for music. A reasonably high level of intelligence is likely to help students on such tasks as learning notation and producing essays on musical history. While a high level of musical talent is a primary qualification for professional training in music, assessment of intelligence and scholastic level might aid selection to colleges of music. Manturzewska (1978) reported that among drop-outs from the Warsaw Music Academy there were some who were overly intelligent, as well as some whose intellectual capacities were too low for the course.

There is some evidence of connections between musical ability and the other arts and with mathematical or spatial ability. These are, however, not overwhelming.

Personality and motivational factors must be critical factors in how far musical talent is realised, even with 'intelligence held constant'. Important new results have recently been obtained in this area.

Part 2

The development of musical ability

7

The development of musical ability

Music begins at birth. Babies have always been lulled to sleep by song or by their own crooning. Where there are many lullabies musical growth and interest are encouraged. In this day, when the crib is never far from the radio, the infant becomes as familiar with the sounds of music as with the sounds of the mother tongue. To shape these sounds into music is as easy as to shape the sounds of language into meaning.

Some children accomplish this with ease and little help. We say they are *talented*. Others show little natural interest in the patterns of musical sound.

These words of M. Emett Wilson (1951) sum up very well both the interaction of the growing child and his environment, stressed by present-day research in child development, and also the differences likely to be found among individual children.

Our knowledge of the responses of very young children to sounds and to music has greatly increased during the past twenty years. However, the observations of such pioneers of child study as Preyer, Shinn and Stern, described at some length in Shuter (1968), were carefully carried out and still have value if only as a base-line of the responses of young children before the days of radio.

As early as 1838 Gardiner tried to represent by musical notation the crying of a child, as well as the calls of birds and animals. Darwin (1872) was interested in the crying of babies and the emotions expressed thereby. In 1906 Flatau and Gutzmann began to describe the acoustic properties of infants' crying from records they made on Edison wax cylinders. Yet Eisenberg (1976) noted that when the programme of the Bioacoustic Laboratory Research Institute was set up in 1961, 'very few studies with neonates had been undertaken and almost no reliable data on hearing capacities in early life were available'. Eisenberg and her colleagues set up experiments using a variety of noisemakers (one of the most effective proved to be the onionskin paper culled from hospital stationery supplies), as well as acoustically precise tonal stimuli and patterned sequences. Methods used were observations of the infants by trained observers and physiological measures such as changes in heart-rate and EEG records. Though primarily interested in auditory competence as the root of linguistic communication and in the diagnosis of auditory abnormalities, Eisenberg included patterned sequences of tones. Such research must help to provide a basis for our understanding of the development of musical abilities.

Among reports specifically concerned with musical development, Michel (1972) summarised research carried out in East Germany and Moog (1976) reported an extensive investigation on the musical experience of the pre-school child. Some differences in method seem to distinguish Michel's from Moog's approach – Michel was interested in the possibilities of conditioning and training to reveal potential, while Moog simply played tapes of his tests to the children and observed their responses.

Moog's tests were very comprehensive. The first test series consisted of three children's songs sung unaccompanied. The second series experimented with three combinations of words and rhythm: (*i*) words spoken rhythmically; (*ii*) words spoken in a different rhythm from the rhythm demanded by their sense; and (*iii*) nonsense-word rhythms, like 'ding-dong'. Test series three used rhythms played on different percussion instruments. In series four, contrasting instrumental items were played: a twelve-tone original melody played on a recorder; an extract from Bruckner's Fourth Symphony; a pop song and a simple string quartet arrangement of 'Sleep, baby, sleep'. Test series five dealt with cacophonies as produced e.g. when the viola part of the 'Sleep, baby, sleep' was raised by a semitone. Finally, the sounds made by a vacuum cleaner and by traffic noise were presented. Whenever it was possible, Moog recorded an example of the child's own singing for critical analysis.

Moog played these tests to 50 children at ten different age levels from six months to five and a half years and also evaluated material contributed by some 1000 parents. He was able to obtain access to families of widely differing socio-economic status (varying from homes where the father was a prominent industrialist or academic to very poor homes where many of the fathers were unemployed).

An important source of data on the musical behaviour of young children is to be found in the reports of Moorhead and her associates at the Pillsbury Foundation School, California. This school was set up to study 'the music of young children, to discover their natural forms of musical expression and to determine means of developing their musical capacities, particularly in the field of spontaneous creation'. Most of the children, whose ages ranged from one and a half to eight and a half years, remained in the school for one or two years. The school was equipped with instruments chosen for simplicity, variety, intrinsic worth and adaptability to the purposes of the children. These included a number of Oriental instruments. In this carefully designed environment the children were left free to sing and play as they pleased with a minimum of guidance. As far as possible all the music produced by the children was noted, or recorded mechanically, and all activities which seemed to be musical were described. A very broad definition of music was adopted. The uses of the voice in speech were considered to be very similar to its use in song. All sounds produced by striking on hollow blocks or on the floor were regarded as sufficiently similar to the rhythmic patterns produced on percussion instruments to be counted as embryonically of musical value. The published reports do not state how the pupils were selected. Pond (private communication) states that they came from all kinds of environments, but predominantly from the professions. Some of the parents were especially interested in the musical activities, but all appreciated the cultural ambience the school provided. It is not usually made clear in the reports at what ages the various activities occurred in the children. No doubt the younger and the less musical pupils learned a great deal from their more talented playmates.

A revival of interest in the work of the Pillsbury Foundation School has led to an observational study being set up in 1978 at the Center for Young Children at the University of Maryland (Pond, Shelley and Wilson, 1978). Seventy children, aged 3 to 5, took part. The aim was to constitute a sample of children balanced as to sex, socio-economic status, age and race; some could comprehend little or no English. Instruments that are likely to be found in kindergarten, such as Chinese tom-toms and Orff instruments, were provided for the children to use during a daily free activity period. So far, the results of the experiment suggest that children are capable of purposeful construction of sound given favourable conditions. Prével (1973) equipped a room with a variety of instruments in order to study how children, aged 4 to 10, would take advantage of the situation to make their own music as a means of self-expression.

Theories of child development and music

The Pillsbury Foundation School would seem to embody the idea of providing an environment in which the talents of the young child can blossom in a free and fruitful way, a principle expounded by Montessori (1959). However, a more 'positive' manipulation of the child by conditioning techniques, both as a method of studying the infant before he can give verbal responses, and as a means of developing his potential, would be advocated for example by the Soviet psychologist Leontiev, and by such Americans as Greer and his colleagues at the Teachers College, Columbia University.

The influence of Piaget has permeated the music development field, though how much of the Piagetian exposition of stages of development is relevant to music is open to question. In so far as Piaget conceives of the child as actively reacting to his environment through the complementary processes of 'assimilation' (accepting a new environmental experience into the existing cognitive system) and 'accommodation' (reorganising internal structures to meet the demands of the environment), his ideas seem acceptable and useful. The boundaries between the stages which Piaget postulates are not to be regarded as sharp dividing lines but as times when intellectual abilities are undergoing considerable change. The ages given are intended to be only approximate; what is important is the sequence of stages. The first, sensori-motor stage, lasts from birth to about two years of age. The first few weeks of this period are occupied by the modification and development of coordinations between the reflexes present at birth. More sustained behaviour directed to-wards a goal follows later. The 'pre-operational representation' stage lasts from about two to around seven or eight. At this stage, judgements are intuitive, ego-centred and made in terms of single relationships. The child tends to 'centre' or focus upon only a single aspect of a situation; hence he can deal with only one problem at a time and is unable to coordinate relationships. Moorhead and Pond observed that 'to combine concepts of timbre and rhythm seems to be somewhat too complex for the small child'. When the child was excited about a rhythm he would pick up, say, the nearest drum whereas he would normally choose an instrument for its timbre with some care.

At about 7 (depending on the task) the child begins to master the principle of conservation – the invariance of a given empirical factor throughout observed changes of state. But concrete thought remains attached to empirical reality and not till the stage of 'formal operations' is reached at 11 or 12, will the child be able to reason deductively from first principles and test them empirically.

It is the acquisition of conservation in music which is the Piagetian stage which has attracted the most effort among music researchers, beginning with the work of Pflederer (later Zimmerman). The suspicion that many children were merely taught to sing by rote or to 'learn their notes' without really understanding the concept of pitch has certainly turned out to be justified (see e.g. Thackray, 1978). Undeniably, too, transformations have an extremely important role in the appreciation of musical form – the 'same-but-different' quality of a melody transposed into another key, a rhythmic pattern presented in augmentation (or diminution) (twice as slow or twice as fast), these would seem to require 'conservation'.

Bruner, too, has been concerned with the development of concepts, though not of musical ones. Cognitive development occurs through the passage from the 'enactive' (not unlike Piaget's sensorimotor) representation, 'a mode of representing past events through appropriate motor responses' to the 'iconic' representation stage where the child is able to replace the action with an image that 'stands for' an object (a tune?), and finally to the 'symbolic'. Growth involves the development of various ways of representing the world and the conflict between these representations may stimulate further growth. Bruner believes that skills can be taught in some form to children of any age but as they develop and their mastery increases then they will need to return to the skills but at a higher level – Bruner speaks of 'the spiral curriculum', rather than the 'ladder' or the 'course'.

How far the development of musical ability can usefully be conceptualised in accordance with any particular theory is still open to question. At least a rich harvest of data has been collected. These will be in the next three chapters. Chapter 8 will deal with the earliest years and the 'foundation' or 'basic' skills. In Chapter 9 we shall look at 'conceptual' or more advanced capabilities. Chapter 10 will deal with music in adolescence including how earlier learnings may be carried over to adult life. The tables of ages at which the various skills are acquired need to be read with due consideration of what the tasks involve.

At the end of Chapter 10, some tentative guide-lines are offered to the musical skills and activities which seem particularly to characterise the various ages. As Leonhard and Colwell (1976) pointed out, 'Most of the research dealing with the relationship between age level and skill is focused on the earliest age at which the skill (concept) can be learned, rather than on the age after which the skill is increasingly difficult to acquire'. The latter would, of course, be difficult to establish. What would seem most important to find out is the *optimum* age or level at which the child should receive the opportunity of acquiring the skill in question, and the best sequencing of musical learnings. In Chapter 11 we shall discuss the development of precocious and unusual talents.

8

The earliest years : foundation skills

Singers often find that their unborn baby seems quieter when they are singing, while mothers who play instruments notice that the unborn child becomes more active while they are playing or shortly afterwards (Oswald, 1973). Whether the musical future of the unborn child can be affected by his mother's musical activities is not known. It is plausible that a serious lack of nutrition during the periods of pregnancy when the auditory neural systems are being formed might affect the child's response to music.

Once born, the infant, having filled his lungs with oxygen, makes himself heard by cries and, a little later, by coos. Oswald notes that a typical pattern of cries during the first month of life is one of rising-falling, and the maximum loudness is achieved at the peak of the cry. Simner (1971) found that 46 three-day-old girls could distinguish the sound of another infant's cry from white noise played at the same volume; 46 boys were less responsive.

Eisenberg (1976) believed that infants absorb more from their sound environment than can be judged from their vocal emissions, and therefore concentrated on studying her subjects' responses to various stimuli. From her own researches and the reports of others, she concluded that 'It now seems fairly well established that most newborns, including premature infants and those with abnormalities of the CNS [central nervous system] ... 'can discriminate sound on the basis of numerous acoustic variables'. All newly born babies have what appears to be a conductive hearing loss of some 35 db, but this soon disappears. The incidence of response to many acoustic stimuli tends to increase directly with intensity – loud noises increase bodily tension in crying babies. Eisenberg believes that the mechanisms for processing intensity may be fully operational at birth, and have their roots in preadapted mechanisms stemming from the history of the species. Data on the effects of differences of frequency on the infant are remarkably consistent. As shown by the researches of Birns and her colleagues (1965), 150 Hz tones could be differentiated from 500 Hz tones and low frequency stimuli (150 Hz), the latter tending to inhibit signs of distress. One of her colleagues, Bridger (1961), studied 50 babies from one to five days old. The tone of a given frequency was sounded till the babies ceased to show any motor response at all. Then a tone of equal loudness but of different frequency was sounded and produced in many babies an increase in movement and heart rate. One baby could discriminate between tones of 200 and 250 Hz. Eisenberg stresses that whether the baby is sleeping or awake, he responds two or three times more frequently to tones below 4000 Hz than to those above the 4000 Hz range. Eisenberg compares these differences in response to affective responses shown later in life. Low frequencies seem to have pleasant associations, high frequencies, unpleasant ones.

A conspicuous element in the prenatal acoustic environment is the mother's heartbeat. It has been suggested that one attraction of 'beat' music is the emotional link with the security of the mother's womb. Spiegler (1967) played 20-minute tape recordings of rhythmic heartbeats (at 75 db), of dysrhythmic heartbeats, of rhythmic clicks and dysrhythmic clicks to 40 babies between 24 and 48 hours old. He found significant differences in activity level as a response to rhythmic as opposed to dysrhythmic heartbeats, and at a lower level of significance between rhythmic heartbeat and rhythmic click. Brackbill (1966) and her colleagues found no difference in the calming effect of heartbeats at 72 beats per minute, the sound of a metronome at the same speed and a foreign language lullaby. *Any* sound was more calming than no sound at all to their two-day-old subjects. Similar results were found by Brackbill *et al.* (1966) in an experiment with the relative effectiveness of such stimuli in inducing 41 nursery school children to fall asleep: again any sound was more effective than no sound in putting children to sleep. However, Salk (1960; 1961; 1962) found that the heartbeat was significantly more calming at bedtime with two-year-olds than no sound or the lullaby or the metronome.

Of special interest from the point of view of music, is Eisenberg's experiment with matched pairs of descending and ascending tonal sequences, e.g. from 2000 Hz down to 500 Hz compared with 500 up to 2000 Hz and 250 down to 75 Hz compared with 75 up to 250

Hz. Like synthetic speech stimuli, these tonal patterns proved far more effective at evoking responses than noisemakers such as a whistle, white noise or onion skin. All 13 babies, judged to be normal, gave immediate and clear-cut responses to such stimuli presented at 10-second intervals and reached peak arousal within seven to eight trials. Whether the babies were awake or asleep, selective motor responses were elicited such as vocalisations or grimaces and small movements of the limbs or the fingers, rather than the startle reactions which might be evoked by constant stimuli. (Some 'suspect' or 'at risk' infants habituated to the stimuli much more slowly or not at all.) Obviously too much weight should not be attached to results with such small numbers before replication of the experiment.

Responses at birth are, however, only a beginning. Michel (1973) claims that whereas infants in the first hours of their life react to only a third of all available acoustic stimuli, the frequency of reactions doubles in the first four weeks, and continues to increase steadily during the following months. In fact, Michel describes the first six months of life as the period of 'learning to hear'.

Evidence from various sources suggest that around 13 to 17 weeks many behavioural patterns are found that are not present before that age. According to the observations of Shinn (1907) and Shirley (1933) as tabulated in Shuter (1968), the median age of 15 to 16 weeks marks the emergence of 'cooing and stopping crying to music', of 'sounds purposefully made by hand', of 'vocal sounds purposefully made' and of 'looking in direction of sound'. From the findings of an early longitudinal study, Eisenberg noted that 'Selective listening behaviour develops rapidly, and in more or less steplike fashion'. The human voice is preferred to noisemakers between 11 and 12 weeks of age. Sensitivity to the mother's, as opposed to a stranger's voice, is evident between 12 and 14 weeks; anticipatory cessation of crying at the sound of the mother's footsteps was reported most frequently between 14 and 16 weeks. Between 15 and 17 weeks, a sharp decline in responsivity to the (relatively uninteresting) noisemakers was noted.

From informal observations of babies younger than those included in his investigation, Moog (1976) noted transitional responses from passive receptivity to active perception of music. Between the fourth and the sixth months, in exceptional cases as early as the third month, the baby listens to music and turns towards the source of the sound. At a somewhat later stage (from two to eight weeks later) the infant begins to move when he hears music, not in an unorganised way, but with clear repetitive movements.

The next development is vocalisation to music. Moog distinguishes between babbling as the precursor to speech and musical babbling. The earliest vocalisations of the child are spontaneous and do not reflect the speech around him. The deaf child babbles for a period as if normal. Such babblings are important in establishing circuits in the infant's brain and nervous system, so that he learns that certain movements of his vocal organs will produce certain sounds. Musical babbling, Moog claims, occurs only if music is played or sung to the child. Sounds of most varied pitch are produced, either on one vowel or on very few syllables (Moog, 1967). From the tests and observations he made, Moog found that the earliest vocalisations to music occurred at just six months and always came after the stages of pure listening and motor response. While speech babbling begins before musical babbling, the child sings his earliest babbling songs before he can say his first word. Before the age of one these songs bear no resemblance to the tunes the baby hears.

When Moog played his tests to six-month-old children, they paid little attention to the rhythmic tests (although these were louder); it was the songs and the instrumental music that attracted the most active attention and motor movements to the music, evidently because of the children's pleasure in the beauty of the sound. At nine months some of the children gave signs of turning away from some items, especially the rhythms and noises. Series 2 began to receive attention, presumably because the children were beginning to be aware of the sounds of speech. By the end of the first year some awareness of the rhythmic motor element was observed, but the children's main interest appeared to be in the sheer quality of the sound.

Very considerable individual differences are found in all the studies of infants, whatever the mode of investigation (see Eisenberg, 1976, p. xxvi). Thus Moog found that an infant who was late in developing, e.g. in the turning of his head towards sound, might be early in producing movements to sound, so that the interval between these activities are unusually short. How far earliness in showing such responses is related to later musical talent has not been established.

Evidence from laboratory experiments suggests that infants are able to discriminate melodic contour. Chang and Trehub (1977*a*) presented a six-tone melody over and over again till their 24 five-month-old subjects habituated to it, i.e. their heart rates having decelerated to the novel stimulus returned to normal. Chang and Trehub then presented a transposition of the melody in a new key, or a new arrangement of the notes that changed the contour. They were careful to keep the first note the same, since previous experiments had used tonal sequences beginning with contrasting notes – thus it was difficult to be sure that it was the tonal configuration as a whole, rather than just to the first note, that the babies were reacting. Chang and Trehub's infants showed deceleration of their heart rate to the new melody, but not to the transposition, demonstrating a sensitivity to change in melodic contour. In a second study Chang and Trehub (1977*b*) demonstrated sensitivity of 5-month-olds to simple rhythmic changes, e.g. -- ---- compared with ---- --.

Kagan (1972) noted from heart-rate evidence that at seven and a half months infants tend to pay most attention to stimuli that are slightly discrepant from one to which they have become habituated. However, he believes that around nine months a change takes place and the first signs of attempts to generate hypotheses to explain novel events appear. But, whereas repetitions of a nonsense phrase followed by a different nonsense phrase produced increased 'mental activity', an ascending scale played on a cello followed by a random arrangement of the same notes did not.

Spontaneous musical activities

Part of the young child's interest in sound-making activities may be due to interest in producing effects by self-activity rather than in filling his ear with sound. Yet Prével (1976) observed that if the first sound explorations often showed a tendency of the children to make use of the potentially noisiest instruments, their choices soon became very diversified. Children's first compositions reflect their motor energy, with uncontrolled gestures. When listening to recordings of their compositions they often repeat the actions involved. After learning control of their gestures, they begin to experiment with variations in timbre and dynamics and, finally, pitch. Eventually, structured forms such as A - B - A evolve in some of the compositions.

Moorhead and Pond noted that the small child 'produces sound from anything and everything around him. And while he does this he listens – it is not an aimless occupation. Some sounds please him more than others; some he will discontinue quickly, others he will repeat many times . . . . Music is, for young children, primarily the discovery of sound.' In the Pillsbury Foundation School it was, of course, much easier for the interest in sounds to acquire musical significance than in an ordinary home.

The deepest interest of the Pillsbury children was in tone-colour. When the young child 'begins to use instruments for specific (e.g. dramatic) purposes he chooses the instrument whose timbre he considers most suitable'. The 29 children aged between 6.5 and 7.5 years, whom Belaiew-Exemplarsky studied, still found their greatest joy in music in timbre or beautiful tone colour. Gesell and Ilg (1943) also noted that the 18-month-old child is 'very much aware of sounds such as bells, whistles, clocks', while the 4-year-old 'likes to experiment with instruments, especially combinations of notes' on the piano.

There are many accounts of spontaneous singing by small children. Moog noted that in the second year there is a marked progress in the intervals used and a decrease in the number of microtonal figures – as in speech music becomes shaped towards the scale of the music the child hears around him. However, the songs still show little relationship to the diatonic system. Some children make movements when singing; others do not. At 18 months, spontaneous songs are dominated by one single note-length. Among three- to four-year-olds, 'imaginative' songs begin to appear. These consist of potpourris of spontaneous songs and snatches of songs known or versions of these. More than half of the three- to four-year-olds sang some kind of original song. Such songs seem to remain poor in rhythmic invention, being usually in duple time and often using only one note in length, unless the rhythm of the words required a difference.

Ninety-five per cent of all spontaneous rhythmic groupings played by twins and matched singletons in a research by Simons (1964) consisted of notes of equal value. More interesting patterns were sometimes produced e.g. ♫♩ ⅞ ⅞ (by a girl singleton of 10 months) and ♫ ⸋ ♫ ⸋ ♩ ♩ ♩ (by a girl twin of one year old). Simons collected his data in the infants' own homes. The 12 pairs of twins and 12 pairs of singletons he studied were aged between 9 months and 2:7 years. Responses to music were significantly less among the twins than singletons.

Among some interesting examples of spontaneous tuneful vocalisations produced by the children during free-play which Simons notated was that shown in Figure 8.1.

FIG. 8.1 Vocalisation produced by a boy singleton aged 2:0

Moorhead and Pond (1942) distinguished two types of music produced at Pillsbury : chant and song. Chant appears to evolve from speech. In fact, the first type of chant is merely heightened speech; its rhythm is that of speech, but it differs from speech in that the most important syllable is strongly accented melodically. The second type of chant has a definite rhythmic pattern to which the words may be forced to conform.

The distinguishing characteristics of the second type are that it seems indifferent to melody; it is rigidly rhythmic and closely associated with physical movement; it is repeated through rises in intensity and pitch till a climax is reached, then stops. A chant may be started by an individual but is most often sung in groups. It occurs when the child is free and happy and it is immediate in emotional origin. The most frequently occurring occasion for chant (44 times out of 135) was motor activity of some sort.

Figure 8.2 is an example of a chant with the 'minor third' said to characterise the music of very young children:

FIG. 8.2

Gesell and Ilg (1943) mention the spontaneous singing of the minor third to such phrases as 'coal man, coal truck' as characteristic of the two-and-a-half-year-old child, while at four the child 'creates song during play – often teases others on a variation of the minor third'.

Moorhead and Pond considered that chant is 'the most primitive musical art form, for such it is *sui generis*, to be found among children and, indeed, among men in general. It is part of the living experience of primitive peoples everywhere, . . . as a primitive, pagan, unsophisticated musical expression *arising from those things which the child feels instinctively to demand such expression.'*

Besides chants, the children produced songs of their own invention. In contrast to chants, 'song is essentially produced by the child for himself'. These experiments in melody are changed and developed as the child wishes. The rhythm is flexible and if accompanied by a drum the song might be at a different tempo. Most seemed not to relate to any observable tonal centre or not to a tonal centre found in western music (cf. Moog, p. 115 and Gardner, p. 117). They tend to progress by small steps, but large intervals are sometimes used to dramatic purpose. (Moorhead and Pond, 1942). Revesz (1953, p. 173) noted that in children with musical talent self-invented melodies that exhibit the first beginnings of musical form can occur 'as early as the fourth year'. In these melodies one finds uncertainty in general pitch, and intervals, but some children reveal a sense of tonality.

Moorhead and Pond believed that the child's world of music is so wide that enforced conformity with the conventions of western music before the child has sufficient background is likely to hinder the growth of vital musical conceptual patterns. Gordon (1979*a*) advises that the pre-school child's spontaneous singing should not be corrected if he has not sung what his teacher or parent thinks he should sing, but that the value of his singing can be increased by using melodic phrases to give directions or answers to questions. Gordon agrees that the pre-school child seems to sing in a tonality he alone understands, but believes that he has at least a sense of tonic as a resting tone on which to end.

The development of rhythmic skills

There appears to be some difference of opinion as to whether rhythmic skills develop before or after melodic skills, or independently.

Revesz (1953) believed that in the period between the second and fourth years 'music and movement go together and cannot be divorced one from the other'. Bentley (1966) also considers that as far as the child's ability to join in with a group is concerned singing in unison seems to occur less spontaneously and at a later stage, than coalescence upon a rhythm.

On the other hand, Wing, while agreeing that the young child delights in physical activity, doubts its value from a purely musical point of view. In his opinion the first aspects of music to develop in the case of many children is melodic shape.

For Moog's subjects, in their imitation of songs sung to them, some resemblance to the rhythm usually preceded acquiring of the pitch. Sometime between the ages of eighteen months and two years about 10 per cent of children begin to be able to match their movements to the rhythm of the music for short stretches of time. Moog found that children can more easily keep time to their own spontaneous singing – partly because it is easier to synchronise voice and motor actions (see further p. 112). Development then seems to progress by the child appearing to match his singing to something sung to him, but only after a number of repetitions. In Test 5 (cacophonies), the rhythm was perceived as the dominant musical element. At the age of two and a half, the child begins to match the movements of another person. Most children can by the age of three to four make a broad distinction beween fast and slow. However, Il'ina (1961) asked 130 children, aged 3 to 11, to move to music in whatever way the music suggested. The older children were better able to correct themselves and change with the music. The younger ones tended to respond to changes in intensity with change of tempo.

Children, aged 4 to 6, would attempt to clap or tap to music but frequently if the child could keep time it was not for very long (Moog, 1976).

The instability of keeping in time was noted by earlier experimenters. Baldwin and Stecher (1924) asked their subjects to keep time to a march by using wooden clappers. The results were not dependent wholly on age: two of the best records were produced by three-year-olds. Good time-keeping might lapse for a few bars and then be recovered. Indeed, Christianson (1938) believed that at pre-school age the more important question was not 'whether or not' but 'for how long' the child could maintain a steady beat. In her research a record player was taken into the playground while the children were engaged in activities of their own choice and their rhythmic responses were recorded and their emotional responses noted. Then they were taken in pairs into an experimental situation where Christianson counted each step that accorded with the music. The children came from Russian, Italian and Spanish backgrounds. However, such differences proved to have little significance compared with differences due to age.

Development with age was reported by Williams (Williams *et al*, 1933) who asked children aged from 3 to 5 to tap in time with the clicks on a Seashore rhythm machine. In the simplest form of the test, regular clicks at intervals of half a second, only about 25 per cent of the 3-year-olds succeeded, while only about 25 per cent of 5-year-olds failed, at 6 there were only 4 per cent of failures. Percentage of errors at ·67 of a second intervals showed similar development. One-second intervals proved more difficult.

Current research includes a three-year longitudinal study of the ability of children aged 3 to 5 to learn specific rhythmic tasks being carried out by Rainbow at North Texas State University and replicated by Frega in Argentina. Preliminary reports (Rainbow and Owens, 1979; Frega, 1979) suggest that for 3-year-olds tasks involving speech rhythms were easiest, followed by keeping a steady beat with rhythm sticks and clapping a steady beat. Speaking a rhythm before clapping it helped to make the clapping more accurate. The 4-year-olds were more successful at all the tasks than the 3-year-olds, though the order of difficulty of the tasks was similar to that found with the 3-year-olds. In general, tasks requiring large muscle movements, e.g. marching to music, were found to be difficult for 3- and 4-year-old children. To aid in the accurate judgement of his subjects' responses, Rainbow is using videotape. Attention was called to the difficulty of judging whether or not children walking or marching to music are in fact keeping in time by Heinlein (1929) and Jersild and Bienstock (1935).

The difficulties of maintaining a steady beat are still notable after the age of six. The children whom Thackray tested found his test of keeping time to music much more difficult than reproducing a rhythm. In Petzold's results, a response was scored as 'correct' only when it occurred simultaneously with the stimulus, according to a visual record transformed from the auditory record. Petzold considered that a less rigorous standard should be adopted in future research. Thackray's and Petzold's results are summarised in Table 8.1.

Table 8.1 Development of ability to maintain a steady beat

Experimenter	Subjects	Task	Results
Petzold (1966)	192 (16 boys and 16 girls at each grade between 6 and 11	Tap with metronome at MM152, 120, 92 and 60	6- and 7- year olds about same; marked improvement at 8, after 8 results stabilised. MM60, the most difficult tempo, improved till 11.
			Mean score (out of 20)
Thackray (1972)	40, aged 8 40, aged 11	Performance test No. 3	9·3 7.6

Thackray found cases of children who produced a perfectly steady beat which, however, did not fit the music; in such cases the beat was usually at the same tempo each time, regardless of the tempo of the music. Others were able to give the beat for a short time, only to lose it.

A much simpler task both from the child's point of view and that of the observer is producing a regular monotonous beat of his own. The first musical attempts of a child are characterised by a 'regular, unaccented beating', probably physical in origin, according to Moorhead and Pond. Thus, Carl, aged 3:8, who attended the Pillsbury School for four months, 'reverted to the usual regular beat, perfectly even, fast and insistent'. A little later the child will begin to introduce 'accentuation within the regular series of beats which he has set up, such accentuation being most often irregular. His rhythms, therefore, are not repetitive nor necessarily symmetrical, but their structure almost inevitably is related to the fundamental pulsation'.

Capacity to produce a regular beat or a rhythmic pattern on one's own is not, of course, inconsistent with finding difficulty in synchronising with the beat of others. Moorhead and Pond remark:

the child has great ability to maintain his own rhythmic concepts against all competition and interference. When he plays simultaneously with other children each child is likely to go his own way. But in a long established, well-integrated group, the children's music is likely to assume the characteristics of a kind of rhythmic polyphony based upon the fundamental co-ordinating pulsation which they feel.

As among African drummers, simultaneous groupings of 2 against 3 are frequently found.

In her experiments with 227 children aged four and five, Zenatti (1976a) found evidence of a developmental stage that occurred at around 4:8, for the task of tapping back a 2-, 3- or 4-note rhythm. If the child failed the first trial (presented on tape), the experimenter tapped the rhythm again. Up to the age of 4:8, the children showed a considerable improvement at their second attempt, helped by seeing the experimenter's movements. By 4:9 70 per cent of the first attempts were successful. Up to 4:8, the children's first attempts were better if the rhythms were presented on the piano. Between 4:9 and 5:2 the results for tapped and melodic patterns were similar. The older children were more successful with tapped rhythms, the musical presentation seeming a distraction. Over 70 per cent of children aged four and five could, after a short period of training, distinguish between a regular rhythm and a varied one (♫♩ ♫♩ ♫♩ versus ♬♩ ♩ ♩♩♪) Of 237 children asked to indicate a preference judgement, the youngest preferred a regular division of the beat. After 4:6 a shift to preference for the varied rhythmic structure was found. However about half of both the 4- and 5-year-olds made judgements too inconsistent to use.

As we have seen, Zenatti has been able to develop a worthwhile test for 4-year-olds by asking them to tap back very short rhythmic patterns. Stamback (1960) used more elaborate patterns than Zenatti, requiring some measure of temporal structuring. She suspected that an important change took place around the age of 6 and that at 5 all would be likely to fail. As we would expect, the number of taps required and the complexity of the pattern affect the difficulty of the task. But the results shown in Table 8.2 suggest a clear development between the ages of 6 and 9 (or even younger). —

The ability to imitate rhythms among 3-, 4- and 5-year-old children improves with age (Klanderman, 1979). Three-year-olds tended to perform the simplest part of the items, while 4- and 5-year-olds responded with the characteristic part, even if it was the most difficult. Klanderman noted that children can perform rhythms with their voices and do not need instruments or hand clapping.

Table 8.2 Ability to reproduce rhythmic patterns

Experimenter	n.	Age	Task	Results
				(median no of errors)
Stamback	48	6	Reproduce pattern	9
(1960)	25	7	of taps, test stopped	7
	50	8	after 4 successive	5·5
	25	9	failures, but not	3
	27	10	before 12th	(little improvement
	25	12	pattern	after 9)
				(mean score)
Gardner	20	6	Tap back patterns	7·35
(1971*a*)	20	8	from 4 to 8 taps	13·00
	20	11	long	16·00
(Significant improvement with age; task too easy for 11-year-olds)				
Petzold	288	Studied	Tap pattern:	No significant differ-
(1966)		from 6	(i) tapped	ence between type of
		to 11.	(ii) sung or	task. No significant
			(iii) sing back	improvement after 8.
			sung pattern	
Rosenbuch	10	5–7	Press key to	Improved up to 9–11,
and Gardner	10	7–9	imitate pattern	then levelled out.
(1968)	10	9–11		
	10	11–13		
				mean score (out of 40)
Thackray	40	8	Performance test	22·6
(1972)	40	11	No. 2	23·6

In the case of a simple 'audiation' rhythm task such as Gordon's, the mean score rises from 22·3 at five to 29·4 at eight, the steepest increase occurring between five and six.

Motor performance

Gilbert (in press) (see p. 48) re-tested after a year 87 of her subjects aged 3 to 6. Improvements related to age were found on all the sub-tests of the motoric music skills test except for motor pattern coordination. In every subtest the greatest gains were made between the ages of 3 and 4. This finding seems to emphasise the need for pre-school children to be given opportunities to exercise motor music skills.

The development of melodic skills

The small child may be happy in his own singing, but how far is he able to reproduce songs that are sung to him or recognise tunes he has heard before? Babies as young as four to six months may try to join in with their mothers' singing (Michel, 1973). Only occasionally do such young children succeed in singing even single notes correctly. Moog found that before one, children do not usually copy the rhythm, pitch or direction of a melody. After a song has been sung to a child many times, he may accompany it with a response that bears some resemblance to the sound of the words. Both Wing (1941b) and Moog observed that after nine months a child may make some specific movement he has been taught such as making appropriate physical signs of clapping to tunes such as 'Pat-a-Cake'. This is evidence of some kind of recognition of the tune. As evidence of the early development of some differentiation between tunes and some memory for their general shape, Wing noted that some children quickly learned to indicate which of certain known records they wished to hear from the colour of the label.

Table 8.3 shows the progress Moog found among the babies he studied: As we can see, the sound of the words was usually picked up first, then the rhythm and finally the pitch of the tunes. Among the one-year-olds, the words that were imitated were those with distinctive sounds, like 'Ding, Dong, Ding, Dong', irrespective of meaning. A few children learn to sing before they learn to talk.

By the age of four, 76 per cent of children could sing more or less correctly, at least one line of the song. Between 4 and 5, half of the children could sing several verses correctly, or with only a few mistakes, sometimes making the intervals too small. About 15 per cent of the 4- to 5 year-old children had difficulty in singing a song they had learnt in tune. (See further p. 192 for a discussion of poor pitch singing.)

Table 8.3 *The development of imitative singing between the ages of two and three*

Years	2·0	2·6	3·0
Songs with no resemblance to model	20%	4%	0%
Songs which resemble the sound of the words	18%	10%	4%
Songs which resemble the words and the rhythm	6%	22%	10%
Songs which resemble the words, rhythm and pitch for part of a song	28% } 40%	26% } 48%	36% } 80%
Songs which resemble the words, rhythm and pitch for a whole song	12% }	22% }	44% }
			(2% of these sing without mistakes)
Songs which resemble rhythm and pitch	16%	16%	6%

[From Moog, 1976]

In a longitudinal study of nine children being followed up for a period up to five years, the emergence of skills such as movement, story-telling as well as music, are being studied by Gardner and his associates (Gardner *et al*. 1979). By 1:7 children are able to produce distinct pitches, but are still more interested in producing spontaneous songs. During the next few months they begin increasingly to 'accommodate' to outside tunes. They agree with Moog that the words are learned first, then the rhythmic structure; by 2:6 children seem to master brief melodic phrases which are sung over and over again. By three the child may have mastered the contour of the song. Five children aged 4 to 5 were taught one song over a year. Some key stability eventually emerged, though the intervals were not always correct.

Further evidence of the kind of melodic tasks which children between 2 and 5 can undertake comes from studies of pre-school children, mostly concerned with how far such skills can be improved by training.

Table 8.4 shows the scores obtained by Updegraff, Heileger and Learned (1938) from pre-school children, whose mean IQ was around 121, but who had had little training in singing.

Many of the 5-year-old children were able to make perfect scores at singing one note and an interval. The children's skill was not, however, too firmly established; they appeared unable to sing a note played on an instrument, though they were quite capable of reproducing it after it had been sung to them. Moreover, especially with the 3-year-old group, performance was inconsistent.

Table 8.4 Results obtained by Updegraff, Heileger and Learned

	Maximum score	Average score at 3 n. = 16	Average score at 4 n. = 14	Average score at 5 n. = 36
Singing one note after it had been sung	9	6·50	5	8
Singing at interval after it had been sung	12	7·75	6·75	10
Singing a phrase after it had been sung	14		10	
Singing a phrase after it had been sung	29			13·25

Williams (Williams *et al.*, 1933) found correlations of over ·9 between two testings of 35 children aged 4:6 to 6:6 and 31 aged 2:6 to 4:6. The average scores and range of scores by ages for repeating the same note or singing back short musical phrases were as shown in Table 8.5.

Klanderman (1979) found a significant difference between 47 three-year-olds and four- and five-year-olds in ability to sing the correct direction of a melody. Her three-year-old subjects tended to continue a set direction or to repeat notes instead of changing the direction of a melody, particularly if the direction had been set by only two notes.

In the case of children of school age, Petzold (1966) carried out

Table 8.5 *Results obtained by Williams* et al.

	Age			
	3	4	5	6
Average score (out of 36)	11·13	11·09	20·15	23·83
Range	2 to 19	3 to 32	2 to 35	10 to 35

an extensive longitudinal study which included a total of over 500 children in the first six grades of Wisconsin schools. He constructed a 45-item test by analysing a large number of songs used in schools in order to find common tonal patterns. A steady improvement in singing back a tune tended to level off among the older children. The most important changes occurred between the ages of 6 and 7. Unscoreable responses or incorrect ones that retained either the general shape of the tune or had the right number of notes decreased from 28 per cent at 6 to 19 per cent at 7; by 10 only about 8 per cent were so classified. Responses that were either completely accurate or contained several correct tones in the proper sequence rose from the quite high percentage of 54 per cent at 6 to 82 per cent at 11. Petzold also used a four-bar phrase test which the child listened to twice and then tried to sing back. The process of listening and responding was repeated till either the child sang the phrase correctly two trials in succession, or till after ten presentations of the phrase. The phrase test was found to be very difficult; even with the 11-year-olds only one-third of the children managed to learn the phrase in 10 trials. Only 8 out of 90 children were capable of learning the phrase by grade four (age 9) and retaining the skill for subsequent years. Furthermore, a second phrase given to these children at 11 showed that they performed at the third grade level of competence, indicating that the learning process had not changed significantly during four years despite experience of a task of this kind. High scores on the 45-item test did not ensure that the phrase, using these same items, would be learned. Children with low or high scores in the initial year of the longitudinal study usually continued to earn low or high scores during subsequent years.

Burroughs and Morris (1962) asked 100 children aged 13 at a mixed-ability school to listen to a four-bar musical phrase and try to sing it back (see p. 66 above). Only five children eventually succeeded in giving a completely correct rendering. Wide individual differences were found at each stage of learning. Nearly half the children reached their peak performance at trial 5 or earlier. In their attempts to sing the whole tune after a single hearing, errors often occurred and these were often perpetuated – it was not what the child heard but what he thought he heard that stuck. Some of the children would be aware of a difference between what they were singing and the tune as played, but could not isolate the note(s) hindering progress.

Though Wassum (1979; 1980) concluded from an extensive study of elementary school children that the concept of tonality and vocal range are not related at a significant level, vocal range must be an important factor in what a child can sing. Welch (1979) has produced a valuable review of research on vocal range. The criterion adopted by some researchers has been the range which the child could produce, with encouragement, upwards and downwards from a note that the child could initially produce with ease (Jersild and Bienstock, 1934; Buckton, 1977). Attention was given not to the quality of the notes sung, only to their pitch. The ranges so found did not mean that the child could sing all the notes effectively in a song or would be able to sing them all in spontaneous singing. Jersild and Bienstock indeed observed each of 18 children aged from 2:7 to 4:0 for 100 minutes in a playground. Ninety-nine per cent of the notes produced were within the range E to E'. The alternative approach is to concentrate on the notes that the child could sing comfortably. Both approaches agree that the child's comfortable range is lower than the range of many songs published for children to sing. This may well be a cause of many children being classed as poor pitch singers by their teachers (see further p. 218).

Perceptual pitch tasks

On the basis of a theory such as Bruner's, we would expect that experiences of the discrimination of pitch would be likely to precede capacity to understand pitch concepts.

The work in the USSR of Yendovitskaya and Repina showed that children between 3 and 5 have considerable difficulty in differentiating pitch relationships. Yendovitskaya (1958) arranged an experimental setting in which children were required to discriminate two sounds differing in pitch to follow directions in their play activities. Only children over 5 could do this. After a programme of conditioning with some 80 or 90 complex sound stimuli with a gradual reduction in the difference of pitch between each pair, the children were able to develop more refined discrimination: of differences between 9 and 25 Hz among the 5- to 7-year-olds and between 8 and 20 Hz among the 6- to 7-year-olds. Repina (1961) obtained correct identification of pitch registers (as high, middle, or low) by using a dramatic scene in which 'father bear' uttered deep sounds, 'mother bear' higher sounds and 'baby bear' who spoke with very high sounds. Even the 2 to 4-year-olds learned to identify where each bear had been hidden by the sound of its voice. This learning generalised to other situations.

Carol Scott (1979) investigated how well children between 3 and 5 were able to group together dissimilar pitches, those 'living together in one house', on the basis of a common critical attribute. Using a play situation with Squeaky, the Mouse, whose nose would light up if the right response was made, she gave 14 children aged between 4:1 and 5:0 and 16 aged between 3:0 and 4:0 tests of pitch register and of melodic contour. Twelve of the most successful were also tested on the concept of interval size. For each concept the stimuli were grouped into sets of three positive and one negative exemplar. Thus, for melodic contour, C F D might be contrasted with F F A. Only one of the younger children reached the criterion of three out of four sets of correct responses on the first two out of three trials, on pitch register and only one on melodic contour. None of the three younger children tested on intervals reached criterion. Ten of the older group succeeded on register, four on melodic contour and two out of the nine tested on interval size. However, partial understanding of concepts occurred and 82 per cent of the older children showed some understanding of register, 56 per cent of melodic contour and 55 per cent of interval size. Of the younger group, 43 per cent completed at least two sets on the register concept and 36 per cent on the melodic contour concept.

A spin-off from an investigation intended to compare the efficacy of a specially developed music curriculum for kindergarten children with the learning which occurred among children attending kindergarten schools where no special attention was given to music is the evidence provided on which musical activities showed little difference when the two groups were tested at the end of the experiment

(Piper and Shoemaker, 1973). After 90 lessons, each lasting 20 minutes, given three times a week, the experimental children were not greatly superior to the comparison group in activities such as correctly identifying at least one out of two ascending and descending phrases, at least two out of three pairs of same or different phrases of songs, and distinguishing between accompanied and unaccompanied music. The experimental children were, however, superior at singing back phrases, especially if the song had formed part of their programme lessons.

Tonal perceptual tasks : pitch discrimination

According to Gilbert (1893) a child improves in pitch discrimination twice as fast from 6 to 9 as he does in the years from 9 to 19. This conclusion was based on testing ten children at each age from 6 to 19 with a pitch pipe adjustable to fine differences. On average the children of 6 could discriminate sounds three-eighths of a tone apart, at 7 sounds less than one-third of a tone could be discriminated, at 8, one-quarter tones, and at 9, approximately one-eighth tones. The 10-year-olds had less fine discrimination than the 9-year-olds. After 10, discrimination improved, till at 14, sounds that were just over one-tenth of a tone apart could be distinguished. All but three of the children could, on the average, discriminate a semitone. Bentley (1966) found that pitch discrimination improved between 7 and 14 by about 30 per cent for 26, 12 and 6 Hz differences, but by only 10 per cent at the 3 Hz difference level. His general conclusion was that the majority of children, including the 7-year-olds, can discriminate a pitch difference of a quarter tone (12 Hz) at 440 Hz correctly, and that about half of 10 and 11-year-olds and the majority of the 12-year-olds and older can judge one-eighth tone accurately. Sergeant (1979), however, contends that, given an appropriate test format, much higher levels of discrimination can be obtained (see p. 36).

However, as we have noted in Chapter 4, Colwell found pitch discrimination tasks, based on semitone differences, sufficiently discriminatory to incorporate in Test 1 of the MAT. Half of his 9-year-old standardisation sample correctly answered only 15 out of the 25 questions. At high school, half could answer 20 out of 25.

Duell and Anderson (1967) attempted to study the pitch discrimination of 168 children aged 6 to 8, by asking them to judge as 'same' or 'different' intervals varying between a sixth of a tone and a major sixth in class-room conditions. Improvements occurred with age. Fifty-nine per cent of the 6-year-olds, but 80 per cent of the 8-year-olds were able to discriminate semitone differences; only 20 per cent of the 8-year-olds managed the sixth of a tone.

Williams (1977) tested 32 subjects aged 7, and 32 aged 12, asking them to push a button to indicate whether two unidirectional tones moved up, or down, or remained the same. The older subjects were superior, but perception was still a function of interval size. The additional of a third tone improved performance and nearly eliminated interval size as a determinant of error. Variations of loudness or timbre could bias judgements of pitch, by distracting the children's attention, especially with the smaller, more difficult intervals.

Hair (1977) also investigated tonal direction in two-, three- and four-tone tasks. These were presented in three ways: a group test where the children had to mark a green word 'yes' or a red word 'no' or a question mark according to whether or not they thought a pair of patterns moved in the same direction. The second task was to match tonal patterns played on resonator bells, given the bells of the pitches required for each item. Finally, the child was asked to verbalise his concept of the directions of the patterns he had heard and played. Most of the 144 subjects were 6-year-olds. Highest scores were made on the performance test. Moreover most of the children who achieved correct answers did so on the first trial. Hardly any of the children could correctly describe the concept of the 'up' and 'down' of pitch either by words or by gesture.

The results obtained on other simple melodic tasks are given in Table 8.6.

As we can see from Van Zee's as in Hair's results, the young child may be able to perceive a difference, but has great difficuly in explaining it. This is a point which we shall discuss further in the next chapter.

The development of absolute pitch

Although the possession of absolute pitch is not a necessary component of a high degree of musical talent, it occurs much more frequently among professional musicians. Bachem (1940) pointed out that this seemed specially true of musicians with early musical

Table 8.6 *Development of ability to perform simple melodic tasks*

	n.	Age		Mean scores (out of 40)
Gordon	127	5	PMMA Tonal Test	24·7
(1979)	202	6		29·8
	280	7		32·0
	264	8		34·6
Simons	71	6	Tonal patterns (same or	2·58 (out of 5)
(1976a and b)	82	7	different)	3·65
	93	8		3·60
	71	6	Melodic direction	2·23 (out of 5)
	82	7		3·04
	93	8		2·84
Van Zee	80	5	Melodic contour same or	
(1976)			different?	41 to 75% correct
			In what way different?	0 to 26% correct
			Demonstrate	40% correct
Zenatti	12	6	Match harmonium tone	
(1969)			while it is sounding	44% correct

training. Attention to musical tones in early youth seems to play a predominant role in its development. Sergeant (1969 *a* and *b*) carried out two surveys on the development of absolute pitch among musicians and music students of varying levels of musical talent and attainment. His first survey included four groups: (1) 36 members of the professional staff of the Royal College of Music; (2) 30 experienced RCM teachers; (3) 145 students training at the RCM and (4) 50 students following general courses at a college of education. Sixty-nine per cent of Group 1, 60 per cent of Group 2, 33 per cent of Group 3, but none of Group 4, claimed to have absolute pitch. Sergeant believes that the age at which music lessons are begun is a critical factor in whether or not the child will develop absolute pitch. As evidence he quoted the figures given in Table 8.7. These figures were supported by a second survey in which information was collected by questionnaires from a representative sample of 1500 members of the Incorporated Society of Musicians. As can be seen from Fig. 8.3, the earlier training was commenced the higher the proportion of subjects with absolute pitch.

Table 8.7 Age of commencement of music lessons

Group No.	Absolute pitch subjects		Non-absolute pitch subjects	
	Mean	Mode	Mean	Mode
1	5·4 yrs	4 yrs	8·7 yrs	9–10 yrs
2	5·9 yrs	6 yrs	7·3 yrs	7 yrs
3	6·4 yrs	6·4 yrs	8·8 yrs	8·0 yrs
4	nil	nil	9·9 yrs	11 yrs
total:	5·9 yrs	5 yrs	8·7 yrs	7–8 yrs

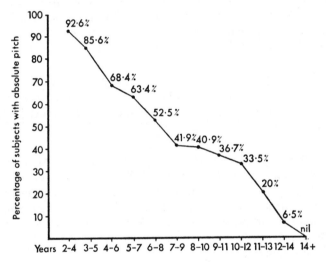

FIG. 8.3 Relation of age of commencement of training to absolute pitch

Sergeant checked the validity of his questionnaire data by testing a representative group of subjects with a pitch-naming test. Groups of five notes were playing on each of 10 different instruments, the subjects being asked the letter name of each note. Results with the test from 96 students at the Royal College of Music showed that:

(*a*) The highest scores were always obtained on notes from instruments with which the subject was familiar.

(*b*) The highest score in all cases except one was obtained on the instrument which had chronologically been the first to be learned.

(c) Where the subject had changed to some other instrument, a higher score was obtained on notes from the instrument learned first than the one which was now of greater importance to the subject.

Sergeant does not of course mean to imply that all children who begin to learn an instrument at a very early age will develop absolute pitch. Indeed he cites the case of a highly talented girl whose development seemed to by-pass concentration on absolute pitches in that she perceived melodic structures at a very early age.

Conversely, some older persons seem not to be aware of possessing absolute pitch before their teens (Vernon, 1977). Sergeant notes the instability of absolute pitch under conditions of fatigue, illness or absence from music. Again, among the middle-aged, pitches seem to become transposed up a semitone, and, later still, by a tone (Vernon, 1977).

Sergeant's data refer to musicians who began to learn an instrument at an early age. Whether a child with little aptitude for music would develop absolute pitch if he started to learn an instrument very young is not clear. Sergeant's work should be considered in the light of the earlier writers, Abraham (1901) and Watt (1917), who expounded the view recently taken up by Ward (1963) that most, if not all, of us might have absolute pitch were it not trained out of us by our hearing the same tunes played in various keys and on various instruments. This is not inconsistent with Sergeant's findings, since learning an instrument and paying attention to the pitch names would tend to reinforce absolute pitch before it had 'died out'. How far it is possible to acquire absolute pitch in later life will be discussed in Chapter 16.

Sergeant and Roche (1973) hypothesised that younger children would show a greater tendency to accurate representation of pitch levels at which they originally perceived stimuli, while older children would show less concern for pitch level, but more for organisational factors such as tonality, melodic shape and interval size.

Over a period of three weeks children were given six training sessions during which they were taught to sing three melodies, 8 to 16 bars long, presented each time at invariant pitch levels. One week after the end of training each child individually sang the three songs. The performances were tape-recorded and rated by two judges on the accuracy with which the following factors were represented:

Perceptual dimension: Pitching The pitch level at which each melody was reproduced was classified as 'accurate', 'accurate within one semitone' or 'inaccurate'.

Conceptual dimensions: Melodic shape Ability to reproduce the outline of the melody with correct directional pitch movement.

Intervals Performance of each pitch interval.

Tonality Security in moving to the dominant or tonic at intermediary or final cadence points.

The results were as shown in Table 8.8. These differences were statistically significant when the youngest group and the oldest were compared. There seemed to be a close inverse relationship between the perceptual and conceptual variables, the onset of conceptualisation imposing an increasingly selective function on perception so that only information relevant to the concepts is attended to.

Table 8.8

	Mean scores		
	n. 13 Age 3–4	n. 10 Age 5	n. 13 Age 6
Pitchings	3·3	1·2	0·23
Melodic shape	15·8	22·5	25·00
Intervals	71·2	98·8	107·10
Tonal sense	13·6	17·6	25·40

Sergeant and Roche sum up their findings by suggesting that the most rapid developments in the years from three to six are in the perception of melodic shape and sense of tonality. Only when these concepts have become established does attention centre on the musical intervals separating the tones of a melody.

Teplov (1966, p. 199), quoting several Russian and German researches, also believes that there are two stages in the development of an ear for melody. At the first stage the child can recognise and reproduce only the melodic contour. At the second stage the child can recognise and reproduce not only the direction of the movement of the notes, but also the correct intervals between them. The first stage, according to Teplov, is attained by all children. If the second stage is reached easily, it is a sign that the child has a good ear for melody. In Teplov's view judgement of intervals grows out of a sense of tonality – which depends on perceiving that certain notes are 'stable' and give a feeling of completion when a tune ends on one of them.

In this chapter we have traced the child's development from birth as far as the time when some basic musical skills are being attained. In the earliest years the child seems to be especially attracted by beautiful sounds, and will seek to explore the sound-making possibilities of his surroundings. Gradually he will learn to pick up from his environment the words, rhythm and melody of at least fragments of songs. His interest in sounds may lead him to acquire absolute pitch if he has the opportunity to learn pitch names on an instrument. As his intellectual abilities mature, he will begin to grasp the organisational features of the music around him, such as its scale system. However, this will be dealt with more fully in the next chapter.

9

The further development of musical abilities

In this chapter, we shall first look at studies that have been especially concerned with the development of musical concepts. Then we shall discuss data relating to the growth of memory for music, the role of a sense of tonality and then of harmonic perception. Finally, we shall briefly consider the earlier stages of development of appreciation of music.

Andrews and Deihl (1967) were pioneers in developing a four-pronged attack on the problem of assessing the musical concepts of elementary school children. They concentrated on three concepts: loudness (louder – softer), pitch (higher – lower) and duration (mainly quicker – slower). Their studies were carried out with 9-year-old children. Two tests were pencil-and-paper ones: a questionnaire which required a background of experience with musical and natural sounds and some understanding of musical terminology ('slow music is like ... running/skipping/creeping/galloping/spinning') and a listening test of 18 excerpts of music for the child to judge, e.g. which of two changes occurred ('higher and louder'). The third and fourth tests had to be administered individually. A manipulative measure required the child to demonstrate the concept (e.g. with a drum 'begin playing fast and gradually get slower'). For an overt measure the child listened to music, then moved with it, changing his movement when the music changed and finally stated what change had occurred. Moderate reliabilities were obtained (with 429 children : verbal ·71; listening ·85; with 214 children: manipulative ·66 and overt ·64).

Finding items difficult enough for the loudness and duration items, especially for the manipulative measure, proved hard. Pitch was the most difficult variable. Indeed, in the overt measure, the majority of the children failed to show overt movements in response to changes of pitch. Though some practice was given beforehand, changes of pitch would seem likely to be not readily expressible in movements, unless the children were accustomed to eurhythmics. In all the overt tests, the explanations showed that a child might be able to indicate a change overtly without being able to verbalise it and vice versa. Laverty (1969) adapted the two written tests for older and younger children. The 9-year-olds were significantly better than 7-year-olds; 11-year-olds gained superior scores to 9-year-olds, but this was not significant for loudness. Like Andrews and Deihl, Laverty found that children confuse labels when trying to describe the musical changes they seem to hear. This is notoriously true of pitch, since higher and lower, up or down have normally acquired spatial connotations before the child encounters them in music.

The research of Taebel (1974) threw some light on the place of verbalisation in the acquisition of musical concepts. His subjects were 260 children between 5 and 7. To demonstrate an understanding of the concept of pitch, the child had to recognise as a positive instance a transposition up a minor third; of loudness, an increase of 6 db; of tempo a change from 84 MM to 112 MM. When duration was relevant, the positive instances had tones with a decay time of ·075 of a second, the negative of ·2 of a second. Before the test all the children were trained to identify consistently the positive instance of a model task. One group had to discover the relevant feature that was different in the test items without further instructions (mode 1). A second group were told what to listen for (louder, higher, etc) (mode 2). A third group were asked to offer their own explanations of the change (mode 3). A fourth group were asked to sing or move to the patterns (mode 4). At all the grades tested, loudness was successfully conceptualised and at first and second grade both tempo and duration were understood. Only the 6-year-olds were successful with pitch. The largest differences due to age were found between the two youngest groups, grade two children being only slightly better than grade one and worse on pitch. When children of different ages were compared on their modes of responding, the 6-year-olds were only 6 per cent better than the 5-year-olds at offering their own explanation of loudness, but the 7-year-olds were 20 per cent better at justifying their choice verbally, though their accuracy was less. On tempo, mode 2 was higher than 3 at all grade levels. The verbal reports of mode 3 closely matched the accuracy means of the test. No significant effect of mode occurred on the pitch test. Percentage incorrect at describing pitch fell from 90 per cent at 5 to 60 per cent at 6 and 54 per cent at 7, though the last were less accurate in their judgements.

How far verbal cues were helpful appeared to depend on the stage. At the earliest stage, when the concept is still labile, words may have little meaning or even be confusing (e.g. 'up' or 'higher' of pitch). Conversely, when the concept is well-established, the child can provide his own cue, e.g. as with volume among the 6- and 7-year-olds. When the concept is reasonably stabilised, the verbal cue may be helpful, e.g. on the tempo tasks all ages found mode 2 easiest.

Six-year-olds do not respond to frequency as a dimension in the same sense as they do to amplitude, nor in the same sense as 8-year-olds do to both. However, an interesting finding suggested that this was more than a matter of terminology, since the 6-year-olds, though they probably knew 'loud' and 'soft' better than they did 'high' and 'low', had great difficulty in following absolute instructions in amplitude. In other words, when asked to remember a pair of pitches 6-year-olds do better than when asked to remember a pair of tones differing in loudness (Riley, McKee, Bell and Schwartz, 1967). This suggested to Dowling (1979) that children of 6 are able to use a stable internal pitch framework as absolute anchor points.

Conservation of melody

Though he did not work within a Piagetian paradigm, the research of Lowery (1929) with his musical memory test is relevant to conservation of melody. A theme was played three times followed by five test items. The task was to recognise whether or not each test was a variation of the theme. The variations used were intended to reflect those to be found in music – they included transposition, various types of ornamentation, and augmentation and diminution. 130 pupils, aged 12 to 14 years, were tested. The themes when transposed up or down an octave were recognised by about 90 per cent of the subjects. Ornamentation consisting of broken octaves resulted in 89 per cent correct judgements; transposition a perfect fifth upwards and presenting the theme in broken thirds was recognised correctly by 67 per cent. Both diminution and augmentation were passed with about 55 per cent of success. Lowery noted a feature that would accord with Piagetian theory: some subjects seized upon some particularly striking figure in a phrase and regarded it as a symbol of the whole, leading to misjudgements.

Many of the Piagetian type of tasks used by Zimmerman and Sechrest (1968) required the child to conserve a melody under different conditions. Eight children aged 5 and eight aged 8 years took part in Pflederer's (1964) pilot study. To arouse the child's interest each task was introduced with a story. The responses to the task and to the subsequent questioning were recorded on tape. One task required the child to conserve the melody when the rhythmic pattern was changed (see example). This the 5-year-olds found difficult; their perception centred on the rhythm. Three of the 8-year-old children still found difficulty. To test ability to grasp the relationships between the tones of a three-note figure, tonal patterns were transposed to different pitches. After listening to the pattern, the investigator and the child sang the melody and used a hand to indicate pitch levels. He was then asked to identify which 'make-believe' child played the tune incorrectly. The 5-year-old children perceived the direction and contours of the patterns, but failed to observe the relationships between the intervals. Even the 8-year-old children's perception centred on the melodic contour.

FIG. 9.1 Task is to identify the item which is *not* tonally the same as the original

In the course of their first experiment, Zimmerman and Sechrest (1968) presented similar tasks to 80 children, 10 boys and 10 girls each at ages 5, 7, 9 and 13 years. For the melody in an augmented or diminished version, there was a slow but steady improvement with age. In the case of the transposition and altered rhythm tasks, scores rose from 5·85 to 12·40 and 6·15 to 12·35 between the ages of 5 and 7; after 9 there was relatively little improvement.

The second experiment was entirely concerned with the conservation of four phrases selected from Bartok's *For Children* against various types of 'deformations', paired with each original phrase. Four tasks were devised. Nearly 200 children in the same age groups as in the first experiment were tested. They were asked whether the original tune and the 'foil' which followed were the same, different, or same in some way, different in others (the correct answer). Half the children were given a brief period of training during which the playing of the first six bars of 'America' was followed by the various deformations to be used in the tests; these were discussed with the children. Consistent differences, though not large ones, were found in the experimental group, especially in the case of the more difficult items. Figure 9.2 shows the results obtained. To check how far memory for the original tune was a factor, in one condition it was repeated. This proved to be the only task at which the 5-year-olds did relatively well. It would therefore seem that whatever abilities are involved in the tasks, they were more than mere recognition memory. Conservation, as judged by the responses given by the children, was rated on a six-point scale. For all the tasks conservation was greatest for the 13-year-olds (see figure 9.3). In general the foils of change of instrument, addition of harmony and change of tempo (augmentation or diminution) were easiest. However, when good conservation responses (rated as 6) were examined, harmony, tempo and the two contour deformations (inversion and contour intact with intervals changed) produced more conservation-type responses than did instrument, rhythm, and mode.

Many of the children, even those aged 13, appeared to have difficulty in verbalising their ideas, perhaps because they had not been taught the correct terminology. Therefore, for their next two experiments, Zimmerman and Sechrest departed from Piagetian interrogation and merely asked their subjects to respond by pressing a black key when variations from the tunes were heard and a white key when the music was completely different from the original. The tasks were similar to those used in the second experiment, except four familiar songs were substituted for the Bartok tunes. In the third experiment, training was again given to an experimental group. For six 20-minute sessions over a two-week period, their attention was directed to invariant qualities from familiar songs, when rhythm, tempo, mode, instrument, etc were changed. However, the training did not produce significant improvements – perhaps because an interval of up to two weeks intervened between the training and the testing, or perhaps the training was too concentrated to achieve significant results. In this experiment, the most marked changes occurred between 5 and 7.

The older children's results were affected by the particular tune chosen. In their fourth experiment, the same tunes were used with double deformations; but no training apart from the test instructions was given. The children were divided into two groups: the first had to press a white key when completely different music was heard and a black key when the music was a variation of the original, the keys being released when the music returned to its original form, an experiment which would seem to reproduce the circumstances of actually listening to a performance. The second group had to press a key only when completely different music was heard. How far the children actually conceptualise what is happening is obscure. In this experiment the ages studied were 7, 8, 9 and 10. No significant age

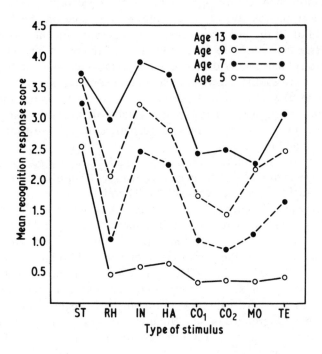

FIG. 9.2 Mean recognition scores for different age groups on different stimuli

Key: ST repetition of stimulus; RH rhythm changed; IN instrument changed; HA harmonisation added; CO_1 melody inverted; CO_2 contour retained, intervals changed; MO mode changed; TE notes augmented or diminished.

differences were found. The task of the second group was shown to be easier, but only in the case of repeated tune and instrument, plus inversion, significantly so. As the Zimmerman and Sechrest research proceeded the situation seemed to become less like a Piagetian study and more like a laboratory one. This does not of course mean that the results are less significant: many people might believe they are more so.

The final experiment was comparison of performance at recognising a tonal pattern under rhythmic deformation with performance at conserving a rhythmic pattern when presented at different pitches. Half of the 160 children were provided with 'visual aids' which proved somewhat helpful. The tonal patterns proved rather easier than the rhythmic ones, but the difference was not great. Of the four age groups tested, the 8-year-olds were significantly better than the 7-year-olds, the 9-year-olds than the 8-year-olds, but the 10-year-olds were not significantly superior to the 9-year-olds, though there was considerable headroom for improvement.

How conservation-type tasks might relate to musical ability did

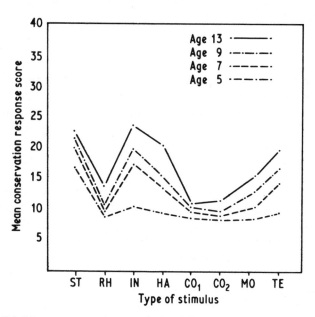

FIG. 9.3 Mean conservation scores for different age groups on different stimuli

not form part of Zimmerman and Sechrest's investigation. Norton (1979) found a correlation of ·44 between auditory conservation and seven of the Simons Measurements of Music Listening Skills among 6-year-old children. The music conservation tasks involved recognising a melody when the rhythm had been altered and recognising a rhythm presented with different melodic patterns. Orientation sessions preceded the testing. Nine out of the 34 children tested were classified as auditory conservers; 14 showed conservation on visual conservation tasks. Only 2 succeeded on both auditory and visual tasks.

Sloan (1973) tried to apply Piaget's model of intellectual development to children's perceptions and conceptions of the patterns and relationships of the C major scale. He constructed a special xylophone of battens of identical length, so that pitch would be the only means of ordering them into a scale. Ten children at each age group from 5 to 12 took part in his study. Before each experiment the child was given time for free play and was introduced to concepts such as 'highest' and 'lowest' in pitch. Sloan recorded the child's responses to questions about his judgements and his general approach to the tasks.

Sloan worked from the simple discrimination of pitch as 'same' or 'different' between two tones struck by the child, through a serial ordering of three battens as 'highest' and 'lowest', to getting the child to build a scale by putting the battens in the right pitch order. Once the scale had been built up, with any necessary corrections, the child was encouraged to play up and down the scale as often as he wished. Each note was allocated coloured crotchet symbols, on a magnetic music board, in order to introduce visual representation of the sounds. The concept of intervals followed, through games with big and little 'musical jumps'.

Sloan interpreted his results in terms of three stages within concrete operations. Before 8, only three children showed any advance from a pre-operational stage. By 8 and 9, half the children had progressed to operational stages, while the two older groups nearly all showed they were capable of decomposition and synthesis of auditory intervals.

Faced by the tasks which Sloan devised, the young child might well tend to exhibit developmental stages of efficiency in dealing with them. Moreover, Sloan himself notes that almost all the subjects brought to bear a unique set of cognitive stratagems in the way they tried to solve the problems. However, from evidence quoted below, it would seem that conception of the scale and of intervals grows from certain notes becoming differentiated from the scale by reason of certain characteristics (such as their contribution to the perception of tonality) rather than being built up from elements.

Larsen (1973) concentrated on studying 8 children at each of the ages, 8, 10 and 12, where he hoped that he might find evidence of a transition stage from concrete to formal operations. He used three forms of melodic permutation – inversion, retrograde, and retrograde-inversion – as likely to require formal operational thought for their conceptualisation. For the first part of the task, the child had to order a set of 5 resonator bells by ear to correspond to a 5-note melody. He was then asked to demonstrate how he might vary the theme. Step three involved the ordering of a second set of pitches to correspond to a contour similar to the original, and step four required the construction of the inversion, retrograde, and retrograde-inversion of the theme. The older subjects were able to complete the various ordering steps faster and with fewer repetitions than were the younger. Only the older subjects accepted inversion, retrograde, and retrograde-inversion as valid means of achieving melodic variation, appearing to use a different method of reasoning for their acceptance than did those subjects who rejected the permutations. Some of the younger children accepted the permutations (in most cases, the inversion) that sounded most like the original. It might be interesting to introduce some pseudo-permutations to see whether they would be detected, as well as to investigate permutations in conditions where the subjects are free to experiment with melodic patterns.

Further development of rhythmic abilities

Conservation of metre. Several studies from Mainwaring (1931) onwards have been concerned with discrimination of duple from triple metre; in some Piagetian studies this task has been called 'conservation of metre'. However, some of these later (such as Pflederer, 1964) were concerned not only with the child's immediate aural perception as with trying to discover from his explanations how the child thinks about what he is hearing.

Serafine (1979) believed that the essence of the concept of metre lay in awareness of a 'beat' that remained constant. To reduce the

Table 9.1 Judging duple from triple metre

			% correct mean	range
Mainwaring (1931)	52 children, mean age 10:6; 29 boys	Rhythm test	42·4	27·7 to 72·2
	23 girls		73·6	50·0 to 94·4
	31 girls, mean age 9:6		59·6	27·7 to 83·3
	34 boys " " 11:5		61·6	5·8 to 82·3
			Mean score (out of 30)	
Colwell (1969)	1237 × 9-yr-olds	MAT: Test 1	15·34	
	1683 × 10-yr-olds	Part 3	15·86	
	1980 × 11-yr-olds		17·58	
	1154 × 12-yr-olds		18·02	
	283 × 13-yr-olds		19·54	
	992 'High School'		21·06	
			Mean score (out of 22)	
Gordon (1970)	2925 9 to 11	ITML rhythmic aural perception Level 1	12·4	
	756 12 to 14	Level 1	14·3	
	1805 9 to 11	Level 2	11·1	
	542 12 to 14	Level 2	12·6	
Simons (1976a and b)	As below (pp. 292–3)	5 items	age 6: 3·27; age 7: 3·49; age 8: 3·23.	
'Conservation of Metre'				
Pflederer (1964)	8 5-yr-olds	6 examples	29% correct	
	8 8-yr-olds	played on drum	54% correct	
		2 played on	44% correct	
		piano	75% correct	
			Mean score	
Zimmerman & Sechrest (1968) Experiment 1	20 5-yr-olds	6 examples	2·75	
	20 7-yr-olds	played on drum	3·75	
	20 9-yr-olds		4·90	
	20 13-yr-olds		5·35	
Jones (1976)	66 5- to 12-yr-olds	12 examples played on drum	10% passed at 8	
			30% at 9	
			38% at 10	
			25% at 11	
			38% at 12	

difficulty of aural memory she devised a test of conservation of metre where the metre is accented by a continual aural or visual stimulus (a loud non-pitched click or a flash of light). In the aural/ aural presentation of the task, the child heard eight clicks at a steady tempo (MM = 60) representing metre. He was asked whether the clicks 'get faster, slower, or stay the same'. Then the test example was presented in which the steady metre clicks were heard simultaneously with repeated tones in various rhythms (the beat was always equal to a crotchet, in some items the duration of notes progressed to demisemiquavers, in others from sixteen notes per click to one; triplets and sextuplets were also used). The child was again asked whether the clicks 'got faster, slower or remain the same' and also 'Why? How can you tell?' The non-conservers were given a similar test with steady flashes of light substituted for the clicks. Those who still failed to achieve a score of three out of four items correct, were divided into experimental and control groups. The experimental groups were given training on moving 'to the beat' to varying speeds of metronome clicks, and on following the experimenter's movements, clapping, tapping or marching to music. The 103 subjects were aged 4, 5, 7 and 9.

Of the 103 subjects, 56 scored as non-conservers on the aural/ aural form of the test; of these 11 passed the aural/visual form. On the post-test after training, 38 out of the 45 still remained as non-conservers on aural/aural, 9 subsequently passing the aural/ visual form. Age was a significant factor in performance. At 4, only 33 per cent of subjects were conservers (and these often guessed). Ages 5 and 7 showed improvement over 4, but with no significant difference betweeen them, hence Serafine considered them to be in a transitional stage. By 9, 76 per cent of her subjects were conservers. The training given was not a significant factor in improving performance. The children's score on Piagetian tasks of weight and number was an even stronger predictor of conservation of metre than was age. The comparison with these other tasks, and the non-linearity with age does suggest a development in stages as proposed by Piaget. Perhaps part of the success of this study was due to its being confined to one aspect of music and the care taken to ensure the reliability of the task. The reliability coefficients calculated by Serafine for the aural/aural part of the task were around ·78.

Serafine (1980) acknowledges in a very useful review article on

Piagetian research in music the difficulties involved in applying Piaget's theories in the area of music.

Other rhythmic tasks

Improvement with age for other perceptual/memory rhythmic tests varies depending on the task. Taylor (1969) devised a test for young children in which a tapped pattern was played followed by three 'variations', the children being required to identify the one which was identical to the original pattern. Improvement was greater among the younger children, viz. age differences were significant at the 1 per cent level between the 7 to 8 and 8 to 9 and the 8 to 9 and 9 to 10 age groups, and at the 5 per cent level between the 9 to 10 and 10 to 11 age groups, but not significant after 11. From the results which Thackray (1972) obtained from testing some 1500 children with his rhythmic perception tests, he commented that development seems to be most rapid about 11 and 12 and much less rapid from 13 onwards; indeed unselected adults made similar scores to 15-year-olds.

Tonal memory

Zenatti (1969) found that as soon as a memory element was introduced into a task, even if it was no more than ceasing to sound a tone after five seconds, or judging which (if either) of two tones had been changed, the difficulty of the task was considerably increased and hence more discriminatory of aptitude. (Cf. Tables 8.4 and 9.2).

While memory for tonal (and rhythmic) tasks increases with age, the progress is by no means wholly linear. Bentley (1966) found that at all ages between 8 and 13, there were some children who could score full marks and others who scored only one mark out of ten, or none at all. The steepest increase in mean scores took place between the ages of 8 and 9, where tonal memory scores improved by 13 per cent and rhythmic memory by 16 per cent. After 9 tonal memory increased fairly steadily by an average of 6 per cent a year till 14. Unselected adults scored only 4 per cent better than 14-year-olds. Rhythmic memory increased rather less steadily, but by an average of 5.5 per cent; the mean score of unselected adults was not higher than that of 14-year-olds. For his own memory test, Wing (1941a) noted that between 8 and 11 memory for the immediate recall of tunes a few notes long develops. With Taylor's task, which was specially devised for research with younger children, the steepest increases occurred earlier. Zenatti found that boys were superior to girls between 6 and 8. Taylor's girls gained somewhat better scores between 7 and 9; around 9 the difference became significant.

Table 9.2 *Development of melodic memory*

	n.	Age	Task	Results		
Zenatti (1969)	13	6	Match tone that ceased after 5 seconds	9% correct		
				% of successes		
Zenatti (1969)	Female subjects			3 tones	4 tones	6 tones
	10	5:6 to 5:9	Tunes played twice.	25		
	20	6:4 to 7:9	Is second playing the	31	23	
	20	8:4 to 9:10	same or different?	48	40	
	20	10:3 to 11:11	If different, which	54	49	
	20	12:4 to 13:9	note is altered?	53	47	
	35	10:3 to 13:5		67	68	42
	62	13:4 to 16:6		75	69	54
	312	Adult		81	78	61
	Male subjects			3 tones		
Zenatti (1970)	25	5:5 to 6:0		30		
	34	6:2 to 7:0		37		
	30	7:2 to 8:2		52		
	34	8:3 to 9:2		50		
	26	9:3 to 9:10		62		
	20	10:3 to 10:11		67		
Taylor (1969)	Nearly 800 children, aged 7 to 11		15 tunes played twice. Which note altered on second playing?	Increases between 7–8/ 8–9 and 8–9/9–10 significant at ·01 level; between 9–10/10–11 at ·05 level		
Hufstader (1977)	Nearly 600 children, grades 1, 3, 5 & 7		Tunes might be changed by inversion, expansion etc. Same or different?	'Above chance' criterion met in two schools by 10, in all four by 12		

One of Zenatti's main interests was comparing the perception of tonal as opposed to atonal melodies, in order to investigate how far 'acculturation' to tonal music affected the child's perception of music. In the case of the girls she studied, it was of little help to them whether or not the items were tonal till the age of 8 was reached. In the case of the 3-note-task, tonal melodies were then significantly better remembered than the atonal ones, up to the age of 13. In the case of sequences four and six tones long, performance on the tonal sequences continued to improve till 16. Different results were obtained from the boys. There appeared to be no difference between perception of tonal versus atonal melodies, nor did any difference appear when she divided the boys into four groups reflecting the percentage of their correct answers. However, when Zenatti considered only those boys whose successes ranged between 41 and 95 per cent, a very significant degree of acculturation was apparent at the age of 6. Admittedly, the number of her subjects was small – only 12 boys were able to achieve this level of success, out of the 25 tested. These 12 children attained a success rate of around 66 per cent with atonal three-tone sequences – the same percentage as was attained for *both* tonal and atonal melodies among the boys in the older groups. Zenatti suggests two possible reasons for the sex difference. Perhaps boys more than girls were interested in listening to contemporary music with its departures from classical tonality, or maybe boys had wider interests so that they heard less music and were less affected by musical acculturation.

Substituting a pentatonic for a major scale made no significant difference at all to girls, though it seemed to produce a somewhat higher degree of acculturation in boys (Zenatti, 1973).

Zenatti (1975) later extended her work to include 396 children with subnormal intelligence, ranging in age from 8 to 16. Tonal acculturation for these children did exist (except for those having IQs between 50 and 59) as a function of their discrimination ability and their mental age. A significant degree of acculturation appeared in both sexes at the mental age of 8 or 9 (chronological ages between 10 and 14:4), about the same as for normal females.

Development of a sense of tonality

Cuddy and Wiebe (1979) postulated that 'the sense of tonality involves the development of a pitch system in which tone relations are specifically defined. That is, even tones not played in a given melody are represented by their inferred relation to the tonic of the melody.' They had in mind experiments in which incorrect transpositions (a semitone changed) of a melody are more easily recognised when the transposition is, for example, from C to G as opposed to from C to F sharp. Bartlett and Dowling (1980) found that even 5-year-old children discriminate between transpositions to near and remote keys. They were not able to discriminate between 'Twinkle, Twinkle' (C–C–G–G–A–A–G) and a tonal imitation (E–E–B–B–C–C–B), but showed a much greater tendency to reject tonal imitations in distantly related keys as opposed to nearly related keys. Thus they seemed able to notice at least gross changes in the scale system.

Imberty (1969) reported a series of experiments on various aspects of the acquisition of tonal structures in children. He concluded from his researches that before the age of 6 the child perceives a tune as complete as soon as the music stops, regardless of the note on which it ends. Imberty's experiments began with a series of studies of cadences. In the first, he asked his young subjects to judge 12 fragments of Bach chorales as 'completed', 'not completed' or 'don't know'. With 6-year-old children, only 56 out of 92 produced usable responses; the others marked the same answer column 11 times out of 12. Between the age of six and a half and seven, the child begins to feel the place of the cadence in a tonal structure. A phrase without a cadence is perceived as 'incomplete'. Differences between types of cadences are not understood. Between 6 and 8, the child is beginning to recognise differences between the degrees of the scale. Tonic and dominant are felt to be important, but not till 10 is the difference in their function grasped. The effect of the perfect cadence (V to I) is felt by 8-year-olds. By 10, the tonic-dominant relation is clear and the half-cadence (I V) is understood. But interrupted cadences (ending on IV or VI instead of the tonic) cause many errors. Even the perfect cadence when the melody ends on the mediant evokes surprise, i.e. perception is still melodic rather than harmonic. The 12-year-olds who took part in Imberty's experiments showed little improvement over the 10-year-olds.

Imberty devised a new experiment to show up the influence of melody on the judgement of cadences. Six short fragments in which the melodic line might or might not reinforce the cadence indicated by the harmonisation were presented in pairs. The children were asked to judge whether the first piece of music was 'completed', whether the second was 'completed', both were 'completed' or neither was. Three weeks later the children were retested with the phrases presented in reverse order, i.e. BA instead of AB. Consistent judgements were obtained from 73 ten-year-olds, except for interrupted cadences where the melody ended on the tonic. In a third experiment six paired items were presented, the harmony always being the same (i.e. a perfect cadence), but the melodies ended on the tonic, dominant, or mediant. Tonic and dominant were clearly differentiated among 63 ten-year-olds, but a melody that rose to E from D instead of falling to C caused surprise. The mediant did not appear to be a strongly differentiated degree of the scale. The melody appeared to be perceived as a 'figure' on the 'ground' of the harmonisation. When some unexpected movement in the melody did not fit in with the structure, attention tended to be forced onto the harmony.

In the course of experiments on the perception of modulations, Imberty found that when the melody was followed by a version in which there was modulation to a different mode (major or minor) the modulation was better perceived than when the modulation was to a key a half or whole tone above. Modulation to a medieval mode was not generally perceived by either the 8- or 10-year-old children involved in the experiment. Imberty also played five tunes well-known to his 7-, 8-, and 10-year old subjects. On the first occasion, the children were asked to note whether there was no change, one change or two changes from the tune (which was not played to them first). For the second experiment the children were provided with the words of the songs and asked to underline the words on which change occurred. Even the younger children were aware of the first 'mistake' in the playing of the familiar tunes. It was perceived as well by the 8-year-olds as by the 10-year-olds. Perception of return to the original key – which seemed more indicative of a musical situation – was more difficult. Significant progress between 8 and 10 seemed to occur.

Imberty went on to study (*i*) the structure of the tunes improvised by 22 ten-year-old children to the words of an old French poem, 'La blanche biche'; (*ii*) the type of mistake they made when they tried to sing back a six-note phrase, and (*iii*) their attempts to provide an ending for a three-note motif. His main findings were that the children tended to centre their singing around several notes, or even one, to follow the direction of notes, slipping from one key to a second as they went along, reducing or increasing certain intervals (without really substituting one note for another). Thus, asked to sing back a phrase that mostly moved upwards, such as D C E F G A, it might be rendered as D C E F (♯?) G ♯ A ♯ or be compressed into D C D E F G. In their improvised songs, the children would 'modulate' by following a melodic 'slope' which led them into a new key. The emotive question in 'La blanche biche', 'What makes you sigh?' could lead to a disruption of rhythm and tonality.

At one stage there seems to be 'continuous modulation' where no one note necessarily need follow another. In contrast a stage is reached where notes follow each other in an organised system. In the intermediate stage of stability combined with instability, order is not based on tonality but on expressive requirements. Imberty quotes the experiment of Reimers in which children between the ages of 7 and 10 would produce songs either in the same key or in a remote key, but never in two closely related keys. Imberty raises the question of whether keeping in the same key was a sign of musical ability. The children described by their teachers as good at music did often tend to do so.

Acquisition of harmonic skills

Though young children seem to be capable of producing polyphonic improvisations in an environment such as provided by the Pillsbury Foundation School (Pond, 1980), an ear for harmony in a more formal sense develops later than an ear for melody. One aspect which has been studied is the effect of the increased difficulty of processing multipart music. Another aspect is the question of acculturation to the conventions of western harmony as evidenced by preference for consonance over dissonance.

To study the perception of polyphonic music Zenatti (1969) used a fugue based on the theme of 'Malbrough s'en va-t-en guerre' and chose subjects who knew the song well enough to be able to sing it correctly. The children were told that the tune would be playing 'hide and seek' behind other notes and that their task was to say 'Yes!' as soon as they spotted it. The tune was presented six times in two voices, nine in three and twelve in four voices, 27 times in all. 55 girls took part in the experiment, producing the results shown in Table 9.3. The youngest group showed little progress beyond melodic perception. But a clear development took place between eight and ten. However, even at twelve, when the tune was played in the bass it was difficult to recognise. They had difficulty with the theme when it appeared in the bass or tenor, either failing to notice it at all, or recognising it less quickly.

Zenatti's results seem to accord with the norms Gordon provides for his tonal (harmony) test, where a judgement has to be made about the lower part. The greatest rise in mean scores seems to take place between 9 and 10, though scores continue to improve till 17.

Table 9.3 Results obtained by Zenatti (1969)

Age	n.	Mean scores (out of 27)
7:0 – 8:3	16	13·7
8:5 – 10:1	21	19·8
10:3 – 12:2	18	21·9

Simple 'vertical' harmonic discrimination tasks, such as judging whether a second chord is the same or different from a first seems to be mastered by 83 per cent of 6-year-olds (Hair, 1973). Zenatti's sample of 10 six-year-olds achieved scores significantly above chance level with two-chord items, but not for three-chord items. But adding quavers to make the task more interesting distracted somewhat from the harmonic changes, for two-chord items, though in the case of the three-chord items, no difference was found between the two types of presentation. Thackray (1973) found that the task of distinguishing between single notes and chords in a series was relatively easy. Between 6 and 7 the average score was 3·5 out of 10, between 7 and 8 it rose to 6·7, 11-year-olds making almost perfect scores. However, ability to locate a change in the harmonisation of a three- or four-note melody or to memorise the sound of a chord so as to recognise its appearance in a short harmonic progression proved much more difficult. The principal factor affecting difficulty in both tests was the position of the chord. In the first the later the change occurred the easier it was to identify, in the second the earlier the chord appeared in the progression, the easier it was to recognise. It is interesting to compare these results with those of Zenatti's 1974 experiment. Zenatti presented two chords played twice, the second time with or without change. Half of the items were consonant, half dissonant. The results obtained were as shown in Table 9.4. The higher percentage correct, compared with Thackray's subjects, was probably due to Zenatti using only two-chord items, compared with Thackray's three- or four-chord items. In Thackray's results, chromatic and dissonant chords seemed to strike the listener more forcibly and were therefore easier to remember. Zenatti found that the age of 5, the consonant series were better perceived than the dissonant (though not significantly so). In Thackray's test, the dissonance occurred in a consonant progression, while Zenatti contrasted items in which every chord was consonant with those in which every one was dissonant. As will become apparent from the discussion below, Zenatti believes that evidence of whether the child's ear is developing towards an appreciation of the conventions of harmony in the idiom of 'western culture' can be gauged from the greater preference the child shows for consonance.

Table 9.4 Results obtained by Zenatti (1974)

Age	n.	% correct
4:6 – 4:11	13	42·3
5:0 – 5:11	50	45·0
6:0 – 6:11	47	56·6
7:0 – 7:11	45	62·7

Experiments on consonance and dissonance. Valentine (1962) concluded from experiments he had carried out in 1910 with 200 unselected children that no preference for concords over discords is found before the average age of 9, but that at 9 a marked advance takes place; by 11 discords are on the average more displeasing than pleasing to the children, while at 12 or 13 changes are suddenly found which result in an order for preferences for the various intervals, that is very similar to that given by adults.

Zenatti (1974) studied the reactions to consonance in children as young as 4. Keeping the upper part identical, she presented ten pairs of chords for comparison, one consonant, one dissonant. She also paired four excerpts from contemporary composers with versions which were identical in rhythm and melody, but had consonant harmonisation. In order to study the consistency of the responses of her very young subjects, the items were presented twice, once with the consonance version first, once with the dissonant one first. 422 children aged from 4 to 10 were tested, individually up to 8, in groups thereafter. The second part of the test was given only to the 201 children of 6 or over. As one would expect, the number of children who changed their judgements on the second presentation decreased with age. Consistent judgements were obtained from boys of about 7, with boys as young as 6 for the chords, very significantly consistent ones at 7 for the first test, significantly consistent ones for the second test at 7 (boys consistent at 7 to 8) and very significantly consistent ones at 8. In the case of girls, judgements became very significantly consistent for both tests at the age of 7. Considering only the children who made consistent judgements, preference for consonance was significant for both girls and boys at the age of 5 in the case of the first test and at 7 in the case of the second.

Zenatti then investigated the effects of giving experience of discrimination between consonant and dissonant chords. Two groups of chords, one consonant ('the song the dog likes'), the other dissonant ('the song the horse likes'), were presented in random order. The child had to identify which animal's song had been heard and was told whether or not his answer was correct. This was much more difficult than comparable melodic tasks and only 10 per cent of 4- or 5-year-olds could score 10 points on a weighted scale.

Not till the age of 7 was the criterion of success (nine successive correct responses) reached by half the children. All those who did attain this standard were retested for their preference for consonance. The 16 children of 4 and 5 years old showed a very significant increase in the number of consistent judgements they made. While preferences for concords increased significantly, preference for discords remained constant. Results for the 6- and 7-year-olds did not significantly improve. A control group of 4- and 5-year-old children were tested and later retested without the training experience; they did not show any improvement.

Bridges (1965) studied whether children between 5 and 7 could notice an 'unsuitable' harmonisation of a tune. She taught them a previously unfamiliar song. This was then played with accompaniments termed 'appropriate' (harmonised as in the teacher's manual), 'slightly altered' or 'radically altered', presented in pairs. A melody which the children did not know was played immediately after the third playing of the original tune. The children were asked to decide which harmonisation sounded better, or if both ways were 'all right'. Preference for the conventional harmonisation developed gradually, being rather better for the unknown tune.

Imberty, too, tried presenting for paired comparisons harmonisations according to 'classical' traditions, according to those used by such composers as Debussy, and atonal ones, By the age of 10, the classical version was preferred, followed by the atonal one. The 'modern' one was least liked.

In an unpublished study, Sloboda investigated acculturisation to the rules of western harmony among 144 children aged from 5 to 12. He asked them to choose the 'correct' member from pairs of musical sequences. ('Correct' was used rather than 'better', since some older children found 'wrong' items amusing and might have chosen them for their novelty.) The 'incorrect' member of the pairs violated *either* rules of consonance in chord construction, *or* rules for sequential ordering of chords, *or* rules of melodic construction, *or* all three types of rule. Rapid improvement was shown between the ages of 5 and 8:4 for the condition where every rule was violated. Dissonant chords were recognised between 8:4 and 10:0. A feeling for the right order of chords did not match adult performance till between 10 and 12. No child reached adult performance with unaccompanied melodies. There was no significant effect for formal instrumental instruction. Though Sloboda's control group of adults was described as 'musically proficient', he believed that even musically untrained adult listeners are able to recognise, categorise, and make appropriate emotional reactions to a wide variety of forms of tonal music, whereas they can 'make nothing of' atonal music.

Development of appreciation

Average scores of Wing's appreciation tests do not exceed chance till about the age of 10 or 11. The median score for 9-year-olds on the Gordon sensitivity tests with musically unselected children is 18 (out of a possible 30). For 11-year-olds it is still only around 19 –

which does not suggest a rapid growth. In the case of younger children, 150 of the most musical of 2700 pupils between 5 and 8 were tested with the phrasing test, a parent marking the answer sheets. Even the 5-year-olds could achieve a mean score of 17, the 6-year-olds one of 20 and the 8-year-olds one of 22.

As noted in Chapter 3, Long adapted the Indiana-Oregon test for use with young children by only requiring a judgement between the correct and the mutilated version of each item. Mean scores showed a rise from 26 for 6-year-olds to 29 for 8-year-olds, then levelling out at 30 for 10-year-olds. Taylor (1969)) developed a somewhat similar test which required an overall discrimination of 'correct' from 'distorted' version of his own original compositions. The distortions were to melody, rhythm or harmony. The child did not have to specify what type of error had been made. After the correct version had been presented, the child was invited to play at being a 'detective' and spotting which of the four following versions was correct or incorrect. Highly significant differences were found between 7- to 8- and 8- to 9-year-old groups and between 8- to 9- and 9- to 10-year-old groups. However, in spite of the levelling off that seemed to occur around 10, Taylor found that some older children and adults that he tested did gain higher scores.

The plateau reached with the Long and the Taylor forms of appreciation tests seem to contradict the findings of Wing and of Gordon. Possibly, tests composed or adapted for younger children tend to lose their effectiveness at a point where those designed for older children take over.

Gardner (1971*b*) presented children with pairs of 15-second long musical extracts and asked them to judge whether the two excerpts came from the same piece of music. Some in fact did, some were taken from music of the same period, others from music of varying periods. Six-year-olds showed some discrimination, but the largest improvement occurred between 8 and 11.

Taylor (1969) included a test of music preference in his researches, the child being asked which of a pair of short extracts he preferred. The composers were grouped into periods – from Byrd and Monteverdi to Stravinsky and Schönberg. Only music that had previously been found to appeal to children was included. From the age of 6 to adulthood there was a broad trend towards adult tastes. Notable was the decline in preference for the contemporary music, shown even between the ages of 7 and 8 and increase in liking for

Bach and Handel. A significant rise in liking for Tchaikovsky and Brahms occurred among the 9- to 10-year-olds, perhaps connected with the increases on scores on harmony tests which Taylor found at that age.

Le Blanc (1979) asked 278 10-year-old children of varying socio-economic status and ethnic background in St Louis to rate on a seven-point 'like to dislike' scale 16 short excerpts of music and ambient sounds. Various styles of popular music were used, as well as electronic music. 'Classical Instrumental' was represented by the Gavotte from Prokofiev's Classical Symphony. The six excerpts that were rated above 5 (7 being highest) all had an easily perceptible beat. The easy-listening pop example was highest (6·15) and had the lowest standard deviation, i.e. there was rather close agreement that it was the most preferred. Rock was placed second. The avant garde example, Penderecki's Threnody for the Victims of Hiroshima, was rated on average 3·69 and in a factor analysis loaded on a factor characterised by novel timbres and mechanical sounds. The Prokofiev was rated twelfth (3·00), but individual responses were highly stable on a retest.

Summary

Though Michel (1973) has suggested that the ages between 5 and 6 are particularly important for the development of musical reproductive abilities, many significant changes take place in the middle years of childhood. This does not mean that essential foundations may not be laid earlier. The concept of pitch is relatively difficult to attain. Ability to cope with polyphonic and harmonic tasks develops even later.

Convergence towards adult judgements on consonance seems to be commonly adopted as a criterion of growth. This implies that adult judgement is superior to that of the child – in Sloboda's results even to the child of 12. However, Imberty found little progress between 10 and 12, and having in mind some research of Francès on the judgements of musically naive young adults, posed the question 'Does musical development cease at 12 or even at 10?' We shall pursue this question further in the next chapter.

10

Music in adolescence and after

Meissner (see Schoen, 1940), who studied the mistakes which children between the years 8 and 14 made when they were asked to sing back tunes, found a marked improvement in the melodic memory at about the age of 13 or 14. Children of this age try to sing with expression and to produce notes of good tone quality. Meissner believed puberty to be a period when an interest in singing as an expression of mood and feeling develops. This deepening of the emotional appeal of music is perhaps the most noteworthy factor in music at adolescence. In many children this may take the form of an increased interest in popular music. This is natural enough and may indeed eventually become the basis of enjoyment of a wider range of musical styles. What would be unfortunate would be for children to lose interest in 'serious' music just at a time when their abilities to listen to, perform and create music are still increasing.

Scores on musical ability tests go on increasing with age up to about 17 in the case of Wing's tests and Gordon's MAP, but up to 20 to 21 years in the case of the Drake memory test, with 'non-music' students. With music students, the improvement with age on Drake's test does not end till the age of 23. The difference is quite substantial; for the student who made 20 errors at 19 years would attain PR 50, while the same score at 23 would be worth only PR 23.

Evidence of increased efficiency with age, indeed into adulthood, on certain musical tasks comes from Funk (1977). His subjects encompassed a wide age range: musically untrained children (aged 6 to 12), younger adults (18 to 37) and older adults (50 to 70). In a series of experiments familiar tunes such as 'Jingle Bells' were varied in order to study ability (i) to recognise a theme when varied; (ii) to discriminate a variation from the theme and (iii) to detect modulations. Recognition of a theme showed a significant increase with age to adulthood; however, the oldest group were the poorest.

Young children relied heavily on rhythmic cues to recognition, older subjects were far superior at detecting variation, especially when the transformation was minimal. The 6-year-olds responded correctly 21 per cent of the time, but with the least varied songs only 50 per cent of their responses were correct. The most severely altered tunes were the most difficult to recognise and the easiest to discriminate. Adults were 78 per cent successful at detecting modulations, the 6-year-olds scoring at less than chance (42 per cent). Williams and Aiken (1975) investigated the auditory pattern perception of 52 subjects at each of five age levels: 8, 12, $15\frac{1}{2}$, 18 and adult. The patterns were made up of five pure tones. Ten patterns from 'Class A' were presented as belonging to one 'family'. Then the subject heard 32 patterns, half being 'Class A', half 'Class B'. His task was to judge whether or not the pattern belonged to Class A. Two levels of similarity to the prototypes A and B were used. Accuracy increased with age but was affected by interactions with difficulty and order of presentation. The greater the similarity to the 'prototype', the more accurately Class A patterns were classified. The reverse was true of Class B patterns.

If we look at achievement tests, we find that on MAT cadence recognition scores show a steady increase with age from medians around 6·2 (out of 15) at 10 and 11 years of age to a median of 8·3 at 17 years. Piano students gained better scores than those learning other instruments, but even at grades 10-12 nearly a quarter of the pianists achieved only a score of 10. These were certainly not impressive increases in the case of a relatively simple cadence task. Tonal memory (part 1 of Test 3) improves from a low mean scores of 5·9 at 9 (out of 20) to 13·1 at 15, thereafter there being little improvement. The largest increases seem to take place between 9 and 10, and between 13 and 14. Melody recognition seems to progress particularly between 13 and 14 and 15 and 16. At the task of recognising musical style, rather little improvement takes places between 10 and 17. Volger (1975) compared the results of testing some 1000 children with two levels of the ITML within a fortnight. The levels concerned with major and minor modes (even when the patterns were more complex) were often found to be easier than where unfamiliar modes were used. Some items in Level 5 may have been found easier because of the two-part harmony may have helped the testee by not requiring him to supply the resting tone through aural imagery. (For details of her findings, see her report and for details of Gordon's own extensive investigations of the relative difficulty of tonal and rhythm patterns and their rate of growth, see Gordon 1974; 1976; 1977 and 1978).

It is clear that while aptitude continues to grow during adolescence, how much this will be reflected in achievement depends on the motivation of the learner and the efficacy of the teaching received.

If we consider the tasks used by Zimmerman and Sechrest, it is evident that there was much room for improvement among their 13-year-old subjects. Studies of comparable tasks, such as the recognition of themes in music excerpts, have been undertaken by Duerksen and by Alan Smith.

Duerksen's (1968) research was concerned with recognition of themes, repeated or in altered form. Using 15 excerpts from classical music, the subjects were required to mark on their answer sheets the number which was being projected at the moment they recognised the first theme of each item; they also indicated whether it was an exact repetition or had been altered, e.g. in melody, harmony, key, etc. The subjects were 378 music majors, 1194 non-music majors and 343 high school pupils. As might be expected, the music majors made superior recognition scores when compared with the other two groups, who were not significantly different. Even the music majors scored on average only 55 out of a possible 124 points. Differences within the groups were small. Duerksen also examined the relationship of the scores to the amount and type of music-making experience of the students. While the mean scores of the music majors with different amounts of performance experience did not differ significantly, among the other two groups those with greater total composite amounts of experience activities generally achieved progressively higher mean recognition scores. Only in the case of the non-music majors did the type of activity show significant differences. The differences of those who had had no performing experience and those who had had piano lessons, or participated in band, orchestra and a combination of band and orchestra were not statistically significant. Those who had participated in chorus work, chorus in combination with band or orchestra, were superior to those who had experience of only piano or band.

Smith (1973) investigated whether 12-year-olds who were musically unsophisticated could be taught to keep track of the unfolding of forms of unfamiliar minuets and sonata-form movements. His subjects' scores on the Seashore measures averaged around the 50th percentile; they were sufficiently interested in music to wish to enrol in a band workshop. After comparatively short periods of training (seven half-hour sessions on the minuet and none on sonata-form) successful tracking was achieved without cost to the observation of briefer musical aspects of the movement.

However valuable such accomplishments may be, the part played by attention to the formal elements of music in the appreciation of music even among experienced music students seems to be rather small. Payne (1973 and 1980) reports experiments on the factors involved in the appreciation of music carried out among young adults who had all had considerable musical training. Six examples were played of a complete work, or part of a work, of 4 to 8 minutes' duration. After listening to each the subjects were asked to choose from statements those most applicable to the music as it had appealed to them, and to rate their enjoyment of the piece. Two of the factors were concerned with 'musical emotion'; the first, a recognition of the emotional subject-matter of the music, and the second, an emotional response to its aesthetic character and value. The other four factors concerned the formal structure of the music, its historical significance, orchestration, and extra-musical associations. Payne concluded from two experiments, one with rather unfamiliar music, the other with music known to many of the subjects, that the primary appeal of music is an emotional one. The first 'human emotion' factor was by far the stronger factor, especially with unfamiliar music, though the aesthetic emotion seemed to be most indicative of how much the music was enjoyed. In the case of familiar music other facets of appreciation tended to come to the fore, for example, the formal aspects of the piece. Personal attitude and preferences may then affect the pattern of appreciation.

Smith 'surprised' a class of music graduates by unexpectedly stopping a recording of a sonata movement and asking them to identify the termination point. Results were no better than chance. However, as soon as they realised that this would happen, they were well able to keep track. The point to be stressed is that training is important so that the ability is available to the listener when he finds it appropriate to exercise it. Without some such training, listeners are likely to give the impression of listening to a text, the language of which is not understood. Such was the conclusion drawn by

Francès (1958) from his well-known experiment which required the listeners to indicate as soon as they perceived a subdivision of the structure. The two compositions were a Schubert impromptu and a Bach fugue. The subjects were 60 young people who had no instruction in the theory of music but most of whom were regular concert-goers and a group of professional musicians. The musically untrained listeners were able to perceive the three-part structure of the Schubert, though not very exactly. The qualified musicians were always able to indicate a meaningful division (perfect chord, re-exposition, etc). In the case of the fugue, the untrained did not seem to possess the frames of reference necessary to cope with the three-part form of the music and their responses to the appearance of the themes were usually late.

Mason (see Zimmerman and Sechrest, 1968, Appendix H) found the teaching of concepts based on Zimmerman's research a valuable approach to music for student teachers with little experience of music. Learning was rapid; the boys in particular declared that the Zimmerman tasks helped them to understand what music was about.

An important consideration in assessing the worthwhileness of the time and effort that the child, his parents and his teachers invest in his music education is how far his musical activities will continue into later life. The results of the survey of the National Assessment of Educational Progress (1974) in the area of music suggests that the adults seem to retain about the level of ability of 13-year-olds on a number of tasks and to be only rather less able than 17-year-olds. Indeed on singing a familiar tune, like 'America', with recorded voices and then alone, 60 per cent of the adults were able to maintain an acceptable pitch when asked to sing alone, compared with 40 per cent of 9-year-olds, 50 per cent of 13-year-olds and 55 per cent of 17-year-olds. The aim of the survey was to compare the attainments of 9, 13, 17-year-olds and adults aged from 26 to 35. The sample of persons tested was claimed to be representative of the United States population. Such an undertaking is obviously a mammoth one. However sound the guidelines for scoring and however conscientious the judges, the results need to be regarded with some caution.

Lawrence and Dachlinger (1967) obtained information on the carry-over of music training into adult life by a postal survey of 1600 parents of children enrolled in instrumental lessons. Twenty per cent filled in a questionnaire; 37 per cent of these still claimed to play often or sometimes. This seems a high proportion, no doubt due to those who played being more likely to return the question-naire. However 39 per cent of the National Assessment adults claimed to play an instrument. Willingness to practise and consist-ency of practicing in childhood did not seem to influence carry-over. For these adults who grew up in the 1920s, 1930s and 1940s, 14 seemed to be the critical age beyond which the child is to play if he is to continue in adulthood. Of those parents who had not kept up playing, 42 per cent felt the training had been of no value to them. Sight-reading and improvisation were rated as the most important skills by the adults who played; only those who have achieved a reasonable competency in sight-reading, improvisation or playing by ear are likely to continue to play if their lessons have been limited to two or three years. Every person who was self-taught still played. Martin (1976), too, found self-taught playing important among variables associated with adolescent appreciation of music.

Increased attention seems to be being given to the need for provision for continuing music education throughout life. (See Leonhard, 1980 and papers from the 1976 International Confer-ence of the International Society for Music Education.) In drawing up a programme for adults, it is important to challenge those with talent (Davidson, 1980) as well as to provide a variety of opportun-ities for everyone who wishes to participate in music. Achieving a high score on the Bentley Measures for example may encourage an adult to take up playing. Gibbons (1980) tested 119 adults aged 65 to 93 and found generally there were no significant age differences in MAP scores. A good foundation of music learning during child-hood is obviously helpful to the adult but even those who may have 'missed out' on music should be encouraged to participate as per-formers as well as listeners.

Attitude to music

Wragg (1974) noted a decline in participation in choral and instru-mental work when she followed up 36 fourteen-year-old children whom she had taught when they were aged 9 to 11. Whereas 31 had rated music as 'very' or 'quite' enjoyable in junior school, only 6 gave music these ratings at the later age. The children's families might have been expected to provide some continuity of support for musical activities. However, most of the families were only marginally interested in music. Eight children who were still actively participating in music had all played in junior school, had higher Bentley test scores and more musically oriented home environments. The average IQ for the whole group was 116; it is possible that they were being pressured to devote themselves to more academic subjects than music. Provision for music in the secondary schools varied. Wragg believed it should be possible to strengthen links between the primary and secondary schools to provide continuity of instrumental teaching.

In the 1950s studies were carried out in which short excerpts of popular and classical music were played for rating for like/dislike by children from 10 or 12 up to 18 or 20 (Rogers, 1956; Baumann, 1960). As we might expect all age groups much preferred popular music – a finding which Le Blanc again reported in 1979 (see p. 151) with 10-year-olds. It is possible, of course, that the emotional appeal was different in character as adolescence proceeded. Adolescence is a time when those who enjoy classical music find its emotional appeal deepening.

It might be expected that college level students would have acquired a preference for classical music over popular if they are studying music seriously. However, Duerksen asked his subjects to indicate on a seven-point scale the degree of their like or dislike of five categories of music. There was little difference between the ninth grade students and non-music graduates, except some tendency for liking for rock and currently popular music to be reduced after second year at college. The music majors showed stronger preferences for classical music and a tendency to dislike rock and currently popular music, though their feelings for jazz and folk music were similar to the other groups. Professed liking for classical music and listening skill did not necessarily go hand in hand. Duerksen expresses concern that high school education does not seem to promote greater liking for classical music. However, the *lowest* mean score was as high as 5·63 (7 = 'like very much' and 4 = 'neutral') – roughly similar to the high school averages for 'currently popular'.

A study of 200 adults in age categories from 21 to 71 and over, taken to represent 200,000 adults in the state of Wyoming, suggested that their 'general music' experience showed little relationship to their attitudes about music. Higher levels of attitude (e.g. 'willingness to respond' and 'commitment') were found among adults with instrumental and/or vocal experience in high school, and in particular among these who had had college courses in music. The current occupation of the adult was also strongly related to the level of his attitude to music (Noble, 1977).

In the following chart an attempt has been made to trace the main developments with age in very general terms. Obviously no two children will follow exactly the same path nor reach the same point at the same age. The chart is intended to be helpful as a guideline that summarises at about which ages certain behaviours are likely to appear and in what sequence.

Whilst some of the difficulties in learning certain skills may be intrinsic to the material, other skills may be later developing due to their neglect by teachers (Colwell, 1970*b*). Development depends not just on 'natural growth' but also on how far the child receives a suitable musical diet. A few examples from the literature indicate what children can do with efficient teaching. Dittemore (1970) taught 29 pupils from each of grades 1 to 6 twelve songs in various modes and rhythms, each for four consecutive days. Five minutes were devoted each day to learning the song for the week. On the

Table 10.1 Guidelines to typical ages for the development of various activities

Ages	
0–1	Reacts to sounds.
1–2	Spontaneous music making.
2–3	Begins to reproduce phrases of songs heard.
3–4	Conceives general plan of a melody; absolute pitch may develop if learns an instrument.
4–5	Can discriminate register of pitches; can tap back simple rhythms.
5–6	Understands louder/softer; can discriminate 'same' from different' in easy tonal or rhythm patterns.
6–7	Improved singing in tune; tonal music perceived better than atonal.
7–8	Appreciates consonance vs. dissonance.
8–9	Rhythmic performance tasks improved.
9–10	Rhythmic perception improves; melodic memory improves; two-part melodies perceived; sense of cadence.
10–11	Harmonic sense becoming established. Some appreciation for finer points of music.
12–17	Increase in appreciation, cognitively and in emotional response.

fifth day, the class sang the song as a group, then each member performed into the tape recorder. All but two of the songs had been published for fifth grade, yet few of them gave the upper grades ceiling to improve. Large improvements were found between grades 1 and 3 with two part-songs. The pupils were drawn from a university school; this almost certainly contributed to their rapid learning of the songs. Also at a university school, Wassum (1980) concluded that the consistent teaching of both songs and the singing of scales is necessary for children to develop a concept of tonality in their elementary school years. De Yarman (1971), with kinder-garten and first grade pupils from schools representative of a cross section of Iowa City schools, found that all could benefit from songs taught in a variety of metres and modes. Miller (1975) found that junior school children might benefit from up to one seventh of a singing period spent learning atonal songs – whether this would lead to better appreciation of contemporary music might be interesting to follow up.

11

Precocious and unusual talents

One of the characteristics of musical ability is its tendency to emerge at a relatively early age, even among not specially talented children, quite apart from the outstanding gifts displayed by many quite young performers.

From data collected by Haecker and Ziehen from 441 cases, Revesz (1953) concluded that nearly half of the children revealed musical aptitude between their second and sixth years. From parents' reports on the age at which various abilities were first noted in his sample of gifted children, Terman (1925) found that, except for general intelligence, musical ability was shown at the lowest age. The average for boys (n = 91) was 4:6 years, for girls (n = 108) 5 to 16 years. The reliability of parents' reports may be thought to vary considerably, but at least the public performance of musical prodigies provide reliable evidence of precocity.

We have already mentioned the early stages at which the professional musicians who filled in Sergeant's questionnaires commenced their musical training. Among the virtuosi instrumentalists studied by Scheinfeld (see p. 175) musical talent appeared at an average age of 4:9 and in the case of the Juilliard music students at 5:6. The average age of their professional debut of the virtuosi (not merely their first public appearance) was 13:9.

The history of music provides many examples of conspicuous musical talent being displayed by young children, not only as performers, but also as composers. For instance, at the age of 12 years Beethoven was already able to read and play difficult scores at first sight. Three sonatas for the piano were published before he was 13. His first composition is said to have been written at 10. A funeral cantata in memory of the deceased English ambassador, this piece apparently aroused great astonishment at its originality. Haydn is said to have begun composing at 5 and at the age of 6 could sing several masses in the church choir and play a little on the piano and violin. Mendelssohn's creative gifts developed rapidly and prolifically after the age of 10. Britten began to write music at 5. By the age of 15 he had over one hundred compositions to his credit.

Mozart was one of the greatest (if not *the* greatest) musical prodigies of all. Pointing out that it is difficult to assess the amount of Mozart's early training and the effect of his musical environment, Richet (1900) reported the case of Pepito Areola whose talent appeared before he had had any training whatsoever. Pepito's father was not musical but his mother had played the piano at the age of 5, while his maternal grandmother is reported to have been a good guitar player. When hardly two and a half years old, Pepito played tunes on the piano. Sometimes they were tunes his mother had played or sung, sometimes they were of his own invention. When investigated at the age of 3:7 by Richet he could play twenty pieces from memory, including the harmonies. His improvisations showed some feeling for form. He appears to have been rather temperamental and refused to play on any instrument except his mother's piano. When Pepito was 6:2, Stumpf found that he could sing any note he was asked for and name any note played to him. The best studied case is that of Erwin Nyiregyhazy whom Revesz (1925) was able to observe from his sixth to his twelfth year. According to Erwin's father, a singer in the chorus of the Royal Opera in Budapest, he tried to imitate singing before he was one year old. In his second year of life he would reproduce correctly melodies sung to him. At the beginning of his fourth year he began to play on the piano everything he heard and at three and a half had already composed little tunes. Regular tuition in music began only when he was 6. When tested by Revesz at 7, his musical ear was already developed to an extraordinary degree. He had absolute pitch and could analyse complicated chords more accurately than a well-known professional cellist. His immediate musical memory was nearly as good as that of a pianist whose musical memory was known to be very good, and his powers of retention for 24 hours were much better. He reproduced faultlessly at the third attempt a 13-note tune played to him by Revesz. He could memorise melodies and harmonise in a simple manner with great ease. Two years later he was able to reproduce without mistake a five-bar theme at the second attempt, the time taken for learning being 22 seconds. He undertook an extensive European tour at the age of 11 and at 15 he had completed his studies and fallen under the spell of Liszt's music. After a highly successful debut in the USA, his professional career began to decline, possibly due to personality problems. Recently at the age of 78 he was persuaded to come out of retirement to make recordings of the music of Liszt (see Sanders, 1979).

Speaking from the experience of having taught over 3000 pupils, Cortot (1935) stated that the proficiency which some children display is no more than the manifestation of dexterity and an extraordinary natural imitative faculty. However, many infant prodigies do become highly esteemed adult musicians. Seventy per cent of the great violinists listed in Leahy's *Famous Violinists* were prodigies (Drake, 1957, p. 13).

Certain individuals have adopted careers outside music and later earned renown as composers. Borodin was a professor of chemistry, Mussorgsky and Cui had military careers. All, however, had shown aptitude for music early in life. This does not mean that training for music must begin at an early age. For example, Malcolm Tillis had sufficient talent to become a viola player with the Hallé Orchestra. His family was not particularly musical. At 11 he was taken to see *Carmen* and fell under the spell of music, but he did not begin to learn an instrument till he was 15 (Tillis, 1960).

Leonard Bernstein had no opportunity to learn a musical instrument till his family acquired a decrepit piano when he was 10. Even when his exceptional talent became apparent, his father tried to discourage him from taking up music as a career. Henry Cowell, the American composer, had had no musical training at all before he was 14. When he was 15 and living in the direst poverty, he scraped together enough money to buy an old piano and taught himself to play it. By the time he was 17 friends, recognising his talent, subscribed to a fund to enable him to receive a proper musical training (Burks, Jensen and Terman, 1930). Whether the talents of these musicians might have developed to even greater heights if they had had opportunities earlier in life is something that we cannot determine.

The idiot savant

A well-known case was that of Blind Tom, who became a vaudeville artist. With no more intelligence than a child of 6, he was evidently able to memorise a piece from one hearing, and to play two tunes and sing a third at the same time. Afterwards he would join the audience in applauding himself. His manager may, of course, have encouraged such signs of 'idiocy' for publicity reasons.

Rife and Snyder (1931) described a blind, imbecile girl who could play a new and difficult piece on the piano after hearing it only once. A musician visiting the Vineland Institution where she lived asked her to play an unpublished composition of his. She was able to do this perfectly after hearing it only twice.

Though according to Tredgold (1922), the special talent shown by idiot savants has rarely been marked in their ancestors, Rife and Snyder decided to study as many of the relatives as possible of such cases as they could locate. By addressing an enquiry to 55 American institutions for the feeble-minded they succeeded in finding 33 idiot savants, of whom 8 showed a special talent for music. They studied personally a case earlier reported by Minogue (1923). XY had developed normally till 3 years old and as soon as he could talk had learned little songs. After contracting spinal meningitis he was left mentally impaired. At the age of 14 his IQ was 62, at 23 (when Minogue described his case) it had fallen to 46. He had remarkable pitch discrimination and an unusually good tonal memory, being able to play jazz or classical music by sight or by ear. He sight-read the *Marche Grotesque* of Sinding and an accompaniment for a singer. Though emotionally unstable, he played well when willing to attend, but produced no original compositions and was unable to learn to dance. When a child he had received two years' piano tuition but had been abusive to his teacher. His memory for time, for places and for events as well as for any composition he had ever learnt was described as 'almost phenomenal'. His parental grandmother and a cousin were said to be pianists of exceptional ability.

Rife and Snyder also mentioned a man aged 35 who could play on the piano any tune sung to him. The chords he used were harmonically correct, although he had never received any training in music. Some of his normal brothers played or sang. Another idiot, aged 19, could play by ear anything he heard. He had a feeble-minded brother with no musical ability and a normal, though blind, sister who played the piano and composed.

Owens and Grimm (1941) reported the case of a woman of very low intelligence whose adult mental age was only two years nine months. She played by ear popular music heard on the radio but seemed to need an auditory stimulus she could copy. Thus she had little ability to play tunes named, but played Brahms's Lullaby in the key in which it was hummed to her. Two of her four sisters played the piano by ear. Her speech was very limited and indistinct.

A more detailed study of an idiot savant with musical talent was reported by Scheerer, Rothmann and Goldstein (1945). This boy was classified as an idiot savant, though a psychiatric consultant believed he might be schizophrenic.

When tested by Scheerer at 11 and at 15 L's IQ was around 50. He first showed signs of remarkable interest and ability in music, rhythm and counting in his third year. He could recognise a melody if any part of it was played. By his sixth year he knew the melodies and names of many compositions and had absolute pitch at least for the notes of the piano. As he grew older he would sit for hours at the piano playing monotonous sequences, but his learning ability was limited to an unreflective manipulation of the keyboard. He reluctantly learnt to read music. For several years he had an almost obsessional interest in an aria from Verdi's *Otello* which he never seemed to get tired of hearing. Without knowing Italian he could sing the words phonetically. At 12 he was taken to a musician who played a piano piece which L did not know. When asked to repeat it the boy did so, according to the musician amazingly well – the melody was correct and the accompaniment adequate. Among his other skills he could spell correctly many words both forwards and backwards. His span for the immediate recall of numbers was seven forwards and six backwards; he could also add up correctly the total of twelve two-place numbers just as quickly as one could call them out. He could very rapidly calculate which day of the week a birthday would fall in five years time. On the other hand, L failed miserably on any activity requiring abstract thought. Scheerer and his colleagues believed that he spent so much time on music and counting because such activities were his only means of self-expression and of being able to come to terms with his surroundings. Both his paternal grandparents were musical; his father was very quick at manipulating numbers.

Anastasi and Levee (1959) described the case of a high-grade adult mental defective with exceptional musical talent. Levee had been employed as his tutor for two years. Both S's parents and his brother were college graduates. Though reported to be normal at birth, while in hospital he contracted epidemic encephalitis which led to permanent brain damage. Before he could speak, S was able to hum tunes. In fact he was eventually taught to speak by a speech therapist through the medium of lyrics. His musical education began at the age of 7, under eminent teachers and concert pianists. His musical ability was judged to be outstanding by his teachers and by musicians who had played with him. At one time he played the piano at rehearsals for a leading chamber music orchestra, being an excellent sight-reader who could also play by ear when the occasion arose. He regarded his own playing as serious work, practising from six to nine hours a day. Apart from his music he was lethargic and had only weak and short-lived affections.

S was also gifted with an outstanding rote memory. For instance, it is claimed that after a single silent reading of a two and a half page article, about George Washington, he reproduced it verbatim. However, he was unable to grasp the significance of Washington's self-sacrifice described in the article. He acquired a large store of information about classical composers.

Viscott (1970) describes the case of a 40-year-old woman about whose family and early life he had been able to gather much detail. Harriet's mother was a singing teacher who isolated Harriet from the rest of the family by placing her crib in the music studio. At four years she could play on the piano the arias her mother's students sang. She later also learned to play violin, trumpet, clarinet and French horn, 'all with feeling, albeit in imitative fashion'. Her younger sister eventually taught her to talk. After some years in a special class at school she learned to read and to draw. Her verbal IQ was 65 and performance IQ 87 (on the Wechsler Adult Intelligence Scale). Her memory for new material was excellent when items were handled in small amounts. She could apparently memorise pages of phone numbers when her father read them to her, at a time when the numbers were virtually meaningless to her. Her detailed knowledge about music was described as 'breathtaking'. When she was tested by Viscott she had absolute pitch and could name all the notes of a four-note chord, change key when asked without losing a beat, play 'Happy Birthday' in the style of Mozart, improvise the right-hand part in the style of one composer and the left hand part in the style of another. Viscott believed that for Harriet music was a means of attaining attention and praise from her mother.

Harriet's musical achievements do seem to have been of a kind superior to most of the other idiot savants described in this chapter.

But like many others, she suffered various emotional problems. Indeed many cases classified as idiot savants may in fact have been autistic or schizophrenic. For a discussion of infantile autism and music see Euper (1968).

Mongols are sometimes said to have a good sense of rhythm. To test this notion, Blacketer-Simmonds (1953) matched 42 mongols with a similar number of non-mongol defectives. The subjects had to listen to three repetitions of three rhythmic patterns played on drums and to try to reproduce them. Eighteen mongols and fourteen of the non-mongols were judged to show 'a good sense of rhythm'. Cantor and Girardeau (1959) tried to obtain a more quantitative measure. They asked their subjects to distinguish between two rates of metronome beats, 120 per minute and 88 per minute. They compared 44 mongols with 24 much younger normal children. The chronological age of the mongols average 12:4 and their mental age 4:4. They were significantly inferior at judging the rate of the metronome test. Unfortunately, the mental age of the normal children was 5:6 and this may have made some difference to the results.

More recently, Peters (1969) worked with 20 mongoloid children who differed in chronological age but not in IQ. She matched 10 children whose IQs were in the normal range with the younger mongoloid group for mental age and with the older mongoloid group for chronological age. A younger normal group was matched with the younger mongoloids in mental age. She played a series of varied musical excerpts to each child individually and videotaped his spontaneous responses. The gross responses of all the subjects to the orchestral music were very similar. Differences between the groups of children at different age levels were found, the difference being more pronounced among the normal children. The study provided no evidence that the mongoloid children had heightened sensitivity to music, or any special sense of rhythm or aptitude for mimicry.

Summary

In this chapter we have looked at some children whose conspicuous early talents have later borne great fruits, and at others whose talents have been inhibited either by emotional stresses, or by limited cognitive strengths, or by both. Such persons are not mere 'prodigies', but merit serious efforts to understand their capacities by any theory of musical ability that makes any worthy claim to be comprehensive.

Part 3

The determinants of musical ability

12

Methods of genetic study

General problems

How far any ability shown by an individual is acquired from the environment and how it is innate is notoriously difficult to assess. Even in the case of general intelligence where the matter has been investigated on a considerable scale over a long period, wide divergences of opinion still exist, in spite of general agreement that intelligence is the product of *both* heredity and environment.

The first systematic attempt to study heredity was made by Galton. He collected data on 997 eminent men in 300 families and demonstrated that the number of eminent relatives was far greater than would be expected by chance. He concluded from this that genius was inherited. The idea of the hereditary transmission of human powers was unfamiliar at that time. As he wrote in the preface to *Hereditary Genius* (2nd edition, 1892), 'the human mind was popularly thought ... to be capable of almost any achievement if compelled to exert itself by a will that had power of imitation'. Failure to learn was liable to be attributed to a lack of diligence on the part of the pupil or to incompetence on the part of the teacher.

But Galton's belief that the fact that talent ran in families necessarily proved that it was inherited, was also open to criticism. The abilities shown by eminent men might, his critics argued, just as easily be explained by the intellectually rich and stimulating environment which many had enjoyed. Unfortunately for the study of the inheritance of human abilities, the closer the genetic relationship, the greater the chance of the members of the family sharing the same home and social environment for long periods, and it is therefore far from easy to determine how much of the family resemblance is the result of common environment and how much is the result of heredity. In fact, wide differences between individuals in the same family may be a more potent argument for heredity than the moderate degree of resemblance which is usually found. The environments of two brothers, for example, are never exactly the same. However, environmental differences can hardly explain the professor's son who is very dull, nor why one brother should be conspicuously bright and another average or below average.

A really scientific study of human heredity would require that either the heredity or the environment was held constant while the other varied. Nature has provided some help in holding heredity constant by producing identical twins. Since these arise from a single fertilised ovum, they have an identical set of genes, while fraternal twins spring from separate ova which happen to be fertilised at the same time and are genetically no more alike than ordinary siblings (brothers or sisters). Darlington (1964) pointed out, however, that the splitting of the one egg often damages one or both parts unequally with consequences for the organisation of the embryos and even of their chromosomes. Conversely, the degree of genetic differences in two-egg twins depends solely on their chromosomes – which are not bound to be greatly different. Thus, comparisons of the two types of twin provide *underestimates* of the effects of heredity. Since fraternal twins share a similar pre-natal environment and are born at the same time, they tend to be more closely associated than siblings. On the other hand, identical twins may acquire differences between conception and birth, e.g. the supply of maternal blood to each may not be equal. However, from a comparison of the average resemblance between identical and fraternal twins, one can at least tell whether or not heredity is of importance for a particular characteristic, and can sometimes estimate how important it is compared with environmental conditions.

Normally, identical twins are brought up in the same home and are particularly liable to be treated alike by their parents and friends; they tend to go around together and may be thought to influence one another in various ways. Occasionally identical twins are adopted into different homes and localities. An extensive study was carried out by Shields who succeeded in locating 44 pairs. Unfortunately for the psychologist, most of the separated twins were raised in homes that did not differ substantially in social or cultural background.

For a detailed discussion of the problems associated with research on heredity and environment, see Vernon (1979). Vernon contends that a reconciliation between the hereditarian and the environmentalist positions that would admit the importance of both factors is possible. A figure of around 60 per cent for the contribution of genetic components to intelligence (i.e. lower than the 80 per cent of earlier claims) with 30 per cent contribution of environmental factors and 10 per cent for the co-variance of heredity and environment would still allow for the large shifts of 30 IQ points obtained in certain studies.

Genetic studies of musical ability

As in the case of intelligence, the heated arguments in the nature – nurture controversy have tended to give way to an appreciation that heredity and environment interact in the development and manifestation of musical ability.

Most psychologists of music would nowadays probably agree with Farnsworth (1969, p. 156) when he says, 'It is now clear that neither nature nor nurture can alone make a musician. Both must be present before musical and other abilities can emerge.' Nevertheless, opinions differ as to which side should be stressed. Wing, Bentley and Drake emphasised the importance of innate factors (see Wing, 1963; 1968; Drake, 1957; Bentley, 1966). On the other hand, Farnsworth himself and Lundin with his 'interbehaviourist' theories (see p. 185 below), seem to lose no opportunities of pointing out the contribution of environmental factors. This may be partly because they have in mind the need to qualify the dogmatic statements of Seashore, Schoen, and Kwalwasser on the hereditarian side. For example, according to Schoen (1940, pp. 161-3), 'Musical talent is first an inborn capacity. Artistic musical performance rests ultimately on innate, inborn equipment'; while Seashore (1919, p. 6) stated, 'Not only is the gift of music itself inborn, but it is inborn in specific types.'

While we may believe that every child should be given the opportunity of developing his musical potential, it may still be of practical importance to try to reach some estimate of how much musical ability can be improved by a favourable environment and efficient teaching. Since music is not a 'bread and butter' subject like reading or arithmetic, it could be argued that if musical talent is largely innate, it is not worth while schools spending too much time on the ungifted. It would be better to encourage the unmusical to pursue other more profitable activities, allowing teachers to devote more time and effort to discovering and fostering the talent of the gifted. Again, the teacher may feel reassured if the failure of some of his pupils to progress can truthfully be ascribed to innate lack of musical ability. The parent may wish to know whether it is worth spending time and money on private music lessons for a child who has not shown definite promise of ability.

The influence of the environment on a relatively specialised ability, such as musical ability, might appear somewhat easier to determine than on general intellectual ability. Indeed, before the days of the record player and the radio, it might have been comparatively simple to obtain an accurate estimate of the music a child heard at home and of the training he had received from school or individual lessons, though interest in music would still have been an important factor. The greatly increased opportunities of hearing good music professionally played in the home which nowadays exist, have enriched the environment to an extent that is difficult to assess.

Two approaches to the study of the heritability of musical ability have been made: (1) genetic studies of family resemblances, and (2) attempts to assess how far environmental influences affect the performance of tests or other musical tasks.

In the next chapter investigations of family resemblances will be summarised. Chapter 14 reviews attempts to study the biological mechanisms by which musical capacity could be passed on from parent to child. Chapters 15 and 16 deal with various types of environmental factors.

13

Genetic studies of musical ability

The earlier attempts to investigate how far musical ability is inherited were mostly pedigree or questionnaire studies. Since the development of musical ability tests some research has been carried out in which parents and children or siblings or twins have been tested and their scores compared.

Pedigree studies

Among the eminent and illustrious men studied by Galton (1869) were 120 musicians. 26 out of the 120, or about 1 in 5, had had eminent kinsmen. As Galton included nine members of the Bach family and two members of four other families, the 26 belonged to only 14 families.

A more extensive genealogical study confined to musicians was carried out by Feis (1910). He attempted to collect information about the parents and children of 285 famous musicians, but found the data on the maternal lines very hard to obtain, so that the material he could assemble was seriously incomplete.

An investigation of professional instrumentalists, opera singers and students of the Juilliard School of Music, was carried out by Scheinfeld (1956). His virtuosi group included such outstanding performers as Yehudi Menuhin and Artur Rubinstein.

An analysis of the incidence of talent in the three groups showed that where both parents had musical talent, more than 70 per cent of the brothers and sisters (in addition to the individual reporting) also had talent. Where only one parent was talented, there was talent in 60 per cent of the siblings. Where neither parent was talented, only 15 per cent of the brothers and sisters had talent.

Among the virtuosi instrumentalists, the majority had talented parents, one or both. Yet quite a number reported no talent in either parent. Nor did the differences in the family backgrounds, or in there being both parents, one parent, or neither parent talented, seem to have anything to do with the calibre or quality of musicianship shown by the individual.

The difficulty in interpreting this type of study is in estimating the relationship between manifest and potential talent which for one reason or another has remained latent.

Sergeant (1969*b*) has also collected some data on the percentages of his professional music groups and of his control group (see p. 124) who had parents that could play an instrument (see Table 13.1).

Table 13.1

	Music groups	General students
At least one parent able to play	Approx. 80%	62%
Both parents able to play	30–42%	24%
At least one parent a professional musician	20–40%	6%

Questionnaire studies

In the 1920s several genealogical studies were carried out on the Continent in which musical ability was assessed entirely or partly by questionnaires.

Haecker and Ziehen (see Revesz, 1953) found that the chance that a child will be very musical is 86 per cent where both parents are talented, about 60 per cent when one parent is musical, and about 25 per cent when both parents are unmusical. Remarkably similar percentages were obtained by Heymans and Wiersma (see Revesz, 1953). That no less than 25 per cent of the children of unmusical parents are described as being very musical might be partly due to the parents making more generous estimates of their offsprings' ability than of their own. Also, the ability may have been inherited from remoter ancestors.

In order to give some degree of objectivity to the assessment of his subjects' musical ability, Mjoen (1926; 1934) used a musical index graded from 0 to 10. In Table 13.2 those described as (P) 'Poor' were rated between 0 and 2. Their ability was limited to being able to recognise a tune (2). The (M) 'Musical' (3-7) ranged from those who knew when they sang or played out of tune (3), to (5), holding a second part, to (7), being able to improvise a second part. The (S) 'Superior' group (8–10) were, at the least, able to play by ear, while the most talented of all could compose and play several instruments.

Table 13.2

Parents	Number of parents	Number of children	% of children		
			S	M	P
S × S	7	23	72	28	0
S × M	40	175	60	34	6
S × P	9	34	26	37	37
M × M	30	113	39	49	12
M × P	21	75	7	40	53
P × P	7	22	0	10	90
Total	114	442			

It is apparent from Table 13.2 that the higher the average talent of the parents, the higher the average talent of the children is likely to be. Mjoen believed that his could be regarded as a demonstration of the inheritance of musical ability. It might be objected that the musical environment provided by the parents is likely to vary roughly with their own talent or lack of talent. Mjoen, however, also presented evidence that where both parents are musical (grade 5 or above), the proportion of children who are musical corresponds to the number of grandparents with talent. Thus, where three of the grandparents are musical, 90 per cent of the children are likely to have musical aptitude, if only one grandparent has talent, only 50 per cent of the children may be musical. Mjoen, therefore, concluded that it is the quality of the stock rather than the quality of the parents which determined the ability of the children.

Among the family trees studied by Mjoen was that of the Norwegian composer, Halfdan Cleve. His father, who was very musical and came from a musical family, married twice. His first wife was unmusical and came from unmusical stock. None of their five children showed musical aptitude. His second wife, however, was musical. All their five children were above average musically, and one, Halfdan Cleve himself, very gifted. Halfdan Cleve married a well-known pianist, who came from a musical family, one of her siblings being highly talented. The four children resulting from their marriage showed promise of exceptional talent.

One performer of international repute conspicuously failed to conform to Mjoen's hereditarian theories. Her family was evidently quite without talent. However, Mjoen later discovered that she was the illegitimate daughter of an eminent musician and had been adopted by unmusical parents.

An example of the converse situation was quoted by Sergeant (1969*b*), of a highly promising young musician from a very musical home – into which she had, however, been adopted. No information was available on her natural parents. Mjoen could say that they might have been musical.

Though many studies of foster children have been carried out, the reports seem not to take account of musical abilities. Re-marriage after divorce or bereavement may often bring into the family a new partner who is more (or less) active in promoting music among the children, but the effects of such situations have apparently not been documented.

Kinship studies based on testing

Parent-child and siblings

Questionnaire surveys, however carefully carried out, depend on the accuracy of the replies. Where instrumental playing is taken into account, less than justice may be done to individuals who have lacked the opportunity to learn to play.

As might be expected the first tests to be applied in genetic studies of musical ability were Seashore's. Felix O. Smith (1914), a student of Seashore, applied an early form of the pitch test using tuning forks to groups of school children. The results were disconcerting to Seashore's belief in the innateness of musical capacities. The correlation obtained from the scores of siblings was ·43 for those without practice and ·48 for those who had been given some practice – not much below the ·5 which is 'typically' found between siblings on intelligence. However when he compared the younger children with unrelated children of the same age and sex as the elder of his pairs of siblings, he obtained a correlation of ·53. Near zero correlations are to be expected from unrelated children; this was found by Kwalwasser (see p. 189).

Stanton (1922) undertook a genetic study with the standarised measures, beginning with the families of six well-known American musicians, since they would be more likely to co-operate than unselected persons. The basis of her sampling was thus rather narrow, though some members of the families were in fact un-musical. She interviewed and tested 85 persons, ranging in age from 8 to 80 years. In five families she was able to study three generations. She drew up talent profiles for each family, though questioned how far the percentile ranks of her older and younger subjects were strictly comparable. When she examined the per-centile ranks of the subtests produced by the mating of parents of various levels of talent, she found that while most of the parents were above average, their children tended to be superior to the average of the parents, perhaps because the children were more adaptable to the testing situation.

Friend (1939) made an interesting, if optimistic, attempt to apply the Seashore tests of pitch, intensity and consonance in a simplified form to kindergarten children and their parents. Only intensity showed any noteworthy parent-child correlation, ·46, probably because the concept of 'loud'/'soft' was the only one the children really understood.

Gedda (1961) tested a group of choirboys from the Sistine Chapel and as many of their relatives as possible, using a modified version of the Seashore tests. The boys were aged between 11 and 15; a group of boys of the same age, but not musically selected, acted as controls. The choirboys were found to be clearly superior in their discrimination of pitch, intensity and time to the control group. Their relatives were also superior. On tonal memory, Gedda asked merely for judgements on whether the second playing was the same or different from the first. Eighty to 90 per cent of the choirboys' answers were correct. Both their relatives and the controls made definitely fewer correct responses.

Kwalwasser (1955) summarised the results of three researchers based on the use of his tests. The correlation of the scores of 255 pairs of siblings was ·48. The 71 pairs of brothers' scores correlated

·56, while the 65 pairs of sisters' scores correlated only ·46. With 151 siblings a correlation of ·53 was obtained. In both cases, when random pairings ignoring the genetic relationship were made, only zero or insignificant correlations were found. Kwalwasser also mentions three attempts to compare parents and children. Unfortunately, all experienced difficulties in securing the co-operation of the parents.

Shuter (1964; 1966) used the Wing tests for a study of parents and children, and of twins.

The aim of the first part of her investigation was to compare the musical ability of parents and children, to see what connections existed which might be related to hereditary and/or environmental factors. Information on the latter was obtained by questionnaires (Shuter 1964; 1966).

The main group tested consisted of 54 pupils of a mixed grammar school and 63 of their parents. (Some of the children were siblings and not all of the parents attended the testing session.) Thirteen pupils of a girls' grammar school and 15 of their parents were also tested. The children's ages ranged from 11:1 to 18:1 (one elder sister, aged 21, was also included). To enable the children's Wing scores to be compared with those of their parents, the raw scores were converted into Musical Quotients (MQs) by the formula given in the Wing Test Manual.

The desirability of including parents and children at all levels of musical ability was stressed to the schools beforehand. Unfortunately, a volunteer group tends to be a self-selective one, since adults are more likely to attend if they themselves are musical, or have some interest in music or feel that their children may show talent. In fact the average MQ of the parents was 112 and that of the children, 132.

However, even with this select group when the MQs of both parents were averaged and compared with their children's, a correlation of ·48 was obtained. With the 14 pairs of siblings, the correlation was ·50. These figures were close to the ·5 'typically' reported between parents and child and between siblings on intelligence. However, comparing each child with each parent yielded a correlation of only ·29. This rose to ·36 when the results from the girls' school, where the self-selective effects were particularly marked, were omitted. Shuter therefore considered that with a more representative sample of parents and children the level of correlation would rise rather than fall. Wing tests 1-3 correlated ·16 – even lower than appreciation tests considered separately (·26).

Shuter also compared the MQs of the fathers with those of the mothers in the 25 cases where she had been able to test both parents. The figure obtained was quite low: ·33 compared with the range of correlations, from ·3 to ·7, cited by Cattell (1965) as found with married couples for a variety of traits such as height, intelligence and interests. One might have supposed that amateur musicians would stand quite a good chance of meeting and marrying spouses with similar interests. Since a high degree of assortative mating tends to raise parent-children correlations (see Vernon, 1979), Shuter's low figures might have been another reason for the modest correlations she obtained.

Figgs (1980) did obtain a correlation of ·56 between the fathers' and mothers' scores for the parents who participated in her study. Her purpose was to investigate whether Galton's law of regression towards the mean[1] would apply in musicality. She used the Seashore pitch and rhythm tests and two of the Gaston subtests with 28 parents and 58 of their children; her study produced evidence that regression did apply in musicality.

Twin studies

Kwalwasser (1955) mentioned a twin study in which a correlation of .77 was obtained with the K-D tests, but did not state how many of the 25 pairs of twins were considered identical.

The validity of studies comparing identical with fraternal twins obviously depends on the accuracy with which the two types of twin can be distinguished. Investigators who have been able to supplement their own observations of the appearance of the twins by such objective measures as blood grouping and examination of finger prints claim to be able to identify as fraternal or identical over 97 per cent of twins. One such extensive investigation was the Michigan Twin Study (Vandenberg, 1962). Batteries of cognitive and perceptual tests were administered to some 33 pairs of identical and 43 pairs of fraternal twins. Vandenberg included Seashore's pitch, loudness and rhythm tests and Wing's pitch and memory test. Only

---

[1] The tendency of offspring to revert towards the average of the group to which their parents belong, i.e. for highly gifted or for below average parents to produce children who are nearer to the average than their parents.

in the case of the rhythm and memory tests were there significant differences between the scores of the two types of twin. The 'heritability indices' (h^2) intended to show the percentage by which heredity contributed to each variable were as follows:

Seashore	Pitch	00%
	Loudness	44%
	Rhythm	52%
Wing	Pitch	12%
	Memory	42%

It is surprising that the two pitch tests should apparently be so little subject to hereditary control. Acuity of hearing, which is, however, not closely related to pitch discrimination (see p. 69) proved highly heritable, but only in the case of the right ear. Any connection betwen this finding and the bilaterality to be discussed in Chapter 18 remains to be traced. If the left hemisphere of the brain *is* more concerned with analytical processing than the right, Vandenberg's results might reflect the innate capacity of humans to deal with auditory patterns analytically. A twin study of dichotic listening produced evidence that right-handed identical twins were *less* likely to be concordant on ear asymmetry than fraternal pairs (Springer and Searleman, 1978). Vandenberg himself suggested that it might only be the exceptional talent of the great composers that has an hereditary factor.

Stafford (1965) reanalysed some twin data collected by Thurstone based on testing 48 pairs of identical twins and 54 pairs of fraternal twins. In this reanalysis the contrast between the types of twin was found to be significant for the Seashore pitch tests. In his case the memory test was found to be less hereditable. Both Thurstone and Stafford found significant degrees of contrast in the case of the Seashore rhythm test.

Later Stafford (1970), reasoned that if heredity and environment interact, some of the differences between fraternal twins could be attributed to environment. He tested 113 identical and 88 fraternal twins with a tonal memory test. He calculated separate h^2 indexes for twins who had received the same amount of musical training and those who had received differing amounts. Those who had received the same training produced an h^2 of ·27, while for those with differing experience the h^2 was ·34 – due not to a difference between the identical twins, but to a greater difference between fraternals who had or had not received training. The h² for the combined group was ·29.

In the second part of Shuter's investigation, 50 pairs of twins ranging in age from 9 to 16 were tested. They were classified as identical or fraternal by general impression and careful inspection. In addition, Shuter obtained Wing scores for 11 pairs of young adult twins who were being studied by the Medical Research Council Psychiatric Genetics Research Unit for another purpose.

Many of the twins were well below average in musical ability and found the appreciation tests particularly difficult. Shuter therefore considered that MQs based on the first three Wing tests to be more reliable. As would be expected if heredity is a factor in musical aptitude, the average difference in MQ between each individual and his co-twin was lower among the identicals and a higher proportion of the identicals had lower intra-pair differences. In Table 13.3 each class of twin is sub-divided by sex and into child and adult, though the number in each category is quite small.

Table 13.3 *Means and medians of intra-pair differences*

MQ Points	Musical Quotients							
	Identical				Fraternal			
	Children		Adults		Children			
	Boys	Girls	Men	Women	Boys	Girls	Mixed	Adults
	n.10	n.10	n.5	n.3	n.9	n.12	n.9	n.3
Means	10·90	13·10	9·20	15·67	16·33	20·04*	13·67	15·67
Medians	9·00	12·00	11·00	15·00	15·00	12·50	15·00	18·00

* would fall to 13·86 if a pair with the difference of 88 points were excluded.

Shuter (1964) compared the extent of intra-pair differences with the twins' attitude to music, amount of training and of listening. No consistent relationships emerged. The majority of the subjects had never had music lessons and only very few listened to classical music.

When the MQ of each identical twin was compared with his co-twin's, the correlation was ·84 for the 20 child pairs and ·79 when the 8 adult pairs were included. With the 20 pairs of fraternal twins of the same sex the correlation was ·72; little difference was made by adding the results from the boy-girl twins and the adult pairs. The heritability indices showed that in the case of the children heredity contributed 42 per cent to their musical ability and in the case of all the subjects, 26 per cent.

The contrast between the two types of twins was considerably less than has been reported in studies of intelligence. But factors such as the level of difficulty of the tests may have affected Shuter's results.

In spite of misgivings about the reliability of the Wing subtests with such unmusical children, Shuter correlated the pitch and memory tests separately to see whether or not the results would confirm Vandenberg's. On the pitch test, the intra-pair correlation of the fraternals was higher than that of the identicals. But on the memory test the identical twins correlated ·77 and the fraternals ·50. The heritability index showed a contribution by heredity of 53 per cent. (This rose to 64 per cent, appreciably higher than Vandenberg's figure, when it was calculated by the formula used by him. For a discussion of the various techniques that have been applied for calculating genetic variance, see Vernon (1979).) Since the Wing pitch test has been found to correlate quite highly (see p. 58) with the memory test, it is surprising that the two tests apparently differ appreciably in the extent to which they are under hereditary control. As some measure of pitch discrimination would appear to be a precondition of melodic memory, one might have expected that, if any difference was found, the pitch test would show the higher degree of heritability.

Identical twins brought up apart

Only one of the earlier studies of identical twins brought up apart included results of testing musical ability, a male pair to whom Vernon administered the K-D tests. One twin apparently showed a definite aptitude for music. At the age of 9 he had chosen to study the violin and had made satisfactory progress. After five years, however, he had to give up his music lessons due to his father losing his job. The other twin's only special talent was playing the trumpet, which he took up at 14. He played in small amateur dance bands. His K-D scores were much inferior to his brother's, which was considered 'not surprising' in view of the latter's superior musical education. 'However, there was no general resemblance between the patterns of their scores on the individual tests, such as would indicate a genetic basis to their musical talents' (Yates and Brash, 1941).

Shuter was able to test 5 of the pairs brought up apart who had earlier taken part in the study carried out by the MRC Genetics Research Unit.

The Wing scores of two of the five pairs differed by only two points. One of these pairs was brought up in rather similar musical backgrounds; both claimed to be interested in music and had one or two years of piano lessons. In the case of the other pair, both had grown up in North of England families where other members of the family played in brass bands. But while one had played brass instruments in a band for 24 years (since he was 14), the other had begun to learn the cornet only a few months before he was tested. Gordon might interpret the close resemblance between their scores in terms of the musical aptitude of *both* having stabilised (at a score close to Wing's median for persons of 17 or over) before lessons were begun (see further p. 232).

The other three pairs had more discrepant scores. In one case the higher scoring twin had enjoyed a much superior musical background, had had piano lessons and conducted an amateur choir. In another case one had become a piano teacher, while her twin had had only two years of piano lessons and much experience of listening to music. In the fifth case, the twin with the greater experience of listening to music made the lower score. Details of these case histories can be found in Shuter (1964).

In an intensive study of separated twins being carried out at the University of Minnesota, Bouchard (private communication) is including a brief questionnaire on their musical activities. Whilst this is of course only a minor part of a very comprehensive study, the results should be interesting.

Summary

The data summarised above might be interpreted as supporting the view that musical aptitude is largely innate because it tends to run in families. Lundin (1967), however, considers that studies of family histories can support a view that musical behaviour is acquired just as well as they can support the inheritance theory. Certainly, Bach and Mozart grew up in highly favoured family backgrounds, and their achievements involved long hours of practice and high motivation to succeed.

The effectiveness of a mere repetition of stimuli is, however, doubtful. Again, many performers and composers were either forbidden by their parents to take up music professionally or had little opportunity to do so. Scheinfeld found that some of the greatest virtuosi whom he investigated came from 'the humblest and least musical homes; . . . some of the lesser ones from highly musical backgrounds, with both parents professional musicians'. Such a lack of consistent correlation between musical achievement and background led Scheinfeld to conclude that musical talent does not arise from any unusual home environment *per se*. That a highly musical environment also (or alone) cannot produce talent was shown by the children of virtuosi, most of whom showed no unusual talent.

The forbears of certain musicians who apparently came from unmusical families may have lacked the opportunities to learn music. Had Gluck not been sent to school at the age of 12 his talent might never have developed. The first 12 years of his life were spent in a completely unmusical background, but as soon as he had the opportunity his ability showed itself very quickly. Whether some of his ancestors would have displayed talent given the opportunity is not known. It would appear to be somewhat more convincing to attribute Gluck's ability to an untraceable hereditary factor than to an environment known to be unstimulating musically.

14

How is musical capacity transmitted?

The studies reviewed in the last chapter were primarily concerned with the question, 'How far is musical ability innate?' But we can also ask, 'By what biological mechanisms is musical capacity transmitted?' The latter question assumes, of course, that musical ability is to some extent under genetic control.

While Galton was engaged on his study of the family trees of eminent men, an Austrian monk was patiently and systematically investigating the effects of crossing different strains of garden peas. Pure strain peas with a pair of genes for tallness were, he found, always tall. When crossed with pure short peas, the hybrids were always tall, the tall gene being the effective of 'dominant' one. More excitingly, when two hybrids were crossed, he obtained one pure tall, two hybrids (tall in appearance, with one tall and one short gene) and one pure short one. The true significance of Mendel's laws was not recognised till 1900. When his work became known, geneticists became eager to find out whether the genes governing the transmission of human characteristics could be identified. This was relatively easy in the case of the kinkiness of hair where the effects were clear cut. But it is now recognised that in so far as most human attributes are genetic they result from the cumulative and combined effects of large numbers of genes situated in different loci of the 46 chromosomes.

Complications of three sorts are found:

1. There may be two or more different genes which produce identical or seemingly identical effects.

2. The same gene may have different effects in different individuals or under different environmental conditions. This may be due to variations in the 'penetrance' and 'expressiveness' of a gene. Every gene has a certain degree of penetrance, and for a given

degree of penetrance may or may not be expressive in the individual.

3. Moderator genes may be determined when the activity of a particular chain of genes will begin or end.

Characteristics dependent on dominant genes will run in families recurring generation after generation, since only one parent is needed to pass them on. Although the degree to which they are manifest in any given individual may vary, an examination of family trees over several generations is likely to reveal inheritance by a dominant gene. Traits determined by recessive genes cannot be identified by following them through several generations since they usually occur suddenly in a lineage as the result of the mating of parents of similar genes. The parents and the children of the individual affected rarely show the recessive trait but it also appears in about 1 in 4 of the affected person's siblings.

Biological mechanisms of the inheritance of musical capacities

The first attempt to apply Mendel's principles to musical ability seems to have been made by Hurst (1912). He concluded that musical ability was a recessive trait and lack of aptitude might be due to an inhibitory factor preventing the expression of the musical talent which is hypostatically present in everyone. Further attempts to follow musical ability through the generations of families were made by Drinkwater (1916), Northrup (1931) and Reser (1935).

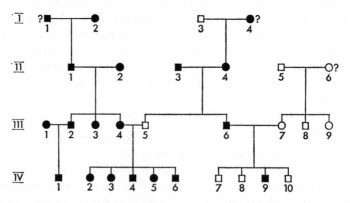

FIG. 14.1 Squares represent males, circles females. Blanks represent no ability in music

(See Shuter, 1968 for further discussion of such studies.)

An interesting attempt was made by Ashman (1952) to trace the biological mechanism of ability to carry a tune, through four generations involving members of three families. Though Ashman quotes Seashore scores for III 6 (PR = 51), III 5 (PR = 15 to 20) and for III 3 (PR = 76) (see pedigree chart in Figure 14.1), most of his information appears to be based on his personal knowledge of the families. His report includes some comment on the individuals concerned.

The brothers, 5 and 6 from generation III, lived up to the ages of 8 and 10 respectively in the mountains of Virginia. They had no schooling and no contact with music. As soon as they were sent to school, 6 rapidly learned to reproduce simple melodies from memory, while 5 never learned to sing more than an occasional two or three bars in tune.

In generation IV, male 7 enjoyed music at school and listening to gramophone records at home. He went to a college where behavourist ideas prevailed and where musical ability was regarded 'as an outstanding example' of an acquired ability. He practised hard, but wholly without success.

IV, 10 was encouraged by his mother, though she was apparently not herself musical, to take lessons. Though he made rapid technical progress, he had no ear for music and no musical memory. His brother, IV, 9 received no encouragement to learn and no musical training, yet he could recall simple melodies.

Ashman put forward the following biological explanation of the pedigree: Individuals known to have had superior musical ability, e.g. II, 1 and 2 and III, 3 and 4, have received from both parents an incompletely dominant gene. Those in whom musical memory is apparently either absent or very deficient have a pair of recessive genes (as Hurst had envisaged). He concluded that 'simple' memory for melody is possibly determined by a multi-factor gene, having other effects which are of survival value. (This is reminiscent of Darwin's idea that music originated as a means of attracting a desirable mate.) Melodic memory is, however, probably not such a simple factor as Ashman supposed, but at least the evidence cited elsewhere in this book shows that it is likely to be closely related to musical ability.

Ashman was, of course, right in thinking that it is likely to be easier to trace the genetic mechanism of a distinctive characteristic that can be isolated and identified as present or not present. 'Tone-deafness' seemed a promising condition for a genetic investigation. Since an inability to perceive or reproduce pitch patterns in a normal fashion is of concern to teachers of speech as well as to music teachers, a joint investigation of tone-deafness was carried out by Kalmus and Fry. A test was developed which appeared to discriminate efficiently between the 'tone-deaf' and the normal, at least among intelligent adults and adolescents. This was a distorted tune test consisting of the first two or more phrases of twenty-five well-known tunes. In one version the tune was played correctly and in the second the melody was distorted by the insertion of several blatantly wrong notes, the rhythm and tempo remaining unchanged. The subjects were asked to decide whether the tunes were played rightly or wrongly. The results showed a clear-cut division into two groups. Ninety-five per cent of some 1200 subjects were considered normal, and the other 5 per cent tone-deaf (Fry, 1948). Performance of the Seashore memory test was invariably found to be bad among the tone-deaf. A significant but weaker correlation with pitch discrimination was found. That the results of the distorted tune test were not unduly influenced by familiarity with the songs chosen was indicated by the fact that Continental students who did not know them made hardly more errors than the English.

The tone-deafness (or tune-deafness as Kalmus called it) appeared frequently to segregate in families and siblings in ratios indicating that it might possibly be caused by a single gene, possibly a dominant (Kalmus, 1949). However, in 1952 he stated, 'We do not know for certain whether tune-deafness is caused by a single gene difference or controlled by many genetic factors.' He thought that there might be several types of tune-deafness and that it was by no means independent of upbringing.

As a result of his enquiry into the musical aptitude of the relatives of professional musicians (see p. 175), Scheinfeld put forward a theory on the inheritance of outstanding talent. He supposed that the highly talented must have in addition to such capacities as measured by Seashore 'certain rarer "special" genes which act either to intensify the effects of the more ordinary "aptitude" genes or to produce some unusual supplementary effects'.

In each of the three groups he studied, the incidence of talent followed the pattern quoted on page 175 above. It is clear, stated Scheinfeld, that no single dominant gene, or no two recessive genes, could account for these ratios. A multiple-gene mechanism would be needed, and the simplest one which might fit the requirements would be, at the very least, two different dominant genes, passed on by only a single parent to a given child, or each parent could give the child one of the required genes.

Scheinfeld's assumption that the great musicians differ from those of lesser talent in possessing a special kind of talent for music for which a special type of gene is required, is open to question. If, however, such a special kind of endowment does exist, Scheinfeld's hypothesis of a double dominant gene might conceivably be correct. In any case he puts it forward merely as a possible theory.

It would seem unlikely that any sex-linked mechanism could be involved in the transmission of musical aptitude when boys and girls make approximately equal scores on musical ability tests (see Chapter 5). Sex-linked inheritance involves a much higher proportion of males showing the inherited characteristic than females. Thus in the case of colour-blindness some 4 per cent of males are afflicted but only ·4 per cent of females. However, Haecker and Ziehen's data seem to suggest that musicality may be inherited to a greater degree from the father than from the mother. Twenty-two per cent of the 74 cases of 'musically productive' individuals seem to have inherited their ability from both parents. In 25 per cent of the cases the talent appeared to have been transmitted by the father alone, and in only 12 per cent by the mother alone (Haecker and Ziehen, 1922, cited Revesz, 1953, p. 191). As we saw on p. 178 it is, however, difficult to assess how far experience of music affected their results. It is possible that the child's opportunity of learning music and becoming musically productive may have depended on whether or not his father, rather than his mother, was musical, in these Continental families earlier in the twentieth century. Swift found that the K-D scores of brothers were more closely associated than those of sisters (see Kwalwasser, 1955).

Shuter, however, found a clear difference between the agreement of the Wing scores between father and child as compared with mother and child, and between male, as opposed to female, twins. The correlation of the children's MQs was quite high (·63) with those of their fathers, but quite low (·26) with those of their mothers. The data from the parents' questionnaires indicated that, even for these children of grammar school age, the mother, rather than the father, set the musical environment. Figgs (1980), however, found a correlation of ·47 between the children's musicality scores and their mothers', but one of only ·13 with their fathers'. With the ten pairs of identical boy twins, a correlation of ·90 was obtained. When compared with the correlation of ·73 for the nine pairs of boy fraternals, a heritability index of 62 per cent was found. Here again, the environmental data did not provide any explanation of the sex difference (Shuter, 1964).

As far as is known, sex-linked characteristics can be passed on only from father to son *or* from father to daughter, but not to both. Some selection effect might be involved in Shuter's results, i.e. men may be more inclined to volunteer to be tested if their children resemble them in being musical and unmusical! The number of male twins was quite small. However, Shuter thought that there might be some connection between her findings and the higher proportion of boys classified as tone-deaf. Bentley (1968) carried out an extensive enquiry among teachers to find out how many children were considered 'monotones'. The percentage of boys was much higher at the age of 7 and failed to decrease with age as much as among girls. At 12, 7 per cent of boys, but only 1 per cent or 2 per cent of girls, were categorised as 'monotones'. Bentley himself thought that the 4 per cent of individuals who are still monotones at 12 may be the same 5 per cent of the adult population of both sexes who are tune-deaf according to Fry. Fry, however, did not give separate percentages for the two sexes.

Petzold (1966) also classified nearly 4 per cent of children of 10 and 11 as being unable to give a scoreable response to his 45-phrase test. Girls improved more than did boys with age, but the sex difference was not significant. An extensive survey of poor pitch singers revealed an appreciably greater proportion of boys compared with girls were so classified by their teachers (Davies and Roberts, 1975). Lewandowska (1978) reported finding four times as many boys as girls who were 'monotones' and that the proportion of girls decreased in the higher age groups. She noted that about 30 per cent of such children came from families where no one is interested in music.

Why many children outgrow their deficiency without special attention calls for explanation. We shall discuss in Chapter 16 research that has been directed towards improving poor pitch singing. However, as there does seem to be a difference in the incidence of problem singers among boys as compared with girls, the possibility of the influence of some deleterious gene or genes should perhaps not be too hastily dismissed. There is now some evidence that at least one major determinant for spatial ability is sex-linked. (See Maccoby and Jacklin, 1974, pp. 120-2 for a discussion of this point.) Thus the lower scores made by girls on tests of spatial ability and the fewer women who have entered occupations like engineering where spatial ability is relevant may not be wholly attributable to social influence.

15

The effects of the home and social environment

In Chapter 8 we noted that the infant comes into the world well equipped to deal with various acoustic stimuli. Before long he finds that his own cries evoke responses from his social environment. But how far are the vocalisations of the newly born significant for their future progress in music?

Fridman (1973; 1976) claims that these early sounds form the basis for building up between mother and baby a relationship of 'sonorous bonds', and that it is important for the mother to sing to her infant and echo back his own sounds. Wisbey in England would support this view. Fridman (1976) found that a month-old baby became motionless and tense when she played back to him his own sounds which she had previously recorded. Soon afterwards he began to enter into a dialogue with her. Mead (1964) tells us that among the Manus tribe a nurse is specifically entrusted with the task of crying in unison with the first cry, so the baby never has the experience of crying and waiting to see what will happen. Later this develops into a lullaby in which the child is put to sleep by crying in tune with the child's cry but louder! This seems to accord with the evidence we noted above that the infant finds sound more comforting than silence. The 'sonorous bond' may later form the basis for a love of music, according to Noy (1968) from his clinical observation of his patients. Noy postulates that aptitude for music may be due to a biological oversensitivity to sound. Due to this oversensitivity, the infant, in order to survive the bombardment by auditory stimuli, learns to use selective attention and hence develops discrimination and the auditory analysis required, for example, by an orchestral conductor. Noy suggests that a longitudinal study might be made of children who exhibit signs of extra sensitivity to sound to find out how many do in fact show signs of musical aptitude later in life.

Noy claims that the mode of communication that a mother adopts towards her baby is different for each baby and is mutual – depending on the response of the child (which may depend on inherent qualities in the infant). When the auditory channel is the supreme mode of communication between the infant and his mother (and through her to the world), the child may be predisposed to develop musical ability. Such persons are, Noy believes, especially sensitive to the auditory non-verbal cues in speech – tone of voice, rhythm, tempo of speech, etc. While Argyle and his colleagues (Argyle, 1975) have demonstrated the greater potency of such cues over verbal content in experiments where, for example, a friendly message is delivered in a hostile tone of voice, whether persons with musical talent are more sensitive to this type of non-verbal cue, has not yet been proven.

Michel (1973) stated that individual differences in the timing of first attempts at 'singing/speaking' and the pace of further development depend vitally on the extent to which people concerned with the child sing and speak to him. Kagan (1972) found from his work with infants that up to six months differences in motor and cognitive development are fairly independent of social class, ethnic origin and even some aspects of how they are reared. By one year of age, however, differences in rearing experience seriously affect cognitive functioning. However, Moog (1976) reported that a very great difference in the quantity of music available to the infant (varying from 8 to 9 hours to a few minutes a day) did not affect the rate of development of active response to music. Indeed, up to about the age of 3, Moog could not observe any significant differences in his subjects' response to music determined by the environment. Children from the poorer homes reacted no differently from those from upper income groups. After the age of 3, Moog agrees that differences in home environment begin to affect the learning of songs and dances. Moog's results refer to children who did not receive any particular attempt to stimulate them musically.

Kucenski (1977) investigated the effects of a systematic musical sensory learning programme in which six folk tunes were introduced to infants between the ages of 3 to 9 months. Training sessions were held twice a month with the 'long-term' group (Group 1) from ages 3 to 9 months and with the 'short-term' group (Group 2) from 6 to 9 months. A control group (Group 3) was tested along with the others but received no training.

During the learning sessions the infants in group 1 were exposed to one new tune twice a month. The programme consisted of 10 minutes of 'Puppet-Song' during which the investigator sang the words of the song synchronised to rhythmic movements of puppets. The song lasted 30 seconds and was repeated ten times. In the 'silent' intervals the tune was sung or played on Orff instruments. Then followed five minutes during which the child was placed on a beach ball and aided by the parent and the investigator to move back and forward to the first beat of every bar of the tune, interspersed with viewing of the puppet faces moving rhythmically to the tempo and metre of the tune. The infant was then exposed to visual stimuli of colours and faces, each of which represented the rhythmic values of each note and musical phrase accents; the tune was played while the film was shown. Finally the tune was played on pitched percussive instruments; the infant was encouraged to strike a drum or tambourine. Sponge versions of the faces, slightly different for each tune, were given to the parents, along with a programmed tape to be played twice to four times a day. The tapes included revision of the tunes learned in earlier sessions. All the infants were tested at 3, 6 and 9 months with the Denver Developmental Screening Tests, and the Bayley Scales of Infant Development.

One month after the end of the learning period all the children were tested with an Infant Musical Response Scale. The six tunes were presented over two sessions. During the presentations of 'Music-Film' and 'Puppet Song', the infant's responses were rated by observers in auditory, visual, vocal, mental, emotional and motor categories. For examples, the observers rated as present or not 'rhythmic sucking' (of bottle, fingers), 'imitates words of song' or 'concentrated attention' (to visual or auditory sources). In the second part of the test the infant was rated for manipulation of melodic and non-pitch percussive instruments to imitate rhythmic patterns of song or for crying or frowning (particularly on removal of instruments), and during a game when, for example, the infant looked at the puppet face corresponding to a particular tune when told to do so. Reliability between the two raters ranged from ·78 to ·99. The Musical Response Scale correlated highly (·7 to ·9) with the Denver Developmental Screening Test, and with the Bayley Psychomotor and Mental Scales (well-established measures of infant growth).

Group 1 infants had increased their scores on the Denver and Bayley scales by 6 months; group 2 improved from six months to a level intermediate between groups 1 and 3 at 9 months. On the Musical Response Scale, group 1 was significantly better than group 2, who were in turn significantly better than group 3, the largest difference being found between group 1 and group 3. The programme was thus highly successful in increasing infants' responses to the tunes.

As Kucenski recognises, there is much in this well-conducted research that ought to be followed up. What would be the long-term effects of such a programme on children's response to music if it could be continued for several years? What other types of music sensory stimulation would also be effective? How far were the visual and kinaesthetic stimulation necessary to the aural learning? The infants showed an unusual increase in language development which was not confined to increase in vocabulary through exposure to the words of the songs; for over half the infants had begun to use three-word sentences. Was this due to the verbal element in the songs or the music or both? Reciting poems might also be tried out.

Home-listening tallies were not significantly correlated to any of the test results. Of the 100 parents approached to take part in the study, 60 were willing and able to do so. The letter requesting parental co-operation made clear the concern of the study with music – this may have meant parents with some commitment to music were recruited. Kucenski proposes that the contribution of the parents should be verified by further research.

In the case of 'intervention' programmes intended to help intellectually disadvantaged children, involving the mother seems to be of crucial importance, so that she may interact more effectively with the child (Vernon, 1979, Ch.9). This should apply in music. Many parents might indeed be eager to help their children to respond to music but lack the confidence to do so. Kessen, Levine and Wendrich (1979) taught mothers to match the vocalisations of their babies and then to respond to vocalisation by singing or playing on a pitch pipe the F above middle C. After about 40 days of such practice at home, on the third visit to the laboratory, the infants made more correct pitch-matchings than incorrect responses. The ages of the 23 infants were between 3 and 6 months. There seemed to be no relation between the musical competence or interest of the parents and the infant's ability to match pitches, though the range of variation was from children with no music in the home to children of professional musicians.

Jenkins (1976) investigated the relationship between the musical development of 2- and 3-year-old girls and their mothers' musical training. Sixty children were tested with rhythm, melody, dynamics, repertoire and other musical items. The results were compared with how much musical training their mothers had received and at what time in life. While the results were positive, they were not statistically significantly so. The general musical home environment (the product of the mother, the father and other adults and the musical activity of the home) did seem to be influential, even before the age of two. Neither socio-economic status nor ethnic origin was statistically a significant influence.

McFie (1973) narrates how he would play or hum the theme of the Andante of Haydn's Surprise Symphony frequently to his son from his fourth month. At about 15 months the son could sing very accurately the first four bars, adding variations such as doubled notes or inverting the melody. This seems to have been the apogee of his musical career. The McFie family was apparently not particularly devoted to music.

One of the difficulties of verifying the influence of music during the first two years of life on the subsequent emergence of musical ability is that the parents who provide rich musical backgrounds in the earliest years of the child's life are likely to continue to do so. An ordinary theory of social conditioning would certainly suggest that any attention to the child and his vocalisations, particularly if associated with affection, is reinforcing.

There is certainly ample evidence that a strong association exists between various musical attainments of the child and the quality of his musical background. How far this is due to purely environmental factors is less clear.

Some indirect evidence of the importance of parents taking an active interest in their children's musical development is provided by the success of the Suzuki music learning programmes. An essential part of the Suzuki method is the enlisting of the co-operation of the parents. The presence of the mother at the child's lessons and the instruction given to her clearly help her to correct the child in between lessons, so that mistakes are not practised. (The progress of the children tends to outstrip that of the parent!) What seems never to have been investigated is the musical ability of the parents who are attracted to the Suzuki method. From his experiences of a year spent in Japan, Kapuscinski (1979), an American cello professor, commented that the Japanese mother is often a strongly involved parent and that the Suzuki system is natural to the Japanese way of life, though it can be transported successfully to other countries. A study of Doan (1973) showed that parental involvement with a child's violin practice tended to be associated with better performance.

Kirkpatrick (1962) found a strong relationship between the singing ability of over 100 5-year-old children and their home environment. From recordings of their repertoire of songs, he classified as 'singers' children who could sing 90 per cent of the notes correctly without change of key, as 'partial singers' those who could sing 75-89 per cent of the notes with only a few changes of key, and as 'non-singers' the children who could sing less than 75 per cent of the notes correctly or who sang without any established tonality. This seems a rigorous criterion to apply to 5-year-olds (cf. Chapter 8). Few non-singers came from homes classified as excellent or good from the point of view of the musical environment. No singers came from musically poor homes. A few children, possibly because of genetic endowment, seemed unaffected by their musical environment. A significant relationship existed between singing ability and the following environmental factors: mothers who sang to and with their children, aid from other adults, family singing and playing, and parents with a musical background. Older brothers and sisters and attendance at a nursery school had less influence on children's singing ability.

Since previous studies had usually been confined to ability to sing, Shelton (1965) tried to obtain classification of children as 'musical' or 'unmusical' on response to rhythm, contrasting tempos and overall musical 'temperament', as well as on their ability to sing in tune and melodic discrimination. He asked qualified music teachers to classify 6-year-old children two months after their entry to school as most or least musical in their class on this basis, a somewhat 'rough and ready' procedure, but probably reasonably satisfactory. Shelton visited the homes of 18 'musical' and of 12 'unmusical' children. Of the 18 musical children, 3 came from homes rated 'musical, 11 from 'average' and 4 from 'unmusical' homes, while 11 of the 'unmusical' children came from 'unmusical' homes and only one from a 'musical' home. The factors which most distinguished the home environments of the musical from the unmusical were: frequent opportunities to hear singing in the home and to sing along with the mother and older children, frequent opportunities to hear records played in the home, and ability of the parents to sing and to learn new songs. Shelton's figures suggest that atypical cases where a musical child comes from an unmusical home are more numerous than the converse.

Moore (1974) tested the pitch and rhythm abilities of 101 five-year-olds during their first week at school. She too found that the musical responses of the children were positively related to having and hearing musical instruments in the home, having parents and siblings who participated in musical activities and receiving help from parents to sing in tune and move to music. Pitch responses were rather more highly related to these environmental factors than were rhythm responses. Twenty per cent of the children who scored at or above the total average score came from homes whose socio-economic level was below the mean socio-economic level for the group.

Freeman (1974) matched 12 musically talented children, 12 artistically talented children with 24 normal children for age, sex, social class and intelligence. The children were of junior school age. The Wing memory test was matched by a colour recognition test. Aesthetic discrimination was tested by asking the children to pair together the beginning and ending of musical extracts in four distinct musical styles and by presenting a set of 14 pairs of art postcards, each pair by the same artist of similar subject matter. The children were required to point out which one card was most like in feeling to the first one they had seen, against the influence of a distractor card by a different artist. The children were also asked to rearrange a set of jumbled chime bars to match two measures of a well-known tune and to draw objects presented on a tray after viewing them for a short time. Freeman then visited the children's homes and completed a detailed questionnaire on family activities and details of parental aspirations. A factor analysis produced, as well as a social factor and an aesthetic involvement factor (with musical interest having a high loading), a music factor loading on the Wing test, the chime bars task, extra lessons in art or music and incentive to play music given by the home. The chime bars and the tray of objects, along with Wing's test, discriminated the talented from their controls. Artistic children were equally influenced to take up art by home and by school. But where there was an incentive to play music, 'the influence of the home appears to have been greater than that of the school, such children of the control group who had received encouragement at school to try a musical instrument often gave it up if home influence was not sufficiently supportive'. The most marked differences between the families of both the music and art groups were in the provision of materials and extent of encouragement given. Some children from the control groups were positively discouraged from aesthetic effort.

Wing (1948), who wished to establish that ability to perform his tests 'was not unduly influenced by opportunity to hear music', collected data on the effects on a child's test scores of the music played by other people in the home. He found that there was a significant difference between the scores made by 333 boys aged 14-18 years who had music at home when their parents played but *not* when persons other than their parents played. He also showed that there was only a very moderate association between interest in music and ability to perform his tests (an approximate correlation was about ·30). As far as awakening the child's interest was concerned, parental playing was very little different from the playing of others. He concluded, therefore, that the most likely explanation of the association between the child's ability and parental playing was that the child's ability had been inherited. This may be the true reason, but it is not the only possible one. Parental playing may be a more potent influence on the child merely because it has gone on for much longer or because the parents have more prestige in the eyes of the child. Wing does not state how the group of 'non-parents' was made up, but it may have included a number of lodgers (Wing – private communication) as well as other blood relatives, siblings with perhaps some grandparents or uncles and aunts. (In so far as the observed significant difference was between the parents' playing and the playing of less close relatives, as opposed to unrelated strangers, that would tend to strengthen the argument favouring heredity.)

As part of her investigation of parents and children (see p. 180), Shuter tried to determine the effect of various environmental factors on the children's musical ability.

She compared the children's MQs with a listening score, derived from questionnaire data. The listening scores correlated only ·18 with MQ. Shuter also made a detailed analysis of the parents' questionnaire answers, tabulated against their children's musical level. An index of the children's musical level was produced by adding the marks for musical knowledge, listening and activity to their Wing scores. On the basis of this total index of musicalness, they were divided into three groups. The parents of the bottom group were, on the whole, considerably less active musically than those of the other two groups. Present parental playing and music lessons were related to the children's musical level to a highly significant degree. It could be argued that the parents who had had music lessons and kept up their playing were those who had talent and that their children had inherited their gifts. But equally it could be held that the parents' playing had contributed to raising the children's musical level and that parents who have themselves had music lessons are more likely to encourage their children to learn.

Similar arguments could be applied to Holmstrom's findings (Holmstrom, 1963). He compared the scores made on his version of Wing tests 1 to 3 by children from musically good homes with those from musically poor environments. The differences in their scores remained statistically significant in favour of the children from the musical homes even when the effects of interest in music and intelligence had been removed by statistical procedures.

Rainbow's (1965) researches threw a little more light on this question. Using a detailed questionnaire, he obtained a separate index of 'home enrichment' and 'participation in music by relatives'. His subjects were pupils at the Laboratory School of the State University of Iowa, whose IQs averaged about 116. Ninety-one were at the elementary school stage (average age 10:9), 112 at junior high school (aged about 13:6) and 88 at high school with an average age of 16:3.

Evidently many of the parents who did not play themselves encouraged their children to take part in music – judging by the quite low correlations between home enrichment and participation in music by relatives (highest $r = \cdot 45$). The effect of home enrich-ment on the scores of Seashore's pitch, memory and rhythm tests and of Drake's memory test was quite small, the test most affected being the Seashore memory test (highest $r = \cdot 34$). The correlation with the teachers' estimates of their pupils' potential capacity for music was also low. Within the three age groups, home enrichment did differentiate between the 20 per cent of the children judged by their teachers to be the most musical and the 60 per cent rated average in musical potential, and also between the lowest 20 per cent and the average group. Home enrichment seemed to have a positive effect ($r = \cdot41$) on the youngest children's interest in music and, as we might expect, less influence on the interest taken by the oldest group in music.

In Rainbow's results, performance of the music tests, and music potential as estimated by the teachers, appeared to be largely independent of participation in music by relatives among both the youngest and eldest children. The difference between this finding and Shuter's may be partly accounted for by Rainbow taking into account *any* playing or singing by the relatives. However, Wing, too, did not assess the amount of parental playing and found, like Shuter, an appreciable association between their musical activity and their Wing scores.

Sergeant and Thatcher (1974) included home musical environment among the variables they compared in their study (see also p. 78). This was assessed by the children filling in questionnaires on their own instrumental playing, number of instruments in the home, and on their estimates of their parents' musical ability and interests. Sergeant and Thatcher regarded the questionnaire data as sufficiently accurate for the purposes of group comparisons. The results showed a tendency to cluster at the very strong or very weak end of the scale. The melody test proved to be linearly related to the children's musical background (which included their own music lessons). i.e. a graph of melody test scores versus musical background scores was approximately a straight line, indicating that the two variables increased together. The rhythm test showed deflections from linear trends which Sergeant and Thatcher suggest may indicate that rhythmic learning is sponsored by other, perhaps genetic, factors.

Martin (1976) tested nearly 200 secondary school pupils using the Wing, the Indiana-Oregon, the Hoffren test and a test of his own designed to discover how well the children could identify a pair of musical excerpts as composed by the same or a different composer. The sample of children was selected so as to have a rather higher-than-normal proportion with musical interests. Indeed nearly a quarter of their families played or sang, nearly 30 per cent of their siblings played. In one out of four families music-making took place regularly or frequently, only in about one out of five was there no instrument in the home. The correlations found between home background and music tests are shown in Table 15.1.

It is perhaps remarkable that it was the number of instruments in

Table 15.1 Correlation coefficients between home background variables and musical ability as measured by music tests

	Total for Wing tests	Total for Indiana-Oregon test	Total for Martin test
Number of instruments at home	·59	·39	·32
Whether parents play an instrument	·50	·34	·29
Whether siblings play an instrument	·38	·27	·14
Amount of family music making	·40	·37	·22

the home, rather than the amount of active music-making that was the most significant variable. Wing would probably have said that the possession of musical instruments was indicative of talent in the family. A variety of instruments was involved: 45 per cent of the household had pianos, and about the same number, guitars. Ability tests seemed to be more highly correlated with home musical background than 'appreciation' tests. In the case of home background compared with performing activities, the most important factor again seemed to be the number of instruments in the home.

In his manual Gordon (1965) reported very low correlations between whether the mothers and the fathers sang or played and the children's MAP scores. In the case of his longitudinal study (1967), he obtained questionnaire answers regarding the home environment of the participants (who, it should be remembered, were volunteer learners). As can be seen from Table 15.2, environmental factors showed much greater influence on the children's achievement test scores (an early version of the ITML) than on their aptitude profiles.

Socio-economic status of the home

How far, we may ask, does the socio-economic status of the home affect the children's musical ability? Is any superior performance of a music test to be attributed to the generally more stimulating environment of a 'better-class' home? Vernon (1979) points out

Table 15.2 Correlations between musical aptitude profile and music achievement test scores with environmental conditions

	Musical aptitude profile				Musical achievement test		
Environmental factors	Total imagery	Rhythm imagery	Musical sensitivity	Composite	Melodic, rhythmic and harmonic recognition total	Symbolic understanding	Composite
1. Sex	·08	·10	·13	·12	·35**	·42**	·39**
2. Instrument	·03	·01	·15*	·07	·21**	·33**	·26**
3. Practice	·15*	·04	−·01	·09	·08	·04	·07
4. Music stand	·10	·13	·18**	·16*	·25**	·30**	·28**
5. Practice days	·13	·06	·14*	·12	·20**	·25**	·23**
6. Like to practice	·25**	·18**	·20**	·24**	·35**	·36**	·37**
7. Extra school activities	·25**	·18**	·24**	·25**	·25**	·22**	·25**
8. Home music activities	·15*	·08	·20**	·17*	·20**	·27**	·23**
9. Summer lessons	·24**	·24**	·27**	·29**	·28**	·29**	·28**
10. Private lessons	·03	·01	·07	·04	·13	·18**	·15*
11. Play another instrument	·18**	·16*	·20**	·19**	·38**	·31**	·38**
12. Parents tell to practice	·12	·03	·11	·10	·03	·02	·03
13. Parents help practice	·11	·06	·11	·11	·11	·08	·11
14. Father play or sing	·14*	·10	·09	·13	·17*	·10	·16*
15. Mother plays or sings	·17*	·12	·13	·17*	·27**	·26**	·28**
16. Siblings plays or sings	·15*	·03	·00	·07	·17*	·07	·15*
17. Piano at home	·18**	·15*	·16*	·17*	·40**	·37**	·41**
18. Record player at home	·08	·09	·07	·10	·15*	·15*	·15*
19. Hear music at home	·13	·08	·07	·12	·24**	·15*	·22**
20. Attend concerts	·20**	·24**	·25**	·24**	·34**	·32**	·35**
21. Head of households	·17*	·17*	·15*	·18**	·38**	·30**	·38**
22. Father attended college	·12	·17*	·17*	·17*	·35**	·28**	·35**
23. Mother attended college	·05	·13	·15*	·14*	·37**	·32**	·38**

*r ≥ ·14 significant at the 5 per cent level   **r ≥ ·18 significant at the 1 per cent level

that the role of socio-economic status in intellectual differences is a complex one and is often misunderstood. (For a detailed discussion, see his Chapter 8.)

At a preparatory girls' school where nearly every girl over 7 learned some musical instrument and all of whom heard good music fairly often, Valentine (1962) found that they developed the power of discriminating between concords and discords as much as three years earlier than did elementary school children. By the age of 9 they gave an order of preference for musical intervals almost identical with that given by adults. This investigation was carried out around 1910. Valentine himself wondered whether very different results would be obtained nowadays. To judge by Zenatti's data (see p. 147 above), they would.

Wing (1936) reported that the average scores of elementary and secondary school boys were almost identical except on tests requiring aesthetic choice. The superiority of the secondary school boys might be due, he thought, to their hearing more good music at home; less time was spent on music at their school compared with the elementary school.

Children from better class homes often have more opportunities for music lessons. Gilbert (1942) suggested that this may improve their music test scores. When he re-analysed his data, classifying by socio-economic status of the college instead of by sex, he found the higher the status of the college, the higher the average K-D test score. However, the higher the status of the college, the greater the percentage of students who had received music lessons. When only untrained students were considered, the difference among the colleges disappeared.

Parker (1978) tested over 1000 Kansas high school children with the Gaston test and with the Wing appreciation tests. With intelligence and the Gaston score held constant, the correlation between the Wing appreciation tests and socio-economic status was zero. Shuter (1964) investigated how far the Wing scores of 189 junior musicians of the Royal Marine School of Music were related to their fathers' occupational level as stated on the entry forms filled in by the boys. When the two top grades of Wing scores were taken together, more than twice as many came from the highest social categories than from the lowest. However, eight out of eighteen boys whose fathers were unskilled manual workers had above average talent. No information was available about the early home background or occupation of the boys' mothers. This might be particularly important with a subject like music.

Rainbow (1965) assessed socio-economic status on the basis of the education as well as the occupation of the head of the household. He found that the correlation between socio-economic status and home enrichment was about ·3. This would confirm the everyday observation that there is a tendency for musical activity in the home to be related to socio-economic status but that higher social status and a regard for music do not always go together – the children of a Welsh miner may be in a more musically stimulating environment than the offspring of a Midland industrialist.

The correlations between socio-economic status and the music tests were low. But when Rainbow analysed his results by a multiple regression technique, socio-economic status was shown to be contributing to a statistically significant extent to the children's musical aptitude as estimated by their teachers.

Analysis of variance also showed socio-economic status to be associated with the teachers' estimates. We may well wonder whether the teachers were in some way influenced in their assessments by factors connected with the socio-economic status of the pupils. Rainbow's result has, however, been confirmed by subsequent research. Sergeant and Thatcher included socio-economic status of the home in their study (see p. 203 above). Besides taking into account the occupations of the two parents, they asked the children to fill in a questionnaire on their parents' hobbies, newspapers read, family visits to places of interest, etc. Both the melody and rhythm tests, IQ, and the home musical environment were all found to be highly significantly related to socio-economic status. Zenatti (1976) reported some similar but much weaker interconnections. She examined data from over 4000 of the children who had taken part in her experiments. She divided the fathers' occupations into an upper and a lower grade. The musical home background was classified from the answers the children over 6 gave to questions on records owned, parental music playing and music heard on the radio or TV. Only 11 per cent of the comparisons with father's occupation were significant, particularly those related to assimilation of musical language – tonal melodies and consonant harmonies were preferred by the upper-grade children, the preferences of the lower grade were more fluctuating. The upper-class children were better at detecting changes of harmony. Thirty-five per cent of her comparisons with musical background were significant, again due to 'aesthetic judgement'. Zenatti believed that the richer musical environment enjoyed by 43 per cent of the upper-class children, compared with only 7 per cent of the lower-class ones, was at least partly responsible.

The influence of father's occupation was greatest between 6 and 7 years. Musical home background and whether the children were having music lessons rose with age up to 10 (the oldest subjects included in the study). Socio-cultural influences were greater on harmonic tasks, less on melodic and least on rhythmic tasks (compare with Sergeant and Thatcher, p. 203 above).

On a task requiring conservation of melodic patterns based on ancient Chinese music chosen for its unfamiliarity, King (1972) found that social class and social environment contributed significantly, but that home musical environment did not. This would seem to accord with Zenatti's finding on the particularly *acculturising* effect of music at home.

Hill (1970) investigated the possible deleterious effects of deprived home backgrounds. He devised a 15-minute test of melodic and rhythmic abilities suitable for 5- and 6-year-old children. High reliability was claimed for the test. He asked the children to echo back single notes, intervals, and phrases, to sing eight bars each of three familiar songs, to recognise familiar songs from the tapped rhythms and to clap back rhythmic patterns. He tested 200 children, half of whom came from low income, often broken, homes and, in contrast, half whose homes were affluent. He also tested 400 9-, 10- and 11-year-old children with an experimental form of the ITML, again half from disadvantaged and half from advantaged homes. Differences in favour of the advantaged children were apparent in almost every subtest used both with the younger and the older children, those depending on aural memory and imitative abilities producing the largest differences. When scholastic-intellectual ability was held constant, a difference in favour of the advantaged group persisted. Hill also found some evidence that there was a consistent, if not statistically significant, increase in the gap between the advantaged and the deprived with age, i.e. 'the poor get poorer, the rich, richer' effect.

Young (1974) investigated the effects of a programme of musical training on the Hill test scores made by advantaged versus deprived kindergarten children. Sixty-four children from two advantaged and 64 from two disadvantaged schools were divided into experimental and control groups. After pretesting with the Hill tests, the experimental groups received twenty lessons spread over nine weeks. These emphasised the learning of melodic and rhythmic concepts and of songs which exemplified these. Though there was much variability within all groups, the pretest means showed considerable superiority for the affluent groups. The scores on the post-test showed no improvement except on rhythm among the control groups and even some regressions. However, the experimental disadvantaged group had improved dramatically (by 62 points out of 200). Little difference was found between experienced and inexperienced teachers in their achievements obtained with Young's programme.

Unfortunately, the disadvantaged control groups were, on average, five months younger than the disadvantaged experimental group; their IQs averaged 86 as compared with the 95 of the experimental group. However age and IQ had only slight relationship to the post-test scores.

A most important question is how far-reaching and how long-lasting are the results of such programmes. We shall discuss this problem in the next chapter.

A much longer project to investigate how far culturally disadvantaged children could succeed in music if given the opportunity of learning an instrument was undertaken by Gordon (1975). The MAP was administered to all fifth- and sixth-grade pupils in four culturally disadvantaged and three culturally heterogenous schools. Every pupil, regardless of his scores, who volunteered to take instrumental lessons and to participate in band activities for five years was lent a woodwind or brass instrument, as far as possible the one of his choice. The musical content of group lessons was similar for all pupils, but the teachers were informed of the MAP scores and taught with regard to individual differences. After one year the culturally heterogenous pupils were found to be superior in achievement to the disadvantaged. However, the disadvantaged had caught up by the end of the second year. Eighty-two of culturally disadvantaged and 96 of heterogenous pupils originally volunteered. At the end of the five years, due to changes of school or time-table clashes, 28 culturally disadvantaged and 35 heterogenous children were still participating. By the end of the experiment the mean scores achieved by the disadvantaged for the performances of studies, composed by the teachers, and for the rhythmic concept part of the ITML were significantly higher than those gained by the hetero-genous group. Their tonal concepts scores were also superior, but not significantly so. The pupils with high musical aptitude aptitude (above the 55th percentile) in both groups achieved more than those with low aptitude. However, the culturally deprived with low MAP scores achieved standards equal to those from culturally heterogenous schools with average musical aptitude. Music thus seemed to be providing, at least for these volunteer students, a means of compensation for lack of achievement in academic studies. Gordon believed that their success was partly due to the teachers giving attention to individual differences, even in the group situation.

Summary

A musically stimulating home is certainly likely to help children to make the best of whatever potential talent they may possess. Whether the parents play or sing and the availability of an instru-ment seem especially important. However, present-day parents who do not perform can encourage their children to sing with recordings or broadcasts and to listen to a wide range of music, thus providing a richer environment than would have been possible in earlier times. Unfortunately, it is only too easy *not* to attend to ambient music. Whatever may be the value of 'Musak' or 'pop' to the setting of moods, too often the child may seem to be receiving training in *not* attending to music in any meaningful way.

Ethnic differences

It has sometimes been suggested that certain groups, such as Negroes, Jews or Germans, have special endowments in music. For many Negro communities music plays an important part in life, but this is by no means universal (Klineberg, 1935). In rural West Virginia where Klineberg lived for some time, he found very little interest in music among the Negroes; such interest as existed was directed towards modern American songs. In the larger cities it seemed that music meant no more or no less to the Negro than to his white fellow-citizen.

In the 1920s and 1930s various efforts were made to use the

Seashore and other music tests to investigate these popular notions about racial differences. The most easily available comparison was between Negroes and white Americans. Since Negro children were, for whatever reasons, usually behind white children of similar age in school grades, the problem arose: should the two populations be compared by age or by grade? To obviate this difficulty, Dorothy van Alstyne and Emily Osborne (1937) tested children aged from two and a half years to six and a half. Their 264 Negro and 307 white subjects were selected to be as nearly comparable as possible. The children were asked to clap blocks together either in time to patterns produced by William's rhythm meter or to reproduce them after listening to each. The Negro children were markedly superior at clapping in time to the apparatus. They were better at simple patterns, and at a slower tempo. Their superiority was less marked at reproducing the patterns, and decreased somewhat with age. When school children and college students are tested, Negro subjects tend to make their best showing on the Seashore rhythm test, and to excel the norms for white populations. However, the differences are usually small. (See Kwalwasser, 1955 for a list of various studies and his interpretation of the findings.) With the other Seashore tests, white students sometimes make slightly superior scores.

More recently, Wilcox (1971) reported that the Seashore scores of 130 inter-city Negro children were all below Seashore's published norms, especially in the case of pitch, but not greatly in the case of rhythm. More importantly, a general decline was found between the ages of 11 and 13, especially in the case of the boys. The girls improved on tonal memory between 11 and 13. Both sexes declined severely on both rhythm and time. The decline seemed to be congruent with a decline found in a longitudinal study on tested intelligence. But would the same be true of all inter-city children? Dawkins and Synder (1972) found culturally deprived children made lower scores on each test than the published Seashore norms, though the white children were rather higher than the black. Culturally deprived children who had studied music scored better than those who had not; their average scores were higher than the norm on tonal memory and about the same on pitch. Walls (1973) gave two tests of the recognition of the concepts of pitch, duration, and loudness to 77 white middle-class and 70 black lower-class fourth graders. One test used excerpts from popular music, the other, standard orchestral music. Both groups scored higher on the popular music listening test, though the scores on both tests were related. The middle-class children did better on both than their lower-class peers, but the latter scored as well on the popular music as the middle-class pupils did on the orchestral. This seems to suggest it was not the concepts *per se* that caused difficulty. Ethnic group was predictive on the orchestral music test, while socio-economic status was not; however, socio-economic status, but not ethnic group, was related to the popular music listening test.

The notable contributions of black musicians to jazz need no comment. That many of the children from disadvantaged schools in Gordon's (1975) study were probably black provides evidence that – given the opportunity – deprived children of whatever ethnic group can succeed with instrumental studies (see p. 209).

Gordon (1980) reported that 167 inner-city children, 98 per cent of whom were black, scored lower than the scores for his standard-ised norms on the PMMA tonal test. On the rhythm test the kinder-garten age group were equal to the norms; grades one to three children were superior.

Within the UK, McLeish and Thomas (1971) compared the Bentley test scores of 18 Welsh-speaking children from Bala, 18 from the mixed Welsh and English town of Wrexham and 18 Cambridgeshire children. The groups were matched for age, sex and non-verbal intelligence. No significant differences were found, except those associated with differences in intelligence levels.

Sward (1933), employing the Drake memory test, as well as some of the Seashore and K-D tests, came to the conclusion that 200 Jewish children were only slightly superior to non-Jewish subjects. He contrasted this very small difference in talent with the very much greater achievement of Jews as professional musicians.

Attempts to apply tests like Seashore's to non-European peoples living in very different cultural backgrounds (Davenport and Steggada, 1929; Eells, 1933) may have provided interest (and frus-tration) to those who carried them out, but unfortunately produced little of scientific value.

Drake has made particularly careful efforts to test primitive and rural subjects whose exposure to western music would be minimal. This must have been particularly difficult in the case of his rhythm test, since any music with a steady beat would be relevant. But certainly, the opportunity for training in music and for casually hearing good quality western music was much less than with most white people. Drake (private communication) collected data on Seminole Indians in Florida, Indians on Guam, natives of the Dutch Antilles, rural Mexicans and a small group of Japanese. He claims that the results he obtained were remarkable in that no real differences appeared. Such variability as was found seemed to be mostly due to error of measurement rather than to any deficiency in any of the ethnic groups.

It is a great advantage if the tester comes from the same country. Igaga, himself a Ugandan, has provided very interesting data on Thackray rhythm tests with Ugandan children, aged between 8 and 17. Comparing 655 Ugandan and 573 English children, aged 10 to 15, on the Thackray perception tests, he found that the English children were superior at first but that at about 14, the Ugandans caught up and went on improving. There were differences in growth rates between the two groups for the subtests (Igaga and Versey, 1977). In the case of the Thackray performance tests, the 398 Ugandans tested showed an average superiority of 8 points over the 246 English children. Both samples showed an improvement from ages 10 to 13, but the Ugandans then levelled off, while the English children's greatest gains were with the 14-year-olds (Igaga and Versey, 1978). A significant sex difference was found – while the English boys surpassed the girls by $1 \cdot 10$ on performance and $2 \cdot 07$ on perception, the Ugandan girls scored, on average, 10 points better than the boys on perception and 8 on performance. The English boys were better by 8 points on perception than the Ugandan (perhaps because English boys listen to 'pop' records) but the Ugandan boys surpassed the English by nearly 10 points on performance. Igaga explains the superiority of the Ugandans on performance in terms of the use of repeating rhythms in much of Ugandan ritual. The Ugandan girls from earliest childhood actively participate in domestic activities that are performed rhythmically. Igaga points out, however, that we must remember that there are many subcultures in Uganda; he was able to test children from thirteen of them.

According to a statement cited by Leontiev (1969, p. 429) tone-deafness is practically unknown among African tribes whose languages entail intoning vowel sounds. He himself was able to test 20 Vietnamese (Vietnamese is a tonal language). Fifteen were as able to detect pitch differences when confounded by the tonal difference between 'u' and 'e' (claimed by Leontiev to be a particularly difficult task) as when pure tones were used. Four out of the five who were less able to do this came from a region where tonal elements are less important in the language.

Farnsworth (1931) tested Chinese and Japanese groups who had been living in contact with western music for varying periods, with the Seashore pitch and consonance, and the Kwalwasser melody and harmony tests. Their scores, especially on pitch and harmony, decreased from American standards in inverse relation to the length of time they had been in contact with western music. White students scored higher on all but the melody test.

Yamamatsu (1974) presented interesting data on the scores made by Japanese living in Japan in 1957 and 1967 compared with the American norms. The results are given in Table 15.3.

Table 15.3

	Japanese scores	
	1957	1967
Pitch	Lower	Lower
Loudness	Lower	Improved to similar
Rhythm	Slightly lower	Much higher
Time	Same	Same
Timbre	Lower	Lower
Tonal memory	Lower	Same (by 1974 higher than American)

(See Chapter 16 for further data from Japan.)

Japan is a country where western music has penetrated ubiquitously. (Indeed, visitors complain of the difficulty of locating traditional music.) A study carried out in Egypt is of considerable interest in showing the confusion that may be caused by trying to teach pupils who hear Arabic music on the radio western music in the schools. Sadek (1968) used the Bentley and Seashore measures along with tests of her own including quarter-tone intervals played on the violin, to test 111 children aged 12 to 15 from ordinary schools and 74 children from music conservatories. With 171 students training to be teachers of music and 59 students at a higher institute of education, she used Wing tests 1-3, the Oregon and other tests. The Egyptian children were considerably superior to the American and British norms on rhythm, and better on time and pitch. But the adult groups were far behind the test norms due, Sadek suggested, to the conflict caused by two different tonal systems. In spite of the years of training on the C major scale, Egyptians often sang a flattened E and B, being influenced by an Arabic mode. However, Sadek believed Arab countries should make use of tests for selection to music schools. With the spread of western music to all parts of the world, it might indeed be useful to develop local norms for British and American musical ability tests. Comparable types of tests could also be produced, based on Oriental or African music.

While the current tendency seems to be to interpret such ethnic differences as are found in terms of differences in educational and cultural background, we cannot be sure that there are not also genetic variations. Negroes may be better at the rhythmic aspects of music because less sophisticated instruments were developed in Africa than in Europe, or because as children they are not discouraged from clapping their hands to music and beating on drums. But there might also be some inherited differences, just as there are in the case of blood groups among the populations of different parts of the world (cf. Vernon, 1979, Ch. 21).

16

The effects of specific practice and music lessons

In the first part of this chapter we shall discuss studies of the effects of specific coaching on various musical abilities. An advantage of such investigations, from the point of view of judging their effects, is that the influence of other variables is less likely to intrude into the results. However, such training programmes usually have to be discontinued after a short period. Questions such as, 'Would longer training have resulted in further improvement? Will any gains achieved persist? Will they transfer to other activities?' are left unanswered.

In the second part of the chapter we shall deal with the effects of music lessons – the only readily available measure of long-term musical training.

Pitch discrimination

Much research effort has been devoted to the possibilities of improving pitch discrimination. Seashore believed that each individual has a maximum potential power for sensory discrimination, determined by the inherited efficiency of the ear, which is reached early in childhood and could not be improved by environmental influences. The results of testing might fail to determine the individual's maximum capacity, due to such factors as lack of concentration or motivation, or a failure to understand the test instructions.

Seashore's position was challenged by Wyatt. In her monograph (1945) she presented a detailed and critical review of the literature and described an experiment of her own, where considerable improvements in pitch discrimination were achieved by her subjects.

The general conclusion to be drawn from the results of such research is that pitch discrimination can be improved in most cases.

However, mere repetition of a test will not necessarily lead to improvement. Indeed the abler subjects may become bored and make lower scores. Prolonged training at one pitch, while it usually improves discrimination and vocal reproduction at that pitch, may not transfer to other pitches. Training may have to be continued for a long period; plateaux of learning are likely to be encountered, but once surmounted, further progress may be rapid (see, e.g., Wolner and Pyle, 1933). Considerable efforts are required to keep the subjects highly motivated. The training needs to be adapted to the needs of the individual, though it may take place within a group. This would make remedial work costly in time, although some form of programmed learning or computer assisted instruction might be applicable. (See Shuter, 1974 for a discussion of the possibilities.)

Singing ability

Granted that gross pitch deficiency can be improved by remedial training, the question arises: what has been achieved that is musically useful? Several studies have reported that there is a relationship between poor scores on pitch discrimination tests and imperfect pitch singing (e.g. Bentley, 1968; Zwissler, 1971). However Fry (1948) and Fieldhouse (1937) suggest that tonal memory is an even more important factor. When Jones (1979) tested 36 uncertain singers with the Bentley measures, half scored average or above on pitch, but only four scored average or above on tonal memory.

Present-day opinion favours the view that poor pitch discrimination may arise from poor vocal control rather than vice versa. Thus, Porter (1977) found that uncertain singers were quickly able to learn to match pitches if allowed to tune a second oscillator against the first but were less accurate on vocal pitch-matching tasks. (See Welch, 1979, for a review of the research on poor pitch singing.)

Gaining control of the voice does seem to lead to improvement in pitch discrimination (see p. 64). Various methods to help the child to learn to sing in tune have been tried: 'conditioning' and 'behaviour modification' techniques; use of a vertical keyboard (Jones, 1979); bone conduction to by-pass the ear (Roberts, 1977). Emphasis has often been placed on the production of in-tune notes at one suitable pitch. For the child who has not found a singing voice at all, this is obviously a milestone. Jones (1979), however, reported that most of the uncertain singers she trained learned to match a pattern more easily than a single tone. Perhaps most important of all is encouraging the child to persist till success is achieved. Thus, Joyner (1969) had to exercise great patience in teaching a 'typical' 11-year-old monotone control of his voice till at the fifth session a breakthrough occurred when the boy suddenly produced a single sound of much improved quality. This boy later learned to sing scales and to imitate short tunes based on consecutive notes.

It should be noted that not all children classified by their teachers as problem singers are 'real' monotones. For example, 10 out of 32 children could sing in tune at lower pitches (Joyner, 1969). Cleall (1970) and Buckton (1977) are among those who attribute much of the difficulties some children find in singing in school to the songs being written in too high a key. Plumridge (1972) found only 14 children out of 500 had a singing range limited to three semitones when they were asked to imitate her singing of 'Three Blind Mice' in a key comfortable to themselves.

It certainly seems important to try to establish how far-reaching and lasting are such efforts. Much may depend on follow-up in the class-room. Thus, Klemish (1974) found that in a campus school with a strong music programme children who had taken part in an experiment to improve their singing by means of a tape recorder continued to gain when tested several months later. Children at a public school regressed to approximately the level obtained by their class-mates who had not received the special training. Again, little information is available on how far improved intonation transfers to such activities as holding a part against an upper voice or learning a pitch-variable instrument.

Evidence from carefully carried out studies in the 1930s showed that training in singing with musically unselected younger children tends to persist. Thus Jersild and Bienstock (1931) trained 18 children (average age 3:2) in the singing of single notes and of intervals during 40 ten-minute sessions spread over 6 months. A significant difference was found between the final scores of the experimental subjects and those of 18 other children paired with them. When the same children were retested several months later (Jersild and Bienstock, 1934) the trained group had retained a reliable superiority over the control group.

The initial scores made by the 3-, 4- and 5-year-old children who took part in Updegraff, Heileger and Learned's investigation

(1938) have been quoted in Chapter 8.

After 15 days, after 30 days, and in the case of the 5-year-olds, after 40 days, the children were retested. Definite, consistent improvement was found among the children given training. The control group improved only slightly, if at all. Not only was the interest of the experimental children sustained throughout the training, but they also began to show increasing interest in the musical activities of the school. The normal music training at the nursery school, though not inferior to average, may have been beneath the capacity of the children to respond, thus allowing considerable scope for the trained group to show improvement. However, it is also possible that the gains made were in the nature of accelerated development. If they lasted, or were boosted by further training, the final result might be that the children would reach musical maturity at an earlier age, with their ultimate maximum of development remaining unchanged.

This seems to be the case with many of the attempts to provide 'compensatory' education for pre-school children in the area of cognitive studies. Typically the children who had received a pre-school enrichment programme for one or two years improved in IQ by approximately 13 points. However, by third grade, differences between them and matched children who had not been given the compensatory education were found to have evaporated (see Brody and Brody, 1976, pp. 158–65).

Some evidence in support of the 'accelerated' maturation hypothesis comes from a study by Boardman (1964), who followed up the work of Robert Smith, at the University of Illinois Child Development Laboratory. Each day for two 16-week terms, Smith had given 15 minutes' practice in singing to 20 three-year-old and 21 four-year-old children. All improved, especially on the lower register, C to A'. Boardman tested 16 kindergarten children, 15 six-year-olds and 15 seven-year-olds. These last were from among the first group trained by Smith, the others having experienced his vocal programme. With these children, Boardman matched groups for age, sex, previous attendance at a comparable nursery school, socio-economic status and grade level. Both groups were given a test of vocal accuracy based on the tonal patterns used in Petzold's research (see p. 118). No significant differences were found between the vocal accuracy attained by the children who had gone through the Smith programme as compared with the control children. Boardman concluded that training improved the ability to reproduce a melody, but that once a plateau of performance had been reached the rate of improvement slowed down, and that the effect of pre-school training at least for the children she studied is primarily to accelerate the developmental process rather than to affect the end-product in any other manner.

However, something valuable may be gained if the child 'finds his voice' at a rather earlier age than he would do without special training. Both Joyner (1969) and Gould (1969) advocate vocal training for 5- and 6-year-olds, especially in the head register, so as to gradually extend pitch range and prevent potential monotones. If the child does not learn the easy command of his voice, physical and psychological strain may come to be associated with singing, possibly adversely affecting his attitude to music. On the other hand, important 'spin-offs' may come from enjoyment of singing well.

Musical ability tests

If the experimental groups mentioned above could have been given further training, for example, in recognising which note in a short phrase had been changed on a second playing, it does seem likely that such long-term practice would tend to improve performance of tests such as Drake's and Wing's memory test.

Some empirical evidence is available on the effects of rather short-term specific coaching and of aural training on tests of musical ability based on musical material. Gordon (1961) investigated the effects of specific coaching on the performance by 14- to 15-year-old children of the two Drake tests. He chose 10 children whose initial PR ranged from between 50 and 75 and 10 whose PR ranged from 1 to 36, on the memory test. Five from each 10 were selected to serve as the experimental group. Seventeen half-hourly instruction periods were devoted to the practice of musical phrases similar to those used in Drake's memory test. The subjects were taught how to listen for the different types of changes in the phrases. Neither group was receiving outside musical instruction. Both groups were retested at the end of one month. The difference between the two groups when their post-test means were compared was 4·32, a result which was found not to be statistically significant. Gordon had tried during the training periods to offer instruction that would help both the high and low scorers. His results did not confirm the hypothesis that training might be more effective with the more musical subjects. Gordon commented that larger groups might have yielded significant differences. Longer-term instruction might lead to greater improvements. Interest could perhaps be sustained by including the study of themes and variations from published music.

Wing (1948) reported that 25 boys, aged 15 to 18, improved their initial score by 4·1 per cent when a second testing was preceded by a 20-minute lesson and discussion on the material of one of the subtests. A control group gained only 3·4 per cent. This very small amount of improvement with practice compares quite favourably with research on intelligence tests. Practice on identical or parallel tests generally produces a rise of about 5 IQ points. Coaching with practice at taking complete tests can produce quite large gains. The total average gain from 2 practice tests plus a few hours coaching is estimated by Vernon (1960) to be about 9 IQ points for the majority of British town children.

Heller (1962) studied the effect of fifteen weeks of music training, where emphasis was placed on the development of listening skills, on the Wing scores of 164 college freshmen. The training periods lasted 50 minutes and were taken three times a week. The gain, though statistically significant, was small when the experimental group and 41 controls were re-tested. There were no differences in the improvement on the first three tests compared with the appreciation part of the battery, and none between the group when subdivided into high, average and low scorers.

Rowntree (1970) did manage to produce highly significant improvements on pitch and chord tests in ten-year-old children by giving them training to reinforce their concepts of pitch and chord analysis as well as practice tests for seven weeks. Tonal memory also improved. A control group who did not receive the training made no significant improvement. As one might expect, with 7-year-olds, training even over the period of one week produced an overall improvement of 23 per cent in mean scores. Rhythmic memory seemed less affected by the training.

Conservation tasks

We noted in Chapter 9 that attempts to train children in conservation tasks met with varying degrees of success. Foley (1975) concentrated on 7-year-olds as being at a stage when conservation was beginning to be established and therefore responsive to training. Training by the usual class music teachers during ten-minute portions of six music periods in activities such as calling attention to a familiar song and then changing the rhythmic pattern and using the children's own original rhythmic patterns in varied tonal contexts resulted in a gain in experimental groups which was significantly higher than the gains made in classes that did not receive the training. Little decrease was found when the post-test was administered again two weeks later.

Botvin (1974) worked with 100 children of low socio-economic status whose average age was 6:8. Non-conservers of a familiar tune were guided by gradual changes ('successive approximation') in tempo to complete diminution (twice as fast) or complete augmentation (twice as slow). One group was taught the verbal rule 'Speeding up or slowing down a song doesn't change it'. Both methods of training were successful in improving performance on the conservation of melody task. The successive approximation training was more effective than the verbal rule method in also improving conservation of mass, weight and number.

Absolute pitch

In Chapter 8 we noted that absolute pitch usually develops in early childhood. Is it possible to acquire this ability later in life?

Seashore (1938) and Bachem (1940) were convinced that absolute pitch was innate, but several experimenters have succeeded in greatly improving their subjects' ability to name notes correctly. Mull (1925) trained her subjects on the twelve sounds in the same octave. They practised attentive listening, followed by testing, three times a week for four months. At the beginning only 7 per cent of the answers were correct, at the end 62 per cent.

Lundin (1963) used a programmed learning technique to teach his subjects to identify a random series of musical tones: 24 chromatic notes from middle C to B[1]. Each subject worked in a booth with a tape. During training he was told immediately when he named a pitch correctly. When he was wrong he was told how far he had erred in number of semitones and in direction from the correct note. He then corrected his error by pressing a button corresponding to the right note. During first part of Lundin's research he trained five male students. After 36 sessions all showed marked improvements. Two of the subjects had gained absolute pitch. During the second part of the research the notes found to be easiest were presented first. Five subjects worked through at their own rate fourteen graded tapes. After ten trials one subject had improved by 700 per cent, another by 600 per cent and a third by 300 per cent. Two subjects who had made only one correct response at the beginning also showed considerable improvement.

Cuddy (1968) proposed that using a reference tone, such as A = 440 Hz, would be more effective than trying to memorise each tone individually. After a year of using this method, Brady (1970) was able to identify randomly presented piano tones on 97 per cent of the trials to within a semitone. One tone was identified each day – to ensure that his judgements were not based on relative pitch.

It certainly seems possible to teach with some success a subject without absolute pitch to name the notes of the piano. Teplov (1966), however, believed that this artificial ear for absolute pitch is fundamentally different from true absolute pitch in being less precise and more unstable. Far from it being improved by contact with music as is the case with true absolute pitch, it tended to be lost in taking part in music. However, at least one of Lundin's subjects improved his singing on pitch and even complained of increased sensitivity to the faulty intonation of others.

Time and rhythmic discrimination

Rhythmic tests seem to be somewhat more resistant to the effects of music lessons than some other tests. But can performance be improved by specific training?

Among the earlier studies, reviewed by Shuter (1968), Coffman's was interesting in providing training to suit the needs of the individual and in covering a variety of rhythmic activities. He selected 36 children from grades seven and eight and 24 college students on their below-average scores on Seashore's rhythm test, on a rhythm discrimination test of Coffman's own, in which rhythmic patterns were presented in musical contexts, and on a motor rhythm test. Half of the subjects received training over three months. Methods used included intensive training in drumming, marching to music, beating time and practice in discrimination. At the end of the training the younger group had improved on both the discrimination tests and the college students on the Seashore test, while the control group showed no improvement. The experimental groups also took a motor rhythm test which required them to tap back 60 rhythmic patterns. Both showed marked gains on this task. Five of the college students were asked to perform piano pieces described as 'rhythmic in character' before and after training. On average they were judged to have improved 'slightly' by five trained musicians.

Shuter mentioned the use of Skinner's teaching machine technique for which considerable improvements in ability to tap in unison with a rhythm were claimed. Shrader has developed, on the principle of Skinner's Teaching Machine, the TAP Master Rhythmic Sight Reading System. This is intended to teach the pupil to tap out exercises printed in the textbook in time with recorded music. Each time he makes a correct response he hears a 'beep' and his score is raised one point on the counter. The ages covered are from kindergarten to advanced levels. Utley (1978) has gathered some evidence that an experimental group working with the system intensively for three weeks improved their note-reading performance significantly. Further research is planned on the use of the system over a longer period and into whether the gains achieved result in improvements in instrumental or choral music performance.

Groves (1969) compared the motor-rhythmic abilities of children, aged 6 to 8, who had been given a period of rhythm training with children who had received none. The experimental group received two half-hour lessons each week for 24 weeks. Each period was devoted to one basic rhythmic pattern. However, no significant difference in the ability to synchronise body movements with rhythmic stimuli was found. Home musical background was not a factor in synchronisation of rhythms. Motor ability, as assessed by a well-established measure, the Brace Scale, did seem important. A follow-up study after 18 months seemed to confirm the original finding that age and maturation are more significant factors than instruction in this aspect of rhythmic ability.

Kuhn (1974) studied the ability of professional musicians to detect changes in tempo (an important ability for conductors and teachers at whatever level of musical activity). Moore (see Kuhn, 1974) carried out a replication among high school students attending a summer music camp. While these students made many more errors than did the professional musicians, results were remarkably similar. The mean correct responses of decrease in tempo were similar to those earned by the professional musicians. However, detection of same and increase in tempo was superior among the musicians, through training/experience and/or age.

Conclusions

Some of the improvements discussed in this section are doubtlessly of a purely 'cognitive' nature in the sense that explanation of what is involved in the concept of pitch may help unsophisticated subjects to make higher scores on Seashore's test.

In addition, there is substantial evidence that specific coaching, if efficiently carried out, can improve specific skills. How far-reaching such improvements can be in later musical development is unfortunately less well established. It is very likely to be affected by how far the teacher is able to make use of such improvements in the class-room or in instrumental lessons.

The effects of music lessons on test performance

Although the only readily available measure of long-term musical training is provided by instrumental lessons, only the fact of whether or not the individual has had lessons or the number of years these have continued has usually been taken into account when comparing the amount of training with test results. Qualititative estimates of the instruction have not usually been available.

In addition to any light which a study of the effects of music lessons on test scores can throw on the theoretical problem of how modifiable is musical ability, it is of some practical importance to the music teacher to know whether or not any allowance need be made for the child who has had music lessons when evaluating test results.

As we noted in Chapters 2 and 3, one way of validating a music ability test is to compare the scores of individuals known to be conspicuously musical with those known to be unmusical. One criterion of success would be being accepted at, and surviving in, a special music school. This needs to be borne in mind in considering the evidence of, for example, the study by Tomita and Kurosu (see below).

The greater opportunities today of talented children receiving lessons than in the 1920s and 1930s when Seashore, Drake and Wing were developing their tests may be another factor tending to produce higher associations between training and test scores.

Most of the group tests were not intended to be applied before the ages of about 8 or 9. If Gordon is right to contend that musical aptitude has stabilised by the age of 9, we should expect test results from older children not to show the effects of music lessons, unless, perhaps, the music lessons were commenced before the age of 9.

The Seashore measures

Reporting on their experiments during the development of the Seashore tests, Seashore and Mount (1918) reported low correlations (up to ·31) between musical training, as carefully estimated from questionnaires, and pitch discrimination for large groups of students. Only low correlations were found by De Graff (1924, cited Farnsworth, 1928) between the number of music lessons and rhythm discrimination among several hundred adults and children. With 20 music students, however, Brennan (1926) found significant correlations between the number of half-hour lessons her subjects had had and the pitch test ($r = ·42$) and the memory test ($r = ·55$). Children who were having lessons gained significantly higher scores than did the children not receiving lessons on the Seashore pitch and memory tests, but not on Seashore's rhythm test (Graves, 1947). Graves commented that it was difficult to believe that the families sorted themselves so definitely in terms of inborn musical aptitude that only children from such families, who also ranked high in musical aptitude, were given lessons.

Stanton (1922) compared the talent profiles of the subjects who took part in her genetic study (see p. 179) with the amount of their previous musical training. While there appeared to be some relationship between musical training and the Seashore profiles, a relatively high proportion of talented persons, even in musical families, had not received music lessons.

Stanton and Koerth (1930; 1933) reported much more extensive data collected at the Eastman School of Music by testing students on entrance and re-testing three years later. Only the 285 pre-adolescent students showed much gain (average 4·7 points). Only those students still at the school were re-tested; a greater increase might have been found among those who had left the course (Wyatt, 1945). Thirty-five per cent had increased their PR from 50 to 90. However, the scores of 57 per cent of the youngest group had not varied by more than 4 to 6 points.

Tomita and Kurosu (1976) in Japan have tried to tease out the effects of maturation from those of musical training by comparing test scores of 44 unselected children aged 12 to 13, 58 unselected students aged 20 to 23 and 87 children aged 12 to 13 from a special music school. In the case of the Seashore pitch and rhythm tests, there was no significant difference due to age, but a highly significant difference due to training. Conversely the time test showed a highly significant difference with age; but the music pupils were very little better than the college students.

The K—D tests

The average total score of some 4,200 children aged 10 to 19 was 11·25 points higher (out of 275) in the case of those who had received six months or more training (Kwalwasser, 1955). This was particularly true of the tonal memory, tonal movement, rhythm imagery and pitch discrimination tests. It is curious that rhythm imagery should be more affected than pitch imagery. Both tests are likely to be susceptible to training influences since they require a knowledge of notation.

Tomita and Kurosu reported no significant differences among their three groups on the quality discrimination test, a moderate difference due to age and a highly significant one due to training on tonal movement. In the case of melodic taste the main difference occurred between groups 1 and 2, the scores of the special music pupils being very similar to the college students.

The Drake musical aptitude tests

Drake (1957) claimed that his tests are measures of 'pure aptitude'. The correlation between number of years of music lessons and the rhythm test is certainly very low (·01 and ·26). The correlations he quotes for the memory test and number of years the pupils had had music lessons, though rather low, are somewhat higher: ·37, ·35 and ·43. In fact, Drake provides separate norms for use with students who have had five or more years musical training.

The differences appear to be quite considerable. They may be partly due to the self-selection of good students tending to continue with their music lessons, while the untalented give up. However, since five years is an arbitrary division, many of the non-musical group must have had music lessons for less than five years and the differences are, therefore, all the more significant. It is, of course, desirable that, where a test is known to be affected by training, definite information should be available, so that the user can make due allowance for previous tuition.

Results of testing 75 Minnesota children, aged between 9 and 17, twice and comparing their scores on the Drake tests with their musical experience were reported by Martin (1964). A significant difference in gain was found in the case of the memory test between a group that had received little or no training as opposed a group who had had less than six months before the initial testing and six months or more after and a third group that had received more than six months' training before and after the first testing. No significant difference was found between the latter two groups. Results on the rhythm test were inconclusive.

Tomita and Kurosu found highly significant differences both for age and for training in their study for the memory test. However, for the rhythm test the differences between their groups were not significant.

Evidence which did confirm Drake's claim that his memory test measured 'pure aptitude', came from an investigation of the effects of systematic musical training on the development of musical memory carried out in Poland by Horbulewicz (1964). The need for such a study arose from the very high percentage – 62 per cent to 89 per cent – of pupils in music schools who failed to complete their courses. This seemed to be due to the adoption of the egalitarian principle that any individual has unlimited possibilities for the development of any ability.

Horbulewicz used the Drake memory test on pupils in music and general schools, aged between 10 and 17, and on groups of professional musicians. For 7-year-old children who were applying for admission to an elementary music school, he devised a test of his own. In all, his subjects numbered 473. He concluded that music training was not the determining factor in the development of musical memory. The tempo of development was not quickened by training. Even after more than ten years of a uniform programme of instruction, great differences remained among individuals. The groups that had undergone training did reach a higher level, making about 23 per cent fewer errors on the Drake test, but this was partly due to the wastage among the less talented. The different abilities involved in the Drake test – memory for time and for pitch – seemed to be subject to the influence of training in varying degrees.

The Indiana-Oregon music discrimination tests

Although Hevner tried to select music which was not likely to be familiar to the ordinary person, a correlation as high as ·64 with musical training was found with 126 college students. With advanced musical students, however, scores were not related to training (Hevner, 1931).

With senior school groups and college students who took the 43-item version of the revised test, Long (1971) found a correlation of ·56 with amount of piano lessons and ·33 with extent of lessons on other instruments. With the 30-item test and junior high school children the correlations were lower: ·36 for piano and ·28 for other instruments. Long (1972) considered evidence of an association with test scores of instrumental and choral performance showed that school music programmes that were oriented towards perform-ance were making significant contributions to the musical taste of youth.

The Wing tests

To find out whether instrumental training made any difference to the performance of his tests, Wing (1968) divided 271 children into three categories: above average, average and below average. Just as many children having instrumental lessons were in the bottom group as in the top group. The children, however, were only 12 years old; some may have been learning an instrument for too short a time for training to have its full effect. Wing claimed that with older children results would be affected by self-selection – the weaker pupils giving up lessons and those who are gifted becoming self-taught if no lessons were available. Shuter (1964) found a correlation of ·65 between Wing scores and a combined measure of their lessons and playing among her sample of grammar school children (see p. 180) perhaps due to the less talented giving up music lessons because of pressure of school work.

Wing also found that the correlations of the scores of several groups re-tested after one to five years were high and unaffected by the fact that many had continued studying an instrument, a few had started to learn while others had given up playing. Even in boys' grammar schools where it was usual for all school music lessons to cease at 14, ability to do the tests continued to improve till the age of 17.

Wing classified his subjects merely into those who had lessons and those who did not, irrespective of the length of training. Newton (1959), however, classified the RMSM junior musicians into three categories: those who had had 3 or less, 4 to 6, or 7 to 15 terms of instruction. As they were undergoing a formal system of organised tuition, it was thought that the amount of their musical experience could be directly related to length of time under training. (Data on their musical experience prior to entry were excluded from statistical assessment as being too unreliable.) No significant difference was found between the mean Wing scores of the boys in the three categories.

Although the proportions of talented, average and unmusical, as reported by Newton, were very close to Wing's norms for the general population and more than half the boys had had less than two years' training, including their terms at the RMSM, it might be true that they had passed the stage where intensive study could improve their performance on the Wing tests.

Holmstrom (1963) compared the grade 2 and grade 4 results of 47 children who had been playing some instrument between grades 2 and 4 with those of 75 children who had not been receiving private lessons. Marked training effects were found for all the subtests used by Holmstrom, especially for pitch. He considered that the improvement might have been greater still if some of the 47 children had not already had lessons before the initial test. (Holmstrom stated that he had other evidence which seemed to suggest that training effects on such tests soon reach a maximum.) The average improvement was actually not very great: roughly 10 marks, compared with 8 marks made by the control group, out of a possible 104. The effect of the training might, of course, be much greater with some individuals.

In the Tomita and Kurosu study, the Wing pitch test was not included. All the other tests showed highly significant differences related to training. The rhythm and phrasing tests also showed highly significant effects of age, as did harmony and intensity to lesser degrees.

Familiarity with the music of the test items appeared to have little difference on Wing scores (Wing, 1968) even when the proportion of known items was quite large. Most boys from a group of 100 who had considerable experience of music knew only between 5 to 15 out of 80 items, but a few knew up to 45. Yet the percentage of correct answers for known and unknown items was almost exactly the same. This is a point which some critics have found hard to believe. For example Davies (1978, p. 123), speaking of Wing's use of Bach chorales in an original and mutilated form, says one 'might surmise that a sample of people who know the originals will do better than a sample who do not'. According to Wing's (1968) account of the development of the material of this test, however, his first efforts to devise the test were found to be too difficult for the average musician. After revision, he produced a version on which the most musical of the subjects could just manage to make a perfect score and the rather less musical solve the easier items. This version was found to be too difficult for 16-year-old schoolboys. Certainly, it would be advisable to check whether 40 years later, the average 11-year-old testee has become too musically sophisticated for this test to work validly. Twenty years ago, the Eastman School students did find it too easy to be discriminating (see p. 25).

The Bentley measures

Whellams (1971) carried out further analysis of data collected by Cleak (1970). 22 children had no instrumental instruction between two testings with the Bentley measures; 10 began to learn an instrument; 8 gave up; and 4 continued learning to play throughout the course of the investigation. The significant differences found in post-test mean scores were claimed to be mainly due to the beneficial effects of instrumental tuition. The mean scores of the children who were having lessons at the time of the first testing were higher than those of the other two groups; those who continued were higher than those who dropped lessons, suggesting that the children who had the higher scores would be more likely to remain interested. Again, the children with higher scores who had not had lessons before the initial testing were more likely to take up an instrument. Instrumental playing appeared to have a dramatic effect on their aural development, since their post-test scores were nearly as high as the children who had been playing throughout the period. The mean score of the 8 children who stopped playing was nearly as low as those who had had no lessons at all. The gains made by the 4 children were about the same as those who did not play at all, i.e., might be reasonably accounted for by maturation. Of the subtests, rhythm appeared to remain the least affected by the training.

As the children were only aged 7, Gordon would probably say that their musical aptitude had not yet stabilised.

The Gordon aptitude tests

Though Gordon provides separate norms for the MAP for pupils who are members of school music performance organisations, the differences are not nearly so large as those in the Drake norms, but the period of learning is not specified. Fosha (1964) found only negligible differences between two testings of 'musically select' students one semester apart; the ages ranged from 9 to 17, and they were continuing their musical activities. Pupils studying different types of musical instruments made similar scores. As noted in Chapter 15 (Table 15.2), the results obtained with the longitudinal study group indicated that the playing of one instrument had no correlation with the MAP except for musical sensitivity, but did correlate significantly with a musical achievement test. Playing a second instrument or attending summer classes, *liking* to practise showed much higher correlations with the MAP and even higher correlations with achievement. All three associations would seem to be what we might expect of the talented child. Gordon also presents the correlation coefficients between the initial MAP scores and those obtained after one and two years of training. The stability coefficients were as shown in Table 16.1. These coefficients, Gordon points out, are of about the same order of magnitude as the reliability coefficients of the test itself. In spite of concentrated musical instruction over two years, MAP scores display only typical increases. More important, pupils retain their same relative position on the test.

De Yarman (1975; Schleuter and De Yarman, 1977) claimed that even as early as 5 or 6 the child's musical aptitude may have

Table 16.1

	One year	Two year
Tonal imagery	·83	·86
Rhythm imagery	·84	·87
Musical sensitivity	·86	·86
Composite	·92	·93

stabilised. Unfortunately, the evidence he puts forward has the disadvantage of being retrospective. It rested upon the scores made at 9 of children who had experienced for from six months up to three and a half years a programme of school music specially intended to develop aural/oral and kinaesthetic skills, being taught as individuals within a group situation. This programme may well have been more effective than that previously available to the children, though De Yarman provides no evidence on this, merely showing that the children who had the benefit of longer as opposed to shorter periods of this curriculum had similar average levels of MAP scores at 9.

Gordon (1979) himself tested two groups of children who might be expected to make scores on the PMMA that were superior to his standardised sample. One group attended a private academic school who enjoyed a high quality and quantity of music instruction at school and came from privileged homes. The other attended a community music school which offered private instrumental lessons and instruction in voice, music theory and ballet. Most of the pupils came from inter-city areas and their home environments were likely to offer limited cultural opportunities. All the 75 private academy children were superior on average to Gordon's standardisation sample, the differences ranging from 4·9 points for 6-year-olds on rhythm to only 0·5 for 5-year-olds on the tonal test. Similarly, all the mean differences favoured the children in the community music school over those in the standardisation group. However, only for the 7- and 8-year-old children on the rhythm test were the differences comparatively pronounced. The differences ranged from 3·7 points for the 7-year-olds on rhythm to 0·7 for 8-year-olds on the tonal test. The scores for the private academy school were only modestly higher than those for the community music school, except for the 5-year-old children on the tonal test, the mean in the community school being 1·2 points higher, and for the 8-year-olds on the rhythm test, where the means for the two groups were exactly the same. Overall, the largest differences among the three groups occurred on the rhythm test for children of all ages with some outstanding exceptions at the extremes.

Gordon interpreted his results to mean that, although the private academy children probably have the same distribution of innate music capacity as the standardisation group, they demonstrate higher overall music aptitude because of their home and school opportunities. The children attending the community music school achieved superior scores due to innate capacity and good music instruction, in spite of their unfavourable home backgrounds.

Summary

It seems to be true that many students with no formal musical training achieve higher scores on musical ability tests than do some subjects with considerable training, but subjects who have had music lessons do tend to gain superior scores.

The question, 'Are the superior scores of those who have had music lessons due to their training or to selective factors?' remains difficult to answer. Kwalwasser (1955) considered that 'it is much more rational and realistic to maintain that training is a by-product of talent (than that talent is the product of training), for those possessed of talent seek and receive instruction.' When using tests for prognostic purposes, it seems reasonable to bear in mind that the scores of candidates who have been learning to play may have been somewhat raised by the lessons.

Other questions are: Is there some critical amount of musical experience which will aid an individual to make a significantly higher score on a musical aptitude test? If so, having reached that plateau do musical aptitude scores then show average maturational growth? If the child gives up lessons, are his future scores likely to drop? Perhaps the reason for giving up is important, e.g. a decline in interest as opposed to pressure to devote more time to vocationally oriented studies.

Part 4

Music, cognition and the brain

Introduction

We have seen that aspects of something called 'musical ability' can be defined and that the extent to which people display them is measurable. The purpose of this section is to provide the reader with an account of the psychological work connected with music and music perception which lies outside the field of tests and testing. This work concentrates on establishing the nature of normal processes rather than on investigating individual differences. However, as we shall see, the two fields of study are connected and it will be argued that the 'psychology of music' has a considerable amount to offer for the testing of musical ability.

Psychology may, in principle, offer us physiological and cognitive descriptions of the processes in the brain which are supposed to underlie musical abilities. Chapter 17 comprises an account of the cognitive research which has been concerned with the constituent parts of musical ability, such as memory for the pitch of tones and for melody. The usefulness of construing the perception of music as a quasi-linguistic process is also suggested. Chapter 18 discusses work on the macroscopic aspects of brain function and structure with respect to music. The chapter closes with a discussion of the relations between the psychology of music and the psychology of musical ability.

17

Cognitive psychology and music

Because this chapter discusses work mainly within the tradition of cognitive psychology it will be as well to provide a brief account of the nature of this kind of psychology.

Cognitive psychology grew out of the need to provide a theoretical framework for various facts which could grow ahead of current physiological knowledge at any given time. An essential element of cognitive psychology is the conceptual nervous system (Hebb, 1949). This comprises a group of linked systems in which, for example, perception and memory may be thought of as a system of filters leading to various types of interlinked memory stores. Although those filters and stores are often represented in diagrams by boxes, they represent functions rather than structures in the brain. Each postulated function is a hypothetical construct. That is to say that we hypothesise its existence (because it seems constructive to do so) and then seek experimental evidence to justify our hypothesis. When we can obtain the evidence we feel surer of the construct. When we cannot we may use the new information to improve the construct, that is to make it better fit all of the available evidence.

Cognitive psychology thus comprises an account of processes in the brain in terms of a series of models (the hypothetical constructs) rather than in terms of physiology. The two types of description of processes in the brain – cognitive and physiological – cannot ultimately be independent. Yet because the nature of their interdependence is largely unknown, and certain to be extremely complex, to a considerable extent the two systems are developed separately with an occasional grateful clutch at a seeming connection.

We begin our account of research conducted within a cognitive framework at a relatively atomistic level. After considering memory for pitch and for melody we shall introduce the idea of music as a language as a useful way of continuing the account. Memory for pitch is a good place for us to start because pitch memory appears to be such a basic ingredient of musical ability, and also for the pragmatic reason that a great deal of work has been done on this topic, largely by one psychologist, Diana Deutsch, on whose efforts any account of the cognitive processing of pitch must heavily rely. We shall later examine studies on memory for melodies and on the perceived meaning of melodies.

It is useful to note at this stage that Deutsch, together with many other workers in this, and other areas of the psychology of music, uses stimuli constructed of sine waves (pure tones). This procedure has two main advantages and one main disadvantage. The first advantage is the superior control attainable by the experimenter over every aspect of the stimulus because its components are electronically generated and can be electronically combined. This control is far in excess of that obtainable with humans playing instruments. The second advantage of sine waves is that they have no overtones, they are a pure fundamental. The overtones of traditional musical instruments are, of course, not random, they play a large part in the auditory identification of the instrument being sounded. The fixed and detectable (by the experienced ear) relationship between the fundamental and overtones gives cues which because of the logic and design of the experiment, the experimenter often wishes to withhold. The principal disadvantage in the use of sine waves is their very artificiality; they, initially at least, put one more veil between the experimental and real situations. A further problem which needs to be considered when sine waves are used in experiments, particularly those concerned with timbre, is the special white (recorder-like) tone which these waves may convey, whereupon their very neutrality becomes a distinctive feature. Nettheim (1979) has most recently drawn attention to this problem.

Memory for pitch

The experiments discussed in this section are about memory for pitch other than that achieved by the possession of 'absolute' pitch. The study of 'absolute' pitch reveals that it is not as absolute as was once thought and that great accuracy is rare (cf. Chapter 8).

Deutsch's work has relied to a great extent on one simple paradigm. The subject in the experiment is presented with a tone and after an interval another tone, the subject's task being to judge the relationship between the two tones. The major variables used have been the alteration of the length of the intervening interval between the two tones and the alteration of the nature of other stimuli given to the subject during the interval.

One of the basic findings of various authors (e.g. Harris, 1952; Wickelgren, 1969) is that although there is some decrement in memory for pitch with the passing of time this is slight even over several seconds. As might be expected by readers familiar with analogous experiments using words, a very potent interferer with memory for tones, producing a considerable decrement in recognition performance, is provided by other tones. Deutsch (1970*a*) pre-selected her subjects by presenting them with two tones which were either of the same pitch or different by a semitone and which were separated by six seconds. Only those who scored perfectly in judging the relationship between the two tones in this task were used for the main experiment which studied the effect of interpolating eight tones in the six-second gap between the two test tones. The subjects were simply asked to make a 'same' or 'different' judgement between the two test tones; they were also instructed to ignore the eight interpolated tones. Despite the seeming simplicity of the task, these subjects, who had been able to score perfectly without interpolated tones, once the interpolated tones were introduced, could not do much better than they would have done by guessing. Deutsch interpolated tones which had been chosen at random from the same octave which contained the two test tones. Had the interpolated tones been very different in pitch from the test tones the results of the experiment would probably have been quite different as some of the work discussed below indicates.

Deutsch performed several further experiments in order to elucidate the mechanisms by which the interpolated tones had so spoilt pitch memory. The possibilities she considered were that the interpolated tones were simply acting as a distraction, preventing rehearsal (listening with the mind's ear) of the first test tone; or that the first test tone entered a limited capacity general memory store and the later tones filled this, thus impairing the memory for the first tone. The last possibility considered by Deutsch was that the tones entered a store which was one specialised for pitch. Using the same basic paradigm, Deutsch (1970*b*) was able to conclude that this last possibility was, in fact, the case.

In further experiments (1972; 1973; 1975), Deutsch showed that the specialised memory store for pitch had considerable internal organisation. Deutsch and Feroe (1975) gathered these findings together by suggesting a model for pitch memory which posits that pitch memory is the function of an array, the elements of which are activated by notes of a particular pitch; the distance between the elements of the array being proportional to the distance between the log frequencies of their corresponding notes. The model also proposes that the elements are arranged as a recurrent lateral inhibitory network, a term borrowed from neurophysiology (see Ratliff, 1965).

One of the implications of such a model is that if a tone which inhibits memory for another tone is itself inhibited then its ability to inhibit the tone should be impaired. Deutsch and Feroe tested this possibility with Deutsch's usual paradigm for this type of work. Using the result of the 1972 experiment they kept the second note of the intervening sequence always at 2/3 tone from the test note (which relation had been found to interfere maximally) and altered the pitch of the fourth note of the intervening sequence to affect in turn to a greater or lesser degree the second note. The more the second note was inhibited the less it disturbed memory of the test tone.

With this series of experiments Deutsch has shown that there is a highly organised specific memory for pitch. Some of the properties of the organisation of the system have also been discovered. Deutsch has investigated the perception of intervals, chords and other higher level attributes of music which may be logically abstracted from pitch; for a summary of this work see Deutsch (1977). It should be remembered whilst considering Deutsch's work on pitch memory that it has used a paradigm in which the context of the test tones is formed by other tones which are often selected randomly from a population which is not very close in frequency to the test tones. If pitch is embedded in more organised material this may affect memory. Deutsch has indeed demonstrated this point in her experiments on interference.

Other, arguably more musically relevant, contexts for tones than those used by Deutsch are possible. Long (1977) has investigated memory for pitch by embedding pitch in melody. She reports a study investigating the effects of: melody length and contour; tonal structure; and music perception ability on memory for certain pitches embedded in short melodies. The melodies used were of three lengths, 7, 9 and 11 tones and of two contours, M-shape and V-shape. As we shall see when discussing the work of Dowling and others below, the contour (shape) of a melody, without regard to the interval sizes (simply their direction) has psychological properties of its own. Two tonal structures were used, tonal and atonal. Subjects, who were from three groups differing in music perception ability, measured by a test developed by Taylor (an account of which may be found in Chapter 5) were given 24 trials each consisting of a melody, an interval and a test tone. The task was to decide if the test tone was the same as one which had occurred in the melody. In the 12 trials for which the correct answer was 'yes' the test tone had the same pitch as the tone adjacent to the centre tone of the melody (either side was always made the same). In fact subjects were asked to respond on a six-point scale from 'very sure yes' to 'very sure no'. Long obtained from this experiment evidence that tonality aids memory for pitches as does (predictably) music perception ability. Three other effects also emerged reasonably strongly from her study: the length of the melody affected the memorability of pitches, 15 pitch melodies giving poorer results than 7 or 11; there was an interaction between contour and tonality such that for tonal melodies the M-shaped melodies provided better pitch recognition than the V-shaped ones; finally, the musically more skilled students were able to do better than the unskilled when provided with atonal melodies.

Whereas Deutsch's studies dealt with randomly chosen extra tones, Long used computer-generated melodies. Long's results point to the view that her subjects were tending to code the pitches for remembering at a higher cognitive level; thus higher musical ability (meaning, one supposes, greater skill at coding notes into melodies or groups of some kind) led to increased memory for pitches as did tonality, perhaps acting as a kind of ready-made code. Further, the musically more skilled were better able to deal with atonality in respect of the task of remembering pitches. It seems that in thinking about pitch memory we need to know whether the subject perceives notes or melodies, a factor likely to be influenced by, amongst other things, simply altering the experimental instructions.

More evidence for the importance of coding of a string of notes for recall of their individual pitches comes from Deutsch (1978*b*).

Using the familiar paradigm she took the randomly chosen notes from a major scale as her interpolated sequences and found that those sequences composed of intervals of smaller size are more accurately and easily processed – thus, she concluded, providing a more effective framework of pitch relationships to which the test tones can be anchored. It seems probable, from this evidence, that memory for pitch occurs via a specialised system which is organised in various ways, one mode of organisation being the ability to code the pitch and its context into a more complex level from which it may later be extracted.

Though these experiments, as do those on melody (below), enable us to form a clearer picture of memory processes in people in general, they are not concerned with individual differences; in this they are typical of much experimental work in the areas of perception and memory. They are, however, important in helping to provide us with a picture of the mechanisms involved in normal pitch memory. The experiments suggest that the results of pitch memory tests may be affected by the context in which the pitches are presented but they also raise a far more general point. To what extent are pitch memory tests relevant to musical ability? The experiments discussed suggest that pitch memory is normally a function of memory for the context in which the pitches are embedded. Further evidence of relevance to this point appears in the following section on memory for melody.

Memory for melody

Some of the work on the perception and remembering of melody regards melody as a collection of intervals whilst other work insists on a view of melody as a cogent unit of analysis having an independent cognitive existence of its own. Melody is a term interpreted very liberally in the psychological literature, stretching from short computer-produced sequences of tones up to well-known folk-tunes. This practice has led to difficulties in interpreting experiments, a point to which we shall have to return.

Dowling and Fujitani (1971) performed two experiments in an attempt to understand the role of melodic contour in memory for melodies. We have met the concept of melodic contour in Long's paper; she distinguished V-shape from M-shape melodies. The idea may be extended to any shape melody. Dowling and Fujitani worked on the idea that if contour was preserved, but interval size was not, then a test melody would be more likely to be recognised as the same as a standard melody than if contour were also altered. They used five-note melodies which were played at the rate of six notes per second. The stimuli were generated by a computer which was programmed to cause successive notes to rise or fall (randomly decided) a semitone (probability 0·50) or two or three semitones (probability of either = 0·25). The initial note for the standard melodies was always middle C (262 Hz). The tones consisted, for a change, of saw-tooth waves, but this does not raise any new matter of principle beyond those discussed for sine waves. (Saw-tooth waves appear on an oscilloscope as sharp-edged, as their name implies, in contrast to the smooth curves of sine waves. Aurally they have a 'rougher' sound.) These details of the stimuli are presented in the hope that the reader may be able to imagine (or reproduce) the type of stimuli used. They are very different from the folksongs used in the second experiment of this paper. The experimental paradigm was simple. Subjects listened to a standard melody, there was a two-second pause and then they heard a comparison melody to which they had to respond on a four-point scale from 'sure same' to 'sure different'. There were three groups of subjects two of whom were asked to use 'same' as meaning just that and another asked to use the word to mean same contour. By giving the groups suitable stimuli, two types in each case, taken from same melodies, same contour melodies and different melodies, Dowling and Fujitani were able to conclude that subjects used different bases for recognition depending on whether or not the comparison melody was transposed from the standard. For untransposed tasks subjects mainly used recognition of pitches, for transposed tasks they mainly used contour. It is interesting to note that in this experiment musical training seemed to bestow no particular advantage on subjects. Dowling and Fujitani's second experiment tested the recognition of distorted versions of familiar folktunes with the same rhythms, played on a soprano recorder. Again, melodic contour was found to be an important element in melody recognition but exact interval sizes were far more important with these tunes than they had been for the computer-generated tunes in the first experiment. This may be, Dowling and Fujitani suggest, because memory for exact interval sizes may depend on extensive learning which existed in the case of the familiar folktunes but not with the computer-generated stimuli; or it may be that the folktunes had in them a far greater range of intervals than the first experiment stimuli, which fact eased discrimination between them.

The view of Dowling and Fujitani that listeners had good long-term memory for absolute interval size when using familiar melodies has been challenged by Davies and Jennings (1977) and Davies and Yelland (1977). Dowling and Fujitani used a recognition paradigm in which interval magnitudes were manipulated and in which recognition was changed. Davies *et al.* point out that it is logically possible but not logically necessary that the manipulation has caused the change. It is only necessary that the method used by the subject to perform the recognition task be compatible with the experimenter's manipulations. Davies *et al.* present an alternative view by means of two experiments.

Davies and Jennings (1977) asked (professional) musicians and non-musicians to draw contours of well-known tunes as well as to estimate the size of the intervals involved from memory. Neither musicians nor non-musicians made accurate interval size estimates although they all knew the tunes, shown by the fact that they could recognise them at the end of the experiments. Thus, the experimenters conclude, people can remember tunes, without necessarily remembering intervals. They go on to hypothesise that subjects compare external tones to an internal representation of a tune. Davies and Yelland (1977) emphasised the conclusion of the last experiment by playing subjects statistically composed tunes which they were asked to remember and then, after a short pause, the subjects were asked to draw a rising and falling line to represent the contour of the tune from memory. The subjects were then split into three groups. The first group spent 15 minutes filling in an irrelevant questionnaire; the second group were asked to draw contours of further tunes as they were played, they were also informed of how well they were doing; the third group selected tunes they thought they knew from a list of titles provided. They were asked simply to think of the tune and draw its contour (they heard nothing), this group were also given feedback. Only this third group improved, a result which Davies and Yelland interpret as indicating that training subjects to think about tunes, i.e. forming internal representations of them, improves their ability to remember them.

There is further evidence that people remember melodies independently of their constituent intervals. Dowling (1971) has investigated the perceptions of the inversions of melodies. His aim, apart from discovering more about the cognitive processes involved, was to establish whether and to what extent inversions of melodies are truly perceived as being related to the original form and to what extent they are simply an empty formalism, mere padding, rather than material lending itself to cognitive processing. He played sets of two five-note melodies (at the rate of 5 tones/sec) to subjects; the first melody was the standard which was followed after a 2-second pause by the comparison melody. The comparison melodies were of various kinds: exact repetitions or inversions; contour preserving (but not exact) repetitions or their inversions or completely different melodies. Dowling was able to conclude that the recognition of exact repetitions and inversions seems to be mainly on the grounds of contour, the exact intervals adding nothing to memory performance in the case of inversions and very little in the case of repetitions. The inversions were certainly recognised at a level better than chance. Because intervals can be recognised about equally well whether inverted or not and also, as Dowling found, contours cannot as easily suffer inversion; he further concluded that the processing of melodic contours and intervals by listeners are different processes. Larsen (1973) worked on the development of the ability to recognise inversions; his work is discussed in Chapter 9.

Cuddy and Cohen (1976) also reached a conclusion which refutes a simple interval view of melody perception. They dealt with material as simple as the three notes of a triad; the triad, they conclude, is a higher order structure which is not merely the sum of the component intervals.

Both Dowling (1978) and Davies (1979) have recently re-stated and developed their views on memory for melody. Dowling has presented a theory in which scale and contour act as two separate components of memory for melody, the overlearned scale acting as a ladder or framework on which the contour is hung. The evidence for the theory comes from a consideration of experiments on short-term and long-term memory using tonal and atonal, familiar and unfamiliar melodies. Dowling posits a 'three-valued dimension of quasi-linguistic marking'. He holds that it is plausible to character-ise the memory storage of the pitch material of a melody as a combination of independently remembered scale and contour, including a specification of the starting pitch level in the mode and the marking of skips and leaps of more than one step in the contour. Dowling argues for the relative efficiency of this method. Even from this very abbreviated account of Dowling's paper it should be clear that he sticks to an atomistic approach to the understanding of melody and to work using the recognition paradigm. Davies (1979) attacks both of these aspects of Dowling's work and believes that the use of the recognition paradigm is largely responsible for what he sees as the artifactual finding that, for familiar melodies, exact interval sizes are remembered. Davies holds that the reproduction of the exact interval sizes caused reproduction of the salient tonal configurations which resulted in the tune being, or not being, recognised as a whole. Davies reiterates a view of melody which has been held by many authors – that melody is not a property of tones as such but rather a function of the listener's ability to code or chunk tones, i.e. to cognitively process them. This view makes the distinction between a melody and a computer-generated tonal sequence crucial because we should expect them possibly to be processed quite differently.

In a sense those results are a pity. If memory for melodies had been clearly and unequivocally reducible to that for intervals, then one would have hoped that ultimately memory for melody may have fitted onto the kind of system Deutsch has suggested for connecting the primary pitch array to a specific interval array and then to a general interval array (Deutsch, 1977). The final answer to what the system of memory for melody looks like will have to be even more complex than that.

One clue as to the nature of memory for melody comes from research on the closely related topic of perception. A possible model for melody perception is that of a system of hierarchical rules similar to current models of language, with a melody being regarded as analagous to a sentence. Such a model would indicate, from the analogy with research using verbal material, that particular basic materials would be stored in the memory together with a set of rules for their combination. Evidence for this linguistic view of melody perception in particular, and music perception in general, comes from many sources. If this view were ultimately regarded as a valid one, subtests of pitch perception, for example, would seem of restricted interest – rather like testing reading ability by measuring phoneme recognition. The remainder of this chapter is concerned with developing the notion of a linguistic model of music perception. Such a model is useful, both as a device for bringing order into evidence from disparate sources as well as in providing us with a way of regarding the testing of musical ability.

Longuet-Higgins (1976) has developed a series of hierarchically arranged rules based on those of musical grammar which enables a computer to write down in the equivalent of musical notation a tune played on a keyboard. The computer program does not simply produce some written account of the notes but produces a grammatically sensible one which generally does not, for example, make blunders in the notation of enharmonics. The program, in fact, is able to 'perceive' music and make similar sense of it as would a musically literate person, thus providing a model of how people perceive melodies which is translatable into the terms of cognitive psychology. This work has been developed by Steedman (1977) who has produced a program intended to act like a human listener in perceiving metre in melody. Simon (1968) has developed another computer program using principles of the same kind which does, to some extent, the reverse task. His program, called LISTENER, extracts patterns from a musical score using an analogy of 'deep-structure' in psycholinguistics. The program is able to announce the key of the group, and using the written rhythm, detect hierarchical phase-structure. Sundberg and Lindblom (1976) were able to describe the style of Swedish nursery tunes in terms of a generative rule system as well as produce grammatically sensible melodic variants on a Swedish folksong.

So far the work mentioned has involved computers rather than people and the reader who is aware of the problems involved in using psycholinguistic theory to explain human language processes (see, for example, Broadbent, 1973) may well fear that the work may be difficult to relate to human musical perception. Sloboda (1977) has provided a clear indication that this need not be the case. He distinguishes between physical and structural markers in language and music. Physical markers are events such as spaces between written (rather than spoken) words. One could reasonably successfully define written words by the spaces between them with no recourse to their meaning or structure. Written syllables on the other hand may only be separated by one who knows (maybe implicitly only) the rules of word construction. A marker which divided syllables would be an example of a structural marker. By taking hymn-like tunes with their clear rhythms and frequent cadences, Sloboda was able to construct four types of stimuli; (*a*) the tunes unaltered with both physical and structural markers coinciding: (*b*) the tunes rhythmically unaltered but with the harmonies not fitting the usual rules, these tunes had physical markers only; (*c*) the tunes harmonically normal but with all gaps closed, these tunes had structural markers only, and (*d*) the tunes with the harmonies not fitting the rules and gaps closed, in which form they had neither physical nor structural markers. Sloboda's procedure was to ask skilled music readers (who had been told what was to occur) to sight-read a short piece which was at some point going to vanish (the piece was projected onto a screen and thus could be simply switched off). His measure was of the eye-hand span, the distance between the note playing at switch-off and that at which playing stopped. Sloboda instructed his subjects not to guess. For experienced sight-readers both physical and structural markers affected the eye-hand span but the increase in the coincidence of the end of the span with structural markers was 27·8 per cent against only 16 per cent for physical markers. Sloboda concludes that the fact that structural markers are used suggests analogies between music and language processing. Certainly these studies taken together point to the possibility of understanding the perception of and the memory for melodies in terms akin to 'deep-structure'. This view of melody would fail, however, when the 'rules' of musical grammar were broken. Whereas this is not permitted in language – nonsense is the result – in music it is. Even the most conservative listener will surely have to allow that not *all* music written with other than diatonic harmony is nonsense. It may well be possible to program the idea of a tone-row for serial music but beyond that the notation of a set of rules becomes less feasible. The implications of this view for composition are profound.

Rhythm as a grouping or chunking principle within melody was, as we have seen, used by Sloboda. Dowling (1973) investigated directly the use of rhythm in this way and found that rhythmic grouping of input determines subjective chunking and memory storage as tested by the facilitation of the recognition of items grouped in the same way. Dowling points out several parallels between his findings and similar ones with verbal material.

Verbal material may be coded in memory in several ways, one of which is semantic coding. Delis, Fleer and Kerr (1978) have demonstrated that coding for meaning can also help in recognition memory for passages of music. They played each subject six from a pool of twenty unfamiliar pieces from the nineteenth- and twentieth-century orchestral repertoire. Each piece lasted for one minute and was accompanied by a false title. The titles were of two kinds, the very abstract (e.g. 'Rebirth of Justice') and the very concrete (e.g. 'Winter Forest'). Subjects were instructed to read the title, listen to the passage and mentally visualise those things to which the title referred which could be related to the sounds of the music. The images generated by the passages were then described by the subjects and rated on a vividness of imagery scale. Once a subject had completed the imagery descriptions for all of the six passages he or she was told, for the first time, of the second part of the experiment. This comprised listening to 24 five-second passages of music, 12 of which came from the 6 previously heard pieces (2 from each piece) and 12 from other similar unfamiliar music. The task for the subject was to say whether or not he had heard the music amongst the passages played in the first part of the experiment. Delis *et al*. were able to demonstrate that the concrete titles induced higher vividness of images ratings and that those titles also resulted in superior recognition. There is, then, evidence that experimentally attaching designative meaning to music may result in a similar enhancement to recognition memory performance as results when meaning is similarly attached to verbal and visual material.

The evidence presented in this section indicates that when pitches and intervals are sounded in a series then the result may be a new entity with its own rules for being perceived and remembered. Several pieces of research indicate that these rules have similarities with some of those suggested by psycholinguists to account for the generation of and the perception of language. Indeed Sloboda (1978) has extended the analogy by arguing strongly for the usefulness of studying the development of and the processes underlying music reading for our greater understanding of the psychology of music.

So far in our analogy between music and language we have considered syntactic parallels. Delis, Fleer and Kerr's evidence, however, suggests a possible semantic parallel. Work on the meaning of music has, in fact, been carried out in experimental psychology for about a century. It is to this area of work we now turn.

Meaning and music

Musicians, philosophers and psychologists have generally agreed that meaning, in art in general and music in particular, may be of two main types. These types of meaning have received many labels, e.g. embodied and designative (Meyer, 1967) and refer, respectively, to that meaning which is perceived in the manipulation of the materials of the art, understood as being for its own sake and that meaning which is perceived as referring to the world outside of the work of art. A painting may be seen as the relationships between shapes and light and dark or as a picture of a shepherd with his sheep; a piece of music may be heard as the relationship between harmonies or as referring to yearning and misery. The strength of the distinction between the two kinds of meaning has recently been emphasised and given a physiological underpinning by Gardner *et al.* (1977) who have investigated the effects of various brain lesions on musical denotation and connotation. They have concluded that there is a behavioural and neurological dissociation between the two forms of musical sensitivity and thus, one supposes, between the two kinds of perceived meaning. The study of the first type of meaning has in general been undertaken by musicologists, that of the second by psychologists. From now on when meaning is referred to in this chapter, it should be taken to mean the second, designative or connative, type of meaning.

One of the attributes of meaning in this sense is that it may be investigated verbally and most psychological studies of music and meaning have attempted to make subjects associate pieces of music with adjectives. Some of the basic work in this area was done considerably earlier than that in the other areas discussed so that we begin around 1930.

Hevner, in a series of papers (1935*a*; 1935*b*; 1936), whilst not the first worker in the field was the most thorough up to that time, being particularly aware of methodological niceties. She drew attention to the importance of very carefully defining the concept of music in any attempt to connect it with meaning. Heinlein (1928), using chords, had found little differential effects of the major and minor modes on conveyed mood. Hevner drew attention to the importance of close definition of the stimuli used, and found (1935*a*) that the effects of the major and minor modes in music were approximately those historically and generally supposed: broadly that the minor would convey sadness and the major happiness.

Hevner's method was one she used successfully to investigate the effects of several attributes of music in separate investigations. Ten musical compositions, dance movements and similar pieces were used, the essential point being that each one constituted a complete musical idea. Some were originally in minor keys and some in major. They were all re-composed in the other modality from which they started, making as few changes as possible (other than modality) in the process of re-composition. The original and re-written compositions were played on the piano to subjects (no subject hearing any one composition in both its forms) who were asked to tick those adjectives from a list which seemed appropriate to the music. The result was that the adjectives ticked for the two different forms of each piece were those which would have been expected from the major = happy, minor = sad hypothesis. Hevner further analysed her data in two ways. By using the results of tests given to her subjects, she was able to conclude that musical training was of more importance than either musical ability (measured by the Seashore tests) or intelligence in leading to discriminating the characteristics of the two modes. More surprisingly, low scorers on all three, training, intelligence and musical ability, were able to discriminate the accepted meanings for the modes. The second additional analysis was to list the ten compositions in the order of size of perceived differences of meaning between the two forms and then to examine their musical characteristics. Comparison of the first five with the second five pieces showed that those compositions whose difference in mode made a great difference to their perceived meaning had a greater proportion of strong beats carrying the third of the scale as well as a simpler structure; they modulated hardly at all. The accepted effect of modality holds good then for real music as distinct from separate chords but only very clearly as long as the music remains very simple. The effect of the attributes of music on perceived meaning will be found to be the result of many interactions. However, to begin to understand these, it is useful, initially, to approach the problem atomistically.

Using her technique of re-composition of the attribute under study. Hevner was able to isolate the effects of modality, pitch, tempo, rhythm, harmony and direction of melodic line. Her main findings were that tempo and pitch had the most widespread and profound influence on the perceived meaning of music. Slow tempo reliably conveys dignity and calm serenity whilst fast tempo conveys meanings from the happy-gay and exciting-restless groups of adjectives; high pitch conveys sprightly-humorousness whilst low pitch causes sad, vigorous-majestic and dignified-serious perceptions. Next in effect come modality, harmony and rhythm. Modality, in more detail than described above, conveys sadness, dreaminess and sentimentality for the minor and happiness, merriness and playfulness for the major. Firm rhythms were found to convey vigour and dignity whilst flowing ones conveyed happiness, gracefulness and dreaminess. Complex, dissonant harmonies were perceived as conveying excitement and agitation whilst simple, consonant harmonies conveyed happiness, gracefulness, serenity and lyricism. Interestingly the direction of the melodic line, varied by inverting the melody, was found by Hevner's method to convey nothing very much at all.

Together with subsequent workers in this field, Hevner is very keen to disclaim belief in music being simply a system of rigid symbols, indeed in her view the flexibility due to interactions and ambiguity, far from being imperfections in musical language, have importance as sources of aesthetic enjoyment.

Modification to some details of Hevner's methods have been suggested (Farnsworth, 1954) but her broad conclusions have remained unshaken by later work.

Before discussing contemporary work mention should be made of that of Gundlach (1935) as one of the earliest users of factor-analytic methods in this field as well as Watson (1942) whose work has especial relevance for music testing.

Gundlach undertook a three-part investigation in which he attempted firstly to determine the consistency and uniformity with which people are able to report the characteristics of a piece; secondly to analyse the musical mechanisms of the piece which may have been partly responsible for its perceived mood and thirdly to analyse the interrelations of the various adjectives used to describe the music excerpts. These excerpts were the first few bars, a simple musical phrase, from gramophone recordings. The scores of the pieces were analysed (by Gundlach and an expert) and allocated ratings for various attributes such as loudness, tempo, range of melodic line, etc. Like Hevner, he found fairly reliable characteristics of each piece of music and, again similarly to Hevner, found speed the most important attribute for distinguishing between his adjectives. After speed came rhythm. Following Hevner's finding that direction of melodic line was not important in conveying mood, Gundlach found that the range of the melodic line was similarly unimportant. Gundlach was able to provide some basic 'formulae' for meaning (recall here Hevner's disclaimers): 'exalted' is loud and slow, 'brilliant' is fast with plenty of fifths and so on. He also factor-analysed the adjectives which he had used and obtained four factors. Unfortunately the methods of factor-analysis used in 1935 did not give a very excellent approximation to a simple solution, (i.e. loadings on a factor ideally all being near ±1 or near 0). However, Gundlach's factor matrix enables one to pick out a bipolar first factor: animated, glad, brilliant versus dignified, tranquil, sombre; a second factor: delicate, sentimental versus (weakly) awkward, grotesque. Gundlach also attempts to name the third factor but this seems now to have been optimistic. Very instructively, Gundlach provides correlations between the factors and attributes of the stimulus music. The first factor correlated with fast tempo, smooth rhythm and loudness and the second with wide melodic range, high pitch and a good representation of thirds, fourths and fifths.

Watson (1942) provided an account of a major study of the relationship of music and meaning. The basis of his work was the development and standardisation of a test of ability to discriminate between musical meanings. The basis of the standardisation was the judgement of twenty expert musicians. Watson was able to conclude that certain types of music can be consistently classified by musicians into at least fifteen different categories of meaning, each of which is represented by definite musical characteristics. Further, the interrelation of the different meanings was consistent with the nature of their musical characteristics. The musical meanings were found not to be determined by a few isolated factors but by constant patterns of the entire array of musical attributes. Using his test, Watson was able to investigate the perceived meanings of music by sixth-, eighth-, tenth- and twelfth-grade children as well as of college and graduate students. There was a consistency found across all ages between musical meanings and the musical attributes which represent them; this consistency applied to the interrelationship of the musical meanings as well. Watson also discovered that there was a consistent growth towards the experts' norms in his subjects' ability to discriminate between musical meanings. Like Hevner,

Watson found that this ability was not closely related to intelligence test scores nor to scores on the Seashore tests. It was related to musical enjoyment.

The work of Hevner, Gundlach and Watson (as well as that of other early workers in this field) can leave us in little doubt about the existence of a language of music which may be primitive and incomplete but which is basic to our comprehension of music. The function of melody in this language remains a problem.

Wedin, in a series of papers (1969; 1972*a*; 1972*b*), has taken up the work just described and using very careful method and measurement has been able to broadly confirm the earlier results. Using factor analysis and unipolar rating scales (1 to 10), Wedin (1969) has identified three factors that represent the dimensional structure of emotional expression in music. The first, bipolar, factor Wedin describes as pleasing relaxation versus violent agitation, the second bipolar factor is gaiety-gloom and the third, unipolar, is solemn dignity. Wedin suggests that the first factor is concerned with motion (tempo and rhythm) and the second with stress and tension (harmony). In a later (1972*a*) study, Wedin found good agreement with these results using a non-metric method of analysis. Wedin (1972*b*) has also attempted to correlate musical attributes with perceived meaning, reaching conclusions which are compatible with Hevner's. These studies are valuable for several methodological reasons, particularly in that they study all attributes of the music simultaneously with short gramophone extracts as distinct from Hevner's one attribute at a time on the piano. Wedin's method of dealing with melody was to distinguish the 'melodious-singable' from the 'unmelodious'. This approach to measuring melody did not cause it to have a very strong influence on any factor although under certain circumstances it had some influence on the second and third factors.

Imberty (1970; 1971; 1976) has attempted to investigate a deeper and more complex stratum of meaning than the other researchers by the use of multifactorial methods. He has been particularly at pains to avoid a totally structured approach to eliciting responses to music from subjects and is critical of other workers in the area who have exclusively used these methods. His own approach has depended greatly, perhaps too much, on a restricted selection from the piano music of one composer, Debussy, and he is willing to interpret subjects' responses more freely than are others in the field. Perhaps for these reasons his work stands rather to the side of the mainstream, with some of the virtues as well as the weaknesses of such a position.

A quite different approach to the problem of meaning in music was made by the musicologist Deryck Cooke (1959). His account of the relationship between music and meaning is complex and only one (but major) section of it attempts to deal with the same problems as the other work discussed here. In this section, Cooke hypothesised the existence of 'basic terms', these are short rows of notes of which Cooke identified sixteen. Considering the varied definitions of melody found in the psychological literature we may regard these basic terms as short melodies. Each of these was supposed by Cooke to have been used by different composers over many centuries to convey the same basic meaning; other aspects of the music such as rhythm, harmony, timbre, according to Cooke, are used to provide nuances in this basic meaning. For example, in the case of 1–2–3–4–5 (major) the message postulated by Cooke is one of 'an outgoing, active, assertive emotion of joy'. Cooke's method has been criticised for being unable to answer the challenge that the music had been chosen to fit the hypothesis (Zuckerkandl, 1960). The only effective answer to this point would be a predetermined sampling procedure or a direct empirical approach. The latter course was taken by Gabriel (1978), who generated Cooke's basic terms using sine waves. Using this method hardly any support for Cooke's hypothesis could be found although a role for the contour of the basic terms was suggested in that they may have played a part in conveying the activity component of meaning (Osgood, Suci and Tannenbaum, 1957). The problem of melody, despite the efforts of several researchers, remains. It is probable that progress with this problem will not be possible until the concept of melody is more thoroughly analysed, allowing for several meanings of the word. In contrast to the other attributes of music, melody is difficult to define and measure and this may well be because it is not so basic as the other attributes discussed. Indeed, as has been suggested earlier, the perception of melody may sometimes be the conscious experience relating to a cognitive coding of other more basic attributes of music rather than being one of the attributes itself.

The evidence on music and meaning indicates that music does seem to be able to convey representational meaning and that the rules for mapping basic attributes of music onto perceived meaning are fairly well, if only broadly, established. This conclusion provides us with a further reason for supposing that one way of regarding music is as a communication system, or a language.

We have discussed some of the research which has been done concerning the perception, remembering and perceived meaning of various attributes of music. The work allows us to begin to understand the kind of cognitive processing of musical stimuli which occurs in humans. It has been concerned with the smaller elements of music as well as with 'real' music. It remains to be seen whether or not the very atomistic work will be of use to our understanding of music perception in the usual meaning of music, Cazden (1979) is among the most recent of several to question its value. It is certainly of use to our understanding of the cognitive processing of non-verbal auditory stimuli, and ultimately to our understanding of the function organisation of the brain.

From the point of view of the researcher or user of tests of musical ability, the work summarised in this chapter suggests that one useful way of construing music is as a language; that is, as a system of communication with its own syntactical and semantic rules. The research at least emphases the view that 'musical ability' is a complex hypothetical construct whose measurement would ideally take account of performance at tasks of disparate kinds, from the mechanical to the quasi linguistic.

18

Lateralisation studies

We saw in the last chapter that studying the psychology of music can offer the researcher a useful context within which to consider problems of testing and test construction. This chapter is concerned with work on gross aspects of brain function which leads us to consider the nature and trainability of musical ability. The investigation of the functioning of the brain is the task of several disciplines. The work reported here is mainly that of psychologists.

The left and right halves of the brain are approximately mirror images of one another. The outer layer of the brain, which is largely concerned with those cognitive abilities which are essentially human, is called the cerebral cortex and the left and right halves are known as (cerebral) hemispheres. The two hemispheres are connected by a large fibre bundle called the corpus callosum which, by means of its 200 million or so nerve fibres, serves to connect the cortical areas in one hemisphere with their counterparts in the other.

One of the major findings of the past twenty years or so (although it had already been adumbrated) has been that the two hemispheres have rather different responsibilities in the processing of information. Psychologists have found that the left hemisphere is generally 'dominant' for the processing of verbal information but not necessarily so for the processing of non-verbal information such as music. One has to say 'generally' because all of the results discussed here apply mainly to right-handed people. Left-handed people sometimes have a different locus of function in the brain (Knox and Boone, 1970). Further, the concept of left- and right-handedness is complex (Rigal, 1974) but it will be sufficient for our purposes to point out that, whereas some left-handers simply have reversed dominance, others have a more complex distribution of function. Therefore, unless the left-handedness is itself the subject of study, researchers use right-handers for their general statements.

Several techniques have been used for the investigation of cerebral dominance, including the study of patients with surgically separated cerebral hemispheres (Sperry, 1974; Scheid and Eccles, 1975; Levi-Agresti and Sperry, 1968). Dichotic listening has been the most frequently used technique in musical studies, the paradigm for this being originally used for verbal material (Broadbent, 1954). A typical experiment involves the presentation of a set of digits through headphones to one ear whilst presenting another set of digits simultaneously to the other ear. For example, the left ear may receive 725 whilst the right ear receives 468. These stimuli are categorised as verbal since they involve the names of numbers. The task for the listener is to say what he heard. A score corresponding to the number of digits reported correctly is assigned to the ear to which the digits were presented and the procedure is repeated perhaps more than thirty times until a total score, out of 100 or so, is the maximum possible for each ear. In this type of experiment performed on right-handed people it has repeatedly been found (Kimura, 1967) that the right ear does better. Because it is believed that the major connections between ear and brain are to the opposite side (contralateral rather than ipsilateral) it is deduced from these experiments that *under the condition of hemispheric competition, which they create*, the left hemisphere is dominant for verbal material.

Kimura (1964) presented a group of normal, right-handed subjects with a task such as that described above and, on a different day, an anologous musical task. From recordings of concerti by Mozart, Telemann, Vivaldi, Bach and Antonini, Kimura took excerpts from solo passages which were mainly of woodwind but occasionally of string instruments. Eighty of these excerpts were recorded and classified into twenty sets of four. Within each set of four, the same instrument was used and Kimura attempted to make the pitch-range and tempo as similar as possible leaving the melody to provide the main cue as to difference. Each excerpt was then trimmed to be of four seconds' duration. Kimura presented two of each set of four melodies dichotically and then after four seconds' silence the four melodies were played one after the other. The listener's task was to say which ('first and third', 'third and fourth', etc) were the two which had just been presented dichotically. Thus each ear was given a score for receiving a recognised melody. Left-ear and right-ear scores were respectively 90 per cent and 94 per cent for the digits but 75 per cent and 63 per cent for the melodies. Thus the right ear (left hemisphere) was superior for digits but the left ear (right hemisphere) was superior for melodies. Both of the differences between ears were statistically significant. By looking at individual listeners' scores the results stand out even more clearly: 3, 2 and 15 were the figures for left-ear superiority, no difference and right-ear superiority respectively for digits, whilst the corresponding figures for melodies were 16, 2 and 2. Whilst the differences between 90 per cent and 94 per cent and 75 per cent and 63 per cent are clear and statistically significant they are not overwhelming. Laterality of function does not seem from these figures to be an all or nothing effect. It can, however, be strengthened by changing the conditions of the experiment, making the task more difficult, for example, but even then the findings demonstrate far from complete lateralisation of function and we shall need to consider the implications of this later.

Many other researchers have since demonstrated left-ear superiority with non-verbal material in dichotic tasks. King and Kimura (1972) attempted to establish if the effect was caused by music as such or whether it would also exist for other non-verbal sounds. They made a dichotic tape of laughing, crying, sneezing, moaning, coughing and sighing. Using right-handed college students as subjects they found that left-ear and right-ear scores were respectively 79 per cent and 73 per cent, hummed melodies giving them scores of 78 per cent and 66 per cent. Both of these results were statistically significant.

Evidence of another type for the greater involvement of the right hemisphere in the processing of musical information has come from McKee *et al.* (1973). They used the technique of electroencephalography (EEG) to measure the brain waves of subjects whilst they were involved in linguistic and musical tasks. EEGs are the records of the electrical activity of the brain. Typical patterns, corresponding to types of activity or state, may be obtained from various sites. The EEG is recorded from electrodes fixed to the appropriate points on the scalp which are able to pick up the electrical currents in the brain from that distance. The type of brain wave they studied was the alpha-wave whose existence is usually interpreted to mean relaxation (but not drowsiness) and little mental activity. They took the waves from temporal-parietal sites which are greatly involved in hearing. The index recorded was the ratio of left to right alpha activity (normally less than one from these sites regardless of task). The tasks were all such as to encourage analytic perception: spotting particular words or parts of speech in readings or a particular two-bar phrase in an unfamiliar Bach concerto. There were three linguistic tasks which were graded for difficulty. The left to right ratios for alpha activity were found to be 0·913 for the musical task and 0·862, 0·808 and 0·801 for the three linguistic tasks in the order easiest to hardest. All of these differences are in the direction of supporting the view that the linguistic tasks are processed in the left hemisphere and musical ones in the right.

The studies presented so far indicate a reasonably clear picture. However, it soon became apparent that the situation was more complex. One of the earlier papers to indicate this was that by Gordon (1970). The study by Gordon produced a great deal of discussion and is perhaps of particular interest to musicians and musical educators. Gordon presented dichotic digit and melody tests (as had Kimura) as well as a chord test; his subjects were right-handed performing musicians and of superior intelligence. Each chord comprised four notes, the tonic triad with either the 7th or the octave. He found no significant difference between ears for either digits or melodies although he did find significant left-ear superiority for chords (scores of 71 per cent and 63 per cent). Two differences between this and previous studies are apparent, firstly the subjects were practising musicians and secondly chords are a more analytic component of music than melodies.

Bever and Chiarello (1974) provided evidence which seemed able to resolve the paradox between Gordon's results and those of previous authors with respect to melodies. These authors started with the view that the left hemisphere of the brain is largely concerned with analytic and serial processing of incoming information whilst the right hemisphere processes holistic and synthetic relations. If this is the case, Bever and Chiarello point out, it must be that melodies are treated by most subjects as a Gestalt, a whole un-analysed experience. As Dowling (1971) and many others have indicated, musically naive listeners do hear melodies in a holistic manner. Bever and Chiarello decided to compare the abilities of musically naive and musically trained listeners at hearing melodies analytically and holistically, taking note in both groups of the effects of using only the left or only the right ear. The listeners for the experiment had, in the naive group, less than three years of music lessons which had taken place at least five years before the experiment; the experienced group were not professional musicians but had all had at least four years of music lessons and were currently playing or singing. The task was to listen to a stimulus tone sequence and, after a two-second pause, a two-note excerpt. The listener was asked to say whether the excerpt was from the sequence and also whether the sequence had occurred in a previous trial – thus the listener's ability to remember analytically and holistically was tested. There were two sets of 36 trials each, the sequences were 12 to 18 notes long.

As expected, naive listeners failed on the excerpt recognition task whichever ear they used; they heard holistically. They did significantly better using the left ear (right hemisphere) on the sequence recognition task. The experienced listeners did fairly but more or less equally well with either ear on the excerpt recognition task. On the sequence recognition task they did better, in contrast to the naive listeners with their right ear. Most of this difference stems from their greatly superior right-ear performance: their left-ear performance was inferior but only slightly so. Thus Bever and Chiarello seemed at the time to have largely resolved the conflict between Gordon's and previous work.

Taken at its face value, Bever and Chiarello's experiment would suggest that the acquisition of musical ability involves major changes in cerebral organisation. But, as we shall see below when discussing the paper by Gaede *et al*. (1978), the musically experienced tend to be those who score reasonably well on a test of musical ability. Thus, in separating the musically experienced from the inexperienced, Bever and Chiarello were also selecting the musically able from the less able.

Support for the view of Bever and Chiarello came from Davidson and Schwartz (1977) who showed that musically sophisticated and musically naive subjects may be differentiated by the hemisphere patterning of EEGs which they display during musical and non-musical tasks. Davidson and Schwartz asked all of their subjects, the musically sophisticated and the musically naive, to list three songs for which they knew well both the tune and words. There were three experimental tasks: whistling the tune, singing the song and reciting the words in a monotone. These conditions were thus purely musical, mixed and purely verbal respectively. Taking EEG recordings from either the left and right occipital or parietal areas of the brain (only one bilateral site from any one subject) they were able to show that non-musically trained subjects show significantly greater left-hemisphere activation during reciting than during whistling. The right hemisphere did not show different amounts of activation for these subjects across the tasks. Davidson and Schwartz interpret this result as indicating that the left hemisphere is more labile and sensitive to a variety of task demands. In support of Bever and Chiarello, the authors found that musically untrained subjects showed greater left-hemisphere activation during talking and singing versus whistling whilst musically sophisticated subjects showed the reverse; i.e. greater left-hemisphere activation during whistling versus talking and singing. Different modes of cognitive processing thus seemed to be involved in the perception and recognition of music depending on the training of the person doing the perceiving.

The Bever and Chiarello result (if not the interpretation) has been supported (Johnson, 1977) and challenged (Zatorre, 1978). Johnson gave a dichotic listening task involving violin melodies to a group of musicians who showed right-ear superiority and a group of non-musicians who showed left-ear superiority. Because the left-ear scores were similar for the two groups, Johnson concludes that as musical skill increases, increasing use is made of the left hemisphere's sequential analytic mechanism. Zatorre, using rather different melodies, shorter and some constructed on different principles, found a clear left-ear advantage for recognising the melodies in both musically naive and experienced listeners. Clearly, the effects of several variables on laterality, such as the details of the stimuli (Stankov, 1980), the definition of 'naive' and 'experienced' and the instructions to subjects need to be clarified and recent work has attempted to do this. (See Chapter 5.)

As remarked above, Gaede *et al.* (1978) have noted that the variables of *musical experience* and *musical ability* are likely to be confounded; that is, those who score highly on one are far more likely to score highly on the other than would be expected purely by chance. They separated out the two variables by assigning subjects to groups according to their scores on a Bever and Chiarello type of test of musical experience and on the Drake musical memory test. The subjects were given dichotic listening tests of musical chord analysis and musical memory sequence analysis (adapted from the Wing tests 1 and 3). Low aptitude subjects showed ear differences (right hemisphere superior for chords, left for sequence analysis) but high aptitude subjects showed only small ear differences. Of great interest to the music educator is that Gaede *et al.* found that musical experience had no effect on the results, which were as true for the experienced musicians (as defined in the experiment) as for the inexperienced. This result suggests that those aspects of musical ability used in the experiment are not trainable to any great extent.

The problems of the definition of training are highlighted by an experiment of Johnson *et al.* (1977). By noting the number of errors made in recognising conventional melodies and random note sequences presented to each ear, they were able to distinguish the performance of trained musicians who were able to transcribe music from other subjects even though these other subjects were able to read music and to play instruments. The subjects trained in transcription made fewer errors with melodies in the right ear and random sequences in the left, the other subjects made fewer errors with the left ear regardless of type of stimulus.

From this recent work on dichotic listening it seems that the former distinction between the 'verbal' and the 'musical' hemisphere is untenable. Musical stimuli of various kinds seem to be processed sometimes in one, sometimes in the other, and mostly in both hemispheres. Gordon (1978) has suggested another, more tenable, functional distinction between the cerebral hemispheres: that between time-independent and time-dependent processes. Certainly the experimental evidence is less puzzling if we drop the notion that the left hemisphere is verbal and the right is musical and if we instead suppose that the left hemisphere deals more with time-dependent, sequential, input and the right with time-dependent, holistic, input. However, these new distinctions are not in themselves an answer to the problems of understanding laterality but, rather, a challenge to develop clear operational definitions of such intuitively appealing concepts as 'holistic', 'sequential', 'time-dependent' and 'time-independent'.

A different kind of evidence for lateral asymmetry of function comes from Dowling (1978), who performed an experiment on the dichotic recognition of musical canons. He varied the time delay between the start of the first and second parts, the number of notes per second, and whether the left or the right ear heard the leading part. The task for the listener was simply to say whether or not the stimulus material comprised a canon. Amongst other findings was the fact that when the right ear led, subjects followed a different strategy for remembering than when the left ear led. The right-ear strategy suggested by Dowling is that of selecting out small chunks of the lead-ear melody for short-term memory storage and later comparison with the trailing melody – the right ear being particularly good at this. So, like many other researchers, Dowling found evidence for lateral asymmetry of function in the brain but like Zatorre he could find no evidence that musicians and non-musicians succeeded better with different ears.

So far we have considered those dichotic listening studies which have used normal humans as subjects, but many studies have been done on patients with damaged brains. These give us yet another route to understanding lateralisation and its implications.

Shankweiler (1966) used Kimura's tapes and procedures described earlier in this chapter. His experiments employed as listeners patients who had epilogenetic temporal-lobe lesions[1], in some cases the lesions were on the right side and in others on the left. Most of the patients underwent an operation for temporal lobotomy which involved removal of part of the temporal lobe concerned. Patients were tested pre- and post-operatively. Preoperatively there were no significant differences in melody recognition between those patients with left and right lesions nor any significant difference between either of these and Kimura's group of normal listeners. Left temporal lobectomy caused no change in listeners' overall score whilst right temporal lobectomy resulted in a significant loss of ability to recognise melodies. Kimura (1961) had found the opposite when presenting patients with digits.

Gordon and Bogen (1974) used a technique developed by Wada in order to study the hemispheric lateralisation of singing. This is one of several studies which are valuable for studying the execution rather than the perception of music. Wada's technique involves the intracarotid injection of sodium amylobarbitone which has the effect of temporarily inactivating the hemisphere on the side of the injection. The procedure was carried out on epileptic patients as a pre-surgical investigation. The expectation from previous work was that right-hemisphere depression would mainly disturb singing rather than speaking whilst left-hemisphere depression would disturb speaking rather than singing. This was, in fact, what Gordon

---

1 These are foci of neurological disturbances which give rise to epilepsy. Lobotomy is the removal of part or all of one of the lobes of the cerebral cortex. The temporal lobes are those primarily involved in hearing.

and Bogen found, but the details of their findings are particularly instructive. Patients were asked to concentrate on the melody by singing 'la la la' rather than the words; the major deficit in singing after suppression of the right hemisphere was the production of correct pitch. Rhythm was hardly impaired by the suppression of either hemisphere and seems to be able to be produced by either hemisphere alone. The production of pitch for melody and for speech seems to be produced by different functional systems because whilst right carotid injected patients sang off-key or in a monotone their speech was inflected normally. Gordon and Bogen conclude that the left hemisphere processes items which come in small units whereas the right processes melodies because they are recalled as a whole.

A further series of experiments which have been valuable in resolving the difficulties in interpreting the lateralisation work have been concerned with the laterisation of the components of music. The first of these experiments was that by Milner (1962). She tested patients with the items of the Seashore scale, before and after unilateral temporal lobectomy, which operation they were having for the relief of epilepsy. Those patients who had the operation on the left side did not show an increase of errors post-operatively whilst those who were operated on the right side did. However, the increase of errors was not uniform over all of the Seashore items: tonal memory and timbre were affected most strongly followed by loudness and time. Neither pitch nor rhythm was affected by removal of the right temporal lobes. In the case of rhythm this will not be surprising because we have already considered the later paper by Gordon and Bogen but in the case of pitch the results are contradictory. The investigation of laterality was furthered by a study by Kallman and Corballis (1975) using a different method involving reaction times. Their stimuli were arrangements of the note A (440 Hz) played on the bassoon, viola, piano and cello. The cello was the target note and subjects were asked to press a button as soon as they heard this note. The experimenters demonstrated a left-ear advantage but only near the beginning of the experiment, no significant difference between ears occurring for later blocks of trials, thus indicating the transitory nature of at least some lateralisation effects.

Gates and Bradshaw (1977) performed a series of six experiments. The first five examined differences between ears of reaction time and accuracy scores for tasks involving the recognition of a change in one component in a musical sequence. The sixth experiment compared differences between ears for recognition of an excerpt from familiar and unfamiliar melodies. Whereas the detection of a changed note in either a single-line melody or in a five-note whole tone sequence happened with equal speed via either ear, accuracy was greater with the right ear. Rhythm changes were detected more rapidly via the left ear but more accurately via the right. The right ear was more accurate in recognising unfamiliar melodies but the left was superior for recognising familiar ones. Gates and Bradshaw use their results to challenge the view that the right hemisphere is a music hemisphere and, like Gordon, they substitute an analytic versus a holistic view.

It should not be understood from this discussion of the different roles which the cerebral hemispheres play in the perception and performance of music that one hemisphere goes its own way without reference to the other. Indeed, from the detailed results shown in this chapter, it will be noticed that the scoring for each ear is far from all or none – the 'inferior' ear often does quite well and sometimes the lateralisation effects seem only temporary (Spreen *et al.*, 1977; Spellacy, 1970; Kallman and Corballis, 1975) or change otherwise with time (Sidtis and Bryden, 1978).

The experimental designs used by psychologists have enabled them to discover tendencies and trends. For successful musical listening or performing there is clearly a working together by the two hemispheres. The experiments are constructive but to some extent artificial, this is not a criticism of them but an indication that they need to be interpreted carefully. From the point of view of the psychologist the results are of interest in themselves; from the point of view of the music educator perhaps their greatest value is the clarity with which they point out the fact that music is sumultaneously synthetic and analytic. There are two modes of perception and performance and, on the face of it, the need is to train the student not only to operate successfully in those two modes but to gain the practice (and pleasure) of frequently switching between them. Indeed Gaede *et al.* (1978) conclude that low aptitude for music may be the result of adherence to a rather rigid hemispheric strategy. Whether the ability to use the holistic and analytic strategies flexibly is a trainable one would seem, from this analysis, to be a question of major importance for music educators.

Damásio and Damásio (1977) and Wyke (1977) both provide excellent, fairly recent, accounts of work concerning musical ability and the brain for the interested reader.

Having briefly discussed the functioning of the brain with respect to musical stimuli and responses, it is of interest to think about the structure of the brain and particularly how this may affect or be affected by its musical functions.

The investigation of the neuro-anatomical localisation of brain function was for long a major occupation of psychologists and neurologists but the methodological problems which arise in the area of study have lessened interest as has the concern that the questions asked are not really meaningful. Localisation of an ability such as pitch or melody perception *may* be anatomical but is much more likely to be functional, that is, the ability may be the result of the working together of various anatomical localisations in the brain some of which may be involved in 'being' parts of other abilities when in different combinations. In the many clinical studies which show correlations between damage to a site in the brain and the impairment of an ability it cannot be concluded that the site contains the function – simply that the site is directly or indirectly involved as one of the many sites whose activity underlies the function. The difficulties in reaching firm conclusions from the brains of musicians examined post-mortem is in the small sample sizes involved as well as the fact that the brains are not working brains.

Scheid and Eccles (1975) have suggested that a particular brain structure, the planum temporale, may be implicated in musical ability. Their argument is that it is usually (in 65 per cent of cases) larger in the left (speech) hemispheres but in about 11 per cent of cases the asymmetry is reversed. There are no significant size differences in the remaining 24 per cent of cases. Speech would explain the left-side enlargement and Scheid and Eccles hypothesise that musical ability may explain right-side enlargement. The hypothesis could be tested, they suggest, by post-mortem examination of those distinguished by musical ability and those who were not. If Scheid and Eccles proved to be correct in their supposition the implications for musical education are interesting because asymmetry of the planum temporale has been shown to exist not only in infants who died at birth but also in a 29-week-old foetus (Wada (in Scheid and Eccles)). However, there is no indication that the asymmetry at such an early stage is precisely maintained to adulthood in any single individual.

For the reader who wishes to know more about the field of neuro-anatomy and musical ability Meyer (1977) and Wertheim (1977) both supply reviews of the literature.

The study of the psychology of musical ability and the study of the psychology of music overlap to a considerable extent. Knowledge of musical ability is used not only in the essentially administrative tasks of selection and assessment but also for the light it throws on human development and even on the nature of music. These last two areas are also concerns of the 'psychology of music'.

Several points have been made in the last two chapters which it is supposed may have close relevance for the study of musical ability. Music as a language is a long established analogy but the experimental evidence suggests that it may be a reasonably detailed and close one with musical equivalents of syntax and semantics. At the very least, the analogy provides a heuristic structure for research into musical ability but it also may provide an aid for defining aims and creating methods for musical education.

The research on laterality is still progressing very quickly and it would be unwise to erect great principles on such a fast-moving basis. At the moment it does seem that people process musical information both holistically and analytically and this fact provides hints for teaching method, as well as for the development and interpretation of tests of musical ability.

Conclusions

The picture we have presented reflects the current state of research. However, as noted in the first edition, research is an ever continuing process. For the efforts of researchers to be of practical benefit in education, it is vitally important that music educators should take an interest in the results and consider how they might be applied. Obviously, careful interpretation is needed and the findings of no one experiment or small area of study should be erected into a universal principle.

Of the many points discussed in this book a few broad issues stand out. On tests, we can say that aptitude tests, though far from perfect, can be helpful to the teacher and to the researcher. The original aim of the Seashore and Wing tests of identifying the talented pupil for special training and saving the ungifted from the disappointment of failure may seem rather elitist in these days. However, the fostering of talent must always remain an important aim of music education. Tests of aptitude and achievement can be useful in helping to show up the talented, but lazy, pupil who is underachieving and also in contributing to a realistic prognosis for the student whose initial efforts may lead him – or his parents – to adopt an excessively high level of aspiration. Whilst a wide range of satisfactory tests have been developed, we should, as Davies (1978) suggested, be prepared to accept that an open-minded approach is needed. Davies himself freely acknowledges that any new testing methods must take their place in the market square among existing ones. From the point of view of education, Farnsworth's (1969) suggestion that there is need to 'study more intensively the minimum level necessary for later success in the several kinds of musical skills' still warrants attention.

Much recent research has stressed the advantages of a musically rich home and educational environment in realising musical potential. However, it seems important to pay attention to what can be achieved by talent and sustained effort in spite of unfavourable circumstances. This is not just true of a few exceptionally talented persons, but also of 'ordinary' children in deprived circumstances.

The teacher can certainly expect wide differences of musical ability among the children who enter school. There is much evidence for the importance of the ages between 5 and 9 as a time when children can master basic rhythmic and melodic tasks and begin to learn some means of reading and writing music. Though teachers will wish to be alert to research that suggests ways of improving their pedagogic techniques, it is above all the skill and enthusiasm of the individual teacher, with the support of high status for music in the school, that leads to success.

Recent developments in tests and analytical techniques have tended to support the view that several factors are involved in musical ability. Certainly, most individuals find some musical tasks are easier than others. However, the various aspects of music are so intimately connected that a minimum level of competence in each one is required for both listening and performing.

The distinction between two complementary methods of construing music, the holistic and the analytic, has been made at several points. Thus, Seashore emphasised the importance of specific capacities whilst Mursell took an 'omnibus' view; in human development a grasp of melodic contour seems to develop before efficiency at processing intervals; in studies of neurological processing the holistic has been distinguished from the analytic. The view was taken that the naive adult, like the young child, was largely limited to processing music holistically.

Modern technology is enabling our daily bread to be gathered with less physical work. If the increase in leisure is to lead to 'self-actualisation' in life, music has a very great role to play. Every child, and also every adult, should have the opportunity to participate in some form of music-making and be enabled to create music. Some amateurs may feel discouraged to perform when their efforts can in no way rival the music they hear on disc, tape or radio. Some may react by improvising their own music, as many young people do already. Obviously not everyone will wish to choose music as a major leisure pursuit. What is imporatnt is that children should receive sufficient basic music education as a foundation upon which they can build later in life, if they want to do so.

Appendix I

Description of tests

Mainwaring tests of musical ability

Three tests: Pitch, Rhythm and Recall.

Details published in Brit. J. Educ. Psych. (1931), I.

Pitch a. 16 items. Two notes are played. Are they the same or different? 20 items. Which two of three or four notes are the same?

  b. Concept of 'high' or 'low'.

9 items. Do three notes go up or down?

5 items. Which of two notes is the higher?

20 items. In which pair of intervals are the two notes farther apart?

Rhythm 25 items presented with a metronome, or pencil tapping, or buzzer, or with rhythmic word groups. In each case the subject has to decide whether the metre is in twos, threes or fours.

Immediate recall 5 tunes, 4-11 notes long, are played. 10 seconds after the playing of each, various questions are asked, e.g. did the last two notes go up or down or were they the same? Was it in two, three or four beats? The ten items are repeated.

Deferred recall The subjects are asked three questions about 'God Save the King' and three on 'While Shepherds Watched'.

Reliability

  Pitch ·81 (Mainwaring); ·77 (Fieldhouse, 1937).

  Rhythm ·74 (Mainwaring); ·62 (Fieldhouse, 1937).

Madison music test

Interval Discrimination (Tonal Imagery) Test described in *Arch. Psychol.* (1942), **206**, 1-99.

Tonal imagery 36 items. Four harmonic intervals are played at different pitch levels. One of the four is always different. Which?

Reliability

·74; ·76; ·84.

Validity

  ·46–·72 (with music students); ·39–·71 (secondary school pupils). ·24–·51; median ·41 (Christy, 1956).

Lundin musical ability tests

Five tests Interval Discrimination, Melodic Transposition, Mode Discrimination, Melodic Sequences, Rhythmic Sequences.

Unpublished

Intervals 50 pairs of items. Is second interval same or different?

Melodic transposition 30 pairs of melodies. Second playing always in a different key but one or more notes may be altered. If transposed back to original key would it be the same or different?

Mode discrimination 30 pairs of chords. Are both either major or minor (same) or is one major and the other minor (different)?

Melodic sequences 30 items each with four melodic patterns. Has fourth pattern been changed?

Rhythmic sequences Similar to Melodic.

Reliability

	167 *Music* *students*	*196* *Unselected* *students*
Interval	·79	·71
Mel. trans.	·65	·71
Mode disc.	·65	·10
Mel. seq.	·70	·77
Rhythmic seq.	·60	·72
Total	·89	·85

Validity Compared with teacher's ratings on Melodic and Harmonic Dictation, written harmonisation performance and general ability in music.

	Range	Total of ratings
Intervals	·32–·66	·48
Mel. trans.	·26–·52	·45
Mode disc.	·35–·51	·49
Mel. seq.	·38–·56	·57
Rhythmic seq.	·10–·33	·26
Total	·43–·70	·69

Very significant difference found between mean scores of 60 music students and 100 unselected students for each test and for total.

Seashore measures of musical talents

1919 version

Six tests Pitch, Intensity, Consonance, Tonal Memory, Time, Rhythm (added five years later).

Reliability

	(1)		(2)	
	Range	Median	Range	Median
Pitch	·51—·84	·71	·58—·90	·77
Intensity	·50—·88	·72	·58—·94	·75
Time	·41—·81	·58	·45—·62	·56
Consonance	·30—·62	·49	·35—·68	·46
Tonal memory	·59—·94	·83	·66—·90	·77
Rhythm	·29—·68	·45	·30—·50	·45

(1) From Lundin (1967)
(2) From Farnsworth (1931), studies not included by Lundin.

Validity (compared with music grades and teacher's ratings)

	Range	Median
Pitch	·01-·60	·23
Intensity	·02-·49	·13
Time	—·14-·36	·17
Consonance	—·27-·41	·05
Tonal memory	·05-·65	·30
Rhythm	—·15-·47	·19
Total	—·15-·73	·27

1960 edition (similar to the 1939 revision)

Six tests Pitch, Loudness, Rhythm, Time, Timbre, Tonal Memory.
Ages 10 to adult.
Time to administer About one hour.
Published by The Psychological Corporation.

A more difficult form of the test, 'B' form, for use with music students was published in 1939, but has since been withdrawn.

Pitch 50 pairs of tones. Frequency differences from 17 to 2 cps. Is second tone higher or lower than the first?

Loudness 50 pairs of tones. Intensity difference from 4·0 to 0·5 decibels. Is second tone stronger or weaker than the first?

Rhythm 30 pairs of rhythmic patterns. Are they the same or different?

Time 50 pairs of tones. Duration differences from ·30 to ·05 seconds. Is second tone longer or shorter than the first?

Timbre 50 pairs of tones. Each tone made up of fundamental and first five harmonies, the intensities of third and fourth being varied. Are the two tones same or different?

Tonal memory 30 pairs of tonal sequences, 10 items each of three-, four- and five-tones. Which note is different?

Norms Percentile for each test separately, none for total score. Grades 4 to 5, 6 to 8, and adult. Based on approx. 3500 for Pitch, Rhythm and Tonal Memory (grades 4 to 5), on 2500 for Pitch, Rhythm and Tonal Memory (grades 6 to 8), much smaller numbers for the other tests for these grades (over 4,000 for all tests at adult level).

Reliability

	(From test manual)	Gordon (1969)	Fleishman (1955)	Tanner and Loess (1967)
Pitch	·82–·84	·92	·86	
Loudness	·74–·85	·85	·63	
Rhythm	·64–·69	·72	·75	·88; ·73
Time	·63–·72	·71	·73	·50; ·78
Timbre	·55–·68	·51	·79	
Tonal memory	·81–·84	·82	·88	

Validity Questionable, except for Pitch, Rhythm and Tonal Memory.

Subjects:	Pitch	Rhythm	Tonal memory	Total	
10-year olds – success at:					
violin	·33	·33	·41		(Manor, 1950)
clarinet	·09	·00	·06		
trombone	·14	·14	·15		
Music students					
'musicality'				·46	(Kyme, 1956)
performance	·13–·15	·18–·31	·14–·27	·34–·42	(Christy, 1956)
theory and					
composition	·12–·19	·19–·46	·27–·41	·34–·49	
Theory grades	·30	·15	·12		(White, 1961)
Theory grades	zero correlations with all tests and total				(Roby, 1962)
291 children (10 to 16 yrs)					
'musicality'	·11–·45	·19–·27	·36–·50		(Rainbow, 1965)

Kwalwasser – Dykema music tests

Ten tests Pitch, Quality, Intensity, Tonal Movement, Time, Rhythm, Tonal Memory, Melodic Taste, Pitch Imagery and Rhythm Imagery.

Ages 10–Adult

Time to administer One hour.

Published by Carl Fischer Inc.

Pitch 40 items. Does pitch of each tone remain the same (S) or does it rise or fall (D)?

Quality 30 items. Two notes are played twice. Is second on same (S) or different (D) instrument?

Intensity 30 pairs of tones or chords. Is second louder or softer than first?

Tonal movement 30 four-note tonal patterns requiring completion. Should a fifth tone be above or below fourth?

Time 25 items of three tones each, first and third are of equal lengths. Is the second same length as first or third or different?

Rhythm 25 pairs of rhythmic patterns from four to nine tones long. Is second (S) or (D)?

Melodic taste 10 pairs of two phrased melodies. First phrases are the same, the second different. Which second phrase makes the more appropriate ending?

Pitch imagery 25 tonal patterns in notation. Are these (S) or (D) from those played on a record?

Rhythm imagery 25 rhythmic patterns in notation. (S) or (D) from those heard on record?

Norms Percentile norms for each test and for total scores for grades 4–6, 7–9, and senior high school. Based on 'thousands of scores'.

Whybrew (1962) after Lundin	Range	Median	Holmes version (based on 237 students, aged 15–18)	
Pitch	−·05–·63	·34	Pitch	·72
Quality	·10–·66	·36	Rhythm	·71
Intensity	−·10–·60	·15	Time	·50
Tonal movement	·37–·85	·68	Intensity	·79
Time	·00–·63	·33	Quality	·70
Rhythm	·04–·48	·29	Tonal memory	·73
Tonal memory	·43–·73	·55	Tonal movement	·88
Melodic taste	·06–·61	·35	Melodic taste	·43
Pitch imagery	·14–·45	·33		
Rhythm imagery	·20–·40	·31	Total	·91

Reliability No information given in the test manual. According to independent studies much lower than comparable tests of the Seashore battery.
Validity Doubtful except for discriminating most musical from least musical of a group.

The comparisons with teachers' ratings and grades.

Whybrew (1962) after Lundin	Range	Median
Pitch	−·18–·23	·00
Quality	−·10–·21	·14
Intensity	−·11–·29	·13
Tonal movement	·00–·31	·18
Time	−·13–·27	·01
Rhythm	−·04–·31	·16
Tonal memory	·02–·45	·26
Melodic taste	−·19–·31	·01
Pitch imagery	·00–·59	·31
Rhythm imagery	·01–·46	·29

The Drake musical aptitude test

Two tests Musical Memory two equivalent forms (A) and (B), Rhythm two forms (B) more difficult than (A).
Time to administer About 20 minutes for each form of each test.
Ages Eight years to superior musical adult.
Published by Science Research Assoc.
Memory 54 items – 12 melodies each played from 2-7 times. Is each repetition same as original or has key, time or notes been altered?
Rhythm 50 items. Subject has to continue to count a beat established by a metronome, during silence till told to stop. Number recorded is compared with correct answer. In (B) form counting is done against a distracting beat.
Norms Memory percentile norms for two-yearly intervals from 7-22 for non-music students, i.e. with less than five years of musical training, based on a total of over 4300 cases; and for three-yearly intervals between 11 and 23 + for music students based on 1400 cases.
Rhythm One set for all ages, but separate for music students, based on approximately 1300 non-music students and nearly 350 music students.

Reliability

	Range	Median			
	from test manual				
Memory (A) + (B) forms	·85—·93				
Rhythm, Form A	·56—·95	·86	·64; ·90	(Tanner and	
Form B	·69—·96	·775	·37; ·88	Loess, 1967)	

Validity from manual compared with teachers' ratings

	Range	Median	
Memory	·32—·91	·55	
Rhythm			
Form A	·31—·82	·58	
Form B	·41—·83	·67	
A + B	·31—·35	·58	
Memory	·09—·50	·42	(Lundin, 1949)
	·17—·32	·24	(Christy, 1959)

Indiana-Oregon music discrimination test

One test Three versions, 43 items, 37 items and 30 items.
Ages 12 to graduate
Published by Midwest Music Tests, 1304 East University St., Bloomington, Ind.

Is first or second playing the correct version, or are both the same? If, different, has the rhythm, melody or harmony been altered?

Percentile norms by age and by grade from grade 6 to graduate. The three sets, for the 30-, 37- and 43-item versions, based on some 4500 cases from the USA and the UK.

Reliability Satisfactory from age 15.
30 items: ·45–·81; 37 items: ·66–·84; 43 items: ·82–·88
30 items: ·81 with 317 pupils aged 17 (Oakley, 1972).

Validity: See p. 23 above.

Correlations with MAT ·46, with MAP ·38, with MAT + MAP, ·49 (Utley, 1970); with MAP sensitivity tests ·28 (Gallagher, 1971).

Wing standardised tests of musical intelligence

Seven tests Chord Analysis, Pitch Change, Memory, Rhythm, Harmony, Intensity, Phrasing.
Ages Eight to adult.
Time to administer One hour.
Published by National Foundation for Educational Research.
Chord analysis 20 items. How many notes in the chord?
Pitch change 30 items. Have the two chords been repeated exactly, or has note moved up, or down?
Memory 30 pairs of tunes from three to ten notes long. Which note has been changed on the second playing?
Rhythm 14 pairs of tunes. Is second the same as the first? If different, which is the better version?
Harmony; intensity; phrasing Similar to Rhythm, except that harmonisation, intensity or phrasing may have been altered.
Norms In five grades for total scores and tests 1 to 3, from 8 to 17 (Adult); based on nearly 10,000 cases. Scores can also be converted into Musical Quotients.

Reliability

·91 (Whole test)
·89 (Tests 1-3)
·84 (Tests 4-7)
·90   (Wing, 1962)

·86 (Whole test) (Bentley, 1955)

·90 (Whole test) (subsests ·65–·85) (Buros, 1966)

·80; ·82 (Whole test)
·78; ·86; ·89 (Tests 1-3)
·28; ·42; ·50 (Tests 4-7) (Heller, 1962)
·82 (Mitchum, 1968).

Validity Good
    With teachers' ratings: ·64 to ·90 (Wing, 1948)
                           ·83   (Cain, 1960)
    Significant differences found between 'above average', 'average' and 'below average' RMSM junior musicians for 127 out of the 136 test items (Newton, 1959).
    Significant differences between actively musical and unmusical groups (Whittington, 1957).
    All members of National Youth Orchestra and all, except one, professional music students at Eastman School of Music achieved grade 'A'.

Gaston test of musicality

Interest in music 17 items
Tonal 22 items
Ages 10-18
Time to administer 40 minutes.
Published by Odells Instrumental Service, Kansas. Available from Paul Gray's Music, Inc. 926 Massachusetts, Lawrence, Ka.
Tonal items
    5 items.   Subject has to find a given note in a chord.
    5 items.   Melody of 4–8 bars answer sheet has to be compared with melody played for possible difference in note or rhythm.
    5 items.   Should final note be higher or lower than last one played?
    7 items.   Melodic memory. Each tune played from 2 to 6 times. Is each repetition same as original or has a note or rhythm been altered?

Separate percentile norms for interest and for aptitude. Separate norms for girls and for boys at Grades 4 to 8 and 9 to 12 for Interest. Separate norms for boys and for girls at five levels (Grade 4 to Grade 12) for Aptitude. Norms based on a total of nearly 6000 cases.

Reliability

From manual Grades 4–6 and 7–9   ·88

Grades 10–12   ·90

Grade 12   ·84 (Bentley, 1955)

Validity From manual – association between teachers' ratings and scores significant at ·05% level only for Grades 10–12 and 4–12.

Items 19-33 Too easy for Bentley's subjects but Melodic memory items most discriminating of all tests investigated in distinguishing instrument from non-instrument playing groups.

The Gordon musical aptitude profile

Three parts Tonal Imagery (Melody and Harmony).

Rhythm Imagery (Tempo and Metre).

Musical Sensitivity (Phrasing, Balance and Style).

Melody 40 items played on violin. Tune and answer. Is answer a melodic variation of tune or is it different?

Harmony 40 tune and answer items played on the cello, upper part played by violin remains the same. Is answer a melodic variation of tune or is it different?

Tempo 40 items. Is end of answer at same or different tempo than end of tune?

Metre 40 items. Is there a change of metre e.g. from duple or triple at end of answer?

Phrasing 30 pairs of items. Which is performed with the better musical phrasing?

Balance 30 pairs of items. Which of the pair has better ending?

Style 30 pairs of items. Which is played in the better style?

Percentile norms based on nearly 13,000 pupils from 18 of the American States, for Grades 4-12, for each subtest, for each of the three parts, and for total scores. Separate norms for musically select students at three levels.

Reliability

	(From manual based on all students in the standardisation sample)	(Over 1000 pupils aged 10–18 (Tarrell, 1965))
Mel.	·73–·85	·67–·84
Harm.	·66–·85	·67–·83
Ton. imag. (Mel. + Harm.)	·80–·92	·80–·89
Tempo	·72–·85	·60–·82
Metre	·66–·85	·60–·84
Rthm. Imag.		·60–·84
(Tempo + Metre)	·82–·91	·76–·90
Phrasing	·67–·78	·60–·67
Balance	·66–·79	·60–·72
Style	·66–·80	·60–·74
Sensitivity (Phr. + Bal. + Stl.)	·84–·90	·70–·84
Composite	·90–·96	·86–·96

	Gordon (1967)	Gordon (1969)	Gordon (1970)	Schleuter (1972)	Froseth (1971)
Mel.	·81	·88	·82	·78	·82
Harm.	·73	·88	·75	·74	·74
Mel. + Harm.	·87	·93	·90	·86	·89
Tempo	·78	·81	·75	·81	·73
Metre	·73	·80	·73	·77	·71
Temp. + Metre	·83	·85	·88	·87	·80
Phrasing	·70	·71	·72	·73	·70
Balance	·70	·72	·75	·73	·73
Style	·70	·80	·70	·74	·65
Phr. + Bal. + Stl.	·86	·90	·90	·86	·–
Composite	·92	·94	·95	·93	·94

Compared with teachers' ratings

	From manual based on 400 students		Culver (1965)	Gordon (1967)
	Range	Median		
Mel.	·37–·88	·52		·30
Harm.	·52–·72	·64		·40
Ton. Imag.	·54–·83	·67		·40
Tempo	·48–·66	·58		·34
Metre	·57–·71	·65		·32
Rthm. Imag.	·64–·74	·66		·36
Phrasing	·19–·66	·36		·25
Balance	·20–·66	·48		·26
Style	·44–·87	·57		·28
Sensitivity	·48–·85	·60	·53; ·72	·36
Composite	·64–·97	·79	·72	·45
Ton. + Rthm. Imag.			·69; ·80	

Compared with performance of selected test pieces

	Tarrell 900 pupils (1965)		Fosha (1964)	
	Range	Median	Range	Median
Ton. Imag.	·25–·43	·380		
Rthm. Imag.	·13–·41	·285		
Sensitivity	·17–·28	·235		
Composite	·24–·43	·380	·12–·55	·290

	Gordon (1967) three-year study	Gordon (1970a) Experimental group	Control group
Mel.	·45–·52		
Harm.	·51–·60		
Ton. Imag.	·52–·63	·37–·42	·41–·46
Tempo	·46–·54		
Metre	·50–·57		
Rthm. Imag.	·52–·60	·49–·56	·44–·50
Phrasing	·38–·44		
Balance	·40–·48		
Style	·40–·48		
Sensitivity	·51–·60	·43–·48	·36–·47
Composite	·63–·73	·51–·60	·47–·58

Compared with Achievement Test (three-year-study)
Range of correlations ·43–·48 (individual tests); ·73 composite score.

Bentley measures of musical ability

Four Tests Pitch Discrimination, Tonal Memory, Chord Analysis and
   Rhythmic Memory.

Age 7 or 8–14.

Time to administer 20 minutes.

Published by Harrap.

Pitch discrimination 20 items ranging from 26 H_2 to 3 H_2. Is second higher,
   lower or same as first?

Tonal memory 10 pairs of 5 note tunes. Is second same as first? If different,
   which note has changed?

Chord analysis 10 items. How many notes in the chord?

Rhythmic memory 10pairs of Time Patterns. Is second same as first or if
   different which note has changed?

Norms divided into five grades, for ages 8–14. Based on testing some 2000
   children.

Reliability

	Bentley (1966)	Rowntree (1970)
Pitch	·74	
Tonal memory	·53	
Chord analysis	·71	
Rhythmic memory	·57	
Total	·84	·60

Validity Significant association between test scores and teachers' estimates
   of the musical ability of three groups of children. Four groups of
   musicians or music students all made high scores. See also p. 30

The Gordon primary measures of music audiation (PMMA)

Two tests Tonal and Rhythm.

Ages 5 to 8.

Time and administer 18 minutes each test.

Published by G.I.A., Chicago.

Tonal 40 items. Do the two patterns (of a pair) sound the same or different?

Rhythm 40 items. Do the two patterns (of a pair) sound the same or
   different?

Norms Based on 873 children aged 5 to 8.

Reliability

	Split-halves	Test-retest
Tonal	·85 to ·89	·68 to ·73
Rhythm	·72 to ·66	·60 to ·73
Composite	·90 to ·92	·73 to ·76

Validity: See p. 31.

Zenatti music tests for young children

Five Tests Reproduction of Rhythms; Identification of Melody; Discrimination of Harmony Changes; Discrimination of Melodic Changes; and Aesthetic Judgement.

Ages 4:0 to 5:5 (rhythm); 4:6 to 7:11 recognition of melody and harmony change; 5:6 to 7:11 pitch change and aesthetic judgement. Also for use in pathology.

Time to administer Individually administered.

Published by Etablissements d'Applications Psychotechniques.

Reproduction of rhythm: 8 patterns tapped by examiner, to be tapped by child (not scored); 8 patterns played on piano, to be tapped by child.

Identifying melodies: Two tunes 'the one that the dog likes' and 'the one that the horse likes' to be identified by child pointing to picture of dog or horse. Scoring takes account of speed of learning as well as number of correct judgements.

Test of harmonic change: 12 items. Two chords repeated. Are they the same, or is first, or second different?

Melodic change: 18 items. Is second the same as the first melodic interval, or has first or second note been changed?

Aesthetic tests of harmonic, melodic, rhythmic elements. 4 pairs of items for each element; consonant v dissonant; tonal v atonal; and simple v varied rhythms. Each pair is presented twice during the course of the test. *Consistency* of judgement is scored.

Norms: In standard scores, based on testing 2300 children between 4:0 and 7:11.

Reliability: ·74 (test-retest) 136 children aged 4:5 to 7:11.

Thackray tests of rhythmic ability

Six tests of rhythmic perception and three of rhythmic performance.
Ages 8 onwards.

Unpublished. Obtainable from the author, Dept. of Music, University of Western Australia.

Perception tests: 10 items.

Counting Count number of sounds in tapped patterns.

Steadiness 10 items. Continue counting silently after 4 clicks till bell is heard.

Long and short 10 items. Match patterns of long and short tones with written patterns of dots and dashes.

Strong and weak 10 items. Mark dot which represents strong (accepted) chord.

Comparing rhythms 10 items. Compare rhythm of two melodies – as same or different. If different, which has more sounds?

Phrasing 10 items. State number of sounds in one phrase of 4-phrase melody.

Reliability Apart from tests 2 and 5, range from ·61 to ·79. Full battery ·88.

Validity Selected groups superior (see p. 34).

Performance tests: Administered individually. Time: 15 minutes.

Synchronisation of rhythms Beat in time with repeated rhythm pattern.

Repetition of Rhythms Beat out rhythm after music ceased.

Beating time Beat in time with the music, showing difference between strong and weak beats.

(Reliability and validity not stated.)

Davies tests of musical aptitude

Four tests Melody, Pitch, Interval, and Rhythm.

Age 7 upwards.

Unpublished. Obtainable from the author, Dept. of Psychology, University of Strathclyde.

Melody 15 items. A sequence of 3 or 4 tones is presented. After 2.26 seconds, a longer tonal sequence of 4, 5, 6 or 8 tones follows. Does the longer sequence contain the shorter one? If so, where?

Pitch 15 items. A sine-wave tone is followed by a 'sweep frequency' tone, divided into two segments by a short period of no signal. In which, if either, segment does tone occur?

Intervals 15 items. Two pairs of consecutive tones are presented. The second note of each pair is higher than the first and the two first notes of each pair are different. Which pair has the smaller tonal separation or are they the same?

Rhythm 15 items. 6 bars of a certain metre (duple, triple or quadruple) produced by a metronome, first beat of each bar accentuated by a bell, are followed by a simple or complex tapped rhythmic pattern. Do the metre and pattern fit together or not?

Reliability

Test-retest	60 children aged 7–9	37 aged 9–11
Melody	·73	·76
Pitch	·41	·58
Intervals	·37	·54
Rhythm	·46	·63
Total	·70	·82

Validity Small groups of choir-boys and of performers significantly superior to non-musical. Correlation with Bentley measures ·66.

Stankov/Horn research tests

Tests 1–12 used in first study (see p. 55); tests 1, 2, 6, 7 and 9 in second study; tests 1, 2, 6, 7, 9 and 10 in third study; tests 3, 9, 13 and 14 in fourth study.
Tests unpublished, but described in Stankov and Horn (1980) and in Stankov (in preparation).

1. *Tonal figures* Four notes ascend or descend, followed by four choices in opposite order of pitch. Which inversion is of the original four notes? Rel. (reliability) ·67.
2. *Tonal re-ordering* Three tones presented to be labelled 1 2 3. Same three notes presented again in different order to be numbered to accord with original order. Rel. ·74.
3. *Loudness re-ordering* Similar to 2, but three pure tones, 1000 Hz, presented with intensities differing by 10 db. Rel. ·73.
4. *Detection of repeated tones* An 8-tone melody played, only 4 of the tones differed in pitch. Identify each the first time it is played and not thereafter. Rel. ·89.
5. *Detection of repeated voices* Similar to 4, except sounds were voices of four different people. Rel. ·70.
6. *Tonal series* Four notes played in series (ascending, descending or other), followed by three notes. Which of the three continued the series? Example:

    Series   Choices (correct answer circled)

        C D E F   E′ Ⓖ D
    Rel. ·69

7. *Chord series* Similar to 6, except series comprised of chords. Rel. ·61.
8. *Tonal analogies* Three notes played, followed by three notes. Which of the three forms the same tonal interval away from the third note as the second from the first? Example:

C F G   E Ⓒ C
Rel. ·77.

9. *Chrod decomposition* A 3-note chord is followed by 3-note arpeggios. Which involved the same three notes as in original chord? Rel. ·78.
10. *Chord parts decomposition* A 3-note chord is followed by 2-note chords. Which contained two notes that were part of original chord? Example:

Item chord   Answer choices
A
F   Ⓐ C G
D   Ⓕ G E
Rel. ·67.

11. *Tonal classification* Series of five chords are presented. Which chord does not belong to the series (is in different key)? Rel. ·67.
12. *Chord matching* Two chords, one major, one minor, are played, followed by a third which may be either. Is third chord more similar to 1st or 2nd? Rel. ·60.
13. *Do-Mi-Sol* Three piano notes e.g. C D E are each repeated several times (maximum 7, 8 or 9 notes). Number of times each note played has to be counted.
14. *The dual task* 3-tone tonal memory test and reordering test simultaneously presented to each ear. See p. 70.

Colwell music achievement tests (MAT)

Times to administer Test 1, 18 minutes; Test 2, 28; Test 3, 32; Test 4, 38, *Publisher* Follett, Chicago.

4 tests, not necessarily given in order 1 to 4.

Test 1

Part 1 *Pitch discrimination*
(*a*) 15 items. Which of two tones is higher or are they the same? (Semi-tone differences)
(*b*) 10 items. Which of three tones is the lowest?

Part 2 *Interval discrimination*
(*a*) 10 items. Do three tones proceed by leaps or steps?
(*b*) 18 items. Does the phrase move scalewise, or by leaps? (In doubt?)

Part 3 *Metre discrimination*
15 items. Does the music move in twos or threes?
(In doubt?)

Test 2

Part 1 *Major-minor discrimination*
(*a*) Chords. 15 items. Are two chords played on the piano major or minor?
(*b*) Phrases. 13 items. Is phrase entirely in major, entirely in minor, or partly in each mode?

Part 2 *Feeling for tonal centre*
(*a*) Cadences. 10 items. Four-chord cadence in major mode is played ending on tonic chord, with key note in both soprano and bass. Three pitches are then played. Which, if any, is key note for cadence?
(*b*) Phrases. 10 items. Four bars of melodic phrase with harmonic accompaniment are played, followed by three tones. Which, if any, is key note?

Part 3 *Auditory-visual discrimination*
(*a*) Pitch. 12 items. In which bar or bars does a difference between pitch as heard and as notated on answer sheet occur?
(*b*) Rhythm. 12 items. Similar to (a) except errors are of rhythm rather than of pitch.

Test 3

Part 1 *Tonal memory*
20 items. Are two chords the same or different, and where different, which note is altered?
A four-note chord is played in block form, followed by arpeggio chord (pitches may be identical with first chord, or one of the four may be altered).

Part 2 *Melody recognition*
20 items. Melody presented on piano, then repeated in 3-part setting (violin, viola or cello). Which part has the melody?

Part 3 *Pitch recognition*
20 items. The first pitch played always identical with the first written note. Testee is then given moment to look at second written note. Three more pitches are played, which one (if any) matches the second written note?

Part 4 *Instrument recognition*
(*a*) Solo instrument. 10 items. Which instrument is being played solo? (Four choices + none of the four.)
(*b*) Accompanied instruments. 5 items. Identify solo instrument when played with orchestral accompaniment.

Test 4

    Part 1 *Musical style*

    (*a*) Composers. 20 items. A short orchestral excerpt is played. Which of four composers' styles does it most closely resemble?

    (*b*) Texture. 20 items. Is texture monophonic, homophonic, polyphonic or (in doubt)?

    Part 2 *Auditory-visual discrimination*

    14 items. Student listens to 4-bar phrase while looking at 4-bar measure on answer sheet. Which bar (or bars) are different in rhythm from melody heard?

    Part 3 *Chord recognition*

    15 items. A four-tone chord is played on the piano. Which, if any, of three following chords sounds like the first?

    Part 4 *Cadence recognition*

    15 items. A short phrase ends with a cadence.

    Is cadence 'Full', 'Half', or 'Deceptive'?

Norms Based on over 20 000 pupils (tests 1 and 2), on 9000 (tests 3 and 4). Percentile norms for grades from 3 to 12, depending on test. Separate and combined norms.

Reliability (from manuals):

    Test 1 Part 1 ·81–85; Part 2 ·56–78; Part 3 ·56–79; Total ·84–92

    Test 2 Part 1 ·65–87; Part 2 ·42–85; Part 3 ·74–96; Total ·80–96

    Test 3 Part 1 ·57–75; Part 2 ·38–73; Part 3 ·43–79; Part 4 ·43–80
        Total ·46–91

    Test 4 Part 1 ·71–79; Part 2 ·40–81; Part 3 ·70–81; Part 4 ·25–46
        Total ·81–88.

Validity (from manuals)

    MAT correlated from ·52 to ·66 with Farnum Music Notation, ·53 to ·84 with Knuth Achievement Tests in Music, and ·42 to ·69 with Gaston Test, in case of 188 children grades 4 to 6.

    Tests 1 and 2 given at beginning of semester predicted final grade within 1 point for 47 out of 52 pupils, and 51 out of 53 pupils.

    (*See also* p. 38).

Gordon Iowa tests of musical literacy (ITML)

Six levels each of which has two divisions: Tonal concepts and rhythmic concepts. Each division has three subtests – Aural perception, reading recognition and notational understanding.

Time to administer 36 minutes each division.

Published by University of Iowa.

Levels 1 and 2.

Tonal concepts.

Aural perception 22 items. Each is performed twice.
Is it major or minor?

Reading recognition. 22 items. Is melody notated on answer sheet same or different from melody performed?

Notational understanding. No of items varies. Short melody is performed three times. Half the blank spaces on answer sheet to be filled in.

Rhythmic concepts

Aural perception. Is passage in duple or triple metre?

Reading recognition. Is notated passage correctly performed? (Yes or No)

Notational understanding. Rhythmic pattern performed three times. Testee to fill in blank spaces on answer sheet.

Level 3. Aural perception melodies may be in usual (major or minor) mode or in an unusual mode (Dorian, Phrygian, etc). Rhythmic concepts may be in usual metre (duple or triple) or mixed metre. At level 4 judgement is between usual and unusual metre. At level, 5 two-part melodies, major or minor.

At level 6 melodies have chordal accompaniments – judgement of major or minor. Reading recognition involves chords.

At levels 5 and 6, rhythmic concepts, choice is between mixed or unusual patterns.

Norms Based on testing 18,680 children. Percentile ranks for each level. For levels 1, 2 and 3 for grades 4 to 6; 7 to 9; and 10 to 12. For levels 4, 5 and 6 for grades 7 to 9 and 10 to 12.

Reliability

Level	Tonal	Rhythm	Composite	
1	·71–·92	·70–·90	·90–·94	(manual)
	·77–·89	·60–·71	·87	(Schleuter, 1972)
	·59–·86	·47–·76	·89	(Mohatt, 1971)
2	·70–·89	·71–·88	·89–·93	(manual)
3	·70–·84	·70–·83	·87–·91	(manual)
4	·70–·81	·70–·85	·90–·91	(manual)
5	·70–·84	·70–·88	·91–·92	(manual)
6	·70–·85	·72–·86	·90–·91	(manual)

(Reading recognition usually the least reliable.)

Validity. See p. 39.

Farnum music notation test

40 melodic phrases.

One of four bars of each melody as played is different from the melody in notation. Which?

Reliability

Range ·78–·91 (from manual) ·89 (Bentley, 1955)

Validity

Compared with Watkins–Farnum performance scale ·40 – ·61 (Manual)

Compared with music grades ·49 (Bentley, 1955)

Farnum music test

Four tests Notation, cadence, patterns and symbol.

Ages Grades 4–9.

Time to administer 40-45 minutes.

Published by Bond Publishing Co.

Notation 40 items. As above.

Cadence 30 items, played once, last tone is missing. Should last tone move up or down?

Patterns 30 items. 4 or 5 tones are played twice. Which tone has been changed on second playing?

Symbol A model presents 9 notes from E (first line of treble clef) to G above treble clef, each note having a block containing identifying dots. For example, block under E has one dot, block under A (second space of treble clef) has nine. Subject is given two minutes to match notation of test items with the model and fill in 65 blocks with the correct number of dots.

Reliability Notation test – see above; Symbol ·87; ·91 (test-retest).

Validity Correlation with Watkins-Farnum Performance Scale ·63. The higher the score, the lower the dropout among 152 students.

The Simons measurements of musical listening skills

Nine subtests, each with six items, five of which are scored: melodic direction, steps/jumps, harmony, harmony (chords), metre, tonal patterns, rhythm patterns, dynamics, tempo.

Ages 6 to 8 (found too difficult for kindergarten).

Published by Stoelting Co., Chicago.

Time to administer Two or three sub-tests in 25-minute class period (playing time = 55 minutes).

Melodic direction Does melody move up, down or straight?
Steps/jumps Does melody move by steps or leaps?
Harmony Is sound made by one or more than one resonator bell?
Harmony chords Circle number of chord which sounds different from others.
Metre Identify as duple or triple.
Tonal patterns Identify two short melodies as same or different.
Rhythm patterns Identify two short rhythm patterns as same or different.
Dynamics Is melody getting louder, softer, or staying on same level?
Tempo Is melody getting faster, slower, or staying at same speed?

Interpretation of test results Chance and passable group scores given by grade level as guide to teacher (see also p. 41). 80 per cent or over considered to indicate good achievement.

Aliferis music achievement test (1954) – College entrant level

Three sections Melody, harmony and rhythm as described on page 43.
Time to administer 40 minutes.
Published by University of Minnesota Press.

Reliability

From manual	Melodic section	·84
	Harmonic	·72
	Rhythmic	·67
	Total	·88

Validity From manual compared with music grades

	Test manual		White (1961)	Roby (1963)
Melodic	·54	·57		·64
Harmonic	·41	·53		·66
Rhythmic	·46	·25		·37
Total	·61	·53	·63	·73
Melodic + harmonic				·77

Aliferis music achievement test (1962) – College midpoint level

Three sections Harmonic elements, melodic and rhythmic idioms.

Reliability

Harmonic	·90
Melodic	·84
Rhythmic	·69
Total	·92

Validity Compared with music grades range from ·40–·51.

Australian test for advanced music studies

Three 'books' Aural imagery and memory; score reading and aural/visual discrimination; comprehension and application of learned music material.

Time to administer 45 minutes for each part.

Published by Australian Council for Educational Research.

Reliability (from manual – based on testing 279 Australian students):
Book 1   ·82
    2   ·80
    3   ·81
Total   ·91

Validity (from manual)

Aliferis (melody plus rhythm elements) and	Book 2	·38
	Total	·73
Dictation test	Book 2	·58
	Total	·62
Aural examination (2 universities)	Total	·69

Correlations between Intelligence Tests and Musical Ability Tests

(In almost every case the intelligence test has been a group test)

Abbreviations: P Pitch; I Intensity; T Time; C Consonance; M Memory; R Rhythm; Ca Cadence; Ph Phrasing; Ch Chords; H Harmony; PR Pitch Recognition; MR Melody Recognition; Ton Tonal; Bal Balance.

Seashore measures

Investigator	Subjects	P	I	T	C	M	R
Weaver (1924)	94 college students	·35	·24	·12	·06	·26	—
Fracker & Howard (1928)	230 college students	·32	·01	·13	·09	·10	·12
Highsmith (1929)	59 female music school students	·58	·35	·39	—·14	·30	—
Salisbury & Smith (1929)	131 training college students	·31	·15	·30	·00	·24	·02
	144 training college students	·39	—	·49	·38	·33	·24
Farnsworth (1931)	150 university students	·14	·11	·10	—·38	·11	·17
Drake (1940)	163 boys; age = 13	·12	·14	·08	·03	·07	·05
Franklin (1956)	(a) 79 training college students	·13				·00	
	(b) 157 training college students	·15				·14	
Hollingworth (1926)	49 children with IQs above 135		Median PR				
		46·7	50·0	58·0		52·3	
Manor (1950)	4th grade children	·21				·27	·11[1]
Christy (1956)	103 college students	·18				·18	·33[2]
Rainbow (1956)	291 children (aged 9–17)	·22				·20	·23[1]

[1] 1939 Revision, Form A.   [2] 1939 Revision, Form B.

Kwalwasser-Dykema tests

Investigator	Subjects	Full battery
Newkirk[a]	1000	·34
Robertson[a]	Over 5000 children aged 8 to 20	·33
Lambert[a]	1024 children aged 11	·33
Lehman (1950)	450 musicians & college students	·18
Chase[a]	82 feeble-minded children (IQ range 45–77)	Average PR = 35·0 (tests 1–8)
Drake (1940)	As above	·06 (Melodic taste) ·13 (Tonal movement)

[a] Cited by Kwalwasser (1955)

Lowery tests

Investigator	Subjects	M	Ca	Ph
Lowery (1929)	Group of school girls aged 12–14	·44	·44	·00
Drake (1940)	As above		·06	

Mainwaring tests

Investigator	Subjects	P	R	M
Mainwaring (1931)	83 elementary school children	·53	·46	·04
	34 grammar school boys	·39	·32	—

Drake tests

Investigator	Subjects	M	R
Drake (1957)	158 college students	·28	
Drake	163 music students (aged 7–16)	·27	
Drake	20 high school children	·05	·10
Drake	61 psych. students		·00
Drake	130 students		−·03
Drake	130 students		·05
Karlin (1941)	120 students	·06	
Christy (1956)	103 students	·21	
Rainbow (1965)	291 children (aged 9–17)	·29	

Oregon music discrimination test

Investigator	Subjects	
Hevner (1931)	74 college students	− ·15 (2 version form)
	74 college students	− ·17 (4 version form)

Indiana-Oregon music discrimination test

| Long (1971) | Group tested with 43 items | | | | | | | | ·47 |

Wing tests of musical intelligence

Investigator	Subjects	Full Battery	Ch	P	M	R	H	I	Ph
Wing (1948)	23 girls	·30							
	42 boys	·32							
	24 adults	·40							
	24 adults	·34							
	454 college students	·20							
Edmunds (1960)	Sec. Mod. school children:								
	60 A & D stream		−·07	·33	·39		·28 (tests 1–3)		
	58 F stream & ESN		−·02	·36	·47		·39 (tests 1–3)		
Coulthard (1952)	32 grammar school boys	·04							
Shuter (1964)	200 Royal Marine School of Music boys		·180 (tests 1–3)			·154 (tests 4–7)			
Whittington (1957)	24 musical adolescents		·36	·18	·42	·40	·47	·52	·20
	24 unmusical adolescents		·21	·63	·32	·20	·17	·00	·40
Bentley (1955)	87 instrument players (a)	·39	·21	·39	·37	·22	·18	·01	·02
	95 non-players (b)	·39	22	·39	·26	·03	·25	·17	·11
Franklin	as above (a)		·09	−·10	−·02	·00	−·19	·20	·04
	(b)		·09	·12	·20	·23	·21	−·03	·08
Beard (1965)	145 children aged 15								
	73 boys		·16	·02					
			·31	·24					
	72 girls		·01	·18					
			·08	·10					
Whellams (1971)	129 children aged 7 : 8 to 10 : 6		·16	−·33	·26	−·40	·37	−·56 (Verbal IQ)	
			·10	−·29	·13	−·32	·11	−·50 (Non-verbal IQ)	
Parker (1978)	1174 high school children	Boys			·134				
		Girls			·054 (Tests 4–7)				
		Both sexes			·075				

Wing-Holmstrom tests

Investigator	Subjects	Ch	P	M	R
Holmstrom	189 children in Grade 2	·25	·28	·23	·33
(1963)	765 children in Grade 2	·16	·32	·29	·33
	651 children in Grade 4	·09	·17	·22	·27
	120 children from unmusical homes				
	Grade 2	·00	·17	·20	·34
	Grade 4	·14	·32	·16	·47

Lundin tests

Investigator	Subjects	Non-language		Language
Lundin (1949)	113 music students	·15	·25	·13
	155 unselected students	·24	·22	·19

Gaston test

Investigator	Subjects	Tests 19–23	Tests 24–28	Tests 29–33	Tests 34–40
Bentley	As above (*a*)	·15	·32	·29	·29
	(*b*)	·11	·18	·16	·25

Franklin TMT tests

Investigator	Subjects	Group	Individual
Franklin	As above (*a*)	—	−·11
	(*b*)	·18	·18

Bentley measures of musical ability

		P	M	Ch	R
Bentley (1966)	166 children aged 10 to 12	·30	·25	·24	·34
	149 children with IQs of 100 or above; age = 11:1	Assoc. signif. at 1% level	No significant association		
Rowntree (1970)	3000 children aged 7 to 11	Assoc. signif. at 1% level			
Whellams (1971)	129 children aged 7:8 to 10:6	Verbal IQ ·46 −·55 ·36 −·52 ·29 −·43 ·45 −·58			
		Non-verbal IQ ·31 −·60 ·20 −·46 ·08 −·37 ·14 −·52			

Gordon musical aptitude profile

	Total of 862 children in:	Mel	H	Tempo	Metre	Ph	Bal	Style	Composite
Gordon	grades 4–6	·27	·23	·36	·35	·19	·33	·28	·39
(1965)	7–8	·30	·30	·40	·26	·25	·33	·32	·40
	9–12	·26	·30	·34	·33	·17	·20	·24	·34
	(Verbal Intelligence)								
	As above	·29	·22	·39	·31	·19	·23	·32	·40
	(Non-verbal	·36	·29	·48	·29	·21	·37	·31	·44
	Intelligence)	·27	·25	·31	·31	·18	·17	·21	·31

Gordon primary measures of music audiation

		Ton	R	Composite	
Gordon	264 children in	·19	·25	·26	Verbal IQ
(1979a)	grade 3	·20	·29	·30	Non-verbal IQ

Colwell music achievement tests

Colwell (1969) p. 90	1400 4th grade children	·28 to ·39

Gordon Iowa tests of musical literacy

		Ton	R	Composite
Gordon (1970)	122 8th grade children	·12 to ·29	−·01 to ·39	·26 to ·39

Correlations between Tests of Musical and other Abilities

Investigator	Subjects	Music Tests	Other Tests	r or range of correlation
Miscellaneous				
Franklin (1956)	179 T.C. students	Seashore P. & M. Wing 1–7;	Vocabulary	−·01 to ·28
		Franklin TMT & Rhythm	Visual Perception	−·11 to ·23
Coulthard (1952)	32 high school boys	Wing 1–7 Wing 1–3	Oral French Oral French	·53 ·42
Edmunds (1960) (a)	60 Sec. Mod. A & D stream	Wing 1–3	Reading	·33
(b)	58 Sec. Mod. F stream & ESN			·24
Drake (1940)	24 to 186 women college students	Drake Memory	Various college subjects	−·13 to ·24
Holmstrom (1963) (a)	About 1000 children aged 8 to 10	Wing-Holmstrom	Reading marks	·06 to ·37
(b)	120 from unmusical homes	Wing-Holmstrom	Reading	−·01 to ·28
(a)		Wing-Holmstrom	Writing	·09 to ·36
(b)		Wing-Holmstrom	marks	−·01 to ·27
Shuter (1964)	200 RMSM junior musicians	Wing 1–3 Wing 4–7	Spelling Spelling Spatial Spatial	·12 ·12 ·21 −·03
Whellams (1971)	129 children aged 7:8 to 10:6	Bentley Wing Bentley Wing	Reading Reading Sentence completion Comprehension	·35 to ·51 ·19 to ·47 ·35 to ·54 ·20 to ·48
Beard (1965)	73 boys 72 girls aged 15	Wing 1 & 2	Various psychological tests	−·14 to ·38 −·18 to ·30
Gordon (1969)	157 college students	Seashore tests MAP tests	American college tests (total scores)	−·03 to ·23 −·11 to ·18
Long (1971)	Groups taking 43-item version	Indiana-Oregon	SAT Verbal	·39
Gordon (1979a)	127 kindergarten children	PMMA	Metropolitan Readiness	·15 to ·30
	202 grade 1	PMMA	Stanford Achievement	·23 to ·37
	280 grade 2	PMMA	"	·29 to ·39
	264 grade 3	PMMA	"	·12 to ·35

Other Arts

Carroll (1932)	133 college students	Oregon	Prose appreciation	·12
				·13[1]
			Art judgement	·16
				·15[1]
Rigg (1937)	71 males students	Oregon	Poetry	·34
				·24[1]
Morrow (1938)	112 males psychology students	K–D	Art	·10 (average)
Williams, Winter & Woods (1938)	Over 200 children aged 11 to 17	Appreciation	Literary	·26
				·18[1]
Karlin (1941)	120 college students	Drake memory etc	Poetry apprec- iation	·12
Drake (1957)	19 music students	Drake	Art	·00
	166 Belgian boys	Rhythm		·14

[1] With intelligence held constant

Mathematic/Scientific

Morrow (1941)	80 college students	Seashore	Arithmetic Thurstone	−·09 to ·19
			Number series	−·08 to ·41
Edmunds (1960)	As (*a*) above As (*b*) above	Wing 1–3	Arithmetic	·11
				·29
Holmstrom (1963)	As (*a*) above As (*b*) above	Wing–Holmstrom	Arithmetic Marks	−·01 to ·23
				−·09 to ·18
Shuter (1964)	200 RMSM junior musicians	Wing 1–3 Wing 4–7	Mathematics	·07
				·05
Gordon (1969)	157 college students	Seashore time	American college test – Maths (the only significant correlation with Maths part of test)	·26
Long (1971)	As above	Indiana- Oregon	SAT – Maths	·39

Bibliography of references cited

ABELES, H. F. (1971) An application of the facet-factorial approach to scale construction in the development of a rating scale for clarinet music performance. Doctoral Diss., University of Maryland.

ABRAHAM, O. (1901) 'Das absolute Tonbewusstein', *International. Musikges.*, **3**, 1-86.

AGNEW, M. (1922) 'A comparison of auditory images of musicians, psychologists and children', *Iowa Studies in Psychology*, **8**, 268-78.

ALIFERIS, J. (1954) *Aliferis Music Achievement Test*. Minneapolis : Univ. of Minnesota Press.

ALIFERIS, J. and STECKLEIN, J. (1962) *Aliferis-Stecklein Music Achievement Test (College Midpoint Level)*. Minneapolis: Univ. of Minnesota Press.

ANASTASI, A. and LEVEE, R. E. (1960) 'Intellectual defect and musical talent: a case report', *Amer. J. Ment. Defic.*, **64**, 695-703.

ANDREWS, F. M. and DEIHL, N. C. (1967) *Development of a technique for identifying elementary school children's musical concepts*. US Office of Education Project 5-0233, Washington, D.C.

ARGYLE, M. (1975) *Bodily Communication*. London: Methuen.

ASHMAN, R. (1952) 'The inheritance of simple musical memory', *J. Hered.*, **43**, 51-2.

BACHEM, A. (1940) 'The genesis of absolute pitch', *J. Acoust. Soc. Amer.*, **11**, 434-9.

BADDELEY, A. D. and DALE, H. C. A. (1966) 'The effect of semantic similarity on retroactive interference in long- and short-term memory', *Verb. Learn. Verb. Behav.*, **5**, 417-20.

BAIN, B. (1978) 'The cognitive flexibility claim in the bilingual and music education research traditions', *J. Res. Mus. Ed.*, **26**, 76-81.

BALDWIN, B. T. and STECHER, L. I. (1924) *The Psychology of the Preschool Child*. New York : Appleton.

BARTLETT, J. C. and DOWLING, W. J. (1980) 'The recognition of transposed melodies: A key-distance effect in developmental perspective', *J. Exp. Psychol., Human Perception and Performance*, **6**, 501-15.

BAUMANN, V. H. (1960) 'Teen-age music preferences', *J. Res. Mus. Ed.*, **8**, 75-84.

BEARD, R. M. (1965) 'The structure of perception: a factorial study', *Brit. J. Educ. Psychol.*, **35**, 210-22.

BELDOCH, M. (1964) 'Sensitivity to expression of emotional meaning in three modes of communication' in J. R. DAVITZ (ed.) *The Communication of Emotional Meaning*. New York: McGraw-Hill.

BELAIEW-EXEMPLARSRY, S. (1926) 'Das musikalische Empfinden im Vorschulalter', *Zsch. f. Ang. Psychol.*, **27**, 177-216.

BELL, C. (1914) *Art*. London.

BENTLEY, A. (1966) *Musical Ability in Children and its Measurement*. London: Harrap.

BENTLEY, A. (1968) *Monotones*. Music Education Research Papers, **1**. London: Novello.

BENTLEY, A. (1970) 'A comparison of a musician's assessments with data from the Bentley "Measures of Musical Abilities" ', *Bull. Council Res. Mus. Ed.*, No 22, 17-24.

BENTLEY, A. (1977) 'International follow-up study of the Bentley "Measures of Musical Abilities" ', *Bull. Council Res. Mus. Ed.*, No 50, 6-10.

BENTLEY, R. R. (1955) A critical comparison of certain aspects of musical aptitude tests. Doctoral thesis, Univ. Southern California.

BERGAN, J. R. (1967) 'The relationship among pitch identification, imagery for music sounds, and music memory', *J. Res. Mus. Ed.*, **15**, 99-109.

BEVER, T. G. and CHIARELLO, R. J. (1974) 'Cerebral dominance in musicians and nonmusicians', *Science*, **185**, 537-9.

BIENSTOCK, S. F. (1942) 'A predictive study of musical achievement', *J. Genet. Psychol.*, **61**, 135-45.

BILLROTH, T. (1895) *Wer ist musikalisch?* Berlin: Ed. Hansick.

BIRNS, B., BLANK, M., BRIDGER, W. H. and ESCALONA, S. (1965) 'Behavioural inhibition in neonates produced by auditory stimuli', *Psychosom. Med.*, **28**, 316-22.

BLACKETER-SIMMONDS, D. A. (1953) 'An investigation into the supposed differences existing between mongols and other mental defectives with regard to certain psychological traits', *J. Ment. Sci.*, **99**, 702-19.

BLACKING, J. A. R. (1971) 'Towards a theory of musical competence' in E. DE JAGER (ed.) *Man: Anthropological Essays in Honour of O. F. Raum*. Cape Town: Struik.

BOARDMAN, E. (1964) An investigation of the effect of preschool training on the development of vocal accuracy in young children. Doctoral Diss., Univ. Illinois.

BOND, M. (1959) 'Rhythmic perception and gross motor performance', *Research Quarterly*, **30**, 259-65.

BOTVIN, G. (1974) 'Acquiring conservation of melody and cross-modal transfer through successive approximation', *J. Res. Mus. Ed.*, **22**, 226-33.

BOYLE, D. J. (1970) 'The effect of prescribed rhythmical movements on the ability to read music at sight', *J. Res. Mus. Ed.*, **18**, 307-18.

BRACKBILL, Y., ADAMS, G., CROWELL, D. H. and GRAY, M. L. (1966) 'Arousal level in neonates and older infants under continuous auditory stimulation', *J. Exp. Child Psychol.*, **4**, 178-88.

BRADY, P. T. (1970) 'Fixed-scale mechanism of absolute pitch', *J. Acoust. Soc. Amer.*, **48**, 883-7.

BRENNAN, F. (1926) 'The relation between musical capacity and performance', *Psychol. Monogr.*, 36:1 (Whole No 167), 190-248.

BRIDGER, W. H. (1961) 'Sensory habituation and discrimination in the human neonate', *Amer. J. Psychiatry*, **117**, 991-6.

BRIDGES, D. (1978) *Australian Test for Advanced Music Studies*. Hawthorn (Vict.): Australian Council for Education Research.

BRIDGES, V. A. (1965) An exploratory study of the harmonic discrimination ability of children in kindergarten through grade three in two selected schools. Doctoral Diss., Ohio State Univ.

BROADBENT, D. E. (1954) 'The role of auditory localisation in attention and memory span', *J. Exp. Psychol.*, **47**, 191-6.

BROADBENT, D. E. (1973) *In Defence of Empirical Psychology*. London: Methuen.

BRODY, E. B., and BRODY, N. (1976) *Intelligence; Nature, Determinants and Consequences*. New York: Academic Press.

BROWN, M. (1969) 'The optimum length of the Musical Aptitude Profile', *J. Res. Mus. Ed.*, **17**, 240-7.

BRUTON-SIMMONDS, I. V. (1969) 'A critical note on the value of the Seashore Measures of Musical Talents', *Psychologia Africana*, **13**, 50-54.

BRYNE, A. (1974) 'Handedness and musical ability', *Brit. J. Psychol.*, **65**, 279-81.

BUCKTON, R. (1977) 'A comparison of the effects of vocal and instrumental instruction on the development of melodic and vocal activities', *Psychol. Music*, **5**, (1), 36-47.

BÜHLER, C. (1935) *From Birth to Maturity: An Outline of the Psychological Development of the Child*. Kegan, Paul, Trench and Trubner.

BURKS, B. S., JENSEN, D. W., and TERMAN, L. M. (1930) 'The promise of youth: Follow-up studies of a thousand gifted children'. Vol III *Genetic Studies of Genius*. Stanford: Stanford Univ. Press.

BURNS, E. M. and WARD, W. D., (1978) 'Categorical perception: phenomenon or epiphenomenon : Evidence from experiments in the perception of melodic musical intervals', *J. Acoust. Soc. Amer.*, **63**, 456-68.

BUROS, O. K. (1953) *The Fourth Mental Measurements Yearbook*; (1959) *The Fifth Mental Measurements Yearbook*; (1966) *The Sixth Mental Measurements Yearbook*; (1972) *The Seventh Mental Measurements Yearbook*; Highland Park, N.J.: Gryphon Press.

BURROUGHS, G. E. R. and MORRIS, J. N. (1962) 'Factors involved in learning a simple musical theme', *Brit. J. Educ. Psychol.*, **32**, 18-28.

CAIN, M. L. (1960) A comparison of the Wing Standardised Tests of Musical Intelligence with a Test of Musicality by Gaston and the Drake Musical Aptitude Tests. Master's thesis, Univ. Kansas.

CANTOR, G. N. and GIRARDEAU, F. L. (1959) 'Rhythmic discrimination ability in mongoloid children', *Amer. J. Ment. Defic.* **63**, 621-25.

CARLSEN, J. C. (1976) 'Cross-cultural influences on expectancy in music', *International Music Education*. ISME Yearbook III pp. 61-5. Mainz: Schotts.

CARROLL, H. A. (1932) 'A preliminary report on a study of the interrelations of certain appreciations', *J. Educ. Psychol.*, **23**, 505-10.

CATTELL, R. B. (1965) *The Scientific Analysis of Personality*. Harmondsworth: Penguin.

CATTELL, R. B., EBER, H. W. and TATSUOKA, M. M. (1970) *Handbook for the Sixteen Personality Factor Questionnaire (16PF)*. Champaign, Ill.: Institute for Personality and Ability Testing.

CAZDEN, N. (1979) 'Can verbal meanings inhere in fragments of melody? A Communication', *Psychol. Music*, **7** (2).

CHALMERS, B. (1976) The development of a measure of attitude toward instrumental music style. Doctoral Diss., Univ. Kansas.

CHALMERS, B. (1978) 'The development of a measure of attitude toward instrumental music style', *J. Res. Mus. Ed.*, **26**, 90-6.

CHANG, H. and TREHUB, S. E. (1977a) 'Auditory processing of relational information by young infants', *J. Exp. Child Psychol.*, **24**, 324-31.

CHANG, H. and TREHUB, S. E. (1977b) 'Infants perception of temporal grouping in auditory patterns', *Child Devel.*, **48**, 1666-70.

CHRISTIANSON, H. (1938) *Bodily Rhythmic Movements of Young Children in Relation to Rhythm in Music*. New York: Teachers College, Columbia Univ.

CHRISTY, L. J. (1956) A study of the relationships between musicality, intelligence, and achievement. Doctoral Diss., Indiana Univ.

CLEAK, R. E. (1970) A study of educational and social factors in the development of musical ability in children of different ages. Master's thesis, Bristol Univ.

CLEALL, C. (1970) *Voice Production in Choral Technique*. London: Novello.

COFFMAN, A. R. (1951) The effect of training on rhythm discrimination and rhythmic action. Doctoral Diss., Northwestern Univ.

COLWELL, R. (1963) 'An investigation of musical achievement, among vocal students, vocal-instrumental students and instrumental students', *J. Res. Mus. Ed.*, **11**, 123-30.

COLWELL, R. (1969-70) *Music Achievement Tests*. Chicago: Follett.

COLWELL, R. (1970*a*) *The Evaluation of Music Teaching and Learning*. Englewood Cliffs, N.J.: Prentice Hall.

COLWELL, R. (1970*b*) 'The development of the Music Achievement Test series', *Bull. Council Res. Mus. Ed.*, No 22, 57-73.

COLWELL, R. (1979) *Silver Burdett Music Competency Tests*. Morristown, N.J.: Silver Burdett.

COOKE, D. (1959) *The Language of Music*. London: Oxford Univ. Press.

COOKSEY, J. M. (1977) 'A facet-factorial approach to rating high school choral music performance', *J. Res. Mus. Ed.*, **25**, 100-14.

COOLEY, J. (1961) 'A study of the relation between certain mental and personality traits and ratings of musical ability', *J. Res. Mus. Ed.*, **9**, 108-17.

CORTOT, A. (1935) 'Do infant prodigies become great musicians?' *Music and Letters*, **16**, 124-8.

COULTHARD, J. W. (1952) An investigation into certain aspects of oral ability in French and musical ability as measured by the Wing Test of Musical Intelligence. B. Ed. thesis, Aberdeen Univ.

COX, C. (1926) *Genetic Studies of Genius*: Vol II *The Early Mental Traits of Three Hundred Geniuses*. Stanford: Stanford Univ. Press.

CRICKMORE, L. (1968) 'An approach to the measurement of music appreciation', *J. Res. Mus. Ed.*, **16**, 239-52 and 291-301.

CRICKMORE, L. (1973) 'A syndrome hypothesis of music appreciation', *Psychol. Music*, **1** (2), 21-5.

CUDDY, L. (1968) 'Practice effects in the absolute judgement of pitch', *J. Acoust. Soc. Amer.*, **43**, 1069-76.

CUDDY, L. and COHEN, A. J. (1976) 'Recognition of transposed melodic sequences', *Quart. J. Exp. Psychol.*, **28**, 255-70.

CUDDY, L. L. and WIEBE, M. G. (1979) 'Music and the experimental sciences', *Human. Assoc. Review*, **30**, (1-2), 1-10.

CULVER, F. (1965) A study of the Musical Aptitude Profile. Masters Diss., Iowa Univ.

DAMASIO, A. R. and DAMASIO, H. (1977) 'Musical faculty and cerebral dominance' in MACDONALD CRITCHLEY and R. A. HENSON (eds) *Music and the Brain*. London: Heinemann.

DARLINGTON, C. D. (1963) 'Psychology, genetics and the process of history', *Brit. J. Psychol.*, **54**, 293-8.

DARWIN, C. (1872) *The Expression of the Emotions in Man and Animals*. London: Murray.

DAVENPORT, C. B. and STEGGERDA, M. (1929) *Race Crossing in Jamaica*. Washington: Carnegie Institute.

DAVIDSON, J. B. (1980) 'Music and gerontology: a young endeavour', *Mus. Educ. J.*, **66** (9), 26-31.

DAVIDSON, R. J. and SCHWARTZ, G. E. (1977) 'The influence of musical training on patterns of EEG asymmetry during musical and non-musical self generation tasks', *Psychophysiology*, **1**, 58-63.

DAVIES, A. and ROBERTS, E. (1975) 'Poor pitch singing: A survey of its incidence in school children', *Psychol. Music*, **3** (2), 24-36.

DAVIES, J. B. (1971) 'New tests of musical aptitude', *Brit. J. Psychol.*, **62**, 557-65.

DAVIES, J. B. (1978) *The Psychology of Music*. London: Hutchinson.

DAVIES, J. B. (1979) 'Memory for melodies and tonal sequences: a theoretical note', *Brit. J. Psychol.*, **70**, 204-10.

DAVIES, J. B. and JENNINGS, J. (1977), 'The reproduction of familiar melodies and the perception of tonal sequences', *J. Acoust. Soc. Amer.*, **61**, 534-41.

DAVIES, J. B. and YELLAND, A. (1977) 'Effects of training on the production of melodic contour in memory for tonal sequences', *Psychol. Music.*, **5**, 3-9.

DAWKINS, A. and SYNDER, R. (1972) 'Disadvantaged junior high school students compared with norms of Seashore Measures', *J. Res. Mus. Ed.*, **20**, 438-44.

DEAN, C. D. (1937) 'Predicting sightsinging ability in teacher education', *J. Educ. Psychol.*, **28**, 601-8.

DELIS, D., FLEER, J. and KERR, N. H. (1978) 'Memory for music', *Perception and Psychophysics*, **23**, 215-18.

DEUTSCH, D. (1970*a*) The deterioration of pitch information in memory. Doctoral Diss., Univ. California at San Diego (reported in Deutsch, 1977).

308   *The Psychology of Musical Ability*

DEUTSCH, D. (1970*b*) 'Tones and numbers: specificity of interference in short-term memory', *Science*, **168**, 1604-5.

DEUTSCH, D. (1972) 'Mapping of interactions in the pitch memory store', *Science*, **175**, 1020-2.

DEUTSCH, D. (1973) 'Interference in memory between tones adjacent in the musical scale', *J. Exp. Psychol.*, **100**, 228-31.

DEUTSCH, D. (1975), 'The organization of short term memory for a single acoustic attribute' in D. DEUTSCH and J. A. DEUTSCH (eds) *Short Term Memory*. New York: Academic Press.

DEUTSCH, D. (1977) 'Memory and attention in music' in MACDONALD CRITCHLEY and R. A. HENSON (eds) *Music and the Brain*. London: Heinemann.

DEUTSCH, D. (1978*a*) 'Pitch Memory: An advantage for the left-handed', *Science*, **199**, 559-60.

DEUTSCH, D. (1978*b*) 'Delayed pitch comparisons and the principle of proximity', *Perception and Psychophysics*, **23**, 227-30.

DEUTSCH, D. and FEROE, J., (1975) 'Disinhibition in pitch memory', *Perception and Psychophysics*, **17**, 320-4.

DEWAR, K. M., CUDDY, L. L., and MEWHORT, D. J. K. (1977) 'Recognition memory for single tones with and without context', *J. Exp. Psychol. (Human Learning and Memory)* **3**, 60-7.

DE YARMAN, R. M. (1972) 'An experimental analysis of the development of rhythmic and tonal capabilities of kindergarten and first grade children', *Exper. Res. Psychol. Music: Stud. Psychol. Music*, **8**, 1-44.

DE YARMAN, R. M. (1975) 'An investigation of the stability of musical aptitude among primary-age children', *Exper. Res. Psychol. Music: Stud. Psychol. Music*, **10**, 1-23.

DITTEMORE, E. E. (1970) 'An investigation of some musical capabilities of elementary school children', *Exper. Res. Psychol. Music : Stud. Psychol. Music*, **6**, 1-44.

DOAN, G. R. (1973) An investigation of the relationships between parental involvement and the performance ability of violin students. Doctoral Diss., Ohio State Univ.

DOWLING, W. J. (1971) 'Recognition of inversions of melodies and melodic contours, *Perception and Psychophysics*, **9**, 348-9.

DOWLING, W. J. (1973) 'Rhythmic groups and subjective chunks in memory for melodies', *Perception and Psychophysics*, **14**, 37-40.

DOWLING, W. J. (1978*a*) 'Dichotic recognition of musical canons: effects of leading ear and time lag between ears', *Perception and Psychophysics*, **23**, 321-5.

DOWLING, W. J. (1978*b*) 'Scale and Contour: Two components of a theory of memory for melodies', *Psychol. Rev.*, **85**, 341-54.

DOWLING, W. J. (1979) Mental structures through which music is perceived. Paper presented to National Symposium on Application of Psychology to the Teaching and Learning of Music, Ann Arbor.

DOWLING, W. J. and FUJITANI, S. (1971) 'Contour, interval and pitch recognition in memory for melodies', *J. Acoust. Soc. Amer.*, **49**, 524-31.

DRAKE, R. M. (1931) Tests of musical talent. Doctoral Diss., London Univ.

DRAKE, R. M. (1933) 'Four new tests of musical talent', *J. Appl. Psychol.*, **17**, 136-47; 'The validity and reliability of tests of musical talent', *J. Appl. Psychol.* **17**, 447-58.

DRAKE, R. M. (1939) 'Factorial analysis of music tests by the Spearman-Tetrad-Difference technique',*J. Musicol.*, **1** (1), 6-16.

DRAKE, R. M. (1940) 'The relation of musical talent to intelligence and success at school', *J. Musicol.*, **2** (1).

DRAKE, R. M. (1957) *Manual for the Drake Musical Aptitude Tests*. Chicago: Science Research Associates.

DRINKWATER, H. (1916) 'Inheritance of artistic and musical ability', *J. Genet.*, **5**, 229-41.

DUELL, O. K. and ANDERSON, R. C. (1967) 'Pitch discrimination among primary school children', *J. Educ. Psychol.*, **58**, 315-18.

DUERKSEN, G. L. (1968) 'Recognition of repeated and altered thematic materials in music, *J. Res. Mus. Ed.*, **16**, 3-30.

EDMUNDS, C. B. (1960) Musical ability, intelligence and attainment of Secondary Modern and E.S.N. children. Thesis, Leeds Univ.

EELLS, W. (1933) 'Mechanical, physical and musical ability of the native races of Alaska', *J. Appl. Psychol.*, **17**, 493-506.

EGGER, G. and IVINSKIS, A. (1969) 'An investigation into the development of melodic interval discrimination', *Austr. J. Psychol.*, **21**, 187-91.

EISENBERG, R. B. (1976) *Auditory Competence in Early Life*. Baltimore: University Park Press.

ELLIOTT, C. D. (1971) 'Noise tolerance and extraversion in children', *Brit. J. Psychol.*, **62**, 375-80.

EUPER, J. A. (1968) 'Early infantile autism' in E. T. GASTON (ed.) *Music in Therapy*. New York: Macmillan.

FARNSWORTH, P. R. (1931) 'An historical, critical and experimental study of the Seashore-Kwalwasser Test battery', *Genet. Psychol. Monogr.*, **9**:5, 291-393.

FARNSWORTH, P. R. (1954) 'A study of the Hevner Adjective List',*J. Aesth. and Art Crit.*, **13**, 97-103.

FARNSWORTH, P. R. (1964) 'New weights for the Seashore-Hevner tests for attitude toward music', *Rev. Psychol. Music*, **3**, 1-6.

FARNSWORTH, P. R. (1969) *The Social Psychology of Music*. 2nd edition Ames: Iowa State Univ. Press.

FARNUM, S. E. (undated) *Farnum Music Test*. New York: Psychological Corp.

FARNUM, S. E. (1969) *The Farnum String Scale*. Winona, Minn.: Hal Leonard Music.

FAULDS, B. (1959) *The Perception of Pitch in Music*. Princeton, N.J.: Educ. Testing Service.

FEIS, O. (1910) *Studien über die Genealogie und Psychologie des Musikers*. Wiesbaden: Bergmann.

FERRELL, J. W. (1961) A validity investigation of the Drake Musical Aptitude tests, Doctoral Diss., State Univ. Iowa.

FIELDHOUSE, A. E. (1937) A study of backwardness in singing among school children. Doctoral Diss., London Univ.

FIGGS, L. D. (1980) 'A study of the law of regression as it pertains to musicality', *Psychol. Music*, **8**(1), 19-24.

FISKE, H. E. (1975) Judge-group differences in the rating of secondary school trumpet players', *J. Res. Mus. Ed.*, **23**, 186-96.

FISKE, H. E. (1977) 'Who's to judge? New insights into performance evaluation', *Mus. Educators J.*, **64** (4), 22-5.

FLATAU, T. S. and GUTZMANN, H. (1906) 'Die Stimme des Säuglings', *Archiv. für Laryngologie und Rhinologie*, **18**, 139.

FLEISHMAN, E. A. (1955), 'Predicting code proficiency of radiotelegraphers by means of aural tests', *J. Appl. Psychol.*, **39**, 150-5.

FLEISHMAN, E. A., ROBERTS, N. H. and FREIDMAN, M. P. (1958) 'Factor analysis of aptitude and proficiency measures in radio-telegraphy', *J. Appl. Psychol.*, **42**, 127-37.

FOLEY, E. (1975) 'Effects of training in conservation of tonal and rhythmic patterns of second-grade children', *J. Res. Mus. Ed.*, **23**, 240-8.

FOSHA, L. (1964) A study of the validity of the Musical Aptitude Profile. Doctoral Diss., State Univ. Iowa.

FRACKER G. C. and HOWARD, V. M. (1928) 'Correlation between intelligence and musical talent', *Psychol. Monogr.*, **39**, 2, No 178, 157-61.

FRANCÈS, R. (1958) *La perception de la musique*. Paris: Vrin.

FRANKLIN, E. (1956) *Tonality as a basis for the study of musical talent*. Göteberg: Gumperts Forlag.

FREEMAN, J. (1974) 'Musical and artistic talent in children', *Psychol. Music*, **2** (1), 5-12.

FREGA, A. L. (1979) 'Rhythmic tasks with 3-, 4- and 5-year-old children: a study made in Argentine Republic', *Bull. Council Res. Mus. Ed.*, **59**, 32-4.

FRIDMAN, R. (1973) 'The first cry of the newborn: Basis for the child's future musical development', *J. Res. Mus. Ed.*, **21**, 264-9.

FRIDMAN, R. (1976) 'Affective communication through the baby's sonorous expression: relation to mental health and future musical activity' in ISME Proceedings of the XI International Conference, *Challenges in Music Education*, Perth: Univ. Western Australia.

FRIEND, R. (1939) 'Influences of heredity and musical environment on the scores of kindergarten children on the Seashore Measures of Musical Ability', *J. Appl. Psychol.*, **23**, 347-57.

FROSETH, J. O. (1971) 'Using MAP scores in the instruction of beginning students', *J. Res. Mus. Ed.*, **19**, 98-105.

FRY, D. (1948) 'An experimental study of tone deafness', *Speech*, **12**(1), 4-11.

FUNK, J. D. (1977) Some aspects of the development of music perception. Doctoral Diss., Clark University.

GABRIEL, C. J. (1978) 'An experimental study of Deryck Cooke's Theory of Music and Meaning', *Psychol. Music*, **6** (1), 13-20.

GABRIEL, C. and CRICKMORE, L. (1977) 'Emotion and music', *Psychol. Music*, 5(1), 28-31.

GAEDE, S. E., PARSONS, O. A., and BERTERA, J. H. (1978) 'Hemispheric differences in music perception: aptitude vs. experience', *Neuropsychologia*, **16**, 369-73.

GALLAGHER, F. D. (1971) A study of the relationship between the Gordon Musical Aptitude Profile, the Colwell Music Achievement Tests, and the Indiana-Oregon Music Discrimination Test. Doctoral Diss., Indiana Univ.

GALTON, F. (1869) *Hereditary Genius*. London: Macmillan.

GARDER, C. E. (1953) A study of characteristics of outstanding high school musicians. Doctoral Diss., Univ. Kansas.

GARDINER, W. (1938) *The Music of Nature*. Boston: Wilkins and Carter.

GARDNER, H. (1971*a*) 'Children's duplication of rhythmic patterns', *J. Res. Mus. Ed.*, **19**, 355-60.

GARDNER, H. (1971*b*) 'Children's sensitivity to musical styles'. Harvard Project Zero, Technical Report, No. 4.

GARDNER, H., DAVIDSON, L, and MCKERNON, P. (1979) 'The acquisition of song: a developmental approach'. Paper to National Symposium on the Applications of Psychology to the Teaching and Learning of Music, II, Ann Arbor.

GARDNER, H., SILVERMAN, J., DENES, E., SEMENZA, C. and ROSENSTIEL, A. K. (1977) 'Sensitivity to musical denotation and connotation in organic patients', *Cortex*, **13**, 242-56.

GASTON, E. T. (1958) *A test of musicality, manual of directions*. Lawrence, Ka.: Odell's Instrumental Service.

GATES, A. and BRADSHAW, J. L. (1974) 'Effects of auditory feedback on a musical performance task', *Perception and Psychophysics*, **16**, 105-9.

GATES, A., and BRADSHAW, J. (1977) 'Music perception and cerebral asymmetries', *Cortex*, **13**, 390-401.

GATES, A., BRADSHAW, J. L. and NETTLETON, N. C. (1974) 'Effect of different delayed auditory feedback intervals on a music performance task', *Perception and Psychophysics*, **15**, 21-5.

GEDDA, L. *et al.* (1961) *L'eredità delle attitudini musicali*. Proc. 2nd Internat. Congr. of Human Genetics, Rome.

GESELL, A. and ILG, F. (1943) *The Infant and Child in the Culture of Today*. London : Hamilton.

GIBBONS, A. C. (1980) 'Musical aptitude scores in the elderly and their relationships to morale and selected other variables'. Paper to Music Educators National Conference National Convention.

GILBERT, G. M. (1942) 'Sex differences in musical aptitude and training', *J. Gen. Psychol.* **26**, 19-33.

GILBERT, J. A. (1893) 'Experiments on the musical sensitiveness of schoolchildren', *Studies from the Yale Psychological Laboratory*, 1892-3, **1**, 80-7.

GILBERT, J. P. (1979) 'Assessment of motoric music skill development in young children: Test construction and evaluation procedures', *Psychol. Music*, **7** (2), 3-12.

GILBERT, J. P. (1981) 'Motoric music skill development in young children: A longitudinal investigation', *Psychol. Music.*, 9(1), 21-5.

GORDER, W. D. (1980) 'Divergent production abilities as constructs of musical creativity', *J. Res. Mus. Ed.*, **28**, 34-42.

GORDON, E. (1961) 'A study to determine the effects of training and practice on Drake Musical Aptitude Test scores', *J. Res. Mus. Ed.*, **9**, 63-74.

GORDON, E. (1965) *Musical Aptitude Profile Manual*. Boston: Houghton Mifflin.

GORDON, E. (1967) *A Three-Year Longitudinal Predictive Validity Study of the Musical Aptitude Profile*. Iowa City: Univ. Iowa Press.

GORDON, E. (1968a) 'The contribution of each Musical Aptitude Profile subtest to the overall validity of the battery', *Bull. Council Res. Mus. Ed.*, No 12, 32-6.

GORDON, E. (1968b) 'A study of the efficacy of general intelligence and musical aptitude tests in predicting achievement in music',

Bull. Council Res. Mus. Ed., No 13, 40-5.

GORDON, E. (1969) 'An investigation of the intercorrelation among Musical Aptitude Profile and Seashore Measures of Musical Talents subtests', *J. Res. Mus. Ed.*, **17**, 263-71.

GORDON, E. (1970*a*) 'Taking into account musical aptitude differences among beginning instrumental students', *Exper. Res. Psychol. Music: Stud. Psychol. Music*, **6**, 45-64.

GORDON, E. (1970*b*) *The Psychology of Music Teaching*. Englewood Cliffs, N.J.: Prentice Hall.

GORDON, E. (1971) *Iowa Tests of Music Literacy*. Iowa City: Bureau of Educational Research and Service, Univ. Iowa.

GORDON, E. (1974) 'Towards the development of a taxonomy of tonal patterns and rhythm patterns: Evidence of difficulty level and growth rate', *Exper. Res. Psychol. Music: Stud. Psychol. Music*, **9**, 39-232.

GORDON, E. (1975) 'Fourth-year and fifth-year final results of a longitudal study of the musical achievement of culturally disadvantaged students', *Exper. Res. Psychol. Music: Stud. Psychol. Music*, **10**, 24-52.

GORDON, E. (1976) *Tonal and Rhythm Patterns: An Objective Analysis*. Albany: Univ. New York Press.

GORDON, E. (1977) *Learning Sequence and Patterns in Music*. Chicago: G.I.A.

GORDON, E. (1978) *Pattern Sequence and Learning in Music*. Chicago: G.I.A.

GORDON, E. (1979*a*) *Primary Measures of Music Audiation: Test Manual*. Chicago: G.I.A.

GORDON, E. (1979*b*) 'Development music aptitude as measured by the Primary Measures of Music Audiation', *Psychol. Music*, **7**(1).

GORDON, E. E. (1980) 'Developmental music aptitudes among inner city primary children', *Bull. Council. Res. Mus. Ed.*, No 63, 25-30.

GORDON, H. W. (1970) 'Hemispheric asymmetries in the perception of musical chords', *Cortex*, **6**, 387-98.

GORDON, H. W. (1978) 'Left hemisphere dominance for rhythmic elements in dichotically-presented melodies', *Cortex*, **14**, 58-70.

GORDON, H. W. and BOGEN, J. E. (1974) 'Hemispheric lateralization of singing after intracarotoid sodium amylobarbitone', *J. Neurol. Neurosurg. Psychiatry*, **37**, 727-38.

GORDON, K. (1917) 'Some tests on the memorising of musical themes', *J. Exp. Psychol.*, **2**, 93-9.

GOULD, A. O. (1969) 'Developing specialised programs for singing',

Bull. Council Res. Mus. Ed., No. 17, 9-22.

GRAVES, W. S. (1947) 'Factors associated with children's taking music lessons, including some parent-child relationships', *J. Genet. Psychol.*, **7**, 65-89 and 91-125.

GRIFFIN, L. R. and EISENMAN, R. (1972) 'Musical ability: the Drake Musical Memory Test', *Educ. and Psychol. Measurement*, **32**, 473-76.

GROVES, W. C. (1969) 'Rhythmic training and its relationship to the synchronization of motor-rhythmic responses', *J. Res. Mus. Ed.*, **17**, 408-15.

GUNDLACH, R. H. (1935) 'Factors determining the characterization of musical phrases', *Amer. J. Psychol.*, **47**, 624-43.

HAIR, H. I. (1973) 'The effect of training on the harmonic discrimination of first-grade children', *J. Res. Mus. Ed.*, **21**, 85-90.

HAIR, H. I. (1977) 'Discrimination of tonal direction on verbal and nonverbal tasks by first grade children', *J. Res. Mus. Ed.*, **25**, 197-210.

HANLEY, C. N. (1956) 'Factorial analysis of speech perception', *J. Speech Hearing Dis.*, **21**, 76-87.

HARRIS, J. (1952) 'The decline of pitch discriminators with time', *J. Exper. Psychol.*, **43**, 96-9.

HATFIELD, W. (1967) An investigation of the diagnostic validity of MAP with respect to instrumental performance. Doctoral Diss., Univ. Iowa.

HEBB, D. O. (1949) *The Organisation of Behaviour*. New York: Wiley.

HEIM, K. (1963) Musical aptitude of senior high school students in residential schools for the blind. Master's thesis, Univ. Kansas.

HEINLEIN, C. P. (1928) 'The affective character of the major and minor modes in music', *J. Comparative Psychol.*, **8**, 101-42.

HEINLEIN, C. P. (1929) 'A new method of studying the rhythmic responses of children', *J. Genet. Psychol.*, **36**, 205-28.

HELLER, J. J. (1962) The effects of formal music training on the Wing Musical Intelligence scores. Doctoral Diss., State Univ. Iowa.

HEVNER, K. (1931) 'A study of tests for appreciation of music', *J. Appl. Psychol.*, **15**, 575-83.

HEVNER, K. (1935a) 'Expression in music: A discussion of experimental studies and theories', *Psychol. Rev.*, **42**, 186-204.

HEVNER, K. (1935b) 'The affective character of the major and minor modes in music', *Amer. J. Psychol.*, **47**, 103-18.

HEVNER, K. (1936) 'Experimental studies of the elements of expression in music', *Amer. J. Psychol.*, **48**, 246-68.

HIGHSMITH, J. A. (1929) 'Selecting musical talent', *J. Appl. Psychol.*, **13**, 486-93.

HILL, J. (1970) 'A study of the musical achievement of culturally deprived children and culturally advantaged children at the elementary school level', *Exper. Res. Psychol. Music: Stud. Psychol. Music*, **6**, 95-123.

HIRIARTBORDE, E. and FRAISSE, P. (1968) *Les aptitudes rythmiques*. Paris: Ed. du CNRS.

HOFFREN, J. (1964) 'The construction and validation of a test of expressive phrasing in music', *J. Res. Mus. Ed.*, **12**, 159-64.

HOLLINGWORTH, L. S. (1926) 'The musical sensitivity of children who test above 135 IQ', *J. Ed. Psychol.*, **17**, 95-109.

HOLMES, J. (1954) 'Increased reliabilities, new keys and norms for a modified Kwalwasser-Dykema test of musical aptitude', *J. Genet. Psychol.*, **85**, 65-73.

HOLMSTROM, L.-G. (1963) *Musicality and Prognosis*. Uppsala: Almqvist & Wiksell.

HOLMSTROM, L.-G. (1969) 'Intelligence vs. progress in music education', *J. Res. Mus. Ed.*, **17**, 76-81.

HORBULEWICZ, J. (1963) The development of musical memory. Doctoral Diss., Higher School of Education, Danzig.

HORN, J. L. (1973) 'Theory of functions represented among auditory and visual test performances' in J. R. Royce (ed.) *Multivariate Analysis and Psychological Theory*. London: Academic Press.

HORN, J. L. and DONALDSON, G. (1980) 'Cognitive development II: Adulthood development of human abilities'. Chapter 10 in O. G. BRIM and J. KAGAN (eds) *Constancy and Change in Human Development: A Volume of Review Essays*. Cambridge, Mass: Harvard University Press.

HORN, J. L. and STANOV, L. (in preparation) 'Auditory and visual factors in intelligence'.

HUFF, J. (1967) An investigation of auditory and visual perception of rhythm and its relation to skill in selected motor abilities. Doctoral Diss., Univ. Utah.

HUFSTADER, R. A. (1977) 'An investigation of a learning sequence of music listening skills', *J. Res. Mus. Ed.*, **25**, 184-96.

HURST, C. C. (1912) 'Mendelian heredity in man', *Eugen. Rev.*, **4** (1), 20-4.

IGAGA, J. M. (1974) A comparative development study of the rhythmic sensitivity of Ugandan and English schoolchildren. Doctoral Diss., London Univ.

IGAGA, J. M. and VERSEY, J. (1977) 'Cultural differences in rhythmic perception', *Psychol. Music*, **5**(1), 23-7.

IGAGA, J. M. and VERSEY, J. (1978) 'Cultural differences in rhythmic performance', *Psychol. Music*, **6**(1), 61-4.

IL'INA, G. A. (1961) 'Characteristics of the development of musical rhythm in children', *Vop. Psikhol.*, **1**, 119-32.

IMBERTY, M. (1969) *L'acquisition des structures tonales chez l'enfant*. Paris: Klincksieck.

IMBERTY, M. (1970) 'Polysémie et cohérence du langage musical I : La polysémie dans les reponses verbales associées à la musique et la construction d'une échelle circulaire des expressivités musicales', *Sciences de l'Art*, **7**, 75-94.

IMBERTY, M. (1971) 'Polysémie et cohérence du langage musical II : structure des connotations verbales de la musique et le cohérence des contenues sémantiques', *Sciences de l'Art*, **8**, 65-81.

IMBERTY, M. (1976) 'Polysémie et cohérence du langage musical, III: Représentation sémantique du style', *Scientific Aesthetics*, **1** (2), 139-59.

JAMIESON, R. P. G. (1951) 'An investigation into songs known by Scottish schoolchildren and their musical preferences'. B. Ed. thesis, Glasgow Univ. Summary in *Brit. J. Educ. Psychol.*, **22**, 74-5.

JENKINS, J. M. D. (1976) The relationship between maternal parents' musical experience and the musical development of two- and three-year-old girls. Doctoral Diss., North Texas State Univ.

JERSILD, A. T. and BIENSTOCK, S. F. (1931) 'The influence of training on the vocal ability of three-year-old children', *Child Devel.*, **2**, 272-91.

JERSILD, A. T. and BIENSTOCK, S. F. (1934) 'A study of the development of children's ability to sing', *J. Educ. Psychol.*, **25**, 481-503.

JERSILD, A. T. and BIENSTOCK, S. F. (1935) 'The development of rhythm in young children', *Child. Devel. Monogr.*, No 22, Teachers College, Columbia.

JOHNSON, P. R. (1977) 'Dichotically-stimulated ear differences in musicians and nonmusicians', *Cortex*, **13**, 385-9.

JOHNSON, R. C. BOWERS, J. K., GAMBLE, M., LYONS, F. M., PRESBREY, T. W., and VETTER, R. B., (1977) 'Ability to transcribe music and ear superiority for tone sequences', *Cortex*, **13**, 295-9.

JONES, M. (1979) 'Using a vertical-keyboard instrument with the uncertain singer', *J. Res. Mus. Ed.*, **27**, 173-84.

JONES, R. L. (1976) 'The development of the child's conception of meter in music', *J. Res. Mus. Ed.*, **24**, 142-54.

JOYNER, D. (1969) 'The monotone problem', *J. Res. Mus. Ed.*, **17**, 115-24.

JUURMAA, J. (1967) 'The ability structure of the blind and the deaf:

Final report', *Amer. Foundation for the Blind Research Bulletin*, **14**, 109-22.

KAGAN, J. (1972) 'Do infants think?' *Sci. Amer.*, **226**, No 3, 74-83.

KAGAN, J. and LEWIS, M. (1965) 'Studies of attention in the human infant', *Merrill-Palmer Quart.*, **11**, 95-127.

KALLMAN, H. J. and CORBALLIS, M. C. (1975) 'Ear asymmetry in reaction time to musical sounds', *Perception and Psychophysics*, **17**, 368-70.

KALMUS, H. (1949) 'Tune deafness and its inheritance'. Proc. Internat. Cong. Genetics, Stockholm, 605.

KALMUS, H. (1952) 'Inherited sense defects', *Sci. Amer.*, **185** (5), 64-70.

KAPUSCINSKI, R. (1979) 'Comment on Suzuki's methods and philosphy', *Music Educators J.*, **65** (6), 40.

KARLIN, J. E. (1941) 'Musical ability', *Psychometrika*, **6**, 61-5.

KARLIN, J. E. (1942) 'A factorial study of auditory function', *Psychometrika*, **7**, 251-79.

KARMA, K. (1975) 'The ability to structure acoustic materials as a measure of musical aptitude 2. Test Construction and Results', *Research Bulletin* No 43, Institute of Education, Univ. Helsinki.

KARMA, K. (1979) 'Musical, spatial and verbal abilities', *Bull. Council Res. Mus. Ed.*, No 59, 50-3.

KARMA, K. (1980) 'The ability to structure acoustic material as a measure of musical aptitude 5. Summary and conclusions', *Research Bulletin* No 52, Institute of Education, Univ. Helsinki.

KEMP, A. (1979) The personality structure of composers and performing musicians. Doctoral Diss., Univ. Sussex.

KEMP, A. (1980) 'The personality structure of musicians'. Paper to 15th Conference of Society for Research in Psychology of Music and Music Education, March.

KESSEN, W., LEVINE, J., AND WENDRICH, K. A. (1979) 'The imitation of pitch in infants', *Infant Behav. and Devel.*, **2**, 93-9.

KIMURA, D. (1961) 'Some effects of temporal lobe damage on auditory perception', *Canad. J. Psychol.*, **15**, 156-65.

KIMURA, D. (1964) 'Left-right differences in the perception of melodies', *Quart. J. Exp. Psychol.*, **16**, 355-8.

KIMURA, D. (1967) 'Functional asymmetry of the brain in dichotic listening', *Cortex*, **3**, 163-78.

KING, C. D. (1972) The conservation of melodic pitch patterns by elementary school children as determined by ancient Chinese music. Doctoral Diss., Ohio State Univ.

KING, F. L. and KIMURA, D. (1972) 'Left-ear superiority in dichotic perception of vocal nonverbal sounds', *Canad. J. Psychol.*, **26**, 111-16.

KIRKPATRICK, W. C. (1962) Relationships between the singing ability of pre-kindergarten children and their home environment. Doctoral Diss., Univ. Southern California.

KLANDERMAN, N. Z. (1979) The development of auditory discrimination and performance of pitch, rhythm, and melody in preschool children. Doctoral Diss., Northwestern Univ.

KLINEBERG, O. (1935) *Race Differences*. New York: Harper.

KLEMISH, J. (1974) 'Testing the uncertain singer through the use of the tape-recorder', *Bull. Council. Res. Mus. Ed.*, No 37, 36-45.

KNOX, A. W. and BOONE, D. R. (1976) 'Auditory laterality and tested handedness', *Cortex*, **6**, 164-73.

KREIS, J. VON (1926) *Wer ist musikallish?* Berlin.

KUCENSKI, D. (1977) Implementation and empirical testing of a sequential musical sensory learning program on the infant learner. Doctoral Diss., Northwestern Univ.

KUDER, G. F. (1956-   ) *Kuder Preference Record*. Chicago: Science Research Associates.

KUDER, G. F. (1970) *Kuder General Interest Survey*. Chicago: Science Research Associates.

KUHN, T. L. (1974) 'Discrimination of modulated beat tempos by professional musicians', *J. Res. Mus. Ed.*, **22**, 270-7.

KWALWASSER, J. (1955) *Exploring the Musical Mind*. New York: Coleman-Ross.

KWALWASSER, J. and DYKEMA, P. (1930) *Kwalwasser-Dykema Music Tests*. New York: Carl Fischer.

KWALWASSER, J. and RUCH, G. (1924) *Kwalwasser-Ruch Tests of Musical Accomplishment*. Iowa City: Bureau of Ed. Res. and Serv.

LANGER, S. (1942) *Philosophy in a New Key*. Cambridge, Mass. Harvard Univ. Press.

LARSEN, R. L. (1973) 'Levels of conceptual development in melodic permutation concepts based on Piaget's theory', *J. Res. Mus. Ed.*, **21**, 256-63.

LARSON, R. (1955) 'Finding and guiding musical talent', *Music Educ. J.*., **42**, Sept., 22-5.

LARSON, R. C. (1977) 'Relationships between melodic error detection, melodic dictation and melodic sightsinging', *J. Res. Mus. Ed.*, **25**, 264-71.

LAVERTY, G. E. (1969) The development of children's concepts of pitch, duration and loudness as a function of grade level. Doctoral Diss., Penn. State Univ.

LAWRENCE, S. J. and DACHLINGER, N. (1967) 'Factors relating to carryover of music training into adult life', *J. Res. Mus. Ed.*, **15**, 23-31.

LE BLANC, A. (1979) 'Generic style music preferences of fifth-grade students', *J. Res. Ed. Mus.*, **27**, 255-70.

LEE, R. E. (1967) 'An investigation of the use of the Musical Aptitude Profile with college and university freshman music students', *J. Res. Mus. Ed.*, **15**, 32-40.

LEHMAN, C. F. (1950) 'A comparative study of instrumental musicians on the basis of the Kwalwasser-Dykema Music Tests, the Otis Intelligence Test and the Minnesota Multiphasic Personality Inventory', *J. Educ. Res.*, **44**, 57-61.

LEONHARD, C. (1980) 'Towards a contemporary program of music education', *Bull. Council Res. Mus.*, No 63, 1-10.

LEONHARD, C. and COLWELL, R. J. (1976) 'Research in music education', *Bull. Council Res. Mus. Ed.*, No 49, 1-30.

LEONTIEV, A. N. (1969) 'On the biological and social aspects of human development: The training of auditory ability' in A. N. LEONTIEV, M. COLE and I. MALT (eds) *A Handbook of Contemporary Soviet Psychology*. New York: Basic Books.

LEUTENEGGER, R. R., and MUELLER, T. H. (1964) 'Auditory factors and the acquisition of French, *Modern Language Journal*, **48**, 141-6.

LEUTENEGGER, R. R., MUELLER, T. H. and WERSHOW, I. R. (1965) 'Auditory factors in foreign language acquisition', *Modern Language Journal*, **49**, 22-31.

LEVY-AGRESTI, J. and SPERRY, R. W., (1968) 'Differential perceptual capacities in major and minor hemispheres', *Proc. Nat. Acad. Sci.*, **61**, 1151.

LEWANDOWSKA, K. (1978) *Rozwoj Zdolnosci Muzycznych*. Warsaw: Wydawnictwa Szkolne i Pedagogiezne. English summary pp. 168-70.

LOCKE, S. and KELLAR, L. (1973) 'Categorical perception in a non-linguistic mode', *Cortex*, **9**, 353-67.

LONG, N. M. (1965) A revision of the University of Oregon Music Discrimination Test. Doctoral Diss., Indiana Univ.

LONG, N. H. (1971) 'Establishment of standards for the Indiana-Oregon Music Discrimination Test', *Bull. Council Res. Mus. Ed.*, No 25, 26-35.

LONG, N. H. (1972) 'Music discrimination tests – their construction, assumptions and uses'. *Austral. J. Mus. Ed.*, **11**, 21-5.

LONG, N. H. (1978) *Indiana-Oregon Music Discrimination Test*. Bloomington, Ind.: Mid West Tests.

LONG, P. A. (1977) 'Relationships between pitch memory in short melodies and selected factors', *J. Res. Mus. Ed.*, **25**, 272-82.

LONGUET-HIGGINS, H. C. (1976) 'The perception of melodies', *Nature*, **263**, 646-53.

LOWERY, H. (1926) 'Cadence and phrase tests in music', *Brit. J. Psychol.*, **17**, 111-18.

LOWERY, H. (1929) 'Musical memory', *Brit. J. Psychol.*, **19**, 397-404.

LOWERY, H. (1952) *The Background of Music*. London: Hutchinson's University Library.

LUNDIN, R. W. (1944) 'A preliminary report on some new musical ability tests' *J. Appl. Psychol.*, **28**, 393-6.

LUNDIN, R. W. (1949) 'The development and validation of a set of musical ability tests', *Psychol. Monogr.*, **63**: 305, 1-20.

LUNDIN, R. W. (1958) 'What next in the psychology of musical measurement?' *Psychol. Rec.*, **8**, 1-6.

LUNDIN, R. W. (1963) 'Can perfect pitch be learned?' *Music Educ. J.*, **49**, 49-51.

LUNDIN, R. W. (1967) *An Objective Psychology of Music*. 2nd edit. New York: Ronald.

MACCOBY, E. E. and JACKLIN, C. N. (1974) *The Psychology of Sex Differences*. Stanford, Calif.: Stanford Univ. Press.

MCFIE, J. (1973) Letter to the Editor. *Devel. Med. Child Neurol.*, **15**, 848-9.

McGUINNESS, D. (1972) 'Hearing: individual differences in perceiving', *Perception*, **1**, 465-73.

McGUINNESS, D. (1976) 'Perception and Cognition' in B. LLOYD and J. ARCHER (eds), *Exploring Sex Differences*. London: Academic Press.

McKEE, G., HUMPHREY, B., and McADAM, D. W. (1973) 'Scaled lateralization of alpha activity during linguistic and musical tasks', *Psychophysiology*, **10**, 441-3.

McLEISH, J. (1950) 'The validation of Seashore's measures of musical talent by factorial methods', *Brit. J. Psychol. (Stat. Section)*, **3**, 129-40.

McLEISH, J. (1968) *Musical Cognition*. London: Novello.

McLEISH, J. and HIGGS, G. (1967) *An Inquiry into the Musical Capacities of Educationally Sub-Normal Children*. Cambridge: Institute of Education.

McLEISH, J. and THOMAS, C. (1971) 'Nationality and Musicality used to test the Lamarckian hypothesis', *Nature*, **230**, 337.

MADISON, T. H. (1942) 'Interval discrimination as a measure of musical aptitude', *Arch. Psychol.*, No 268.

MAINWARING, J. (1931) 'Experiments on the analysis of cognitive processes in musical ability' *Brit. J. Educ. Psychol.*, **1**, 180-203; 'Tests of musical ability', *Brit. J. Educ. Psychol.*, **1**, 313-21.

MAINWARING, J. (1933) 'Kinaesthetic factors in the recall of musical experience', *Brit. J. Psychol.*, **23**, 284-307.

MAINWARING, J. (1948) 'Review of H. D. Wing's Tests of Musical Ability and Appreciation', *Music and Letters*, **29**, 290-3.

MANOR, H. C. (1950) 'A study of prognosis', *J. Educ. Psychol.*, **41**, 31-50.

MANTURZEWSKA, M. (1978) 'Psychology in the Music School', *Psychol. Music*, **6**(2), 36-47.

MANTURZEWSKA, M. (1979) 'Results of psychological research on the process of music practising and its effective shaping', *Bull. Council Res. Mus. Ed.*, No 59, 59-61.

MARTIN, J. (1964) 'Changes following musical training', *J. Educ. Res.*, **44**, 440-2.

MARTIN, P. J. (1976) Appreciation of music in relation to personality factors. Doctoral Diss., Univ. Glasgow.

MARTIN, P. J. (1979) 'Distinguishing school orchestra members', *Bull. Council Res. Mus. Ed.*, No 59, 62-7.

MAWBEY, W. E. (1973) 'Wastage from instrumental classes in schools', *Psychol. Music*, **1**(1), 33-43.

MEAD, M. (1964) 'Comments' in T. A. SEBEOK, A. S. HAYES, M. C. BATESON (eds) *Approaches to Semiotics*. The Hague: Mouton.

MEYER, A. (1977) 'The search for a morphological substrate in the brains of eminent persons including musicians: a historical review' in MACDONALD CRITCHLEY and R. A. HENSON (eds) *Music and the Brain*. London: Heinemann.

MEYER, J. (1978) 'The dependence of pitch on harmonic sound spectra', *Psychol. Music*, **6**(1), 3-12.

MEYER, L. B. (1956) *Emotion and Meaning in Music*. Chicago: Univ. Chicago Press.

MEYER, L. B. (1967) *Music, the Arts, and Ideas*. Chicago: Univ. Chicago Press.

MICHEL, P. (1973) 'The optimum development of musical abilities in the first years of life', *Psychol. Music*, **1**(1), 14-20.

MILLER, P. H. (1975) 'An experimental analysis of the development of tonal capabilities of first grade children', *Exper. Res. Psychol. Music: Stud. Psychol. Music*, **10**, 77-97.

MILNER, B. (1962) 'Laterality effects in audition' in V. B. MOUNT-CASTLE (ed.) *Interhemispheric Relations and Cerebral Dominance*. Baltimore: Johns Hopkins Press.

MINOGUE, B. (1923) 'A case of secondary mental deficiency with musical talent' *J. Appl. Psychol.*, **7**, 349-52.

MJOEN, J. (1926) 'Genius as a biological problem', *Eugen. Rev.*, **17**, 242-57.

MJOEN, J. (1934) *Die Vererbung der musikalischen Begabung*. Berlin: Metzner.

MOHATT, J. L. (1971) 'An investigation of the criterion-related validity of the Iowa Tests of Music Literacy', *Exper. Res. Psychol. Music: Stud. Psychol.* **7**, 144-67.

MONTESSORI, M. (1967) *The Absorbent Mind.* Trans. C. A. Claremont. New York: Dell.

MOOG, H. (1967) 'Der Bildungsinhalt Musik und seine Bedeutung für die Heilpädagogik', *Päd. Rundschau*, Jahrgang 21, Ratingen.

MOOG, H. (1976) *The Musical Experience of the Pre-School Child.* Trans. C. Clarke. London: Schott.

MOOG, H. (1979) 'On the perception of rhythmic forms by physically handicapped children and those of low intelligence in comparison with non-handicapped children', *Bull. Council Res. Mus. Ed.*, No 59, 73-8.

MOORE, D. L. (1973) A study of pitch and rhythm responses of five-year-old children in relation to their early music training. Doctoral Diss., Florida State Univ.

MOORHEAD, G. E. and POND, D. (1941-1951, reprinted 1978) *Music of Young Children*, Santa Barbara, Calif., : Pillsbury Foundation for Advancement of Music.

MORROW, R. S. (1938) 'An analysis of the relations among tests of musical, artistic and mechanical abilities', *J. Psychol.*, **5**, 253-63.

MORROW, R. S. (1941) 'An experimental analysis of the theory of independent abilities', *J. Educ. Psychol.*, **32**, 494-512.

MORTON, J. (1979) 'Rhythm and handedness'. Paper to Society of Research in Psychology of Music and Music Education. March 1979. Summary in *Psychol. Music*, **8** (2), 50.

MUELLER, J. H. *et al.* (1934) *Studies in appreciation of art*, 4, No 6, 1-151.

MUELLER, K. HEVNER (1956) 'Studies in music appreciation', *J. Res. Mus. Ed.*, **4**, 3-25.

MULL, H. K. (1925) 'The acquisition of absolute pitch', *Amer. J. Psychol.*, **36**, 369-93.

MURSELL, J. L. (1937) *The Psychology of Music.* New York: Norton.

MURSELL, J. and GLENN, M. (1931) *The Psychology of School Music Teaching.* New York: Silver Burdett.

NATIONAL ASSESSMENT OF EDUCATIONAL PROGRESS (1974) The First National Assessment of Musical Performance. Reports 03-MU-00, 03-MU-01, 03-MU-02, 03-MU-03. Education Commission of the States.

NETTHEIM, N. (1979) Comment on a paper by Gabriel on Cooke's theory. *Psychol. Music*, **7** (2), 32-3.

NEWTON, G. DE C. (1959) *Selection of Junior Musicians for Royal Marines School of Music: An evaluation of H. D. Wing's Test.* Senior Psychologist's Dept., Admiralty, London.

NIELSON, J. T. (1930) 'A study in the Seashore Motor Rhythm test', *Psychol. Monog.* **40**, 74-84.

NOBLE, R. F. (1977) 'A multivariate analysis of factors in attitudinal levels of Wyoming adults toward music', *J. Res. Mus. Ed.*, **25**, 59-67.

NORTHRUP, W. C. (1931) 'The inheritance of musical ability. Student Pedigree Studies', *Eugen. News*, **16**.

NORTON, D. (1979) 'Relationship of musical ability and intelligence to auditory and visual conservation of the kindergarten child', *J. Res. Mus. Ed.*, **27**, 3-13.

NOY, P. (1968) 'The development of musical ability', *Psychoanal. Study of the Child*, **23**, 332-47.

NUNNALLY, J. C. (1978) *Psychometric Theory*. New York: McGraw-Hill.

OAKLEY, D. (1972) The cumulative attainment by Missouri high school seniors of the musical learnings stated in the Music Curriculum Guides published by the Missouri State Department of Education. Doctoral Diss., Indiana Univ.

OLDFIELD, R. C. (1969) 'Handedness in musicians', *Brit. J. Psychol.*, **60**, 91-9.

OSGOOD, C., SUCI, E. and TANNENBAUM, P. (1957) *The Measurement of Meaning*. Urbana, Ill.: Univ. Illinois Press.

OSTWALD, P. (1973) 'Musical behavior in early childhood' *Devel. Med. Child Neurol.*, **15**, 367-75.

OWENS, W. A. and GRIMM, W. (1941) 'A note regarding exceptional musical ability in a low-grade imbecile', *J. Educ. Psychol.*, **32**, 636-7.

PARKER, O. G. (1978) 'The relationship of musical ability, intelligence and socioeconomic status to aesthetic sensitivity', *Psychol. Music*, **6**(2), 30-5.

PAYNE, E. (1973) 'The nature of musical emotion and its place in the appreciative experience', *Brit. J. Aesthetics*, **13**, 171-81.

PAYNE, E. (1980) 'Towards an understanding of music appreciation', *Psychol. Music*, **8** (2).

PEGGIE, A. (1980) 'Reading the dots', *Classical Music*, August 2, 14, 31-41.

PETERS, M. (1969) A comparison of the musical sensitivity of mongoloid and nonmongoloid children. Doctoral Diss., Univ. Illinois.

PETZOLD, R. G. (1966) *Auditory perception of musical sounds by children in the first six grades*. Cooperative Research Project No 1051, Univ. Wisconsin.

PFLEDERER, M. (1964) 'The responses of children to musical tasks embodying Piaget's principles of conservation', *J. Res. Mus. Ed.*, **12**, 251-68.

PHILLIPS. D. (1976) 'An investigation of the relationship between musicality and intelligence, *Psychol. Music*, **4** (2), 16-31.

PIPER, R. M. and SHOEMAKER, D. M. (1973) 'Formative evaluation of a kindergarten music program based on behavioural objectives', *J. Res. Mus. Ed.*, **12**, 145-52.

PITMAN, D. J. (1965) 'The musical ability of blind children', *Rev. Psychol. in Music*, **2** (2), 19-28.

PLUMRIDGE, J. M. (1972) The range and pitch levels of children's voices, in relation to published material for children's voices. Diss. Diploma in Advanced Studies in Education, Univ. Reading.

POLLOCK, T. (1950) Singing disability in school children. Master's Diss., Univ. Durham.

POND, D. (1980) 'The young child's playful world of sound', *Music Ed. J.*, **66**, March.

POND, D., SHELLEY, S. J. and WILSON, B. D. (1978) 'The Pillsbury Foundation School revisited'. Paper to the Music Educators National Conference, 26th National Conference, Chicago.

PORTER, S. YANK (1977) 'The effect of multiple discrimination training on pitch-matching behaviour of uncertain singers', *J. Res. Mus. Ed.*, **25**, 68-81.

PRÉVEL, M. (1976) 'Helping children build their own music'. In ISME Proceedings of the XI International Conference, *Challenges in Music Education*, Perth: Univ. Western Australia.

PREYER, W. (1901) *The Mind of the Child* Part I : *The Senses and the Will*. New York: Appleton.

RADOS, K. (1980) 'The structure of musicality'. Paper to 22nd International Congress of Psychology. Abstract guide p. 563.

RAINBOW, E. L. (1965) 'A pilot study to investigate the constructs of musical aptitude', *J. Res. Mus. Ed.*, **13**, 3-14.

RAINBOW, E. L. (1977) 'A longitudinal investigation of the rhythmic abilities of pre-school aged children', *Bull. Council Res. Mus. Ed.*, No 50, 55-61.

RAINBOW, E. L. and OWEN, D. (1979) 'A progress report on a three year investigation of the rhythmic ability of pre-school aged children'. *Bull. Council Res. Mus. Ed.*, No 59, 84-6.

RAKOWSKI, A. (1979) 'The magic number two: Seven examples of binary apposition in pitch theory', *Humanities Association Review*, **30**, (1, 2), 24-45.

RATLIFF, F. (1965) *Mach Bands: Quantitative Studies of Neural Networks in the Retina*. San Francisco: Holden Day.

REPINA, T. A. (1971) 'On some techniques of studying pitch sensitivity in preschool children'. *Dokl. Akad. Pedag, Navk. RSFSR*, Nos. 4-6, 1961 *a*, *b*, *c*, cited in A. V. Zaporozhets and D. B.

Elkonin, *The Psychology of Preschool Children*. Trans. Shybut and Simon. Cambridge, Mass. : MIT.

RESER, H. (1935) 'Inheritance of musical ability. Student Pedigree Studies', *Eugen. News*, **20**.

REVESZ, G. (1920) 'Prüfung der Musikalität', *Zsch. f. Psychol.*, **85**, 163-209.

REVESZ, G. (1925) *The Psychology of a Musical Prodigy*. New York: Harcourt Brace.

REVESZ, G. (1946) 'Beziehung zwischen mathematischer und musikalischer Begabung'. *Schweiz. Zsch. f. Psychol.*, **5**, 269-81.

REVESZ, G. (1953) *Introduction to the Psychology of Music*. London: Longmans, Green.

RICHET, G. (1900) 'Note sur un cas remarquable de précocité musicale'. IV Congr. Internat. de Psychologie.

RIFE, D. C. and SNYDER, L. H. (1931) 'A genetic refutation of the principles of behaviouristic psychology', *Hum. Biol.*, **3**, 547-59.

RIGAL, R. A. (1974) 'Determination of handedness using hand-efficiency tests', *Perc. and Motor Skills*, **39**, 253-4.

RIGG, M. (1937) 'The relationship between discrimination in music and discrimination in poetry', *J. Educ. Psychol.*, **38**, 149-52.

RILEY, D. A., McKEE, J. P., BELL, D. D. and SCHWARTZ, C. R. (1967) 'Auditory discrimination in children: The effect of relative and absolute instructions on retention and transfer', *J. Exp. Psychol.*, **73**, 581-8.

ROBERTS, E. (1977) Tonal deafness in children: Studies of remedial treatment. Doctoral Diss., Univ. Liverpool.

ROBERTS, E. and DAVIES, A. D. M. (1975) 'Poor pitch singing: Response of monotone singers to a program of remedial training', *J. Res. Mus. Ed.*, **23**, 227-39.

ROBY, A. R. (1962) 'A study in the correlation of music theory grades with the Seashore Measures of Musical Talents and the Aliferis Music Achievement Test', *J. Res. Mus. Ed.*, **10**, 137-42.

RODERICK, J. L. (1965) An investigation of selected factors of the creative thinking ability of music majors in a teacher training program. Doctoral Diss., Univ. Illinois.

ROGERS, V. R. (1956) Children's expressed musical preferences at selected grade levels. Doctoral Diss., Syracuse Univ.

ROSENBUSCH, M. H. and GARDNER, D. B. (1968) 'Reproduction of visual and auditory rhythm patterns by children', *Perc. and Motor Skills*, **26**, 1271-6.

ROWNTREE, J. P. (1970) 'The Bentley "Measures of Musical Abilities" – A critical evaluation', *Bull. Council Res. Mus. Ed.*, No 22, 25-32.

SACHS, C. (1957) *The Lore of Non-Western Music. Essay in Some Aspects of Musicology*. New York: Liberal Arts Press.

SADEK, A. A. M. (1968) A factor-analytic study of musical abilities of Egyptian students taking music as a special subject. Doctoral Diss., Univ. London.

SAKURABAYASHI, H., SATO, Y. and UEHARA, E. (1956) 'Auditory discrimination of the blind', *J. Psychol. Blind*, **1**, 3-10.

SALISBURY, F. S., and SMITH, H. R. (1929) 'Prognosis of sight-singing ability of normal school students', *J. Appl. Psychol.*, **13**, 425-39.

SALK, L. (1960) 'The effects of the normal heartbeat sound on the behaviour of the newborn infant: Implications for mental health', *World Ment. Health*, **12**, 168-75.

SALK, L. (1961) 'The importance of the heartbeat rhythm to human nature: Theoretical, clinical, and experimental observations', *Proc. Third World Cong. Psychiat.*, Montreal: McGill Univ. Press, **1**, 740-6.

SALK, L. (1962) 'Mother's heartbeat as imprinting stimulus', *Trans. New York Acad. Sci.*, **24**, 753-63.

SANDERS, A. (1979) 'Ervin Nyiregyhazi', *The Gramophone*, **57**, No 674, 175-6, 230.

SCHEERER, M., ROTHMANN, E. and GOLDSTEIN, K. (1945) 'A case of "idiot savant": An experimental study of personality organization', *Psychol., Monog.*, **58** (4), 64.

SCHEID, P. and ECCLES, J. C. (1975) 'Music and speech: Artistic function of the human brain', *Psychol. Music*, **3**(1), 21-35.

SCHEINFELD, A. (1956) *The New Heredity and You*. London: Chatto & Windus.

SCHLEUTER, S. L. (1972) 'An investigation of the interrelation of personality traits, musical aptitude, and musical achievement', *Exper. Res. Psychol. Music: Stud. Psychol. Music*, **8**, 90-102.

SCHLEUTER, S. L. (1977) 'The development of a college version of the Musical Aptitude Profile', *Psychol. Music*, **5**(2), 39-42.

SCHLEUTER, S. L. (1978) 'Effects of certain lateral dominance traits, musical aptitude and sex differences with instrumental music achievement', *J. Res. Mus. Ed.*, **26**, 23-31.

SCHLEUTER, S. L. and CHAMBERS, V. (1976) 'Relationship among musical aptitude and musical achievement test scores of non-select college students enrolled in a music fundamentals course', *Psychol. Music*, **4** (1), 24-8.

SCHLEUTER, S. L. and DE YARMAN, R. (1977) 'Musical aptitude stability among primary school children', *Bull. Council Res. Mus. Ed.*, No 51, 14–22.

SCHOEN, M. (1923) 'The validity of tests of musical talent', *J. Comp. Psychol.* **3**, 101-21.

SCHOEN, M. (1925) 'Tests of musical feeling and musical under-standing', *J. Comp. Psychol.*, **5**, 31-52.

SCHOEN, M. (1940) *The Psychology of Music*. New York: Roland Press.

SCOTT, C. R. (1979) 'Pitch concept formation in pre-school children', *Bull. Council Res. Mus. Ed.*, **59**, 87-93.

SEASHORE, C. E. (1919) *The Psychology of Musical Talent*. New York: Silver Burdett.

SEASHORE, C. E. (1937) 'The psychology of music: XI', *Mus. Ed. J.*, **24** (3), 25-6.

SEASHORE, C. E. (1938) *Psychology of Music*. New York: McGraw-Hill.

SEASHORE, C. E., LEWIS, D. and SAETVEIT, J. C. (1960) *Manual of Instructions and Interpretations for the Seashore Measures of Musical Talents*. 2nd revision. New York: The Psychological Corporation.

SEASHORE, C. E. and LING, T. L. (1918) 'The comparative sensitiveness of blind and seeing persons', *Psychol. Monogr.*, **25**, 148-58.

SEASHORE, C. E. and MOUNT, G. H. (1918) 'Correlations of factors in musical talent and training', *Psychol. Monogr.*, **25**, 47-92.

SEASHORE, R. M. (1926) 'Studies in motor rhythm', *Iowa Stud. Psychol. Music*, **9**, 142-9.

SERAFINE, M. L. (1979) 'A measure of meter conservation in music, based on Piaget's theory', *Genetic Psychol. Monogr.* **99**, 195-229.

SERAFINE, M. L. (1980) 'Piagetian research in music', *Bull. Council Res. Mus. Ed.*, No 62, 1-21.

SERGEANT, D. C. (1969*a*) 'Experimental investigation of absolute pitch', *J. Res. Mus. Ed.*, **17**, 135-43.

SERGEANT, D. C. (1969*b*) Pitch perception and absolute pitch : A study of some aspects of musical development. Doctoral Diss., Reading Univ.

SERGEANT, D. C. (1973) 'Measurement of pitch discrimination', *J. Res. Mus. Ed.*, **21**, 3-19.

SERGEANT, D. C. (1979) 'Vocalization as a substructure for discriminatory and cognitive functioning in music : A pilot study', *Bull. Council Res. Mus. Ed.*, **59**, 98-101.

SERGEANT, D. C. and BOYLE, J. D. (1980) 'The effect of task structure on pitch discrimination', *Psychol. Music*, **8** (2), 3-15.

SERGEANT, D. C. and ROCHE, S. (1973) 'Perceptual shifts in the auditory information processing of young children', *Psychol. Music*, **1** (2), 39-48.

SERGEANT, D. C. and THATCHER, G. (1974) 'Intelligence, social status and musical abilities', *Psychol. Music*, **2** (2), 32-57.

SHANKWEILER, D. (1966) 'Effects of temporal lobe damage on perception of dichotically presented melodies', *J. Comp. Physiol. Psychol.*, **62**, 115-19.

SHELDON, J. M. (1964) Prediction of success in pitch reproduction for the non-music major in college. Doctoral Diss., Univ. Southern California.

SHELTON, J. S. (1965) The influence of home musical environment upon musical response of first-grade children. Doctoral Diss., Nashville, Peasbody College for Teachers.

SHERBON, J. W. (1975) 'The association of hearing acuity, diplacusis, and discrimination with music performance', *J. Res. Mus. Ed.*, **23**, 249-57.

SHIELDS, J. (1962) *Monozygotic Twins Brought Up Apart and Brought Up Together*. London: Oxford University Press.

SHINN, M. W. (1907) *The Development of the Senses in the First Three Years of Childhood*. Univ. Calif. Publ. in Educ., Vol. 4.

SHIRLEY, M. M. (1933) *The First Two Years*: II *Intellectual Development.*. Univ. Minnesota Press.

SHRADER, D. L. (1970) An aural approach to rhythmic sight-reading, based upon principles of programmed learning, utilizing a stereo-tape teaching machine. Doctoral Diss., Univ. Oregon. (The TAP Rhythm System published by Temporal Acuity Products, Seattle.)

SHUTER, R. P. G. (1964) An investigation of hereditary and environmental factors in musical ability. Doctoral Diss., Univ. London.

SHUTER, R. P. G. (1966) 'Hereditary and environmental factors in musical ability', *Eugen. Rev.*, **58**, 149-56.

SHUTER, R. (1968) *The Psychology of Musical Ability*. London: Methuen.

SHUTER, R. (1974a) 'Singing out of tune: A review of recent research on this problem and its educational implications', *Sci. de l'Art*, **9**, 115-20.

SHUTER, R. (1974b) 'The relationship between musical abilities and personality characteristics in young children', Paper to Fourth Internat. Seminar on Res. in Music Educ., Christchurch, N.Z.

SHUTER-DYSON, R. (1979) 'Unisex or "Vive la difference"? Research on sex differences of relevance to musical abilities', *Bull. Council Res. Mus. Ed.*, No 59, 102-6.

SHUTER-DYSON, R. (in press) 'Musical ability' in D. DEUTSCH (ed.) *The Psychology of Music*. New York: Academic Press.

SIDTIS, J. J. and BRYDEN, M. P. (1978) 'Asymmetrical perception of language and music: Evidence for independent processing strategies', *Neuropsychologia*, **16**, 627-32.

SIEGEL, J. A. (1972) 'The nature of absolute pitch', *Exper. Res. Psychol. Music: Stud. Psychol. Music*, **8**, 54-89.

SIEGEL, J. A. (1976) 'Judgment of intonation by musicians: Further evidence for categorial perception', *Research Bulletin* No 375, Univ. Western Ontario.

SIEGEL, J. A. and SIEGEL, W. (1977*a*) 'Absolute identification of notes and intervals by musicians', *Perception and Psychophysics*, **21**, 143-52.

SIEGEL, J. A. and SIEGEL, W. (1977*b*), 'Categorical perception of tonal intervals: musicians can't tell sharp from flat', *Perception and Psychophysics*, **21**, 399-407.

SIMNER, M. L. (1971) 'Newborns' responses to the cry of another infant', *Devel. Psychol.*, **5**, 136-50.

SIMON, M. A. (1968) 'Perception du pattern musical par "Auditeur" ', *Sci. de l'Art*, **5**, 28-34.

SIMONS, G. M. (1964) 'Comparisons of incipient music responses among very young twins and singletons', *J. Res. Mus. Ed.*, **12**, 212-26.

SIMONS, G. M. (1976*a*) *Simons Measurements of Music Learning Skills*. Chicago: Stoelting.

SIMONS, G. M. (1976*b*) 'A criterion-referenced test of fundamental music listening skills', *Child Study Jour.* **6**, 223-34.

SLOAN, W. B. (1973) 'The child's conception of musical scales', *Psychol. Music*, **1** (1), 10–18.

SLOBODA, J. A. (1977) 'Phrase units as determinants of visual processing in music reading', *Brit. J. Psychol.*, **68**, 117-24.

SLOBODA, J. (1978) 'The psychology of music reading', *Psych. Music*, **6**, (2), 3-20.

SLOBODA, J. (in press) 'Music performance' in D. DEUTSCH (ed.) *Psychology of Music*. New York: Academic Press.

SLOBODA, J. (unpublished) 'Children's Perception of Harmony in Music'.

SMALL, C. (1977) *Music — Society — Education*. London: Calder.

SMITH, A. (1973) 'Feasibility of tracking musical form as a cognitive listening objective', *J. Res. Mus. Ed.*, **21**, 200-13.

SMITH, F. O. (1914) 'The effect of training in pitch discrimination', *Psychol. Monogr.*, **17**(3), 49-57.

SMITH, I. M. (1964) *Spatial Ability : Its Educational and Social Significance*. London: Univ. London Press.

SMITH, I.M., HOWES, R. and SHEPHERD, K. (1976) 'A study of the abilities and interests of overseas students', *Vocational Aspect of Education*, **28**, 55-6.

SOLOMON, L. M., WEBSTER, J. C., and CURTIS, J. F. (1960) 'A factorial study of speech perception', *J. Speech and Hearing Research*, **2**, 101-7.

SPELLACY, F. (1970) 'Lateral preferences in the identification of pattern stimuli', *J. Acoustic. Soc. Amer.*, **47**, 574-8.

SPERRY, R. W. (1974) 'Lateral specialization in the surgically separated hemispheres' in F. O. Schmitt and F. G. Worden (eds), *The Neurosciences: Third Study Program*. Cambridge, Mass.: MIT Press.

SPIEGLER, D. M. (1967) Factors involved in the development of prenatal rhythmic sensitivity. Doctoral Diss., West Virginia Univ.

SPREEN, O., SPELLACY, F. J. and REID, J. R. (1970) 'The effect of interstimulus interval and intensity on ear asymmetry for non-verbal stimuli in dichotic listening', *Neuropsychologia*, **8**, 245-50.

SPRINGER, S. P. and SEARLEMAN, A. (1978) 'Hemispheric asymmetry of function in twins' in W. E. NANCE *et al.* (eds) *Twin Research* : Proc. Internat. Congress in Twin Studies. Part A. New York : Liss.

STAFFORD, R. E. (1965) 'Nonparametric analysis of twin data with the Mann-Whitney U test', *Res. Report* No 10, Louisville Twin Study Child Development Unit, Univ. Louisville School of Medicine.

STAFFORD, R. E. (1970) 'Estimation of the interactions between heredity and environment for musical aptitude of twins', *Human Hered.*, **20**, 356-60.

STAMBACK, M. (1960) 'Trois épreuves de rhythme' in R. Zazzo (ed.) *Manuel pour l'examen psychologique de l'enfant*. Neuchatel: Delachaux et Niestle.

STANKOV, L. (1978) 'Fluid and crystallized intelligence and broad perceptual factors among 11 to 12 year olds', *J. Educ. Psychol.*, **70**, 324-34.

STANKOV, L. (1980) 'Ear differences and implied cerebral lateralization on some intellective auditory factors', *Appl. Psychol. Measurement*, **4**(1), 21-38.

STANKOV, L. (in preparation) The role of competition in human abilities revealed through auditory tests.

STANKOV, L. and HORN J. L. (1980) 'Human abilities revealed through auditory tests', *J. Educ. Psychol.*, **72**, 19-42.

STANKOV, L. and SPILSBURY, G. (1978) 'The measurement of auditory abilities of blind, partially sighted, and sighted children', *Appl. Psychol. Measurement*, **2**, 491-503.

STANTON, H. (1922) 'Inheritance of specific musical capacities', *Psychol. Monog.*, **31**, (1), Whole No 140, 157-204.

STANTON, H. (1935) 'Measurement of musical talent: the Eastman Experiment', *Univ. Iowa Stud. Psychol. Music*, **2**, 1-140.

STANTON, H. and KOERTH, W. (1930) 'Musical capacity measures in adults repeated after musical education', *Univ. Iowa Stud. Aims Progr. Res.*, **31**. No 189.

STANTON, H. and KOERTH, W. (1935) 'Musical capacity measures in children repeated after musical training', *Univ. Iowa Stud. Aims Progr. Res.*, **42**: 259.

STEEDMAN, M. J. (1977) 'The perception of musical rhythm and metre', *Perception*, **6**, 555-69.

STENDHAL, H. C. (1956) *Life of Rossini*, trans. Coe. London: Calder.

STERN, W. (1924) *The Psychology of Early Childhood up to the Sixth Year of Age*, trans. Barwell. New York: Henry Holt.

STIVERS, J. E. (1972) A reliability and validity study of the Watkins-Farnum Performance Scale. Doctoral Diss., Univ. Illinois.

STRONG, E. K. (1959) *Vocational Interest Blank for Men, Vocational Interest Blank for Women*. Revised as *Strong-Campbell Interest Inventory*, 1974, Stanford, Calif.: Stanford Univ, Press.

STUMPF, C. (1883-90) *Tonpsychologie*. Leipzig: Hirzel.

STUMPF, C. (1909) 'Akustische Versuche mit Pepito Ariola', *Z. ang. Psychol.*, **2**, 1-11.

SUNDBERG, J. and LINDBLOM, B. (1976) 'Generative theories in language and music descriptions'. *Cognition*, **4**, 99-122.

SWARD, K. (1933) 'Jewish musicality in America', *J. Appl. Psychol.*, **15**, 675-712.

TAEBEL, D. K. (1974) 'The effect of various instructional modes on children's performance of music concept tasks', *J. Res. Mus. Ed.*, **22**, 170-83.

TAN, N. (1979) 'Tonal organisation in the perception of melodies', *Psychol. Music*, **7**(1), 3-11.

TANNER, J. and LOESS, H. (1967) 'Correlations among rhythm tests', *Perc. and Motor Skills*, **25**, 721-6.

TARRELL, V. (1965) 'An investigation of the validity of the Musical Aptitude Profile', *J. Res. Mus. Ed.*, **13**, 195-206.

TAYLOR, E. M. (1941) 'A study of the prognosis of musical talent', *J. Exp. Psychol.*, **10**, 1-28.

TAYLOR, J. A. (1976) 'Perception of tonality in short melodies', *J. Res. Mus. Ed.*, **24**, 197-208.

TAYLOR, S. (1969) The musical development of children aged seven to eleven. Doctoral Diss., Univ. Southampton.

TAYLOR, S. (1973) 'Musical development of children aged seven to eleven', *Psychol. Music*, **1**(1), 44-9.

TEPLOV, B. M. (1966) *Psychologie des Aptitudes Musicales*, trans. Deprun. Paris: Presses Universitaires de France.

TERMAN, L. M. *et al.* (1925) *Genetic Studies of Genius*: I. *The Mental and Physcial Traits of a Thousand Gifted Children*. Stanford, Calif.: Stanford Univ. Press.

THACKRAY, R. (1969) *An Investigation into Rhythmic Abilities*. London: Novello.

THACKRAY, R. (1972) *Rhythmic Abilities in Children*. London: Novello.

THACKRAY, R. (1973) 'Tests of harmonic perception', *Psychol. Music*, **1**(2), 49-57.

THACKRAY, R. (1974) *Some Research Projects in Music Education*. Interim Report – Univ. Reading and Schools Council Research and Development Project Music Education of Young Children.

THAYER, R. W. (1972) 'The interrelation of personality traits, musical achievement, and different measures of musical aptitude', *Exper. Res. Psychol. Music: Stud. Psychol. Music*, **8**, 103-18.

TOMITA, M. and KUROSU, M. (1976) 'A preliminary study on the assessment of musical aptitude', *Waseda Univ. Psychol. Report*, **8**, 25 March 1976.

TILLIS, M. (1960) *Chords and Discords: The Life of an Orchestral Musician*. London: Phoenix House.

TREDGOLD, A. F. (1922) *Mental Deficiency (Amentia)*, 4th edit. London: Bailliere, Tindall and Cox.

TREDGOLD, R. and SODDY, K. (1956) *A Textbook of Mental Deficiency*. 9th edit. London: Tindall and Cox.

TROTTER, J. R. (1967) 'The psychophysics of melodic interval: Definitions, techniques, theory and problems', *Austral. J. Psychol.*, **19**, 13-25.

UPDEGRAFF, R., HEILEGER, L. and LEARNED, J. (1938) 'The effect of training upon the singing ability and musical interest of three-, four-, and five-year-old children', *Univ. Iowa Stud. Child Welfare*, **14**, 83-121.

UTLEY, E. (1971) The development of a musical perception test free of technical vocabulary for use in grades six through twelve. Doctoral Diss., Indiana Univ.

UTLEY, E. (1978) The effectiveness of the Shrader TAP System in improving music reading and general reading comprehension. Unpubl. report, Norfolk, Va.

VALENTINE, C. W. (1962) *The Experimental Psychology of Beauty*. London: Methuen.

VAN ALSTYNE, D. and OSBORNE, E. (1937) 'Rhythm responses of Negro and White children two to six', *Monogr. Soc. Res. Child Devel.*, **2**, 4.

VANDENBERG, S. G. (1962) 'The hereditary abilities study: hereditary components in a psychological test battery', *Amer. J. Hum. Genet.*, **14**, 220-37.

VAN ZEE, N. (1976) 'Responses of kindergarten children to musical stimuli and terminology', *J. Res. Mus. Ed.*, **24**, 14-21.

VASIL, T. (1973) The effects of systematically varying selected factors on music performing adjudication. Doctoral Diss., Univ. Connecticut.

VATER, H. (1934) 'Musikalische Produktion', *Arch. ges. Psychol*, **90**, 1-60.

VAUGHAN, M. M. (1977) 'Musical creativity: Its cultivation and measurement', *Bull. Council Res. Mus. Ed.*, No 50, 72-7.

VAUGHAN, M. M. and MYERS, R. E. (1971) 'An examination of music process as related to creative thinking', *J. Res. Mus. Ed.*, **19**, 337-41.

VERNON, P. E. (1931) The psychology of music with especial reference to its appreciation, perception and composition. Doctoral Diss., Cambridge Univ.

VERNON, P. E. (1960) *Intelligence and Attainment Tests*. London: Univ. London Press.

VERNON, P. E. (1968) 'What is potential ability?' *Bull. Brit. Psychol. Soc.*, **21**, 211-19.

VERNON, P. E. (1977) 'Absolute pitch: A case study', *Brit. J. Psychol.*, **68**, 485-9.

VERNON, P. E. (1979) *Intelligence: Heredity and Environment*. San Francisco: Freeman.

VIDOR, M. (1931) *Was ist Musikalität?* Munich: Beck.

VISCOTT, D. S. (1970) 'A musical idiot savant: A psychodynamic study, and some speculations on the creative process', *Psychiatry*, **33**, 494-515.

VOLGER, T. (1975) 'An investigation to determine whether learning effects accrue from immediate sequential administrations of the six levels of the Iowa Tests of Music Literacy', *Exper. Res. Psychol. Music: Stud. Psychol. Music*, **10**, 98-181.

WALLS, C. (1973) The identification of musical concepts by elementary children from contrasting racial groups and socioeconomic environments. Doctoral Diss., Ohio State Univ.

WAPNICK, J. (1980) 'The perception of musical and metronomic tempo change in musicians', *Psychol. Music*, **8** (1), 3-12.

WARD, W. D. (1963) 'Absolute pitch I', *Sound*, 2(3), 14-21; 'Absolute pitch II', *Sound*, **2** (4), 33-41.

WARD, W. D. (in press) 'Absolute pitch' in D. DEUTSCH (ed.) *The Psychology of Music*. New York: Academic Press.

WARD, W. D. and BURNS, E. M. (1978) 'Singing without auditory feedback', *J. Res. in Singing*, **1** (2), 24-44.

WASSUM, S. (1979) 'Elementary school children's vocal range', *J. Res. Mus. Ed.*, **27**, 214-26.

WASSUM, S. (1980) 'Elementary school children's concept of tonality', *J. Res. Mus. Ed.*, **28**, 18-33.

WATKINS, J. G. and FARNUM, S. E. (1954) *The Watkins-Farnum Performance Scale*. Winona, Minn.: Leonard Music.

WATSON, K. B. (1942) 'The nature and measurement of musical meanings', *Psychol. Monogr.*, **54**(2).

WATT, H. J. (1917) *The Psychology of Sound*. Cambridge: Cambridge Univ. Press.

WEAVER, A. T. (1924) 'Experimental studies in vocal expression: II. The prediction of talent for vocal expression in reading', *J. Appl. Psychol.*, **8**, 159-86.

WEBBER, G. H. (1974) The effectiveness of musical and nonmusical measures as predictors of success in beginning instrumental music. Doctoral Diss., Univ. Texas.

WEBSTER, P. R. (1979) 'Relationships between creative behaviour in music and selected variables as measured in high school students', *J. Res. Mus. Ed.*, **27**, 227-42.

WEDIN, L. (1969) 'Dimension analysis of emotional expression in music', *Swed. J. Musicology*, **51**, 119-40.

WEDIN, L. (1972a) 'Multidimensional scaling of emotional expression in music', *Swed. J. Musicology*, **54**, 115-31.

WEDIN, L. (1972b) 'A multidimensional study of perceptual-emotional qualities in music', *Scand. J. Psychol.*, **13**, 241-57.

WEINERT, L. (1929) 'Untersuchungen über das absolute Gehör', *Arch. ges. Psychol.*, **73**, 1-128.

WELCH, G. F. (1979a) 'Poor pitch singing: A review of the literature', *Psychol. Music.* 7, (1), 50-8.

WELCH, G. F. (1979b) 'Vocal range and poor pitch singing', *Psychol. Music.* 7(2), 13-31.

WERTHEIM, N. (1977) 'Is there an anatomical localisation for musical faculties?' in Maconald Critchley and R. E. Henson (eds.), *Music and the Brain*. London: Heinemann.

WHELLAMS, F. S. (1970) 'The relative efficiency of aural-musical and non-musical tests as predictors of achievement in instrumental music', *Bull. Council Res. Ed. Mus.*, No 21, 15-21.

WHELLAMS, F. S. (1971) The aural musical abilities of junior school children: A factorial investigation. Doctoral Diss., Univ. London.

WHELLAMS, F. S. (1973a) 'Musical abilities and sex differences in the analysis of aural musical capacities', *J. Res. Mus. Ed.*, **21**, 30-9.

WHELLAMS, F. S., (1973b) 'Multiple correlation in music education research studies', *Bull. Council Res. Mus. Ed.*, No 33, 34-45.

WHITE, A. (1961) 'The Aliferis Music Achievement test as a predictor of success in music theory at St Olaf College', *J. Ed. Res.*, **54**, 315-17.

WHITE, B. W. (1954) 'Visual and auditory closure', *J. Exp. Psychol.*, **48**, 234-40.

WHITE, R. K. (1931) 'The versatility of genius', *J. Soc. Psychol.*, **3**, 460-89.

WHITTINGTON, R. W. T. (1957) 'The assessment of potential musical ability in secondary school children', *J. Educ., Psychol.*, **48**, 1-10.

WHYBREW, W. E. (1971) *Measurement and Evaluation in Music*. Dubuque, Iowa: Brown.

WICKELGREN, W. (1969) 'Associative strength theory of recognition memory for pitch', *J. Mathem. Psychol.*, **6**, 13-61.

WILCOX, R. (1971) 'Further ado about Negro music ability', *J. Negro Educ.*, **40**, 361-4.

WILLIAMS, D. B. (1977) 'An interim report of a programmatic series of music inquiry designed to investigate melodic pattern identification ability in children', *Bull. Council Res. Mus. Ed.*, No 50, 78-82.

WILLIAMS, E. D., WINTER, L. and WOOD, J. M. (1938) 'Tests of literary appreciation', *Brit. J. Ed. Psychol.*, **8**, 265-84.

WILLIAMS, H. M., SIEVERS, C. H. and HATTWICK, M. S. (1933) 'The Measurement of Musical Development', *Univ. Iowa Stud. in Child Welfare*, **VII**, 1, 191.

WILLIAMS, T. M. and AIKEN, L. S. (1975) 'Auditory pattern classification: continuity of prototype use with development', *Devel. Psychol.*, **11**, 715-23.

WILSON, M. E. (1951) *How to Help Your Child With Music*. New York: Schuman.

WING, H. D. (1936) Tests of musical ability in school children. Master's Diss., London Univ.

WING, H. D. (1941a) 'A factorial study of musical tests', *Brit. J. Psychol.*, **31**, 341-55.

WING, H. D. (1941b) Musical ability and appreciation. Doctoral Diss., London Univ.

WING, H. D. (1955) 'Musical aptitude and intelligence', *Education Today*, **5**, No. 1.

WING, H. D. (1960) *Manual for Standardised Tests of Musical Intelligence*, Windsor: Nat. Found. Educ. Res. Publ.

WING, H. D. (1963) 'Is musical aptitude innate?' *Rev. Psychol. Music.*, **1**, 1-7.

WING, H. D. (1968) 'Tests of musical ability and appreciation', 2nd edit: *Brit. J. Psychol. Monogr. Suppl.* No 27 (1st edit. 1948).

WITKIN, H. A., OLTMAN, P. K., CHASE, J. B. and FRIEDMAN, F. (1971) 'Cognitive patterning in the blind' in J. HELLMUTH (ed.), *Cognitive Studies II: Deficits in Cognition*. London: Butterworth.

WOLNER, M. and PYLE, W. H. (1933) 'An experiment in individual training in pitch-deficient children', *J. Educ. Psycho.*, **24**, 602-8.

WOODROW, H. (1939) 'The common factors in fifty-two mental

tests', *Psychometrika*, **4**, 99-108.

WRAGG, D. (1974) 'An investigation into some factors affecting the carry-over of music interest and involvement during the transition period between primary and secondary education', *Psychol. Music*, **2** (1), 13-23.

WYATT, R. F. (1945) 'The improvability of pitch discrimination', *Psychol. Monogr.*, **58**: 267, 1-58.

WYKE, M. A. (1977) 'Musical ability: A neuropsychological interpretation' in MACDONALD CRITCHLEY and R. E. HENSON, *Music and the Brain*. London: Heinemann.

YAMAMATSU, T. (1974) *Musical Talent*. Tokyo: Dainippon-Tosho.

YATES, N. and BRASH, H. (1941) 'An investigation of physical and mental characteristics of a pair of twins reared apart from infancy', *Ann. Eugen.*, **11**, 89-101.

YENDOVITSKAYA, T. V. (1958) 'Concerning differentiation of pitch in pre-school children', *Dok. Akad. Pedag. Navk. RSFSR*, No 5, Cited in A.V. Zaporozhets and D.B. Elkonin, *The Psychology of Preschool Children*. Cambridge, Mass.: MIT, 1971.

YOUNG, W. T. (1972) 'Musical Aptitude Profile norms for use with college and university nonmusic majors', *J. Res. Mus. Ed.*, **20**, 385-90.

YOUNG, W. T. (1973) 'The Bentley Measures of Musical Abilities: A congruent validity report', *J. Res. Mus. Ed.*, **21**, 74-9.

YOUNG, W. T. (1974) 'Musical development in preschool disadvantaged children', *J. Res. Mus. Ed.*, **22**, 155-69.

YOUNG, W. T. (1976) 'A longitudinal comparison of four music achievement and music aptitude tests', *J. Res. Mus. Ed.*, **24**, 97-109.

ZATORRE, R. J. (1978) 'Recognition of dichotic melodies by musicians and nonmusicians', *J. Acoust. Soc. Amer.*, **63**, 551.

ZENATTI, A. (1969) *Le développement génétique de la perception musicale*. Paris: C.N.R.S.

ZENATTI, A. (1970) 'Perception mélodique et acculturation tonale: Etudie expérimentale de l'influence du sexe sur les performances d'enfants agés de 5 à 10 ans', *Sci. de l'Art*, **7**, 71-6.

ZENATTI, A. (1973) 'Etude de l'acculturation musicale chezl'enfant dans une épreuve d'identification mélodique', *Psychol. norm. et pathol.*, **4**, 453-64.

ZENATTI, A. (1974) 'Perception et appréciation de la consonance musical par l'enfant entre 4 et 10 ans. *Sci. de l'Art*, **9**, 74-61.

ZENATTI, A. (1975) 'Melodic memory tests: a comparison of normal children and mental defectives', *J. Res. Mus. Ed.*, **23**, 41-52.

ZENATTI, A. (1976a) 'Jugement esthétique et perceptive de l'enfant, entre 4 à 10 ans, dans des épreuves rythmiques', *Année psychol.*, **76**, 93-115.

ZENATTI, A. (1976*b*) 'Influence de quelques variables socio-culturelles sur le développement musical de l'enfant', *Psychol. Franç.*, **21**, 185-90.

ZENATTI, A. (1980) *Tests Musicaux pour Jeunes Enfants*. Issy-les-Moulineaux: Editions Scientifiques et Psychologiques.

ZIMMERMAN, M. P. and SECHREST, L. (1968) 'How children conceptually organize musical sounds', *Cooperative Res. Proj. No 5 — 0256*. Evanston, Ill.: Northwestern Univ.

ZUCKERKANDL, V. (1960) Review of *The Language of Music* by D. Cooke, *Music Theory*, **4**, 104-9.

ZUCKERKANDL, V. (1973) *Man the Musician*. Princeton, N. J. : Princeton Univ. Press.

ZWISSLER, R. N. (1971) An investigation of the pitch discrimination skills of first grade children identified as accurate singers and those identified as inaccurate singers. Doctoral Diss., Univ. California.

Name index

General index

absolute pitch, x, 162, 165–6
  acquired by training, 222–3
  development of, 123–6, 128
  experimental studies of, 60
  instability of, 126–239
  tests of, 125–6
  theories of, 59–60
'accommodation', 100, 117
acculturation in music, 61–2, 142,
  145–9, 206–8
acoustic structure, test of, 36, 90–1
adopted children, 178
aesthetic enjoyment of music, 253,
  255
aesthetic judgement in music and
  the other arts, 88
aesthetic response to music, test of,
  33–4
age
  and absolute pitch, 126
  development of musical ability
    with, 97–160
  differentiation of general ability
    with, 81
  guide lines to music development
    with, 159
  optimum for learning, 102
  and perceived meaning of music,
    254
  stabilisation of musical aptitude
    with, 30–1, 226, 232–3
Aliferis Music Achievement Tests,
  43, 45, 50, 293–4
American negroes, musical abilities
  of, 210–12, 215
analytic v. holistic listening, 55,
  182, 261–4, 271

anthropological studies of music,
  4–5
appreciation of music
  development of, 149–51, 155
  factors of, 56
  tests of, 21–9, 32–4,
  see also aesthetic enjoyment;
    aesthetic response to music
aptitude v. attainment, 5–7, 12–13
'assimilation', 100
assortative mating, 181
attitude to music, 157–9
  assessment of, 48–50
auditory acuity, 68–70, 182
Auditory Cognition of
  Relationships (ACoR), 57,
  68
auditory immediate memory
  (Msa), 57, 68
Australian Test for Advanced
  Music Studies, 38, 44–6, 50,
  294
autism, 167

babbling, 106
Bach family, xi, 175
behaviour modification, 217
Bentley Measures of Musical
  Abilities, 29–30, 35, 37, 122,
  140, 157, 284
  effects of training on, 221, 231–2
  relation to other abilities, 77–80,
  298–300
binaural diplacusis, 69–70
Bioacoustic Laboratory Research
  Institute, 97–8
blind persons, musical abilities in,

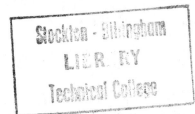